Radicalism
IN THE MOUNTAIN WEST, 1890–1920

Socialists, Populists, Miners, and Wobblies

D1356385

DAVID R. BERMAN

UNIVERSITY PRESS *of* COLORADO

© 2007 by the University Press of Colorado

Published by the University Press of Colorado
5589 Arapahoe Avenue, Suite 206C
Boulder, Colorado 80303

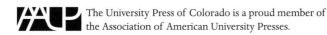 The University Press of Colorado is a proud member of
the Association of American University Presses.

The University Press of Colorado is a cooperative publishing enterprise supported, in part,
by Adams State College, Colorado State University, Fort Lewis College, Mesa State College,
Metropolitan State College of Denver, University of Colorado, University of Northern Colorado,
and Western State College of Colorado.

∞ The paper used in this publication meets the minimum requirements of the American
National Standard for Information Sciences—Permanence of Paper for Printed Library Materials.
ANSI Z39.48-1992

Library of Congress Cataloging-in-Publication Data

Berman, David R.
  Radicalism in the mountain West, 1890–1920 : socialists, populists, miners, and Wobblies / David
R. Berman.
    p. cm.
  Includes bibliographical references and index.
  ISBN 978-0-87081-884-4 (hardcover : alk. paper) 1. Radicalism—West (U.S.)—History. 2.
Populism—West (U.S.)—History. 3. West (U.S.)—Politics and government. I. Title.
  HN49.R33B47 2007
  303.48'4—dc22

                                                                              2007024033

Design by Daniel Pratt

16   15   14   13   12   11   10   09   08   07   10   9   8   7   6   5   4   3   2   1

To Susan, Wendy, and Zoe

Contents

Tables

Preface

Historian W. J. Cash observed some years ago that the South is not simply a geographic division of the United States. Rather, one finds in this region "a complex of established relationships and habits of thought, sentiments, prejudices, standards, and values, and association of ideas," shared by most people, that distinguishes the area from others.[1] While one is not altogether certain the same can be said of the Mountain West—Arizona, Colorado, Idaho, Montana, Nevada, New Mexico, Utah, and Wyoming—these states do share a common history of interest to students of radicalism.

The Mountain West in the last decade of the nineteenth century and the first two decades of the twentieth century was a place where radicals—people who wanted to replace the capitalist system, not simply reform it—were active on both the political and industrial fronts. While previous work suggests that the nature and impact of the radical movement in the United States during this period varied considerably from region to region, little has been done to examine the Mountain West in this regard. This book aims to fill this gap and to help not only to complete the story but also to increase our understanding of the strengths and weaknesses of the radical movement as a whole.

My central focus is on Socialist party activities in the area and events that conditioned party development and the broader environment in which the Socialists functioned. More specifically, the study focuses on (1) the relationship between the Populist and Socialist movements and how both were related to the emergence of a streak of radicalism in the union movement, particularly in mining areas; and (2) the development, characteristics, limitations, and accomplishments of Socialist party organizations in the area. Along the way I touch upon several themes of interest to western historians—free silver, labor relations, violence, woman suffrage, and Mormonism among them—and, for political scientists as well as historians, the utility of third parties as vehicles for change.

I found an emerging labor force central to the development and growth of both the Populist and Socialist parties, a force that at various times, particularly in mining areas, had a radical component based not so much on radical doctrine as on the workers' experiences. On the industrial front, Mountain West radicals stood out from their counterparts in other regions of the country in their willingness to confront employers and in the extent to which they were willing to engage in violence. At the same time, Mountain West Socialist parties did well compared with their counterparts in other regions, in terms of membership, picking up votes, and winning elections. Clearly, the parties had something special going for them.

The study suggests that radicals benefited from an ongoing anti-corporate reform effort that was all the more potent because of its ties to anti-colonial sentiment; the momentum built up by a relatively successful labor-centered Populist crusade; the strong emphasis in the labor movement on industrial unionism and the resulting worker solidarity, which included unskilled as well as skilled labor; the emergence of discontent in mining areas (a discontent radicals did not just take for granted but actively cultivated); and the existence of a party system that, for various reasons, was unusually favorable to third parties' efforts. The last factor may have been especially significant.

The fact that the parties did not do better in an absolute sense may be attributed to a variety of factors, some of which in varying degrees affected Socialist parties elsewhere and some, such as the opposition of the Mormon Church, of which were unique to the region. When it comes to barriers the story is much the same throughout the region—the disinterest or downright hostility of workers; the opposition of newly enfranchised women voters and of church leaders; town builders' fear that radicals would scare off investors; the determined, sometimes ruthless, resistance of mining companies; the use of state and federal troops to subdue workers; and the popularity of conspiracy theories linking radicals to Germany's side in World War I all presented formidable barriers for the radicals. In particular, the impact of the party movement was sapped by the thunder-stealing reformers and the patriotic surge of World War I, which, because of the party's opposition to the war, was used against it. The radicals' principal achievement may have been in capturing enough votes and causing enough disruption on industrial fronts to wring concessions from those in power.

In these pages I describe the broader environment in which the radicals functioned, the havoc they raised, and the reaction to them. Included are accounts of a variety of dramatic events, including violent strikes and murders that are of interest in and of themselves but are also important because they functioned as defining moments that shaped opinions and guided future conduct and events. One finds ideological polarization, anger, fear, violence, and, in part because of participants' efforts to shape or "spin" the news in their favor, sharply different firsthand accounts of various events. Much of the battle was over which side, the radicals or their opponents, could win over public opinion to their point of view. On this count, the opponents generally came out on top.

In the blizzard of slanted information, employers' anxieties were sometimes needlessly aroused by information coming from Pinkerton and other detectives they hired to spy on workers and their economic and political organizations. In some cases, the undercover detectives working for the companies were agent-provocateurs urging workers to commit acts of violence. Radicals, on the other hand, also saw the world to be pretty much as their ideology led them to expect, seeing conspiracies everywhere and viewing events as confirming their worst suspicions about the other side.

This account rests on extensive archival research and a variety of materials, including radical newspapers and pamphlets and reports filed by labor spies and government agents. I have attempted to depict the various events as the participants saw or depicted them, drawing upon their own words and thoughts when possible. To better document events, I have also examined election returns, membership records, newspaper subscriptions, votes taken at conventions, and votes in national party referenda.

I would like to thank the many archivists and librarians who have helped me over the years on this project; there are simply too many to thank individually. I would also like to thank several people for taking the time to give me the benefit of their thoughts on various versions of this manuscript: Amy Bridges,

Richard Foster, James McBride, and John Sillito. I also thank my wife, Susan, who accompanied me on several trips to out-of-state and, in some cases, out-of-the-way archives and who proofread the manuscript and added several valuable suggestions as to how it could be improved.

Radicalism

IN THE MOUNTAIN WEST, 1890–1920

Introduction

DURING A SWING THROUGH the Mountain West in the winter of 1915, a nearly exhausted Eugene Debs demanded to know how Socialist party staff workers could have expected him to make it from Tooele, Utah, in time for his next engagement in Burley, Idaho. Debs complained: "The place is almost inaccessible—no earthly way to get from there to Burley and the latter is lost to us, notwithstanding I have been up all night and am about half dead in the vain struggle to get there. . . . I can't go out of a hot hall, covered with sweat, and climb into an open buggy on a bitter cold, raw night and ride 17 miles over half-frozen roads and then stand waiting for a train until I'm frozen numb—nor can anyone else."[1] Debs did not make it to Burley, no doubt disappointing hundreds who saw the notices of his visit that were prominently displayed in local newspapers. At the time—February 1915—Debs was on one of his many educational tours, which he described as "lecturing my way into insanity." He much preferred rushing into some strike where he could take a direct part in the class struggle, something he had frequently done in the Mountain West.[2]

The region—encompassing the states of Arizona, Colorado, Idaho, Montana, Nevada, New Mexico, Utah, and Wyoming—from 1890 to 1920 was a hotbed of radical activity on both the political and industrial (economic) fronts. The radicals wanted not to simply reform the capitalistic system but to replace it with something they felt was better, be it a cooperative commonwealth or a system of industrial democracy built around one big union.[3] Radical thought was, for some, based directly or indirectly on a Marxian analysis of the capitalist system. Perhaps more often, though, it simply reflected the thoughts and experiences of the people who had only a vague awareness, if any, of Marx. Mountain West Socialists were a somewhat unsophisticated bunch who, as eastern Socialists liked to point out, "did not know surplus value from long division and did not care to know."[4] As a miner in Kingman, Arizona, told a comrade from New York, being a Socialist had nothing to do with reading or going to lectures—all one had to know is that he or she "is being robbed."[5]

Radicals were far from a monolithic group. Indeed, much of the story of the movement in the Mountain West as it unfolds in these pages is one of tension and destructive conflict among radicals and radical groups.[6] Radicals differed in the extent to which they focused on the end objective of fundamental change and in the intensity of their beliefs and commitment. They differed in basic approaches or attitudinal tendencies, for example, over whether to work primarily through the political system or directly at the point of production on the industrial level, whether to press for immediate and complete revolutionary change or focus on ameliorative reforms and wait for fundamental change to set in gradually, and whether to use violent or unlawful methods to advance the cause.

Within the Socialist party, members leaning to the right had a hunger for respectability, an inclination to work for the utopian objective gradually through the political process, and a willingness to make alliances with or work through craft unions and go to the voters with platforms featuring immediate reforms. Those on the left wanted to emphasize the messages of class conflict, worker solidarity, and the need for revolutionary action. They wanted to abandon the capitalist-accepting craft-union–loving American Federation of Labor and the focus on reform—the latter in part out of fear that making reforms would improve conditions and make developing a revolutionary spirit more difficult. The left wing of the Socialist party and the radical labor organization, the Industrial Workers of the World (IWW), had much in common, although the IWW had its own particular guiding radical ideology. The IWW was not entirely opposed to political activity (realizing, for example, that a friendly sheriff came in handy) but channeled its energies directly on the industrial front.

Previous studies have suggested that the radical movement in the United States varied from region to region.[7] Yet our knowledge of the movement in the Mountain West as a whole and how it compared to the movement elsewhere is very limited. Fragments of the story told here are found in the vast literature on Populism and labor conditions in the various states and territories in the region and in a relatively small number of studies on Socialist activity in those places.[8] This work constitutes the first attempt to focus on radical activities in the region as a whole. The broader goal is to increase our understanding of the strengths and weaknesses of the radical movement not only in the region but across the nation. Scholars have advanced numerous reasons for the Socialist party's failure to become a major party in this country. Indeed, a recent study noted, "Explanations of socialism's weakness in America are as numerous as socialists were few."[9] Here I work to isolate some of the more salient forces that both strengthened and weakened the movement. More generally, this book focuses on a series of questions: What were the characteristics of the Socialist movement in the region? In particular, how did it relate to the Populist movement and the union movement that took place in mining areas? What were its strengths and limitations compared with the movement elsewhere in the country? Why was it not more successful?

In addressing these questions, the book deals only tangentially with the national Populist and Socialist movements in this period and does not attempt to offer anything close to a comprehensive political history of the region at the time or of labor conditions and the everyday lives of workers in the region. I join what is now a long line of scholars who see Populism in the region as a whole as far more than a free-silver cause.[10] I also join those who emphasize the radical streak in the Populism movement and how that movement fed into the Socialist movement.[11] When it comes to mine labor, this work is in the tradition of Vernon Jensen in highlighting labor tensions and wars in which unions were pitted against mine owners.[12] This is not to suggest that conflict generally characterized labor-management relations in the region. The focus is placed on these events because they help illuminate the activities of the radicals or the environment in which they functioned. Still, a broader theme in this study is the importance of violence—including labor and land wars and sometimes overlapping ethnic and racial physical clashes and murders—in shaping the character of radical activity in the region.

The Mountain West provides a particularly useful laboratory for examining the rise and fall of American radicalism. The region in the late 1890s and early

1900s offered several advantages to the radically inclined. They had an opportunity to build upon widespread anti-corporate sentiment, which was all the more intense because it was coupled with resentment based on anti-colonial, anti-eastern feelings. The Mountain West too was a place where industrialization was just beginning and working conditions were in some respects among the worst in the country—the type of conditions out of which one might expect revolutions to be made. On the political level, Populists and Socialists working in the Mountain West had a head start over their counterparts in other parts of the country in picking up votes because their movements came to life in an environment that for various reasons, such as its newness and small population, was relatively receptive to third-party activity.

The newness of the region gave parties on the left another advantage because there was less tradition and fewer entrenched institutions and, thus, fewer barriers to new ideas, such as what appeared to some to be "radical" notions of woman suffrage, open primaries, and direct democracy. To offset corporate control of the political system, Mountain westerners were in a mood to experiment with political reform. By adding the initiative and opening up party primaries, Mountain West states gave political radicals additional tools; and by adopting woman suffrage and, thus, doubling the size of the electorate, they gave the struggling new parties an opportunity to dramatically expand their bases. For Mountain West Socialists, another benefit was having a relatively strong left-leaning and labor-centered Populist movement to build upon. Further supportive of the cause were the inclinations and activities of the industrial mining unions, the Western Federation of Miners (WFM) and the United Mine Workers (UMW). The former played an especially strong role in promoting Socialism in the area.

Given all they had going for them, one is not surprised to find that compared with Socialist parties elsewhere in the country, Socialist parties in the region generally did better when it came to gaining membership, picking up votes, and winning elections (albeit mostly at the local level). However, not all the factors they presumed or hoped would be working in their favor actually gave them much of an advantage. Looking at the related question of why they did not do even better gives us an opportunity to identify forces—some of which confounded the movement nationally and some of which were relatively unique to the area—that stunted the growth of the movement.

In telling the story of what happened in the region in regard to radical activity, why, and with what effect from roughly 1890 to 1920, I offer an analysis of events—elections, strikes, trials, deportations—and, relying on archival material, the thoughts and actions of individuals caught up in these events. We see radicals as political candidates, campaign workers, party and union organizers, sidewalk orators, preachers, and people coming to the aid of other radicals, be they schoolteachers or miners, who were about to lose their jobs or were in trouble with the law.

Along the way we encounter several fascinating characters, some well-known, others whose place in radical history thus far has been largely neglected. Some of the radicals or near radicals were national agitators who came into the region only periodically to stir things up. Others made homes in the region but moved from state to state, city to city, or mining camp to mining camp. Many radicals, though, were well-established members of their communities rather than transients.[13] They found a home in the party system, especially the Populist and Socialist parties but also the Non-Partisan League and various labor parties. Some wound up in Communist organizations. Within the labor movement, radicals were found in the Knights of Labor, many unions affiliated with the American Federation of Labor, and, especially important in this study, the WFM, UMW, and IWW. Radicals operated on two fronts, the political and the industrial, and spent a great deal of time debating which of the two was the most worthwhile.

Debs was among the most prominent and effective of the radicals frequently visiting the area. Born in Terre Haute, Indiana, in 1855, one of ten children, he began organizing railroad workers in his twenties and came to national prominence after the 1894 Pullman railroad strike. He traveled to the region on several occasions in the early 1900s, lecturing on behalf of Socialism and encouraging striking workers. Debs had also frequently visited the area as a presidential candidate of the Socialist Party of America (aka Socialist party) and, before that, the Social Democratic party. Debs, though, was hardly the conventional presidential candidate. In 1908 he told the muckraking journalist Lincoln Steffens: "I am not fitted either by temperament or by taste for the office, and if there were any chance of my election I wouldn't run. . . . I am running for president to serve a very humble purpose: to teach social consciousness and to ask men to sacrifice the present for the future, to 'throw away their votes' to mark the rising tide of protest and build up a party that will represent them. When Socialism is on the verge of success, the party will nominate an able executive and a clear-headed administrator; not—not Debs."[14] Still, many voters in the Mountain West took him seriously in his various campaigns. He often did much better as a presidential candidate in this region than anywhere else in the country.

Davis H. Waite, who became not altogether affectionately known as "Bloody Bridles Waite," stood out among the earlier set of "calamity-howling"

5

Populists. Born in Jamestown, New York, in 1825, Waite began his political life as a Democrat, turned to the new Republican party in 1856, and served in the state legislatures in Wisconsin and Kansas before being lured west by the silver boom. He arrived in Colorado in the late 1870s, settling first in Leadville and later in the silver mining camp of Aspen. Waite held a variety of jobs, prospector, lawyer, and newspaper editor among them. In 1892, to the horror of many, he became governor of Colorado on the Populist ticket. Waite found the existing economic and political system corrupt—a situation he blamed on monopolies, be they of the land, transportation, money, or any other variety. He also stood for the rights of labor and used the power of his office as governor on behalf of striking miners. Waite, to say the least, was a colorful character. Historian John Hicks described him as "headstrong and obstinate. His whole personal appearance as well as the occasional frenzy of his rhetoric suggested the narrow-minded fanatic."[15] Others looked at Waite as a sharp-tongued "moral absolutist" who "saw the world in terms of a cleavage between the robbers and the robbed."[16] To some extent his speech-making style worked against him. As historian Karel Bicha noted: "On a podium he thrived on the response of audiences and his utterances were more extreme than his intentions. Enemies regarded him as a madman, and he often played into their hands."[17] Waite aroused unskilled workers and furthered the cause of the WFM but was also used by those eager to brand Populists as wild-eyed and crankish.

William Owen O'Neill, commonly known as Buckey O'Neill, also gained considerable prominence among the plain-speaking Populist politicians. O'Neill, born in 1860—historians are uncertain whether in Saint Louis, Missouri, or Washington, D.C.—came into the Arizona territory about the same time Waite was heading for Colorado. O'Neill also engaged in newspaper work before running for office. Settling down in Prescott, he won office as tax assessor and collector, county sheriff, and mayor of Prescott. As a Populist, he made two unsuccessful bids for the office of territorial delegate to Congress on a platform condemning the "moneyed aristocracy" running the country. He later gained fame as a founder of Troop A, First Territorial Volunteer Calvary, later to become famous as Theodore Roosevelt's Rough Riders. Described by those who knew him as a wild and reckless fellow, he died while commanding Troop A in combat in Cuba in 1898, at age thirty-eight.

While Waite governed, or tried to govern, in Colorado and O'Neill contended in Arizona, rebels like Henry W. Lawrence, 1835–1924, a Mormon who broke with the church, and Warren Foster, a newspaper editor fresh from Kansas, were trying to round up Populists in Utah. Both, like many other Populists, went on to become Socialists. Foster, like other radicals, called them as he saw them.

Responding to J. D. Rockefeller's claim that "God gave me my money," he contended that this had to be "the meanest thing that we have ever heard charged up against God. We have read a great deal of the writings of avowed infidels against the Lord; but we search in vain for one that has ever accused Him of going into partnership with a thief and using His powers to rob the poor and give it to the rich."[18] When Foster died in 1909, a radical paper noted: "He was a man of fine ability who might have won distinction, but who gave himself to what he conceived to be the cause of the people and died poor. . . . There is an element of heroism in such a life as his, and he really accomplished more than he seemed to have done. Honor to Warren Foster."[19]

On the labor side, one of the leading radicals during the 1880s—a time when unions were struggling for recognition in the area—was Joseph R. Buchanan of Denver (1851–1924), known as the "Riproarer of the Rockies." Born in Hannibal, Missouri, in 1851, Buchanan moved to Colorado in the late 1870s where he became editor of a labor paper, the *Labor Enquirer*, and tried to organize workers in the Rocky Mountain region into trade unions and Knights of Labor assemblies. He led a Socialist group, the Rocky Mountain Social League, and moved in and out of various political parties, including the Socialist Labor party (from which he was eventually expelled), the Democrats, and the Populists. Like countless other radicals, Buchanan had many disappointments along the way, especially with the workers' voting habits. In his autobiography he noted: "It will not surprise the thoughtful reader, especially if he be a student of human nature, to be told that disappointment and discouragement reduced me at times to a very pessimistic frame of mind. More than once I lost hope that the wrongs of labor would ever be righted by peaceable means. The workingmen could not be made to appreciate the power the ballot gave them; they were, it seemed to me, slow to take advantage of the opportunities opened to them by the labor organizations, and I sometimes thought the majority of them were not only too stupid to raise themselves, but too weak to stand if raised by others."[20] When it came to elections, Buchanan noted, "I have always observed that only a slight fog was necessary to obscure the political vision of the average workingman."[21] Deeply disappointed with the outcomes of elections, many other radicals also frequently blamed the workers, although one might contend that much of the fault rested with the radicals themselves.

Ed Boyce stands as a leading figure in the history of labor and political reform in the Mountain West through the 1890s to the early 1900s. Born in Ireland in 1862 and migrating to the United States in 1882, he became an underground miner and an active member of the Knights of Labor. After being imprisoned for his participation in the labor conflicts in the Coeur d'Alene district in 1892, he went on to help organize the WFM and became a successful Populist politician in Idaho. Like many of his fellow Populists, he later became a Socialist and tried to move the WFM in that direction. This effort frightened mine owners in the region badly enough that they came after both the union and the Socialists with full force. Boyce was one of the radicals who dropped out in time: by 1909 he had moved into the world of prosperity as a manager of an exclusive hotel in Portland, Oregon.

Frequently traveling to the area in the early 1900s and having an almost uncanny ability to find her way into the middle of the most violent labor mining strikes—confrontations out of which she would wind up in jail, deported, or both—was Mary Harris Jones, better known as Mother Jones. Born in Cork, Ireland (best guess is 1836), she came to the United States as a child. After losing her husband and four children in a yellow fever epidemic, she spent sixty years roaming the country as a labor agitator, mostly for the UMW. Over the years she went from strike to strike being arrested, deported, and hunted by the police and state militia. Jones was also a Socialist and a campaigner for that cause. Her fame, however, rests on her labor activities and, on occasion, gaining sympathy for workers by playing the role of John D. Rockefeller's victim. Although she did not look the part, Jones was a fearless agitator and dramatic speaker and something of a pioneer in enlisting women, especially immigrant women, into protest activity. Elizabeth Gurley Flynn, another radical, first heard Mother Jones at a Bronx open-air meeting in the summer of 1908, giving the city slickers hell for, among other things, not helping western miners. In her autobiography Flynn noted that Jones's "description of the bull-pen, where the miners were herded by federal troops during a Western miner's strike, and of the bloodshed and suffering was so vivid that, being slightly dizzy from standing so long, I fainted. She stopped in the middle of a fiery appeal. 'Get the poor child some water!' she said, and went on with her speech. I was terribly embarrassed."[22]

Flynn herself went West in quest of justice for workers. In the summer of 1909, while agitating for the IWW, or Wobblies, she appeared in Butte, Montana, a place where mines were in the heart of the city and the city was blighted because the practice of burning the sulfur out of the copper had produced poisonous fumes that destroyed all vegetation. Butte, she said, was "a sprawly, ugly place, with dusty shacks for the miners," which, because life was cheap in this great copper camp, had an ever-expanding cemetery.[23] Moving on, she helped organize an IWW free-speech fight in Missoula, Montana, directed against an ordinance banning street speaking. Working alongside her was Frank Little, later lynched in Butte. As part of her tour she also tried to rally miners in Colorado, Idaho, and Utah. In Utah she visited Joe Hill, a Wobbly awaiting execution for a crime many claimed he had not committed. Flynn later wrote that by 1914: "I had been in daily contact with workers and their struggles for eight years. I saw their honesty, modesty, decency, their devotion to their families and their unions, their helpfulness to fellows, their courage, their willingness to sacrifice. I hated those who exploited them, patronized them, lied to them, cheated them and betrayed them. I hated those who lived in idleness and luxury on *their* sweat and toil."[24]

When one thinks of radicals who roamed the Mountain West, the first name that comes to many historians' minds is someone born and raised in the area: William D. ("Big Bill") Haywood. Born in Salt Lake City, Utah, in 1869, Haywood was a big man, more than six feet tall, who had a slightly sinister appearance because of the loss of sight in one eye as the result of a childhood accident. From a poor family, he went to work in Nevada mines at age fifteen, joined the WFM when he was twenty-five, and became secretary-treasurer of the union at age thirty-one. He presided over the founding of the IWW and not long after was kidnapped along with two others by Idaho authorities, who placed him on trial for murdering a former governor of that state. Acquitted of that charge, Haywood for a time became a celebrity, touring the country on speaking engagements; but as an IWW leader he also became an advocate of general strikes, boycotts, and even sabotage to achieve labor's objectives. The IWW under Haywood spread fear throughout the Mountain West. During the early 1900s Haywood helped shape the image of the Mountain West as home to some of the most dangerous radicals in the country—people who believed in making revolutionary change through sabotage and industrial violence rather than achieving gradual change through political means. Haywood wound up fleeing the country.

Rivaling Haywood in ferocity, if not notoriety, were Thomas J. Hagerty and Vincent St. John. In 1902 Hagerty, a Catholic priest, abandoned his church duties in Las Vegas, New Mexico, so he could try to win over to Socialism miners who were meeting in Denver. Later, he toured Colorado mining camps with Debs on behalf of the American Labor Union and the Socialist ticket. In Telluride he told his audience: "That railroad is yours; the trains are yours; those large businesses blocks and office buildings down-town that bring in big rents are yours; the mercantile stocks of goods are yours; the banks and the moneys there on deposit are yours; if you want them, go and take them."[25] For such utterances, he was suspended by his archbishop. Later, he showed up at the founding of the IWW. He literally vanished from the radical scene in 1905.

Capitalists, especially mine owners, equally feared and detested Kentucky-born Vincent St. John, known as "The Saint." Saint John went to work in 1895 as a seventeen-year-old miner for the Bisbee Copper Company in Arizona and proceeded to build his labor career in Colorado, Nevada, and Idaho. Saint John, like Father Hagerty, saw little value in political action. According to a report of an operative working undercover for mine owners in January 1906, he told a small group of colleagues at a union meeting that "if the working men waited until they got relief through the ballot box they would never get it."[26] Continuing, he reportedly warned that "the day is not far distant when they will have to enforce their wishes by the torch and the bomb as they are now doing in Russia."[27] He organized for the IWW and became the organization's general secretary in 1908, a position he held until 1915. St. John retired to work a small copper claim in New Mexico but was sought out by federal officials, arrested, tried, convicted, and sent to prison.

David Coates and Guy E. Miller were other radicals who popped up in Mountain West states in various capacities. Coates, born in England in 1868, immigrated as a teenager with his family to Pueblo, Colorado, where he worked for a time in the steel mills. He later became active in Colorado and Idaho as a hard-nosed left-winger who divided his time among being a newspaper editor, a union official, and a Socialist party organizer. Technically speaking, he was the nation's first Socialist governor. The highly effective writer, speaker, and organizer Guy E. Miller, born in Iowa in 1870, came to Colorado where he took a variety of jobs—schoolteacher, farmer, newspaper editor, and mine worker among them. He represented the WFM and joined the Socialist party in 1902 after hearing Debs speak. Also spending much of his time among the miners and Socialists, particularly in Arizona, was the articulate and forceful Joseph D. Cannon, organizer for the WFM. Debs described him as "a thoroughly fine fellow, clear headed and sound to the core."[28] At one time, though, many Arizona Socialist party leaders saw him as a traitor to the cause.

In surveying the cast of radical characters in the region over the period, on the political side one needs also to note the elegant lawyer and former minister Lewis Duncan, the "Eugene Debs of Montana," who delighted the Socialist world by becoming mayor of Butte. Like Cannon and many of his fellow radicals, however, Duncan also got caught up in bitter internal squabbling, and some especially vitriolic supporters in the labor movement turned against him. In Montana one also finds party builder James D. Graham. Born in Scotland, he came to America as a teenager in 1886 and settled in Livingston, Montana, working as a machinist. He moved from Populism to Socialism, becoming Socialist party secretary, although a controversial one. He also was an organizer for the United Brotherhood of Railway Employees and a member of the executive committee of the Montana Federation of Labor.

Colorado, meanwhile, had Socialist A. H. Floaten who, like many of his co-workers, spent much of his time getting arrested, beaten up, jailed, or deported. Nevada had A. Grant Miller who almost made Socialism respectable, as did Herman V. Groesbeck in Wyoming who, before turning Socialist, had been elected as a Republican to the Wyoming Supreme Court and served as chief justice. Also among the Wyoming Socialists was the mysterious German-born F. W. Ott who, among other things, got on the bad side of the law by running off with the instruments and receipts from a children's band concert he had organized and, on another occasion, for trying to blackmail a political opponent. Equally filled with fire but less erratic was A. B. Elder, a Salt Lake attorney who coupled being a Utah Socialist leader with being an American Labor Union organizer, a reporter for *Appeal to Reason,* and legal counsel for the UMW.

One, finally, has to make special mention of Ida Crouch Hazlett, born on a farm near Kirkwood, Illinois, who was one of the most active radicals in the region. Over her career, Hazlett served the cause of reform as a member of the Knights of Labor, an organizer for the Woman Suffrage Association, and a newspaper reporter who covered the labor wars throughout the region and the Haywood trial. As a Socialist she served as a traveling organizer and agitator, party candidate, and newspaper reporter/editor in Utah, Colorado, and Montana, especially the latter. The skills Hazlett developed as a suffrage agitator helped her advance in the ranks of the Socialist movement. As a Socialist agitator, moreover, she made good use of the network of women sympathizers she had created during her suffrage years.[29] As editor of the Montana party's newspaper, the *Montana News,* she traveled around the region, writing reports on the Socialist movement in neighboring states. She was one of the most persistent critics of the radical movement's failure to make progress on political and economic fronts.

Some radicals, including Lewis Duncan, identified themselves as full-time agitators. On a paying basis, the job of agitator was often coupled with the job of being a party or union official or a publisher, editor, or journalist. People in these positions were the "brainworkers," the articulate leaders of the movement.[30] Several radicals at one time or another had been priests or ministers. In some cases their radicalism cost them their positions. The region also had its share of Christian Socialists. These included Congregationalist minister Myron Reed, a friend of Debs, who, working out of Denver in the 1880s and 1890s, spoke out against injustice and exploitation. He saw the West as open to new ideas and providing an opportunity to build an ideal community worthy of the kingdom of God.[31] Franklin Spencer Spalding, Episcopal bishop of Utah, also believed the aims of Socialism were embraced in Christianity's message, although this had somehow gotten lost. In 1914 the bishop wrote: "The Christian Church exists for the sole purpose of saving the human race. So far she has failed, but I think that Socialism shows her how she may succeed. It insists that men cannot be made right until the material conditions be made right. Although man cannot live by bread alone, he must have bread. Therefore the Church must destroy a system of society which inevitably creates and perpetuates unequal and unfair conditions of life. These unequal and unfair conditions have been created by competition. Therefore competition must cease and cooperation take its place."[32]

Whatever their status in life, many on the left were shocked and outraged by the industrial conditions they saw around them. A young Franklin Spencer Spaulding, who came to Utah in 1905 already committed to Socialism because of working conditions he had seen in Erie, Pennsylvania, became even more committed to Socialism after frequent contact with workers in Utah mining camps.[33] About the same time, a young lawyer named William Brooks had a similar experience in Arizona. Before heading west, he had heard Debs speak about labor conditions. At the time, this made little impression on him, but, according to his correspondence, he later saw the truth in what Debs was saying when he got to Arizona in 1903 and saw firsthand what he found to be the deplorable condition of workers in mining camps.[34] In a letter of September 18, 1904, he wrote that the workers got a little pay and nothing else: "They don't get pleasure or happiness out of their work, for they leave it at the first opportunity and it is their greater desire to have their children escape it. . . . Their physical labor is bought and sold in the market just as is any other commodity without regard to the fact that they are human."[35] Much of many radicals' focus was on the job. What was the "job" problem? As a Nevada Socialist party candidate put it: "When we have got the job we know not the minute we will be deprived of the job; a job subject to some one man's will, one man's anger. When we are deprived of the job we are denied the right to live."[36]

Radicals were concerned about what industrialization had done to workers but were not equally concerned about all workers. Radicals often carried the racial and ethnic biases common in the West against Asians and Hispanics. Anti-black sentiments were also often expressed, evident on an everyday basis and during strikes, as in Coeur d'Alene in 1899, when black soldiers came in to restore order. The bias against blacks, though, had a less pronounced impact on shaping the general pattern of the radical movement in the Mountain West than it did in the South simply because of the relatively small size of the black population. At the same time, the movement, both on the labor and political fronts, was conditioned by the "Chinese question" and the "Hispanic question" and, indeed, by the existence of any foreign nationality from which employers could recruit strikebreakers. Racism and perceived threats to job security proved a powerful combination.

Debs too was guilty of prejudices against blacks and immigrants, although his views mellowed over time.[37] Questions of racial equality became important to Debs, as did the subject of women's rights, but, as historian Nick Salvatore has written, his central message was aimed at white workingmen—urging them to stand up and, in fact, to be what men should be and refuse to allow the boss to push them around. Debs would blame the system, but he would also blame the workers for their inability to think for themselves, for being satisfied with miserable, degrading jobs, and for tolerating their treatment as slaves. As Salvatore put it: "At the core of Debs's appeal lay a spirited defense of the dignity of each individual."[38] Radicals throughout the Mountain West shared this perspective.

Following a general overview chapter in which the basic context and themes are set forth, the book proceeds largely in chronological order, built around election cycles but shifting back and forth from the political and industrial fronts. Chapters 2, 3, and 4 focus on the broad shape of the Populist movement in the area during the 1890s to portray the political and economic context out of which radicalism emerged. Chapter 2 covers the years 1890–1892, when the Populist movement was coming together in the Mountain West and during which land wars in Wyoming and New Mexico and labor wars elsewhere fed into the movement. Populists' organizations at the time were unstable coalitions of various groups, although in some places the organizations were undergoing a transition from essentially agrarian to more labor-focused parties. By 1893, as Chapter 3 illustrates, events had pushed the Populist movement in a more radical direction.

Unemployment, tramps, and strikes raised the specter of revolution, with the Populists in the forefront. Movement to the left came to a halt, however, with the decision of the national party and Populist parties in the area in 1896 to focus on free silver and to fuse with the Democratic party. With the collapse of the Populist parties, many radicals switched to Socialist parties in the region. Chapter 4 focuses on the fusion debate and the exodus of radicals and others out of the Populist party.

Chapters 5, 6, 7, and 8 look at the early years of Socialist party building in the area and how this was related to the miners' agenda, radical tendencies in the WFM, labor wars (especially in Colorado), and the emergence of the IWW. Chapter 5 examines Socialist party building and electoral progress in the early 1900s, years characterized by considerable enthusiasm and confidence in the triumph of the cause in the not too distant future. The early 1900s, though, also showed the range and depth of disagreement among Socialists and indicated the type of resistance they could expect. Chapter 6 switches the focus to the WFM, which, under Ed Boyce, was a major force driving radicalism in the late 1890s and early 1900s. On the political field WFM leaders had backed the Populists, and, when that party failed, they turned to the Socialists. At the same time, the union became more confrontational with mine owners. The most important labor wars involving the WFM took place in Colorado. As Chapter 7 indicates, the Colorado Socialist party was severely weakened as a result of these conflicts. It had been abandoned by the WFM, and other unions and party members spent much of their energy fighting among themselves. The party, though, was doing relatively well in other parts of the region. At the same time, the WFM set out to strengthen its labor ties through the creation of the IWW. This organization and the emergence of Big Bill Haywood dominate Chapter 8. Here again, though, the full force of state power was directed against the radicals. For Haywood this meant being kidnapped and put on trial for murder. For Wobblies in Nevada it meant military repression.

While the obstacles Socialists encountered in the early years of the movement served as a harbinger of the future, in the short run the party continued to make progress in the region as a whole, building up to a peak of electoral success in 1912. Chapters 9, 10, 11, and 12 look at the strength and character of the movement from roughly 1908–1914. Chapter 9 follows Debs's Red Special as it chugs through the region and also examines the activities of Mountain West Socialists centering around the 1908 elections. We also find the IWW successfully engaging in nonviolent free-speech campaigns. Chapter 10 makes the point that in contrast to the growing image of Socialists in the area as left-wing extremists—an image fed in part by press coverage of conflict in mining areas—party leaders in much of the region were trying to build respectable reform-minded parties that would appeal to the middle class as well as the working class. Many were shooting for mainstream status and trying to separate the party from those on the extreme left. Socialists, though, were also aware that their parties were perceived to be radical. In violation of party rules, some found it necessary to work outside the party organization or through organizations with a less radical image. Going the latter route, Socialists had a significant impact on the Arizona constitution. In Chapter 11 we find Socialists presenting broad municipal reform programs and settling down to do the day-to-day tasks necessary to run cities—doing the best job they could to prove they could be trusted to run the government. There was considerable dispute within the party, however, as to whether this was the best way to spend limited resources. The party nationally and in a good many states, including those in the Mountain West, made a leap in 1912; but, as Chapter 12 indicates, shortly thereafter party leaders began worrying about the loss of momentum and became bogged down in disputes concerning whether to build a mass party or to focus on political or direct action on the industrial field.

While Socialists did not lose all hope after the 1912 election, this event was followed by more setbacks on the industrial front, fallout among radical forces, and poor performances at the polls. Chapter 13 covers the relevant events, including the Ludlow Massacre in Colorado; a miners' riot in Butte, Montana, that helped topple Mayor Duncan; the execution of Joe Hill in Utah; and, on the bright side for radicals, the actions of a heroic governor in Arizona. Chapter 14 accounts the diminishing effectiveness of the campaign on the political front, in part because of the Socialists' inability to attract women voters, and offers an account of the activities and problems of the few Socialists who served as state legislators. Finally, in Chapter 15 we arrive at the period following the entry of the United States into World War I and the harsh environment this created for Socialist parties, the IWW, and the newly emerging Non-Partisan League. The concluding section extends the discussion into the 1920s and offers final observations on the rise and fall of the party and its legacy in the region.

Overview

THE MOUNTAIN WEST FROM 1890 TO 1920 was a place where, as historian John Caughey once noted, the environment had "to be taken into account."[1] Writer Harvey Fergusson, son of a prominent New Mexico Progressive reformer with the same name, observed that the Mountain West towns of this period, when seen from a distance, looked "small and insignificant, completely dominated by a landscape that lends itself but grudgingly to human use."[2] When coming to the region, Fergusson had the impression "of leaving a world of men and buildings and entering one dominated by mountains."[3]

The area was vast, often bleak and desolate, with abundant natural resources but little water. One found rugged terrains and long distances between settlements. Socialist and labor organizers were commonly struck by how far they had to go just to find someone to talk to about joining up. Hundreds of agitators before and after Eugene Debs grumbled as they tried to get to remote mining camps and isolated farms, forced to depend on trains that frequently broke down or followed an unpredictable schedule. The region was sparsely settled. According to the 1890 national census, Nevada had only around 45,000 people, Wyoming had only a few more at 60,000, while Idaho had approximately 84,000. Colorado was the largest, with 412,000 residents. In most states and territories of the region, the foreign born constituted a relatively high percentage of the populations. Some of the foreign born, especially Western Europeans, were among the most active participants in Mountain West politics during the years in which the territories and states were still in the process of formation. Others, however, as noted later, did not fit in.

Politically, the region was a place of highly personal politics, of small settlements where everyone knew everyone and character often counted more than party when it came to getting elected to office. The area, though, was also subject to sudden and unsettling changes—boom-and-bust periods were common, with the latter leaving considerable economic distress. Often settlements came and went within a matter of months. At any given time the area was also a place of considerable cultural, social, and political contrasts—for example, farms with straitlaced and family-centered Mormon communities sometimes coexisted with "spiritually feeble" mining camps filled with unattached males. Within mining camps one commonly found dozens of languages spoken and a complex, sometimes explosive combination of ethnic and racial groups. Economically, the region existed largely to supply raw materials to the rest of the country. Its prosperity was highly dependent on eastern and foreign investors and the federal government. Along with this dependency came resentment.

If the people of the Mountain West shared anything in the 1880s, it was the desire for economic development, much of which rested on extracting the mineral resources found there. To develop the region, state and local officials requested help from the federal government to subdue Indians, improve mail service, and provide better transportation facilities. On their own, state and territorial legislatures chartered railroads and, unable to directly finance road construction, granted franchises to toll companies and allowed them to charge whatever rates the market would bear. Meanwhile, boosters conducted promotional campaigns through newspapers and books aimed at readers in the more settled parts of the country or in foreign countries, providing them with a continual flow of information—some of dubious accuracy—about the region's economic potential. By the 1880s, the developmental and promotional efforts began to pay off—in came the railroads and in came the capital from the eastern United States and Europe necessary for large-scale deep mining operations.

The intrusion of large corporations—often eastern or foreign owned—into the affairs of Mountain westerners, however, produced a backlash. The economic and political dominance of these corporations, often referred to as "the beasts," alarmed observers throughout the region. Wyoming became known as a satrap of the Union Pacific Railroad. Critics charged that political power in Nevada resided with wealthy San Franciscans who controlled the Southern Pacific Railroad. Reformers in Colorado saw the state as well on its way toward becoming a colonial economy controlled by absentee capitalists who had invested in deep shaft mines. In Montana, the dominant force became the Anaconda Mining Company, which was purchased by Standard Oil Company in 1899 and stayed under its control until 1915. Arizona reformers focused on the "big four"—two copper companies, the United Verde located in the north and the Copper Queen in the south, and two railroads, the Santa Fe and the Southern Pacific—which had shown their ability to work together to block any legislation that adversely affected any of their interests. In Utah the powerful Mormon Church backed corporate interests by strongly supporting the capitalist system and condemning unions. In New Mexico power was said to rest in a political ring tied to an economic elite made up of railroad, mining, and livestock interests. Similar interests prevailed in Wyoming. Nearly everyone in the Mountain West had grievances against the railroads, while farmers had additional enemies in land and water monopolies and small ranchers, particularly in Wyoming and New Mexico, struggled against large ranchers. Office holders throughout the region were more than eager to do the bidding of the dominant economic interests. Many looked at the existing political arrangements with contempt.

Throughout the Mountain West, the concentration of economic power threatened the individualism of farmers, ranchers, miners, and other workers. They encountered big business, if not monopolistic conditions. The fact that the corporations were big was bad enough; the fact that many of them were also controlled by easterners made them even worse. As Richard D. Lamm and Michael McCarthy noted years later, people in the area "settled the land, lived on it, died on it. But they seldom owned it. . . . They blazed the trails, dammed the rivers, built the cities. But it was eastern power—mining combines, cattle cartels, railroads, banks, smelters, and political coalitions—that ruled."[4] The Mountain West, then, as it remained for decades to come, was a place with a chip on its shoulder.

By the late 1880s the once heavily courted corporations, particularly the large railroads and mining companies, became in the eyes of reformers throughout the Mountain West the outside, eastern "money interests" who were exploiting the wealth of the sparsely settled area, taking far more out of the local economy than they put in. Local politicians also charged the giant corporations with mistreating workers, farmers, and small businessmen and corrupting the political system. The railroads faced additional charges of receiving unfair tax advantages, hoarding the millions of acres of land given to them by the federal or state governments, being partial to particular shippers (through kickbacks and preferential shipping allotments), and charging excessively high rates for both passengers and freight. Anti-corporate reformers called for shifting a greater portion of the tax burden to large business concerns, regulating the rates and services of large enterprises, adopting measures to protect or advance the interests of the working class, and adding reforms such as the initiative, referendum, and recall that would ward off corporate control of the political system.

Anti-corporatism was not the whole of reform politics in the Mountain West. It was, however, an important element and one that linked the Populists, Socialists, and an emerging labor movement—the most reform-minded, if not radical, component of which existed in mining areas. Radicals, working from the anti-corporate perspective, argued that workers deserved better jobs and better government and that the solution was to give them greater control over both. Although Socialists had broader aims, they, like the Populists, had an important place in the anti-corporate political movement that ultimately produced a variety of economic and political reforms identified with the early-twentieth-century Progressives.

The impact of industrialization was first felt in the mining areas of the Mountain West. During the last few decades of the nineteenth century, prospectors and, later, large-scale development companies found several minerals—particularly silver, gold, lead, and copper—throughout the Mountain West. Small companies and even individuals could profitably mine and transport gold and silver. Mining, for many, was an individual activity that required little more than a pick, a shovel, and a pan to go into business. By the 1890s and even earlier in some places, however, placer mining began to give way to deep shaft mining. With the advent of deep mining, miners became the employees of large corporations, often owned by absentee capitalists. The character of mining changed from an occupation that offered "to all the world the chance to be one's own master" and an "equal opportunity for wealth" to one whose "attractions were only those of an eastern factory town."[5]

With the transition, the miner turned from a self-reliant prospector who stood a chance of striking it rich to an industrial worker or wage miner dependent on the absentee owners of a large corporation for his livelihood. Miners, both new and old to the profession, often found employment in isolated company towns where virtually everything, including the homes in which they lived, belonged to the mining companies. Miners in some camps received scrip redeemable only at overly expensive company stores as pay. Those who thought about striking knew they risked losing their company-owned homes and having their credit denied at company-owned stores. Absentee ownership made matters worse in that it ended the rather close relationship that had existed between employees and employers in locally owned mining companies. With absentee ownership, those who profited the most were far removed from conditions under which profits were made. Employees discovered that owners were more difficult, if not impossible, to reach, and owners found it easier to ignore workers' demands. Local managers, critics charged, were incompetent, especially in personnel matters, and too eager to please owners with bottom-line results.[6]

Within mining communities, tensions grew because of the divisions between those who had become wealthy from mining activities and those still struggling. Company officials, leading merchants, and professional people separated themselves from the less successful. Society in the sense of class consciousness came early to the new industrial communities.[7] Worker solidarity, however, was frustrated by friction among racial, ethnic, and religious groups—divisions owners were eager to exploit. In some mining camps, thirty or more nationalities were represented. Writing about divisions in the copper camp of Bingham Canyon, Utah, for example, one observer in a leftist publication noted that, with the help of mine owners stirring things up, "The Finns dislike the Greeks, the Greeks look askance at the Slavonians, the Slavonians are distrustful of the Americans and the Americans proudly flout the whole batch of 'ignorant foreigners' and stand on their American birthright and supremacy."[8]

Each group had its own particular characteristics and problems. In several camps, the Finns were among the more radically inclined and among those more likely to favor direct action against their employers. Historians estimate that about a quarter of the Finnish immigrants were attracted to Socialism.[9] Finns played a strong role in Socialist party and Industrial Workers of the World (IWW) affairs in various parts of the region, especially Montana and Wyoming. Other immigrant groups, such as the Greeks, were less radically inclined but could be aroused into strike activity.[10] On the bottom of the heap were the Chinese and Mexicans. The Chinese, first arriving in the 1850s to do railroad work and later turning to mining and other occupations, were unwelcome in many mining towns. In some places they were kept out of the towns altogether. Sometimes they were the targets of violence, the most notorious instance of which occurred in Rock Springs, Wyoming, in the fall of 1885, when white workers turned on strikebreaking Chinese, killing twenty-eight and driving hundreds of others out of the area. Much of the hostility resulted from the fact that in competing for mining jobs, the Chinese undercut the wages of white miners.

Indeed, one of the driving forces behind the first miner unions was to protect against such competition.

Mexican miners initially were better off than the Chinese. Their experience in the deep silver and gold mines of northern Mexico gave them a prominent place in the early days of deep shaft mining in the Mountain West. By the 1880s, though, they had been replaced in the elite ranks by Cornish miners, who brought newer and more efficient techniques, and Mexicans began a slide to the bottom ranks of mine labor.[11] Anglos showed their sense of racial superiority by refusing to work side by side with Mexican workers.[12] Many immigrant workers from Mexico, Greece, Italy, and other places who sought unskilled railroad, construction, and mining jobs were virtually forced to work through agents known as *padrones* to secure employment. These immigrant bosses extracted high fees and regular payments from workers who got jobs through them. To keep their businesses going, they also arranged with employers for frequent firings to occur. In time, many immigrant workers rebelled against this coercive labor system.[13]

In the early years of industrial mining, several factors reduced worker stress. For one, workers and their leaders were slow to accept the new industrialism as a permanent condition. Many of those who worked for mining companies also worked at mining their own claims in their free time, still hoping to "strike it rich" on their own. Others acted as though they were still in business for themselves by "high-grading," that is, pilfering from their employers. Discontent in many mining areas was further staved off because individual miners were often able to find employment with mine owners they knew. Moreover, if they were unhappy with their wages, they could often find a new camp where, because of the scarcity of labor, employers were willing to pay more. Many miners were single males and thus were relatively free to follow the labor market wherever it took them. Many regularly moved around the region, taking advantage of seasonal differences (going south in the winter, north in the summer) and sometimes working in coalfields, sometimes in copper mines.

By the early 1900s, however, many miners had begun to accept wage earning as a permanent condition (although Socialists continued to protest this situation), and with this came growing class consciousness and a move toward unionism to make the best of this situation. Surplus labor caused by increased foreign immigration and by the introduction of labor-saving machinery further stimulated unionization. Organization became necessary, if for no other reason than to protect wages from those willing to work for less. Although a genus of "hobo miners" continued to move from place to place, the mining workforce by the early twentieth century had generally become less mobile and more composed of family people who wished to stay in their communities. Miners, however, had little, if any, control over pay, hours of work, or safety conditions. They had to constantly guard against employers' efforts to find cheaper labor by hiring immigrants. They had to worry about pay cuts. Employers frequently took such action in response to downturns, as an attempt to increase returns to investors, or simply to reduce the level of compensation to that for which the least demanding were willing to work. Miners were caught up in dangerous and insecure employment situations. Employers sometimes refused to do anything about the conditions and were willing and able to use the state against workers who protested.

Industrial conditions and the reputations of mine owners and their status among workers varied greatly from time to time and place to place. In 1899, miners were helping put out a fire in W. A. Clark's United Verde Mine in Jerome, Arizona, while Idaho miners were blowing up a mill owned by the Sullivan and Bunker Hill Company. The difference, according to a miner quoted by an undercover operative in Leadville, Colorado, had to do with the fact that Clark "is a gentleman and treats his men right, while the owners of the Sullivan and Bunker Hill are genuine s--s of b--s and won't recognize the fact that a workingman has any rights."[14] To quickly even up the record, in another camp a few years later, one miner volunteered within hearing distance of an operative that Clark "was a cheap old cuss and would never do anything for a laboring man."[15]

Miners commonly complained about their pay and hours, how much it cost to rent company-owned housing, the high prices charged by company-owned stores, the prices and services of company doctors and hospitals, and nonexistent or inadequate safety measures. How bad conditions in mining areas actually were is a matter of some dispute among historians, but obviously they were often bad enough for many workers and those sympathetic to the workers to want to do something about them. Much of the time discontent stemmed from feelings of relative rather than absolute depravation—those aroused by differences in income between mine owners or managers and mine workers, between skilled and unskilled workers, or between workers from different ethnic groups, such as Mexicans and Anglos. Miners frequently complained that they were not getting their fair share of the profits.

Most of the early industrial conflicts in mining areas starting in the 1890s grew out of the owners' refusal to bargain with unions or anyone other than individual workers. Mine owners banded together through associations and used several techniques and strategies to combat union activity. These included hiring strikebreakers ("scabs"), often Mexican or Chinese who would work for reduced wages; mine guards who would make sure the scabs could get to work without being hindered by union men; and labor spies supplied by such outfits as the Pinkerton Service to infiltrate the unions. The owners also secured court injunctions against union activities, closed down operations until workers got hungry and gave up their demands for union organization, circulated blacklists of those suspected of being union troublemakers to keep such people from finding employment, and made workers sign "yellow dog" contracts in which they agreed not to join a union once hired. When the chips were down, the corporations could often depend on the local sheriff or the state militia or federal troops to settle their disputes with workers. Governors regularly came down on the side of mine owners by sending in the militia to protect mining property and the scab workers who defied strike activity. The same was sometimes accomplished by duping presidents into sending federal troops into strike areas.

A scenario commonly played out in the Mountain West had union and non-union men pitted against each other and a governor threatening to impose martial law if violence should erupt. When violence erupted (and sometimes even when it did not), governors called out the state militia or asked the president to send federal troops into the area. Striking workers were arrested and incarcerated in warehouses and other enclosures known as bull-pens. State militia, local sheriffs, or bans of armed citizens would sometimes load labor troublemakers on a train and deport them to another state, with New Mexico a favorite destination. Deportation, however, was sometimes only a short-term solution. As one deportee shouted to soldiers who had just pushed him and other suspected agitators off a train in New Mexico, "Ten to one we beat you back to Colorado."[16]

Early on, many emerging mining groups became affiliated with the Knights of Labor (KOL), a large national working-class reform organization that was first formed in 1869 but did not make its existence known to the public until 1881. KOL leaders sought to build an organization that would represent the interests of all wage earners and "real producers." The latter term included all gainfully employed persons except lawyers, bankers, stockbrokers, and a few others in suspect occupations.[17] The Knights refused to accept the notion that the wage system was a permanent condition of labor. Leaders such as Terrence V. Powderly looked forward to the day when the system would be replaced by self-employment and ownership of small parcels of property. Joseph R. Buchanan of Denver and others who were much more militant than Powderly headed the Knights in the Mountain West.

The Knights initially were very revolutionary, advocating close to a total makeover of American society.[18] Several radicals emerged from their ranks. As it grew, the organization became much more of a "pure and simple" labor organization bent on improving wages, hours, and working conditions, but at the leadership level the organization never fully abandoned its idealistic goals. In the 1880s the KOL had more members than the rival American Federation of Labor (AFL), much of its growth stemming from a wave of strikes in the years 1884–1886 that brought in thousands of unskilled workers. Yet, it failed to consolidate these gains and declined as rapidly as it had grown.

Meanwhile, further organization among miners and others who worked in the mining industry led to the creation of United Mine Workers (UMW) and the Western Federation of Miners (WFM). Membership in both unions was subject to sharp and frequent fluctuations, reflecting the results of strike activity and organization campaigns. The UMW was formed in 1890, three years earlier than the WFM, but its failure to make much headway west of the Mississippi provided an opening for the WFM. Both the UMW and the WFM were organized on an industrial, rather than a craft or trade, basis. While initially competitive, they worked out an agreement whereby the UMW organized workers employed in and around coal mines, while the WFM organized workers employed in and around other mines mostly, but not exclusively, in the Mountain West region. Both were members of the AFL, except for a brief period when the WFM, at the height of its radicalism, dropped out and created organizations to compete with the AFL. AFL leaders were not completely comfortable with industrial unions— most AFL members came from the exclusive skilled-worker craft-union type— but they made an exception in regard to mining unions, no doubt influenced by the emergence of the UMW as the organization's largest affiliated union.

The WFM for a time, especially under Ed Boyce, veered sharply to the left and became a major driving force behind the growth of Socialist parties in the Mountain West region. Membership in the WFM grew rather steadily from 1893 to 1903, fluctuated for several years, reached a peak in 1911 of over 50,000 members, and, although rallying from time to time, was caught in a downward spiral thereafter.[19] The organization also experienced ups and downs in the numbers of locals (Appendix, Table 1). In 1916 it changed its name to the International Union of Mine, Mill, and Smelter Workers. Prior to this, it helped give birth to the radical IWW, or Wobblies, in 1905. The IWW spread fear throughout the Mountain West. It was active not only in mining areas but also among workers in lumbering, agriculture, railroading, marine transport, and construction.

In the 1890s, early 1900s, and even later, miners and their unions held sway in numerous communities, finding support within the broader community, even among the relatively small but important class of business and professional people. Over time, however, the situation was more likely to fit the description given by a special agent reporting to the U.S. Justice Department from the mining community of Globe, Arizona, in 1917: "I do not think any man can come here in this country and try to reach the true facts, without feeling that the big mining companies dominate public opinion. Their managers are much smarter than the workmen, and one can feel their influence in the official life of the State and county. They pay eighty-five percent of the taxes of this county, and are furnished with copies of the reports made to the County Attorney."[20] The agent further noted, "The fact that the IWW and Western Federation of Miners are fussing among themselves, of course, rebounds to the benefit of the companies."[21] Throughout the period of review in Arizona and elsewhere in the region, one found considerable destructive tension and outright warfare between the various unions trying to represent the miners.

On the political front, both Populist and Socialist parties found much of their voting strength in the mining communities, including those built around coalfields as well as gold, silver, and copper mines. The third parties benefited by the tacit, if not official, endorsement of mining unions. This and several other factors—the shock of changes in miners' occupational status, from independent entrepreneurs to industrial workers; the harshness of the working conditions; increased class consciousness; and the failure of existing parties to deliver on the miners' demands—appear to have worked for a time in favor of the third parties.

The Mountain West during the period under review was unusually friendly to third parties in general. Attachment to the Republican and Democratic parties was relatively weak in the region, in part because of the underdeveloped nature of major party organizations in the area and in part because of their general failure to address the problems that concerned Mountain West voters.[22] The small size of the populations in the region also made major party ties somewhat less meaningful because it was relatively easy for citizens to get to know candidates personally and to judge them as individuals. The small size of the populations further encouraged third parties because only a relatively few votes had to be mobilized to bring about an electoral victory. Given these conditions, it comes as no surprise that the Mountain West in the late nineteenth and early twentieth centuries featured much third-party activity, with third parties frequently coming and going and, with the notable exception of the Socialists, often fusing with another third party or with a major party as the occasion warranted.

Third parties—the Populists, Socialists, and the less threatening Bull Moose Progressive parties—carried a great deal of the burden of building the agenda for anti-corporate, or what is customarily thought of as "Progressive," reform in the region. Because of the third-party influence, there were swings, sometimes substantial ones, in voter support for the major parties. These patterns contrast with the South, where fear of dividing the white majority dictated that reform activity be funneled through the dominant Democratic party, and with the East and Midwest, where voters tended to remain loyal to one of the two major parties, largely ignoring the minor parties' claims.[23] In the end, though, many radicals in the Mountain West questioned the efficacy of the third-party route in bringing about radical change. As they saw it, the Populist and Socialist experience indicated that, at best, third-party pressure might prompt some change in the platforms of the major parties, but this was likely to produce only modest regime-saving reform. Looking for another route, the Non-Partisan League set out to capture one or another of the major parties through participation in its primary. This, though, also had limited results.

The Populists were the first to articulate the anti-corporate program. In the region, as nationally, the Populist, or People's, party initially represented the efforts of a variety of groups, some more radical than others, that, having given up on the major parties, were looking for a political vehicle to power. Mountain West Populists rallied behind a broad anti-corporate platform that rejected much of the new industrial order beginning to take root in the region. Mountain West Populists also generally sought to defend and promote the interests of the new class of industrial workers, although the interests of farmers and ranchers were not ignored and, indeed, were prominent in many of their platforms. Underneath, though, Populism in this part of the country had as natural a relationship with the emergence of an industrial labor movement, especially in mining areas, as Populism in the Midwest and South had to the emergence of a farm movement.[24]

The Populists' commitment to the goals of labor and more radical ends was obscured, especially in the mid-1890s, by their simultaneous commitment to "free silver." This took the form of a demand that the federal government purchase silver bullion for conversion into silver dollars at a ratio of sixteen grains of silver to one grain of gold. The federal government had once followed a silver purchase policy but abandoned it in 1873 and allowed the price of silver to vary in the open market. In later years, westerners commonly referred to this abandonment as the "crime of '73." The policy change caused little problem until the late 1870s when the production of silver greatly increased, largely because of new discoveries, causing the price of silver to plummet. Pressure from the silver-producing states in the Mountain West helped prompt Congress to increase its purchase of silver for coinage, but these steps, taken in 1878 and 1890, did not satisfy the silver forces and, indeed, did not prevent a further decline in the price of silver. Unhappy with the status quo, Silver Clubs or Silver Leagues, dedicated to free coinage at the ratio of sixteen to one of gold, sprang up around the Mountain West.

Although support for the silver cause cut across party lines, the issue was particularly effective for Populists in the Mountain West because of the national major parties' stand on the subject. Much of the momentum behind the silver cause was supplied by mine owners in an effort to increase their profits (a fact that aroused the opposition of some radicals) and people in mining communities who saw it as essential to job creation and economic health. The silver issue also fit in well with the aims of a long line of farmers and workers who, in the antimonopoly tradition, saw the cause as a way to ensure economic opportunity and political equality.[25] As following chapters indicate, the silver cause deeply influenced the Populist movement in the Mountain West. Yet, the movement was in its essence about far more than free silver. In the end, the Populist movement passed along to the Socialists an anti-corporate program, a core of leaders, a stirred-up working class, and lessons on what to avoid and look out for, particularly in regard to fusion. It also passed along some enemies in the corporate world, a determined opposition that had been aroused and put on guard by the Populist experience, especially in Colorado.

The states and territories of the Mountain West first caught the attention of nationally prominent Socialists not so much because they saw these places as filled with potential radicals but because the places had so few inhabitants that the leaders felt they would be great areas in which to establish Socialist colonies. Debs and other prominent radicals dreamed of the Socialist electoral victories that could be realized by moving large numbers of radicals into sparsely settled states such as Nevada and Idaho.[26] As the region began to grow in the late nineteenth century, however, national leaders thought less about the size of the population and more about the possibility of immediate and fundamental political and economic change growing out of the emerging anti-corporate reform effort, at the core of which, as they saw it, were the grievances of a new class-conscious industrial workforce in mining areas.

Radicals liked to think of the workers in the Mountain West as something special in both their willingness to stand up to the boss on the job and their eagerness to use the ballot to pursue revolutionary ends. Writing about workers in the West in general, one radical expressed the view that their spirit of independence was a result of the rough frontier environment that stripped away a man's "effete artificialities" and forced him "to stand upon his own two feet if he would stand at all."[27] The end product, at any rate, was a "strong and courageous race," eager for freedom, that would not give in to the new industrial system or to capitalist bosses.[28] People working in and around mines, the radicals argued, stood to be the most radical of the radicals because of their experiences in the East, the severity of the industrial conditions they faced, or both.

Socialist parties burst on the scene in the Mountain West during the late 1890s and early 1900s as part of both a national movement and a continuation of the regional anti-corporate political reform effort. The Socialist movement as a whole was decentralized. State and territorial organizations generally ran their own campaigns without a great deal of interference or assistance from the national organization. State and territorial organizations, moreover, had difficulty exercising control over local chapters, which often hovered around the minimum membership requirement of four or five people and were widely scattered over large land areas. Foreign language federations also generally acted independent of state organizations. In addition, there were numerous unaffiliated "bushwhackers," including Christian Socialists, doing their own thing.

Mountain West Socialists absorbed much of the Populist platform, some of their leaders, and some of their following in the electorate, especially in mining areas. Yet, while Socialist parties in the Mountain West took up the "lost cause" of Populism, they also added their own particular ideological interpretations and prescriptions and, partly because of this, wound up with a more limited, class-conscious constituency.[29] They contributed to the Populists' anti-corporate platform by giving it a deeper, more theoretical underpinning, rooted in what they offered as scientific theory. They also offered fundamental reform—a way out of wage slavery through the establishment of a cooperative commonwealth that would replace capitalism. Members, though, differed somewhat over how and how soon this was to be done. Compared to the Populists, Socialists proved far less flexible, more divided over the value of political action, and—seeing themselves as part of a national and international movement with a historic mission—less focused on the politics of particular states and communities. Many had their eyes on a bigger prize and saw little value in state and, even though the chances of success were considerably greater, local politics.

By the early 1900s the Socialist movement in the Mountain West began to acquire the reputation of being home to the most radical of the radicals, the stronghold of the IWW and revolutionaries like Bill Haywood whose version of direct action meant sabotage and industrial violence and, in the end, one big union that would overthrow the capitalist system through a national general strike. One does indeed find a broad streak of revolutionary direct action in Mountain West radicalism—a willingness to go to a no-holds-barred war to the finish with the capitalists at the point of production—that made the region somewhat unique.[30] Still, the extent and importance of this aspect of the radical element in the movement can be overstated. This reputation stems largely from the widespread attention given to the violent labor wars in the region's mining areas—wars in which Socialists as union leaders and members were frequently involved and in which Socialist party leaders expressed support for the work-ers—and by the widespread attention the media gave to the IWW and prominent radicals associated with that organization. Radicals like Haywood called atten-tion to themselves by their public utterances and manifestos advocating vio-lence. They were easily depicted, in President Theodore Roosevelt's words, as anarchists, dynamiters, and all-around "undesirable citizens." The mainstream, corporate-owned, or corporate-supportive press drew upon these experiences and the revolutionary rhetoric of Wobblies such as Haywood to shape the image of radicals in the region as extreme and dangerous. Given the influence of the press, Mountain West radicals may have been generally perceived as far more confrontational, strident, dangerous, or violent than many or even most actually were. While many Wobblies were Socialists, in their own definition of the term, not all Socialists were Wobblies.

On the left-wing–right-wing scale, Mountain West Socialist party members tended to be directed toward the left. This is generally shown, for example, when we compare how Socialists in the area stood on issues voted upon by party mem-bers on a national basis. On the other hand, party functionaries throughout the region generally took party building and electoral contests seriously. In practice, they championed a variety of reform proposals (immediate demands), sought out middle-class as well as working-class support, and developed close relations with craft unions as well as industrial ones. While militant direct action and strike activity that characterized the radical movement on the industrial front may have helped build a sense of worker solidarity that benefited the parties, party leaders in the region often felt that the resulting violence and the revolutionary utterances of radical unionists, especially those who led the IWW, got in the way of party building. When it came to membership, the parties in many places attracted respected middle-class members of society. The IWW as it developed had an altogether different membership base than the Socialist parties, drawing unskilled drifters and seasonal workers uninterested in party politics or voting.

The typical Mountain West Socialist party in its heyday seemed less like a group of dangerous outcasts, failures, and incompetents—descriptions often found in the capitalist press—and more like, in Leon Trotsky's words, "a party of dentists." Speaking for her generation, a youthful Socialist Elizabeth Gurley Flynn found the IWW a definite improvement over the maturing Socialist party: "We felt it [the Socialist party] was rather stodgy. Its leaders were, if you will par-don me for saying so, professors, lawyers, doctors, ministers, and middle-aged and older people, and we felt a desire to have something more militant, more progressive and more youthful and so we flocked into the new organization, the IWW."[31] Wobbly Ralph Chaplin echoed a similar view: "I didn't think much of the politicians in the Socialist party. Too many of them looked like frustrated old businessmen or foxy young lawyers. Too many of them carried briefcases or bulged too comfortably at the waistline to suit me. I frequently asked myself bitterly, 'What are such petty-bourgeois characters doing in a revolutionary proletarian movement?' I have never been able to figure out the answer."[32] Mountain West parties were often led by middle-class people, many of whom had deep roots in their communities and felt comfortable getting involved in civic and political activities. While not abandoning long-term radical goals or the interests of working people, they set out to build moderate reform-minded political parties under the Socialist banner.[33]

Over time, the greatest electoral success in the region occurred in Nevada, where the suppression of industrial radicals and left-wing Socialists had created an opening for right-wing Socialists eager to retain and cultivate their strength in mining areas but, at the same time, eager to construct a moderate and respectable reform party with wide appeal. Their effort was showing relatively significant results before being cut off by the super patriotism and fear that accompanied World War I. Socialist candidates in the Mountain West also did relatively well on the local level, again showing a moderate side. These victories often came by riding a protest vote against corruption in local government and incompetent local administrations. Downplaying revolutionary rhetoric, Socialists pledged clean and efficient administrations and focused on such practical problems as getting the government out of debt, improving the local water supply and sewer system, and making gains in health and sanitation standards.

Rather than label the radical movement in the area as a whole somewhere on a scale of extremism, it is better viewed as proceeding along two competing fronts—the relatively peaceful political front and the often violent industrial front. Failure to quickly make gains on the political front fed a shift to the industrial front, but the ensuing violence there reverberated badly for Socialists on both battlegrounds. Still, the political effort was relatively strong. Along with being distinctive as home to a relatively large number of strident, direct action radicals, the region stands out as a place where Socialists were generally more successful than their counterparts in other regions of the country when it came to gaining party membership, winning votes, and securing elective office. This had less to do with the message—right- and left-wing parties did equally well in the region—than with the underlying industrial conditions found there, especially in mining camps, and a variety of factors mentioned earlier that made the area favorable to third-party activity.

For much of the period under review, party fortunes were on the rise, there was reason to hope, and hope helped keep the political movement alive. The strength of the Socialist party nationally and in most of the Mountain West rose rather steadily, peaking in 1912. Following the entry of the United States into World War I in 1917, the appeal of the Socialist party both nationally and in the region fell to a new low. The party's opposition to the war branded it as unpatriotic, indeed to many as being—along with the IWW—part of a pro-German conspiracy. The party's position on the war even alienated many of its leaders in the Mountain West and set off a wave of repression—led by government agents and aided by various patriotic, veterans', and church groups—against radical organizations. Parties in the region, as elsewhere, were badly crippled by this repression. Many Socialists left the party, opting out of politics or drifting into one the mainstream parties, the Non-Partisan League, or, following the Russian Revolution, one of the Communist organizations.

Long before these events, though, many Socialists had become bitterly disappointed by the failure of workers, especially miners, to rally to the Socialist cause in large numbers. Socialists were initially very enthusiastic about the revolutionary potential of the labor force in the Mountain West. For a time, they saw workers as playing the messianic role prescribed to them in Socialist theory. Yet, even in the euphoric period of growth in the early 1900s, it was apparent that the working class was not joining the Socialist cause in large numbers and was showing little gratitude to the Socialists for their efforts on labor's behalf. Workers had been willing to join a union and fight the boss for more money and better conditions, but this did not take them to Socialism. They had been willing to back Socialists for union offices but not willing to take the next step and support them for political offices.[34] In Butte, Socialists ran up against a trio of forces that limited their appeal to workers: the Catholic Church, which was particularly effective among the many Irish workers; the conservative Butte Miners' Union, which, in alliance with management, controlled the jobs; and the Democratic party, which had cultivated and drew upon the support of the miners.[35]

The failure of the industrial mining wars in Colorado at the beginning of the twentieth century to drive workers into the party's camp prompted Socialists everywhere to shake their heads in puzzlement—why, they wondered, were workers turning their backs on those trying to help them, and why were they willing to endure economic conditions so detrimental to their interests. Throughout the region, Socialists declared, they had discovered that "[i]f you help a laboring man he will kick you, if you kick him, he will help you."[36] Workers, radicals concluded, were not only ungrateful but easily intimidated—caring only about holding on to their jobs. One might argue that the Socialists were misled in the first place by their own doctrinal needs and misread the situation or saw it as they wanted to see it, not as it was—that, in fact, workers were not all that unhappy and conditions were not that bad in most mining camps. The large amount of strike and near-strike activity, however, suggests the existence of widespread and deeply felt grievances.

The fact that worker discontent did not always translate into Socialist votes seems attributable to several factors discussed in more detail later—the co-optive strategies of other parties, the workers' tendency to see the choice as boiling down to Republicans and Democrats as the likely winners and to vote against the lesser of two evils, and the Socialists' inability to articulate a meaningful message or to get their message out were high among them. For a time the Socialist parties, like the Populists before them, were attractive to union leaders looking for a new vehicle to power. The failure of Socialist parties to gain the support of workers and, more generally, to win statewide elections, however, led reform-minded union leaders to turn to other parties or to shun electoral politics altogether and engage in traditional interest group activity.

In the Mountain West, the "calamity howling" Socialists, like the Populists before them, alienated local boosters who cared deeply about economic growth and making their communities attractive to settlers and investors. Socialists, in turn, liked to think of the boosters as "prosperity howlers" who would do anything to attract investors, even sell their souls to the out-of-state corporate beasts. In the end, the anti-colonial and anti-corporate backlash against development created strong pressure for reform but never went deep enough to muster a movement strong enough to even seriously question the overall value of growth, let alone challenge the foundations of the corporate system and the economic-political system upon which it was built. Socialists, while making some inroads among the more rural populations—as in New Mexico, where the poverty of dry farmers was a way of life—often encountered an intense patriotism, made all the more intolerant by the war, and blind hatred of organized labor and of any group, Socialists included, associated with labor. On the electoral level, Socialists in much of the region tried but failed to make inroads with the farmers, although many farmers were drawn to the radically inclined Non-Partisan League. Socialists worked hard for woman suffrage, but, like the Populists before them, failed to gain much support from women voters. Many Socialists concluded that this was because women generally were not yet ready, that their movement to Socialism awaited their entry into the industrial workforce.

Mountain West Socialists faced the opposition of church leaders, with the Catholic and Mormon hierarchies the most noticeable. Catholic Church opposition made life difficult for Socialists throughout the region, including in Montana among Butte's Irish and in New Mexico among the Hispanic population.

Organizers frequently accused mine managers of paying priests and ministers to warn workers of the danger of joining unions and the Socialist party. Several church leaders apparently needed no prompting to take on the Socialists.

In Utah, and to a lesser extent in Idaho and Arizona, a major obstacle was the Mormon Church. In the 1870s and 1880s the Mormon Church had encouraged the establishment of communalistic economic systems in various communities through which activities were performed by cooperative enterprises. In some places, there was no private property.[37] Socialists later referred back to the cooperative systems established by the church as reflective of a culture consistent with radical thinking. By the mid-1890s, however, these systems had generally collapsed. By this time, moreover, the church was making a conscious effort to enter the mainstream of American life, and, as part of this, it became strongly supportive of the capitalist system. This commitment carried with it a rejection of unions and radical politics. The church never really waged war on the Populists or Socialists but was rapidly moving away from its own cooperative tradition toward the mainstream of American life, a move that carried with it a high regard for "rugged individualism" and capitalism and a dislike of unions, strike activity, and radicals.[38] In Utah, scholars have noted, "The Mormon Church was such an important presence in the state and it so pervaded the entire fabric of society that no movement could have succeeded in the face of its opposition or at least without its passive support."[39]

Also along the road Socialists encountered the hostility of the mainstream press (often corporate owned), to which they largely lost the battle for public opinion. Socialists were usually ignored by media sources owned by or sympathetic to corporations. When they mentioned Socialists at all, Republican papers regarded them with scorn but also as a potential threat to the Republic that could only be avoided by voting Republican. When mentioned in Democratic papers, editors were more likely to treat them with respect but also to outline the threat Socialists posed to the Democratic party—warning that Democrats were losing or might lose out in the competition with Socialists for the same voters and that they needed to increase their efforts or adjust their platform. Republicans would sometimes secretly subsidize Socialist party publications and campaign efforts in hopes that this would drain support from Democrats, but, in print, they had nothing good to say about the Socialists, if they said anything about them at all. Socialists struggled with all their might to establish their own press, but parties in several of the states and territories fell far short in this regard and had to depend on labor organizations for what favorable publicity they received.

On top of all these opposition forces, Socialists hurt themselves by constantly fighting among themselves. Often these were no-holds-barred struggles. In Utah, for example, the struggle among competing factions brought out maneuvers that, in the opinion of the party's national secretary, "would put the old party politicians to blush."[40] Socialists argued over goals and tactics and just about everything else. Even the occasional electoral victories brought conflicts growing out of party leaders' efforts to make sure successful candidates stayed loyal to the party and its campaign pledges. Socialist parties changed direction rapidly as one ideological wing drove out the other, leaving a trail of conflicting messages.

Socialists also often demonstrated considerable inflexibility by following a strict policy of nonalignment with other political organizations, a principle they applied to prohibit virtually any type of cooperative activity. Aloofness was partially the product of the felt need for doctrinal purity and for keeping the focus on the ultimate, if not immediate, goal of overthrowing the capitalist system. Socialists also looked to the Populist experience as proof positive of the dangers of fusion. This experience, however, could also be taken as evidence that third parties from the left were not likely to make much of an impact without fusing with other parties. Going it alone lessened the chance that Socialists would have any form of electoral success or opportunity to share in party-building patronage. Going it alone also increased the probability of dividing the radical or reform vote, to the advantage of the most conservative candidates. Aloofness put Socialists on the political sideline and reduced the incentive of those seeking a sense of immediate accomplishment to join the party.

When it came to party membership, the word was "fluidity." Socialist party officials in the Mountain West undertook their organizing campaigns in states where the population levels were constantly changing—often growing but, with the depletion of mines, also shrinking. Noting the frequent surges, declines, and shifts in population, an Arizona organizer observed: "It is possible to build up a local of considerable size, and in three months perhaps those people are practically all gone."[41] Membership rolls throughout the region rose and fell with the movement of workers, particularly miners, from location to location. The unusually high level of worker movement in the region—some voluntary in quest of a better opportunity, some forced by mining shutdowns or employer action aimed at troublemakers—made membership stability a particularly severe problem for party builders. Many members also left the party because of ideological disputes. Mountain West Socialists took their differences seriously, and one can find wholesale defections by dissenters who set up rival organizations, rival newspapers, and sometimes rival political parties.

A more general problem in retaining members was that being a member of the Socialist party was not for everyone and, for most people, was not that attractive. Membership came at a price in terms of time, effort, and, often, financial well-being. Often simply being known as a party member was equivalent to prompt dismissal or another economic hardship. The possibility of losing one's job for joining the Socialist party was a serious threat to those who worked for the mines, railroads, and a variety of other employers. Yet, while some found membership too dangerous, others found it too boring—too much theoretical stuff and too little work on immediate issues and practical problems.

The work of the radicals, finally, was also made difficult by an intricate web of surveillance. Operatives from Pinkerton and other detective agencies hired by companies and government officials regularly infiltrated radical parties, unions, and working units. The operatives were not altogether reliable. As an agent attached to military intelligence remarked about the private detectives, "From my own experience in working [with] men of this type I feel justified in the suspicion that they are pretty sure to find just what is desired."[42] To justify and prolong their employment, operatives may well have generally exaggerated the danger they found and, in the process, encouraged overreaction by employers and government officials. Labor radicals charged that private detectives were responsible for the outbreak of strikes, both by supplying inaccurate information and by acting as agents-provocateurs, encouraging radicals into activities likely to rebound against them.

Socialist parties in the Mountain West undoubtedly had more support within the adult population than showed up in official election returns.[43] Potential supporters were lost because they were not citizens, because they frequently moved from place to place and failed to meet residency requirements for voting, or because they were intimidated. Socialist candidates further suffered from the reluctance of many potential supporters, working class or not, to waste their votes by casting them for candidates who did not appear to have the slightest chance of winning. While naturally inclined toward Socialist candidates, many may have concluded that their vote would do a lot more good elsewhere. For potential supporters in the Mountain West, voting for a major party candidate was often not simply a case of trying to avoid wasting their vote but of trying to avoid cutting their own throats by helping to put a truly terrible person in office. Given the political forces at work, most often behind Republican candidates, the goal of potential supporters became largely defensive—that is, to defeat a particular candidate—and they turned to the party, usually Democratic, with the best chance of doing so.

Over time, Socialists also lost supporters because many of the more popular reforms they championed were co-opted by "thunder-stealing" Democrats and progressive Republicans and enacted into law. As political and social reforms were enacted into law, the party was left with a message that to many people may have appeared too extreme, strident, or filled with unattainable "pie in the sky" promises far removed from the everyday concerns of working people. Some parties shrank to a cultlike status. Yet, for all this, one cannot ignore the historic accomplishment: Socialists in the Mountain West played an important role in building the agenda for reform by expressing economic discontent, agitating for change, educating the public, and, perhaps most important, putting the fear of God into the capitalist class.

CHAPTER TWO

Coming Together

The Populist Protest

W RITING IN FEBRUARY 1896, Joseph H. Kibbey, a Republican party leader in Arizona, noted that political life in the territory was in flux. Since the late 1880s, Kibbey contended, more and more people had been willing to experiment with radical changes in governmental functions and to think beyond what the Republican and Democratic parties were offering them. "The people," Kibbey concluded, "are thinking hard, are thinking rapidly, and more than ever are less disposed to adopt party policy simply from mere party adherence."[1] Political activists in the Mountain West, even in the remote and lightly settled territory of Arizona, had picked up on Edward Bellamy's view of a future world in which cooperation had replaced competition. Many, too, had seen confirmation of Henry George's theme that progress for a few had been accompanied by poverty for the many.

Hoping to turn things around, reformers and radicals of various stripes had come together in the early 1890s under the banner of the Populist party.

Mountain West Populists borrowed freely from Populists elsewhere, but they were not simply trying to be fashionable in advancing ideas imported from the East or West Coast. On the contrary, they were groping for remedies to real problems that had begun to emerge in the region. They were also helping to set the stage for anti-corporate reform and radical activities.

At the time Kibbey wrote, Populists nationally were preparing for their second try at the presidency. The emergence of the party five years earlier was the culmination of a long history of farmer and worker protest. Greenbackers, prohibitionists, urban reformers, free-silver advocates, single-taxers, and Socialists of various stripes were among those who joined agrarian reformers and labor leaders in founding the new party. Although leaders of the country's only Socialist party, the Socialist Labor party (SLP), wanted nothing to do with the Populists, several members of that group were drawn to the new organization. So too were the nationalists who, inspired by the publication of Bellamy's *Looking Backward* in 1888, called for government ownership as a solution to the problem posed by monopolies and trusts.

The Populist party platform adopted in Omaha, Nebraska, in 1892 condemned the concentration of wealth and corporate power. The preamble to the platform referred to the United States as a nation where "the fruits of the toil of millions are boldly stolen to build up colossal fortunes for a few."[2] To the Populists, this land of "tramps and millionaires" was on the "verge of moral, political, and material ruin."[3] One witness to events at the Omaha convention declared, "No intelligent man could sit in that audience at the Coliseum building in the city of Omaha on July 4 last, and listen to the wild and frenzied assaults upon the existing order of things, without a feeling of great alarm at the extent and intensity of the social lunacy there displayed."[4] The witness, writing for a national magazine, found the Populist party "an aggravated symptom, a surface manifestation of a disease which has fastened itself firmly upon the mental constitutions of the people of the great West." Although stopping short of portraying the region as "in a condition of volcanic socialistic fury," he contended that the principles of Socialism had already become embedded in the thinking of many people in that part of the country.[5]

Specific remedies in the party's platform called for the free coinage of silver at a ratio of sixteen to one, more paper money, a sub-treasury produce storage plan intended to raise farm prices, a graduated income tax, government ownership of the railroads and other monopolies, the right of labor to organize, an eight-hour workday, and political reforms such as the secret ballot, popular election of United States senators, and the initiative and referendum. These reforms seem mild when compared with the rhetoric in the preamble and on the convention floor, but contemporary critics considered many to be radical changes. This view, though, was not shared by leaders of the SLP, the principal competitor of the Populists on the left. Since its origins in the late 1870s, the SLP had been built around a core of German immigrants steeped in Marxist ideas. The party, which had virtually no following in the West, lashed out at the Populists with as much vigor as had those on the right, but for opposite reasons. Speaking at a party open-air meeting in October 1892, just before it was broken up by the police, SLP leader Daniel De Leon said he suspected the motives of the farmers and silver advocates behind the new party and branded it as just as antagonistic to the interests and aims of the proletariat as were the Democrats and Republicans.[6]

The Populists, however, moved on, demanding what they saw as fundamental reform. In 1892 they chose James B. Weaver of Iowa, a former Republican and general in the Union Army who had been the Greenback nominee for president in 1880, as their presidential candidate. He toured the country offering a broad-ranging reform program organized around the theme "Equal rights for all and special privileges for none." While on a tour of the Mountain West in the summer of 1892, Weaver told a gathering at an auditorium in Helena, Montana: "I want to testify to you tonight that from actual observation I know that the American people are today in the midst of the most tremendous upheaval that the world has ever known about; a political upheaval that extends into every county in the Republic"—a movement that, he felt, was "invigorating the people and giving courage to the lowly and downcast."[7] Weaver said he had just come from an eight-day visit to Colorado, where he was greeted by large and enthusiastic crowds. Turning to his Helena audience, he predicted: "I want to tell you today that three out of every four votes in Colorado are for the Peoples Party. And I am not overestimating it either, that is a conservative estimate. And the other fourth are asking 'Lord, what shall we do to be saved?'"[8]

Weaver went on: "This is a battle between the people and the corporations. The corporations have driven the people to the wall, and flesh and blood amounts to nothing unless it has got dollars behind it now a days. . . . You know the corporations of this country today . . . dominate every state institution in this government and the Federal government . . . that they are corrupting your legislatures and corrupting your ballot box."[9] Turning to the silver issue, particularly hot in the Mountain West, Weaver declared: "We say you haven't got money enough in this country . . . and we are going to give you more just as soon as we get into power. . . . We are going to give you more silver. Can you get it in the Republican party? Can you get it in the Democratic party?"[10] According to reports, the two questions received a resounding "no" from the audience.

Weaver's themes, while well received, were familiar to Mountain West audiences. They had been articulated by speakers representing various groups—Farmers' Alliances, Silver Clubs, labor organizations, and some fledgling Populist parties on the local, state, and territorial levels—since the late 1880s. Agrarian reformers, working through Farmers' Alliances, complained about abuses of water monopolies and railways and sought free silver as a way to ease the farmer's debt burden. Free silver was the single issue of the Silver Clubs that sprang up around the region in the 1890s, although the driving force behind such groups had less to do with easing the farmers' debt than with increasing mining company profits and general prosperity in silver mining districts. Labor leaders, meanwhile, had been shopping around for a party to champion such causes as the eight-hour day, the elimination of blacklisting, increased safety standards for miners, and restrictions on immigration as a way of eliminating low-wage competition. Leaders valued the eight-hour day as a way of reducing hours without sacrificing income and of increasing the number of available jobs.

By the late 1800s, workers' discontent had produced considerable union activity and some violent labor-management confrontations in mining areas. One confrontation, although very mild compared with what was to come, occurred in 1880 after the Miner's Cooperative Union, a Knights of Labor local in Leadville, Colorado, called for a strike because of mine managers' decision to lower wages to take advantage of a surplus of labor in the area. The union was far from a hotbed of Socialism, and the striking members showed no inclination toward violence—their walkout had been peaceful. As the strike proceeded, however, a committee representing the business community and the "better element" of Leadville sent a telegram to Governor F.W. Pitkin asking him to send troops "if you want to prevent the destruction of the city by the mob."[11] The governor immediately sent in several companies of the militia from around the state and declared martial law over the area. The strike was broken. The miners, faced with overwhelming force, voted to return to work on management's terms, and the militia returned to Denver. The governor later reportedly remarked that he had been deceived by the telegram's senders—he discovered that the disorder was minimal and could have been easily handled by city and county authorities.[12] In the Leadville strike, however, mine owners and public officials set a precedent they frequently drew upon in later years by showing a no-nonsense, law-and-order attitude toward strikers and an inclination to quickly use force to keep workers in line. Radical leader Joseph Buchanan, working with a newspaper in Leadville and a strong supporter of the strike, was as much bothered as the other side was cheered by ease with which organized capital had crushed the workers' effort.[13]

Along with labor wars, the region experienced violent and politically signifi-cant land wars in the 1890s in which small farmers and ranchers were locked in combat with super-landholders—big ranchers, railroads, syndicates of one type or another—who were monopolizing the land or trying to do so. In northern New Mexico, Populism emerged as part of a movement in the "good outlaw" tradition of the West. Here the Populists were aligned with protestors known as "White Caps," who engaged in night-riding guerrilla warfare against land-grab-bing, prosperous Anglos and Hispanics. The White Caps, and to some extent the Populists, became the folk champions of the underdog group of poor Hispanic grazers (discussed later).

The Johnson County War of 1891–1892 received more attention in the region as a whole and served to those on the left as a prime example of the evils of large corporations. This conflict grew out of the decision of large stock grow-ers, represented by the powerful Wyoming Stock Growers Association, to take the law into their own hands by sending a punitive expedition of 46 men, half of whom were hired gunmen from Texas and Idaho, into Johnson County in north-ern Wyoming to track down cattle rustlers. Such action was needed, the official story went, because small stockmen on the state's public lands were rustling cattle from the larger growers to start their own operations. The large growers argued that because of community pressure in the county, it was almost impossi-ble to get a jury to convict anyone for stealing cattle. The gunmen sent in by the large growers engaged in several skirmishes, killing two suspected rustlers, but they eventually had to be rescued from a sheriff's posse of 200 citizens by federal troops sent into the area by President Benjamin Harrison at the request of lead-ing politicians—including both Wyoming senators and the acting governor—on behalf of the Wyoming Stock Growers Association. Later, a jury dismissed the murder case against the gunmen for lack of evidence.

The events in Johnson County provoked a wide reaction. Populists in the region, and indeed throughout the nation, used the episode as a prime illustra-tion of what was wrong with the economic and political system. Populist Davis Waite, running for governor in neighboring Colorado, contended that during the Johnson County War the federal government had acted to protect criminals. The Populist party, meeting at its national convention in Omaha, saw fit to "condemn the recent invasion of the territory of Wyoming by the hired assassins of plutoc-racy, assisted by federal officials."[14] Wyoming Populists undoubtedly were pleased with the national party's resolution, although they probably wished someone had told its drafter that Wyoming was now a state (it had been since 1890).

Beyond all the talk about cattle rustling, many suspected that the large growers, who already had a virtual monopoly on the state's grazing lands, were simply trying to oust the homesteaders and small stock grazers who had begun to organize and challenge the large cattlemen's monopoly. As the leftist *The New Nation* described the situation in April 1892:

> The civil war in miniature which exists in Wyoming, and has already led to the intervention of the United States troops, is ominous of the increasing bitterness of the issue between capitalism and the people. In this fight on one side are arrayed the pioneers and settlers who are seeking to homestead places on the public lands. These are described by the associated press dispatches as "rustlers," and represented as bands of robbers. On the other hand are the great cattlemen, who, without right or title of any sort insist on keeping the public lands a waste for their cattle-herds to range on, and employ gangs of armed mercenaries, frontier "Pinkertons," to drive out, burn out, and kill out all would-be settlers. That is the precise size and shape of the issue, and as might be expected, President Harrison and the state authorities are on the side of the cattlemen against the settlers.[15]

On the heels of the Johnson County War came a second major disturbance in the area, which helped set the stage for the 1892 elections: a violent strike involving around 3,000 miners in the Coeur d'Alene silver mining district in Shoshone County, Idaho. In January 1892 mine owners, citing an increase in railroad rates to ship ore out of the district, announced they were going to reduce mining wages. Members of the Coeur d'Alene Miners' Union responded by walking off the job. Mine owners tried to replace them with nonunion "scabs" and hired Pinkerton detectives and armed guards to protect the scabs. Pinkerton detectives also infiltrated the unions. One of these men, who rose to the position of union recording secretary, helped inflame the situation by reporting that union leaders were "as a rule, a vicious, heartless gang of anarchists."[16]

Open fighting between union and nonunion men resulted in several deaths. When it appeared the pro-union forces would prevail, the mine owners elicited the support of Republican governor Norman Willey, who proclaimed martial law in Shoshone County and sent the state militia into the area. At Willey's request, President Harrison, as he had already shown himself willing to do in Wyoming, dispatched federal troops to the district—around 800 soldiers, both cavalry and infantry, were rushed in by rail from Montana and Washington. Their presence, in effect, broke the back of the strike. With the protection of military forces, the scabs, who had been driven from the county by union supporters, returned and went to work at the wage the mine owners were willing to pay. Meanwhile, soldiers arrested hundreds of union men and placed many of them in warehouses called "bull-pens." According to Haywood: "A bull-pen was built in which the prisoners were confined for more than six months. This was a rough lumber structure two stories high. There was no sanitation provided, and the excrement of the men above dripped through the cracks in the plank floor on the men below. They became vermin-infested and diseased, and some of them died."[17] Ed Boyce, later a mine union leader, was among those confined to the bull-pen. The event confirmed for many what the radicals and reformers had been saying about the evils of big business and its collusion with government. It also set in motion activities that led to the creation of the Western Federation of Miners.

On the political front, Knights of Labor Unions, Farmers' Alliances, Silver Clubs, and other reform organizations in the Mountain West during the 1890s found the existing major parties unsatisfactory instruments for pursuing their aims. They started shopping around for new political vehicles, and many eventually collaborated in the formation of Populist parties in the region's states and territories. They frequently formed coalitions resembling those found on the national level—sometimes including, for example, single-taxers, Socialists, former Greenbackers, and nationalists. In places such as Colorado and Idaho, agrarian organizations played a prominent role in the formation of Populist parties, although within a few years these parties became more labor centered. Even though the area mostly involved mining and cattle, Farm Alliance organizations were also active in the early stages of Populist organization in Arizona in the early 1890s.[18]

In the early 1890s Populist parties, consisting of loose coalitions of various groups, were found throughout most of the region, although sometimes only on the local level. They pledged themselves to the Omaha platform and generally offered a broad program in which silver, anti-corporate, and pro-labor issues dominated. Many, though, were also conscious of farmers' rights in regard to such matters as rates charged by water monopolies and railroads. Some contended that free silver was in the farmers' best interest because their interests were tied to prosperity in the mining communities. The importance of different planks varied from party to party: silver played a central role in the Populist campaigns in Colorado and Nevada, while labor themes stood out in Idaho and Montana, and large rancher versus small rancher issues moved to center stage in Wyoming and New Mexico. Several parties, though, used the Johnson County War as a battle cry and, addressing another regional problem, saw value in restricting immigration. Some of the parties, such as in Colorado and Montana, were strongly associated with the woman suffrage cause. Montana Populists nominated a women's rights advocate for attorney general who turned out to be the party's best vote getter.

In some places the radical presence in the movement rose to the surface. In Wyoming, for example, Knights of Labor and Populist leader Henry Breitenstein declared that the money interests had stolen the government from the people and that these interests—banks, bondholders, speculators—were ticks living off laboring people.[19] At other times, the Populist parties sounded like anything but left wingers. The People's party of Globe, Arizona, endorsed the national People's party's Omaha platform but combined its anti-corporate rhetoric with more conservative complaints that, for example, county expenditures were too high (largely because of unnecessary officials and offices) and that the rate of taxation "was burdensome and oppressive, deterring capital from investment and retarding the development of the natural resources of the [county]."[20] Populists elsewhere were also critical of excessive government spending and taxing, although, on reflection, this seems to have had less to do with a desire to generally reduce the size of government or promote development than it did with the desire to combat the efforts of corrupt "special interests" to feather their own nests through unnecessary expenditures and to shift the tax burden for these expenditures to the general public.

Political conditions for the emergence of Populism varied—for example, in Utah, Populism was shaped in a somewhat hostile political environment dominated by the Mormon Church and took on a somewhat anti-Mormon tone, while the nature of the movement in New Mexico reflected Hispanic resentment of Anglo encroachments. Throughout the region, though, Populists presented a threat to the power structure and were branded "radical" even when the reforms they advocated clearly fell into the category of reform. The emerging parties also had difficulty holding competing interests, such as those of labor and agricultural groups, together. Along with this was the difficulty of forging satisfactory relations with other political parties, particularly the Democratic party, which was often close to the Populists in basic orientation. Democrats were close to Populists on many issues, particularly as they affected labor, and had the most to lose through the growth of the new party. In some places Democrats viewed emerging Populist parties as a Republican plot to draw away votes from Democrats. The two parties had considerable reason to pool their resources— often, this represented the only way they could defeat the dominant Republicans. Still, fusion meant a loss of control over the agenda. Populists were torn over the lifetime of their movement in the region by the dilemma of fusion.

Given the economic-political context, it is not surprising that Weaver, who polled more than a million votes nationally, did unusually well in the Mountain West in 1892. Although portrayed as a lunatic by the major party press, he carried Colorado, Idaho, and Nevada; the only other states he carried were Kansas and North Dakota. Weaver lost in Montana and Wyoming and, in so doing, left two lessons for the Populists: the need to fuse efforts with other parties, which was apparent in Montana, and the folly of doing so, which appeared to be the case in Wyoming. Electoral victories on the state level were few in 1892, but Populists made a significant breakthrough in Colorado and showed some strength in Idaho, Montana, Nevada, and Wyoming. Having no presidential election around which Populists could organize, the movement was weaker in the territories of Utah, New Mexico, and Arizona. Populists in these places, however, competed in territorial elections and sometimes showed surprising strength.

The major state-office victory in 1892 came in Colorado. Here, the Populists nominated and elected sixty-seven-year-old Davis H. Waite as governor. Waite at this time was known as the crusading anti-monopoly, pro-labor editor of the *Aspen Union Era*. He constantly referred to the Populist Omaha platform as the basis of his beliefs.[21] Free silver, though, was a secondary matter to Waite. He found its chief value was as a means of achieving political power. When it came to the money supply, he was closer to the Greenback position that the issuance of paper money would bring prosperity.

Most of Waite's support at the Populist party nominating convention in Pueblo came from the party's farm element, which had been central to the founding of the organization a year earlier and still was in control in 1892, not yet giving way to the ever growing influence of delegates from mining areas. Waite turned back the challenge of Julius Thompson, a Silver League activist and a late convert to Populism, in securing the nomination. Old-time Populists feared Thompson was only interested in silver, and, as it turned out, most of his delegate support did come from mining areas where Silver Clubs were active. Following Waite's nomination, the party formed an alliance with the State Silver League, which had around 25,000 members statewide, even though the league was somewhat hesitant about the "calamity howler" Waite. Sometime after the convention, the state central committee of the out-of-power Democratic party also endorsed Waite, although a group of anti-fusionist Democrats decided to nominate their own candidate.

Blending ideology, policy preferences, and strategic considerations, the Colorado Populist party came up with a platform that featured free silver, greater regulation of railroad passenger and freight rates, the eight-hour day, and, in the interest of both economy and fighting political graft, the reduction of state officials' salaries. The convention too, much to the delight of the nationalists, also included a plank in the platform demanding "A law forbidding the future sale of any coal lands by the state and providing for the working by the state of its own mines upon such terms as will secure fair wages and humane treatment to miners." Another plank of the Colorado Populists came out strongly for woman suffrage: "We favor, and if given the power will secure equal rights at the ballot box[,] to all citizens of the state without distinction of sex."[22]

Shortly after the convention, an editor of a Republican newspaper passed along these thoughts: "It is difficult to see how any sensible person can expect the ticket nominated by the populists convention at Denver to win. . . . The people's party convention had a chance to nominate a strong ticket—but they didn't. It is composed of a lot of mongrels from top to bottom."[23] When the votes were counted, however, the People's party, fused with the Democrats, swept the state offices and won the state's two seats in the U.S. House of Representatives. Populists also placed twelve of their candidates in the state senate and twenty-seven in the state house.

Waite's victory was not overwhelming—he came up with 47 percent of the vote in a three-way contest, and, while Weaver carried the state by 15,000 votes, Waite had a plurality of just over 5,000. Nevertheless, many in Colorado and around the nation were shocked to learn that such a reliable Republican state, and one where the Populists had received just 6 percent of the vote in 1890, could change direction so dramatically. Following the election Waite declared, "We have gained a great victory in Colorado, and it has been won by the people regardless of former political ties and influences solely by a patriotic effort to act for their own interests and the prosperity of the state."[24] Waite felt the Populists in Colorado had rallied the sentiment for silver and the rights of the people, "which have been outraged by the governmental policy of the last twenty years." Moreover: "We have compelled the recognition of a line of division between the privileged classes and the common people, which both the old parties, controlled substantially by the same monopoly power, have heretofore ignored or opposed."[25]

In explaining the Populist party's success, one observer wrote for a national magazine, the *Forum*, a few years later: "Thousands of Colorado voters turned to it, not because they accepted its doctrines on other subjects—for they ignored them—but for the purpose of protesting against the attitude of the two dominant parties on the one subject of coinage."[26] The Populists in 1892 no doubt benefited by being the only party pledged to free coinage of silver. This helped them carry the mining areas, although in these places they may have also benefited, as they had anticipated, by their call for labor reforms such as the eight-hour day. Support in mining areas came from protesting miners. Waite and the Populists had little support among the mine owners and their business allies.[27] Populists also owed part of their success to their exploitation of the irrigation issue in agricultural areas.[28] Overall, the Populists lacked much of a following among skilled craftspeople in places like Denver. They also failed to secure the support of trade union leaders. These people opposed independent labor politics and were happy to confine their activities to nonpartisan lobbying efforts at the state capitol. The party, though, had begun to arouse considerable support among unskilled workers.[29]

The Populist victory in Colorado brought to power a strongly reform-minded group whose views reflected grievances building up over the years against the domination of the state's economic and political system by corporations and out-of-state financial interests.[30] At the heart of the party one did not find, as commonly charged, a group of professional reformers or third-party veterans. Most leaders of the new party had previously identified as Republicans or Democrats. Although the party spoke for the interests of miners and farmers, evidence indicates that people in these occupations did not lead the movement. Rather, the party's leadership consisted of professional and semiprofessional people, successful businessmen, and a healthy sprinkling of newspaper editors and educators.[31] The movement also attracted the support of Christian Socialist Myron Reed. The reverend, though, turned down a chance for the party's nomination for a seat in Congress because of his current obligations and his feeling that he could better serve the cause through his profession. He later accepted appointments to various boards in Waite's administration.[32]

To contemporaries, the party may well have sounded radical. Willingly adding to that impression was J. A. Wayland, later famous as the owner-editor of the widely circulating Socialist paper *Appeal to Reason*. Wayland, born in Versailles, Indiana, in 1854, was among the radicals who chose Populism as a way of venting their discontent with the capitalistic system. He became a Socialist about the time the Populist party was being organized, having been guided in that direction by an English shoemaker he met shortly after moving to Pueblo, Colorado, in the early 1890s.[33] Wayland became a strong admirer of Davis Waite and his stand against plutocracy and monopoly and volunteered his assistance to the Populist cause in 1892. Initially, the Populists did not trust him because he was a capitalist who sold real estate, but he eventually gained their confidence. Wayland contributed money, worked as an unpaid editorial writer for a Populist-labor paper in Pueblo—*The Coming Crisis*, which he felt was as radical as anything published by the Socialist Labor Party—and distributed party propaganda leaflets. Wayland claimed the Populist party he saw in Colorado and elsewhere in the West was something other than a capitalistic reform party. Indeed, he claimed that "all the speeches by the populists were socialistic . . . and nearly all our candidates were avowed socialists."[34] The Populist party he saw was serving as the means through which "the socialist platform will be carried into effect. . . . Socialism by any other name will be as sweet."[35]

With the Johnson County War, Wyoming's Populists, who had largely functioned until now as a small club concerned with making resolutions on national issues, suddenly had a local anti-monopoly issue around which to build a following. They condemned the large ranchers in no uncertain terms for causing the "murderous invasion" into Johnson County.[36] By the fall of 1892 several Republicans as well as Democrats had defected to the Populists, and the new party had made inroads with small homesteaders, ranchers, and others anxious to challenge the large ranchers.[37] Wyoming, like Colorado at the beginning of 1892, was a Republican state—the GOP held all state executive offices and controlled both legislative houses. Democrats looked at pooling their efforts with the Populists as a vehicle to success. From the Democrats' point of view, the Populists were worth a courtship because they appeared to have a following in both the agricultural areas where the Farm Alliance was active and railroad towns such as Cheyenne and Laramie, strung along the tracks of the Union Pacific Railroad, among those who worked for the railroad and those who belonged to the Knights of Labor. Considerable disagreement existed within the Populist party, however, over whether they should go it alone or work with the Democrats in an attempt to bring down the Republicans. Following a heated and prolonged debate, the 1892 Populist convention, by a twenty-seven to seventeen vote, agreed to a proposal from the Democratic party under which Populists would support the Democratic candidates for congress, governor, and other state offices and the Democrats would support Weaver's bid for the presidency. Delegates from several counties walked out of the Populist convention in protest of the decision to accept the Democratic proposal.

In November the Democratic candidates emerged victorious, but the state went Republican in the presidential race. Democrats, some Populists contended, had not adhered to their bargain as faithfully as the Populists did—although, in fact, the election outcomes may have been more attributable to the decision of many Republicans in the northern part of the state, where the Johnson County War had occurred, to support the fusion ticket for state offices but remain loyal to the Republican presidential candidate.[38] At any rate, both the Populists and Democrats benefited in congressional and state elections by allying themselves with the small settlers in their battle with the Wyoming Stock Growers Association. The Republicans, widely perceived as tied to large ranchers, wound up on the wrong side of the Johnson County War issue. Two of the four legislators Johnson County sent to the state capitol were Populists.

Wyoming Democrats on the campaign trail often sounded every bit as anti-corporate as the Populists. One of the most prominent Democratic candidates that year who fell into this category was Henry A. Coffeen, who successfully ran for the sole seat in the U.S. House of Representatives. Coffeen, Ohio born, had been active in the Knights of Labor in the late 1870s and early 1880s. Like many others from the Midwest, he had been attracted by the notion of western pioneering and moved to northern Wyoming in the late 1880s. He soon became a prosperous businessman, one of the wealthiest men in northern Wyoming. Coffeen, though, had a strong Populist bent. A firm foe of "organized greed" and the "cunning avarice of the money powers," he felt comfortable running with the support of Populists. In 1892 he denounced the large cattlemen and proudly stood for silver.[39]

During the 1892 campaign, the Populists threw in the silver issue (there was little silver mining in the state, but many were hopeful that this would soon change), as well as, through the rampages of leaders like Henry Breitenstein, considerable class warfare rhetoric along with an anti–large stockman attack. The Populists, although part of a victorious fusion, received only about 13 percent of the votes cast. In the house, the Democrat-Populist combination had enough representatives to take control, but only five of these people were Populists. Still, following the 1892 election a Wyoming Populist paper proudly announced: "The people's party have met the enemy on Wyoming soil and the enemy is ours. . . . The next legislative assembly for our state will be composed of [the] people's party and democrats. Good bye to the Wyoming Stock Association."[40]

While the news from Colorado was very encouraging and that from Wyoming somewhat encouraging, the messages from Idaho, Montana, and Nevada in 1892 were more mixed. As in Colorado, Idaho farmers in the 1890s worked through the Farmers' Alliances in their battle against water monopolistic irrigation companies for lower water rates. Farmers also sought rail reduction rates and free silver as a way to ease their debt burden and end deflation. They eventually joined with Free Silver Clubs behind the Populist party.[41]

The Idaho People's party, in its first state convention in May 1892, adopted a platform vigorously protesting the governor's decision to proclaim martial law and send the national guard to Coeur d'Alene and extending its support and sympathy to the miners' union. More broadly, the Populists condemned the old parties for ignoring laboring men as well as farmers. For the workers came calls to prohibit cheap foreign labor and yellow dog contracts under which an employee had to agree not to join a union. For farmers, the Populists produced planks protecting their water rights and opposing the abuses of railroads and monopolies.

In August the party nominated its candidates, including James Gunn, an ex-Republican who edited an influential Populist newspaper, for Congress and Abraham Crook, another former Republican and mine owner who had played a prominent role in the formation of the Populist party in Idaho, for governor. Neither candidate won, although both did relatively well in mining areas and agricultural counties where Farmers' Alliances were active.[42] During the election the silver issue was neutralized, as all three parties supported free coinage, and both Populists and Democrats condemned Republicans for imposing martial law in Coeur d'Alene. In the end, the Populists sent ten members to the state legislature and, working with the Democrats, delivered the state to Weaver.

Matters did not work out as well for the Populists in neighboring Montana. Although various groups, including Farmers' Alliances and single-taxers, had been involved in the formation of the Montana Populist party in a January 1892 convention in Anaconda, the party was dominated by labor, especially the labor force emerging in mining areas in the western part of the state. In 1892 the party sprang to life early in protest of the legislature's failure to approve an eight-hour-day law. The party platform put together in Butte in June of that year emphasized the need for a legal workday of eight hours for "all employers of labor, thereby reducing the hours of labor and increasing the number of employees."[43] In a move toward nationalization, the party declared: "We hold that where free competition becomes impossible, as in telegraphs, telephones, railroads, water and gas supplies, etc., such business becomes a proper social function, which should be controlled and managed by and for the whole people concerned, through their government, local, state, or national, as may be."[44]

Other major planks in the platform called for the free and unlimited coinage of silver, the election of federal officer holders (president, vice president, and senators) by popular vote, and the restriction of immigration to "such classes as will make good citizens," an anti-Chinese labor plank. Populists also demanded that the land grant of the Northern Pacific Railroad Company in Montana "be declared forfeited by reason of the failure of the company to build the road within the time period specified in the charter."[45] In emphasizing free silver, Montana Populists felt they had an economic development and employment issue that was attractive to both miners and mine owners. They also argued that Montana farmers had much to gain through free silver. In making the argument, however, the Populists focused less on the reform as a cheap money solution to the farmers' debt problems than on the notion that farmers would suffer if the silver industry was killed because this would destroy the state's economy, dry up the only market farmers had for surplus products, and severely depreciate the value of farm property.[46]

Montana Populists went into the 1892 election with considerable enthusiasm—thinking, as a base, they would do well among the 17,000 voters connected with organized labor and Farmers' Alliances.[47] Unlike their counterparts in Colorado and Wyoming, Montana Populists in 1892 refused to fuse with Democrats for any offices. The Populists, running on their own, came up with a state ticket representing a variety of reform-minded groups. It included William Kennedy, a newspaper editor and single-taxer, for governor; Harvey H. Cullum, a mining foreman and union leader from Butte, for lieutenant governor; Ella L. Knowles, a New Hampshire–born lawyer, for attorney general; and Caldwell Edwards, a single-taxer associated with the Gallatin County Farmers' Alliance, for Congress. Kennedy was the most seasoned politician of the group, having served in the Montana Territorial Legislature as a Republican where he was credited with securing passage of a bill calling for the secret ballot. The party depicted itself as a dynamic, new, pro-labor, pro-silver reform party. On the silver issue, though, its stand differed little from the Democrats and Republicans.[48]

The failure of Montana Populists and Democrats to fuse hurt both parties. It allowed the Republican Harrison to carry the state, despite the already-noted campaign appearance by Weaver, and Republicans to carry several state offices they might otherwise have lost.

The top vote getter in the November election was Knowles, who spoke on women's rights issues as well as the silver issue and received 11,465 votes in finishing third in her race, a little better than 26 percent of the vote. While failing statewide, voters sent three Populists to the state house. The party did particularly well in Silver Bow (Butte), where it had some success among working-class voters in mining areas—two of the house members came from there—and Deer Lodge (Anaconda) counties, where labor was strong.[49]

Tracing the success of the Populist movement in Nevada in the early 1890s is more complex because many people identified it with a new party, the Silver party, which, in fact, was not truly committed to Populism. Unhappy with the position of the major parties on the silver issue, members of various Silver Leagues and many of the state's most prominent politicians from both major parties met in Reno in June 1892 and formed the Silver party to push for the unlimited coinage of silver at a ratio of sixteen grains of silver to one grain of gold. The new party drew Democrats and Republicans in relatively equal numbers.[50] Among those switching to the new party was U.S. Senator William M. Stewart, a Republican, who was eager for another term. Stewart saw free silver as the major issue in the state and wanted to be on the winning side by helping build a party that could ride this issue to power. The Silver party in 1892 nominated electors pledged to the Populist national ticket and not only swept the state for Weaver but sent Francis G. Newlands to Congress, won the gubernatorial contest and several other statewide offices, and took control of the state assembly. The legislature gave Stewart another term.

To the electorate at large, the Silver party may well have appeared radical or, at least, little different from the ordinary Populist party. The Silverites endorsed the national Populist platform demands for such measures as government ownership of railroads and telegraph lines, compulsory arbitration of labor disputes, and direct election of senators. Contemporary observers, however, noted that the Central Pacific Railroad's main lobbyist, C. C. Wallace, had played a key role as a party founder and suspected that the Central Pacific Railroad actually controlled the Silver party. All in all, as Nevada historian Russell Elliott has noted, "It seems apparent that the railroad's support of the Silver party in Nevada was a practical way to assure control of the state."[51] In fact, the Silver party's sweep of the state in 1892 did not produce anything that gave the railroads much trouble. The tide of public support for the Silver Party in 1892 had, no doubt, caught up many sincere Populists, some of whom would have organized a Populist party had the Silver party not emerged. Following the 1892 election, some of these people rebelled against the Silver party, which they had come to think of as "the Wallace combine of free silver and railroad supremacy," and established what they contended was a genuine Populist party.

While Populists in most of the Mountain West states were making considerable noise in 1892, the territories in that region—Utah, New Mexico, and Arizona—with no presidential election around which to rally the troops, were relatively quiet. There were probably some Populists in the Utah territory in 1892, but formal organization of the party was still a year away. Since the creation of the Utah territory in 1850, the Mormon Church had dominated Utah electoral politics, although there were scattered signs of opposition. From 1870 to 1890 the church's People's party—tied nationally to the Democratic party and having no connection with the Populist movement—had some opposition as non-Mormons, whose ranks had begun to swell because of the completion of the transcontinental railroad in 1869 and the subsequent development of mining, found a political outlet in the Liberal party. Church leaders, in an effort to enhance the territory's chances for statehood, abandoned the People's party in 1890 and, drawing upon several methods, divided the church membership between Democrats and Republicans.[52] Some also may have moved on to the new Populist party. A more likely source of support for the Populist party, however, was the Liberal party, which dissolved in 1893. Indeed, one does find evidence of some of its leaders and members becoming Populists.[53]

By the early 1890s, the backbone of the Populist party-to-be—the growing unionized labor force in the cities and mining areas—had begun to make itself felt in Utah politics by pressuring for labor reforms. Mormon Church leaders, who had created and controlled the first unions in the territory, were openly critical of the new unions as represented by the rabble-rousing Knights of Labor allied with the Liberal party. Many church leaders were businesspeople who held an anti-union bias common among employers. Church leaders were especially anxious to keep members of their own faith away from unions. The church, they argued, could provide for its members' needs, negating the necessity for any of them to turn to unions for help. Further, unions were to be avoided because joining them violated church policy at the time of nonassociation with Gentiles (non-Mormons). Such association, church leaders felt, could only weaken Mormon workers' loyalty to the church. Moreover, Mormon leaders asserted, association was to be avoided because union organizers were people of questionable motives and character.[54]

As Utah began to develop the rich ores found in the territory, it experienced a succession of immigrants—Finns, Italians, Serbs, Croatians, Slovenians, Greeks, and Japanese came into the territory to fill the demand for unskilled labor in developing mining areas. The church was alarmed by the influx of newcomers—some of whom, it felt, were drawn to radical ideas—and depicted mining towns as sinful places, filled with liquor, gambling, violence, and prostitution.[55] Anti-Mormon politicians, business leaders, and clergymen encouraged the importation of non-Mormon miners in the hope that this would help them break the Mormons' hold on the territory. On occasion, Mormon versus non-Mormon conflict was evident in labor confrontations. Such was the case in an 1893 strike by hard-rock miners at the Bullion-Beck Mine at Eureka, Utah, in the Tintic Mining District sixty miles south of Salt Lake City. The mine owners, who were prominent in the Mormon Church, took their cue from the mine owners' victory in Coeur d'Alene and decided to lower wages. The mine workers struck but soon found themselves in violent conflict with strikebreakers brought in by the company. The fact that the owners and many of the strikebreakers were Mormon created considerable anti-Mormon feeling among the strikers. In the end, the workers gave in—the union was not recognized, and workers accepted the reduced wage—and Mormon leaders, particularly those who had invested in the company, emerged even more hostile to organized labor.[56]

While the Knights of Labor worked to arouse class consciousness among workers and the organization's efforts were paying off to some extent with miners and railroad workers, little pressure for reform was coming from rural areas. Utah farmers were not protesting currency deflation or railroad gouging. Nor were they in debt or suffering low prices for their products. The Utah farmers produced mainly for a local market and, thus, were less insecure than farmers of other regions tied to the national market. Farm Alliance members, moreover, had to operate within a theocratic social framework imposed by the Mormon Church, which limited their access to the farmers, many of whom were Mormon.[57]

New Mexico in the early 1890s was also dominated by a conservative political order. In this case powerful land, cattle, and railroad interests were allied with old-guard Republicans and prominent Hispanic leaders in what is known as "the Santa Fe Ring." Yet, as in Utah, the arrival of railroads and the influx of immigrants from other parts of the country had begun to change things. Especially important in New Mexico was the movement of farmers from the Midwest and the South, where Populism had caught fire, into the eastern and southern parts of the territory. These dry farmers, most of whom were Democrats, were going broke trying to raise crops without irrigation. New Mexico, which also had a silver mining industry in the southwestern section, became a place where agrarian protest merged with the cause of free silver.[58]

During the 1890s New Mexico Populists enjoyed some success on the county level, spurred on by local assemblies of the Knights of Labor or of the Southern Alliance. New Mexico farmers and ranchers had grievances concerning hauling charges, land prices, water rights, and access to the public domain. In the late 1880s and early 1890s farmers and ranchers in the southeastern part of the state, working through a Southern Alliance organization, challenged the powerful Cattle Association.[59] In the northern and eastern part of the territory, populism revolved around land grabbing and an alleged cattle monopoly. Populists first came alive in San Miguel County in northern New Mexico (where Las Vegas, New Mexico, was located), after large landowners, often Anglo-Americans new to the territory, began fencing off community grazing lands. This enclosure provoked considerable resentment among Hispanics and led to the organization of a Hispanic gang or vigilante group called the Las Gorras Blancas, the White Caps, Whitecappers), because they wore white hoods during nighttime raids in which they cut fences and often burned the property of large landowners. Juan Jose Herrera, the leader of the White Caps, was also a district organizer of the Knights of Labor. The Knights claimed, unconvincingly to many, that there was no relation between their organization and the White Caps.[60] In the early 1890s conservative papers linked the White Caps to nearly every incidence of violence in the territory. The Populists were strongest in counties where the White Caps were most active, although not all White Caps were Populists or all Populists White Caps. In a broad sense, New Mexico Populists fed off the general discontent Hispanics felt toward the Anglo regime in the territory.[61]

In 1890, Herrera and the Knights put a Populist Party–like organization together in San Miguel County, and voters sent six of the party's representatives to the territorial legislature, two to the council and four to the house. Among the council members was Pablo Herrera, the brother of Juan Jose. Theodore B. Mills, later the most prominent Populist in the territory, was another Populist council member. Mills, a former Republican, had served in the Kansas legislature as a member of that party. He had also been a newspaper editor and a mine investor. In the house the Populists had enough votes to affect the outcome of legislation. Much to the disgust of the party's more doctrinaire members, however, the Populist legislators wound up working closely with Democrats on legislative matters and produced little in the way of reform. By 1892 the Populist party in New Mexico had expanded into only the southernmost county of Dona Ana. The Populists in San Miguel, meanwhile, had become junior partners with the Democrats, receiving just five of the sixteen places on the joint ballot.

Populists in Arizona were also active on the local level, but with less success. Populist candidates for office first appeared in Arizona in 1892, although, as one Populist organizer later noted, the party at that time was only a little club "burning for liberty."[62] Perhaps best indicative of the status of the movement in Arizona in the early 1890s was a report in a Democratic paper on a Populist convention held in Phoenix on October 6, 1892. This Sunday gathering, the reporter noted, was attended by around 100 people, a mix of Democrats, Republicans, Mugwumps, and Populists—the reporter claimed not over 30 were Populists—who had gathered to discuss nominating their own candidates as opposed to endorsing nominees of other parties. Failing to reach a decision, they decided to put off the discussion. "At this point," the reporter noted, "the feeble pulse beat of the convention ceased, and those present carefully tiptoed down the stairs."[63] The same paper two days later, however, seemed to take the new party more seriously—attributing the emergence of Populist parties in Phoenix and around the territory to a Republican plot to draw away votes from Democrats. Best organized in Arizona in 1892 was the People's party in the mining town of Globe, where miners had established a union in 1884. Globe was destined to be at the heart of reform and radical activity in Arizona for many years.

The Arizona Populists came to life in an environment where they had plenty of competition on the silver issue: both Arizona Republicans and Democrats claimed they were the true and only champions of silver. In 1891 members of both parties even went so far as to shape a proposed state constitution that called for the establishment of silver as well as gold as legal tender for the payment of all debts in what would become the state of Arizona.

Populists also had to face the fact that, overall, the Democratic party in the territory was positioned on the left and on the side of labor. This was reflected in the party's platform and newspapers. Democratic editors, for example, were eager to blame the Republicans for siding with employers and "trying to pauperize American labor."[64] Anson H. Smith, the fire-eating editor of a Democratic paper in Mohave County (a thinly populated mining area), asked (and answered): "Why is it that so many manufacturers are Republican, if politics does not cut a big figure in the manufacturing industries? The Democratic party is the party of the masses, the Republican, the party of the classes. The classes propose to rule by whatever methods circumstances suggest."[65] Arizona Democrats, though, differed from both Republicans and, as time would demonstrate, the Populists in one important respect—they were far more in tune with the relatively conservative Mormon population. Populism in Arizona, as in Utah, took on an anti-Mormon tone.

Overall, in the early 1890s Mountain West Populists offered an essentially anti-corporate platform that appeared to some contemporary observers from both the right and the left to reflect radical objectives. If there was a common denominator among Populist activists in Mountain states, it was concern over large corporations or monopolies, be they of the land, money, transportation, or another variety.[66] If, too, there was a common complaint against Populists (and later the Socialists), it was that their anti-corporate "calamity howling" could kill off development by alienating key players in that process, such as eastern investors and the owners of mining companies and railroads. Beyond this, though, the nature and development of the parties varied considerably within the region in the early 1890s, and their success depended largely on the willingness or ability of Populist parties to fuse with other parties. Although a radical element was usually discernible, Populist parties in some places were not, on balance, much different from the Democratic parties. Indeed, in Nevada, one can argue that the Silver party posing as a Populist party actually drove out a more reform-minded Democratic party.[67]

During this period, however, third parties found fertile ground in the region. The major parties offered little to appease radicals or reformers or to entice voter interest. As the editor of an Arizona paper described it in 1890, the platforms of both major parties were "not only tiresome as to quantity but equally fatiguing in quality."[68] For the editor, the excessive length and meaningless flourishes of the major party platforms could not hide the fact that "the lines separating the two great parties are in substance the same that have existed for a quarter of a century."[69]

By the end of 1892, Populists had benefited from this sentiment. Populism in the region made its biggest splash in Colorado and showed some strength in Idaho, Montana, Nevada, and Wyoming. It was weaker in the territories, existing there largely only on the local level. Populism was at its potentially revolution-ary best in Colorado. Here, one can reasonably argue, there was "no perfected scheme of Marxian theory, no imported philosophy of European proletarians, but in essence an indigenous radicalism induced by the dilemma of pioneer indi-vidualists confronted with the menace of full-blown industrialism."[70] Here, too, the Populists had begun to arouse unskilled workers.

Although the overall message was mixed, in the early 1890s one found Populist leaders throughout the region who were concerned with problems of inequality and injustice and the plight of individuals caught up in the transforma-tion from an era of frontier individual enterprise to one in which corporations, often eastern owned and controlled, with monopoly powers had taken over. In 1893–1894 the movement's anti-corporate focus and radical component would become even more important throughout the region as events played into the hands of those on the left, but problems regarding fusion and the performance of Populists in office, which had already begun to surface, became more acute.

CHAPTER THREE

Moving Left

Stopping the Trains

THE YEAR 1892 WAS A BREAKTHROUGH ONE for Populists in much of the Mountain West, but the years 1893 and 1894 were initially even more exciting as events seemed to confirm what the more extreme Populists had been asserting about the capitalist system. Several national and regional disturbances in these years—affecting economic conditions, labor-management relations, and the silver issue—played into the Populists' hands, helping them build further support for the party from labor, farmers, and the middle class. During this period, too, many Socialists joined the Populist cause, though how many did so is difficult to estimate.

Editorial writers for *The New York Times* attributed this to the discovery by the Socialists that the call for free silver was actually a call for Socialism, the idea being that in calling for free silver, proponents were acting on the Socialist principle "that the Government, as the agency of the whole people, should be made to promote the interest of those who, unaided, do not get on as well as they would like to, or, to put it in another form, that the Government should take care of the distribution of the total wealth of the people so that all shall have what they consider an equal share."[1] The newspaper's equating silver with Socialism appears to have had less to do with an effort to identify the appeal of the silver cause than with a desire to discredit it. At any rate, the editorials were off the mark as far as Socialists were concerned. While Socialists were attracted by much of what was in the Populist platform, they did not always embrace the silver crusade. Many were suspicious of the motives of some of silver's most prominent supporters in the corporate world and saw it as a distraction from the more central revolutionary goal whose time, given present economic and political conditions, seemed to be coming.

The nationwide depression set off by the Panic of 1893 brought considerable hardship in the Mountain West and, coming on the heels of booming prosperity, much disappointment and disillusionment. The depression lowered farm prices, caused mines to close, and forced banks and stores out of business. Some miners and smelter workers turned to farming because of depressed conditions in their industry, only to find that farming offered little, if any, improvement in the way of rewards. Many of the newly unemployed became tramps. In Kingman, Arizona—a town said to be so tough that people shot other people just to see which way they fell—the editor of a local paper noted on August 12, 1893, "More tramps have passed through Kingman the past week than in any like time in the history of the town."[2] To the editor, the problem rested on the national government's policy with regard to silver. He warned, "A government that will make paupers of its workingmen will not long hold together and our national government is doing its best to arrive at this stage."[3]

Industrial armies of the unemployed roamed the country, raising the specter of revolution. The best known of these was a group headed by Jacob Coxey, who led a march to Washington, D.C., to pressure for unemployment relief. This turned into a fiasco when police arrested Coxey for walking on the grass on the Capitol grounds. One stream of unemployed from the West Coast, hoping to join up with Coxey's army, became stranded in Idaho because their free railroad ride ended there and the railroad threatened to have them arrested if they tried to take possession of the train to continue their journey. In Reno, Nevada, city officials refused to allow a special train of 23 cattle cars filled with unemployed workers to stop in town. As a result, 300 recruits for Coxey's army planning to join the train in Reno were left behind. The sheriff ordered the tramps to get out of town. Most did so by hopping rides on freight trains. In Colorado and Montana, detachments of unemployed or striking workers attempting to hook up with Coxey did steal some trains but were eventually arrested and dispersed by United States marshals. Governor Waite and other Populist leaders took the side of the unemployed workers and drew upon the enthusiasm the episode generated to build their party organizations.

In Montana, close to a third of the state's workforce was unemployed. This amounted to around 20,000 men, many of whom were idle on the streets of Butte and Helena. Following the lead of William Hogan, a labor leader soon to be known as "General" Hogan, several hundred striking railroad workers seized a train at Butte and attempted to link up with Coxey. Hogan's effort fell short, but he became a hero to many in the community, business leaders as well as workers. His seizure of the train led to a sentence of six months in jail, but he was released after serving three months on the petition of 10,000 citizens of Butte.[4] According to newspaper accounts, most Montana Coxeyites and many of their friends and sympathizers, especially those who resided in Butte, were affiliated with the Populist party.[5] The Massachusetts-born Hogan remained active in the Butte labor movement before moving on to the state of Washington, where he ran in 1900 as a Socialist candidate for Congress.

In 1893–1894 the nation also witnessed labor disturbances, especially the Pullman strike of 1894 led by Eugene V. Debs of the American Railway Union, which tied up railroad traffic throughout the county. It was put down by federal courts and President Grover Cleveland's sending federal troops to Chicago, over the strenuous objections of Governor John Peter Altgeld. The strike was a defeat for Debs and demonstrated to workers throughout the country how the powers of government—injunctions, imprisonment, and military force—could be marshaled against organized labor. It helped send Debs on his way to international Socialism. In the long run, it helped foster a new politics of Progressive reform. In the short run, it helped mobilize people in the Mountain West behind the striking workers and, by creating an atmosphere of class conflict, further radicalized the area. Populists saw themselves benefiting from the disturbances, becoming the vehicle for protest, and, in particular, having a great opportunity to pick the support of working-class Democrats offended by Cleveland's actions.[6] Some of this support was forthcoming, but not as much as the Populists had hoped.

Tieups and explosive strike conditions were common in the Mountain West, causing much concern for U.S. attorneys and marshals who bore much of the burden for restoring order. They commonly had to deal with mobs sympathetic to strikers—people more than willing to destroy railroad property and take over trains. They faced the hostility of ordinary citizens, merchants, and local sheriffs and felt it necessary to equip small armies to keep order, protect railroad property, and get the trains moving again. During the summer of 1894, in the railway center of Ogden, Utah, a U.S. attorney found a mob of several hundred people in possession of a train. They were in no mood to listen to his plea to return to their homes and let the train depart. Fearing a riot if he tried to arrest anyone, he simply bided his time until troops arrived.[7] In defense of spending what some of his superiors felt was an excessive amount, a marshal from the Colorado district reported to Washington in late 1895 that an emergency existed and he had no option but to raise, equip, and maintain a small army of 600 men.[8] He reported: "[T]he condition of affairs at Grand Junction were [sic] extraordinary, my deputies were met not only by the strikers at that point but by the citizens who met in a public hall prior to their arrival and resolved to not only resist the entry of the deputies to the town, but also to give them no quarters or sell them anything to eat!" All the hotels and boardinghouses, as well as stores, were closed to the deputies, so they were compelled to go to a nearby town for provisions.[9]

In August 1894 a marshal in Carson City, Nevada, also defended hiring a large number of deputies—some acted as guards on the mail trains, others guarded bridges because threats had been made to burn or blow them up. The marshal said he had to act alone: "It was impossible to obtain any practical assistance from the local civil authorities, many of whom were in sympathy with the strikers, as were, in fact, ninety per cent of the people of the State."[10] In Nevada, a young Bill Haywood stood looking at sidetracked railroad cars when it suddenly dawned on him that the strikers possessed "a great power . . . they could stop the trains."[11] The strike gave life to a new, more genuine Populist party in Nevada but also set the Nevada Populists up for disappointment a few months later when votes were counted.

Meanwhile, Debs and others leading the strike paid for stopping the trains: they were arrested and sent to jail. Debs spent six months in jail in Woodstock, Illinois, for violating a court injunction requested by U.S. Attorney General Richard Olney that forbade him from doing anything to encourage the boycott. His confinement, if anything, made Debs more popular with western labor leaders. He and other strike leaders were stoutly defended by the region's Populist leaders. In Shoshone County, Idaho, for example, Populists overwhelmingly approved a resolution offered by Ed Boyce: "Be it resolved that it is the sense of this convention that we extend our sympathy to Eugene V. Debs and his associates of the A.R.U. [American Railway Union] in their arrest and imprisonment under the unjust and unlawful rulings of Attorney General Olney, and we hereby demand the impeachment of the said attorney general."[12] While in the Woodstock jail, Debs was visited by Victor L. Berger and other leading Socialists who attempted to bring Debs over to their way of thinking. As the story goes, Debs went to jail a Populist and came out a Socialist.

Along with the disturbances accompanying the Panic of 1893 and the Pullman strike came another development on the labor front: the creation of the Western Federation of Miners (WFM) on May 15, 1893, at a convention in Butte, Montana. A dozen or so mine union leaders had worked out the idea in the fall and winter of 1892 while serving time in the Ada County jail in Boise for their involvement in the Coeur d'Alene miners' strike that year.[13] Friends who stopped by helped develop plans for the new union. One of these was the miners' lawyer, James H. Hawley. While Hawley was conferring with the jailed union leaders about a new union, similar discussions were taking place among mine union leaders in Butte. The Butte Miners' Union at the time was a driving force in the mine workers' movement—it had strongly backed the Coeur d'Alene strikers, making nearly backbreaking assessments to provide relief and legal defense funds—and its leaders saw considerable wisdom in broadening the base of labor support should there be another such crisis. The Coeur d'Alene experience had made it obvious to mine union leaders that the only way to fight the mine owners was through a strong association of mining unions.[14]

The WFM brought together fourteen local miners' unions, with a total membership estimated at 10,000. About half of these members were in the Butte Miner's Union, which, appropriately, was designated charter number one. The organization proceeded to get involved in violent strikes, particularly in Colorado and Idaho. It met with some success—particularly, as discussed later, in Cripple Creek—but efforts to build and maintain memberships were frustrated by mine closures and employer lockouts in the depression years. From the start, the union was politically minded and endorsed candidates, usually Populists or Democrats, who supported labor causes. At the 1894 convention, the union endorsed the Populists' Omaha platform.

Adding fuel to the political fire in the Mountain West, President Cleveland provoked a new round of agitation over the silver issue by leading a successful effort in 1893 to have the Sherman Silver Purchase Act repealed. He believed silver purchases had contributed to the depression. This action, however, along with the closing of mints in India to the coinage of silver, produced a tremendous decline in the price of silver, which, in turn, had a devastating effect on the economies of several Mountain West states. Mountain westerners saw congressional repeal of the Sherman Silver Purchase Act as a disaster for the silver industry, one that compounded the problems already caused by the Panic of 1893. Protesting President Cleveland's proposal to Congress that the act be repealed, Governor Waite told a large and boisterous gathering called by the State Silver League in Denver's Coliseum Hall in July 1893 that the state would use force if necessary to resist "the strong hand" of the "money power." The governor added that "it is better, infinitely better, that blood should flow to the horses' bridles rather than our national liberties should be destroyed."[15] A hostile press seized upon the speech to nickname the governor "Bloody Bridles Waite" and to depict him as a bloodthirsty radical who was staging a revolution in Colorado.

Waite, a leading symbol of Populism in the Mountain West, had already had a rough go in Colorado. On the legislative level, the governor, as one historian put it, had "found the road to reform strewn with rocks."[16] Although he proposed only a modest reform program—his rhetoric would have predicted a much more revolutionary one—he had little success with the legislature. Waite faced the opposition of a Republican-controlled house and had to work with a highly fragile coalition of Populists and Democrats in the senate. The Populist legislators themselves were divided between rival farming and labor factions. The former group thought little of the governor's programs—compulsory arbitration, employers' liability, the eight-hour day—that reflected the interests of the working-class segment of the party. Waite got nowhere with a proposal to create a strong railroad commission (indeed, the legislature even abolished the rather weak one already in existence) or with a somewhat bizarre scheme that would have made silver dollars legal tender in the state.

One of the governor's few legislative victories was the submission of the equal suffrage question to male voters. With the support of unionists and Populists, the amendment received an overwhelming majority on November 7, 1893. Writing in *The North American Review* in the summer of 1894, Waite took pains to point out: "[T]here is no doubt that in Colorado the women owe suffrage to the Populists. The Populists in the General Assembly nearly all supported the bill, but a majority of the members of both the old parties voted in opposition. The law was recommended by a Populist governor, the bill was introduced by a Populist Representative, at the general election the Populist party in the State supported the measure; but nearly all the Republican counties and all the Democratic counties voted largely against it."[17] Waite later blamed women for his failure to get reelected and said he regretted the expansion of suffrage.

As chief executive, Waite had difficulties in both hiring—bickering over patronage appointments took up most of the first few months of his administration—and firing administrators. Critics railed against many of his appointees, charging cronyism and, in the case of his son's appointment as a prison official, nepotism. Waite regretted some of his selections but sometimes found it difficult to get rid of his appointees. In what became known as the "City Hall War," he attempted to remove some of his appointees from the Denver police and fire board. He felt they were trying to protect the illegal business of gambling by refusing to investigate charges that gamblers had bought protection from the police. The board members refused to vacate their offices; to protect themselves from being forcibly ousted, they fortified City Hall with around 300 armed men. Waite responded by ordering the national guard into the area around City Hall. For a time it looked as if violence might break out. Matters were resolved, however, when, at Waite's request, national troops were sent into the area to maintain order while the dispute was settled in court. Nevertheless, newspapers condemned Waite for imperiling public safety by jumping to the use of military force. *The New York Times*, among others, noted the incident and commented that while the Populist party said it stood against the arbitrary exercise of power by people in authority, Waite was guilty of that very thing.[18]

Waite, decidedly pro-labor but also hoping to shore up his political support in mining areas, sided with the WFM and miners at Cripple Creek who had gone on strike in 1893–1894 for an eight-hour day and an increase in the minimum wage. Waite, unlike other governors of the time, sent in troops to protect the strikers. He put the national guard between armed strikers and armed county deputies—the latter had sided with the mining companies—and acted as a representative of the strikers in negotiating a settlement.[19] The success of the Cripple Creek strike increased greatly the WFM's prestige in mining areas.[20] It also demonstrated to the WFM how important state support could be to the workers' cause and the value of engaging in political action to secure that support.[21] Encouraged, the WFM began a strenuous organization effort in Colorado and other states in the Mountain West.

For Populist party officials in Cripple Creek, the outcome was also positive. Many of the striking miners were Populists, and Republicans had hoped to use the deputies to drive them out of the county and thus weaken the Populist party at election time.[22] They failed to do so. For Waite, his performance during the strike brought an outpouring of praise around the country from the left side of the political spectrum, but, in the long run, it produced only questionable political gains, if any, for him in Colorado.

Waite had spoken up for the lowly and downcast in their battle against the rich and powerful and, by protecting striking miners, encouraged WFM activity in the state. He was, in turn, condemned by critics as a Socialist (a label he rejected) who badly frightened employers, arrayed class against class, and scared investors away from putting needed capital into the state. Republican papers also sought to attack the Populists at what they thought was the base of the third party's support by charging: "There is no greater mistake than to call the populists a silver party. It is true that they talk in favor of silver, but the true populist is a Greenbacker."[23] Republican papers also noted that the Populists had made a strong move to enlist the support of women about to vote for the first time. This effort, they predicted, was doomed to fail: "Women are not fools and it will not take long for them to see that while some of the evils that the populists complain of really exist, the remedies they suggest are impracticable and if applied would bring about still greater evils. . . . Parties which cannot recognize prosperity when they see it and can bring nothing but disaster when they get into power, will be supported by neither men nor women of sense, except those that can get into office by it."[24]

Waite also had critics within the Colorado Populist party who feared his radicalism, or what they or others perceived as radicalism, would take down the party. Some also felt he should give the silver cause more prominence as a way of generating support from more conservative middle-class voters. Waite, though, had the votes to get the Populist nomination without making any concessions to the right, and he refused to do so. In the general election, he continued to have strong support among workers and in mining areas but went down to defeat under a Republican attack that branded "Bloody Bridles" a dangerous radical. One Republican editor put it clearly: "Waite is a blot upon Colorado's fame and a cancer eating out its vitality."[25] Republicans enjoyed playing the role of "redeemer" against Populism and Waiteism in Colorado. Breaking away from the Populists were the farmers and those who had joined the ranks only because of the silver issue. Populists had, indeed, made an attempt to secure the women's vote but were out-campaigned in this regard by the Republicans.[26] Reported one newspaper, "The women worked earnestly at the polls all day for the success of the Republican ticket and the result is largely due to their efforts."[27] Looking back, one radical contended: "In every mill and factory where large numbers of women were employed, there were placed placards bearing about these words: 'If the Populists re-elect Waite, this factory will be closed.' The politically inexperienced, frightened, and brow-beaten women slaves voted against Waite to save, as they thought, their jobs."[28]

Summing up the election from a broader perspective, historian James Wright concluded: "There seems little reason to dispute the judgment that the issue in 1894 was clear. Waite challenged the political and economic norms with his unabashed class appeal and with his concept of an active state aiding the oppressed and deprived. He lost."[29] Writing a few years after the election, Waite blamed his failure on the lack of commitment to basic reform within the state Populist party. He wrote to Wayland at *The Appeal to Reason* in 1897: "By skillful management in 1892 we elected the populist state ticket in Colorado. I expended my whole time and the greater part of my salary as governor in building up the populist party of the state upon populist principles, but it was in vain, and mainly because the so-called populist party of Colorado never believed in any principle of the Omaha platform except the free coinage of silver."[30] Wayland, in response, suggested to Waite that the problem was rooted in the party's failure to educate the electorate: it had put Waite in power on the basis of the silver issue, but the voters had not been prepared in advance for more radical changes. He suggested that the lesson concerning the all-important need to educate the public to accept change should not be lost on the Socialists.[31]

The years 1893–1894 also brought a letdown for Populists in Wyoming. Populists had hardly distinguished themselves in the 1893 legislature, where they had the balance of power. In an effort to bring the Populists into a governing coalition, house Democrats joined the five Populists to elect Populist Lewis Cass Tidball as speaker. Tidball, born in Ohio, was a rancher from Sheridan and a former Greenbacker. He was a highly vocal proponent of the initiative and referendum. He was not, however, successful as a legislative leader. The session was bitter and faction-ridden. The Populists were unable to work out an agreement with either of the major parties as to who should be sent to the U.S. Senate, leaving the state with only one member of that body for a two-year period. At times the Populists were able to work with the Democrats in the lower house, but with Republican control of the upper house Populist proposals such as a railroad commission to control rates and the initiative and referendum failed. The Populists themselves were often divided; those elected from Johnson County, because of the invasion, were essentially conservatives and greatly differed from other party members on matters of reform.[32] Contrary to the Populist prediction following the 1892 election, at no time was the Wyoming Stock Growers Association in danger.

Municipal elections in 1893 resulted in Populist losses around the state. Still, as the 1894 elections neared, the Populists thought they would do well because of depressed economic conditions. Filled with confidence and not altogether pleased with the way fusion had worked out in 1892 or with the Cleveland-led anti-populist, anti-labor, anti-silver Democratic party, they refused to join with the Democrats on a statewide ticket. They viewed the Democrats as weak, having little to offer.[33] At the same time, they saw themselves as rapidly gaining ground, indeed, as so successful that the Republicans were holding daily meetings to find some way to check the spread of Populism.[34] In fact, though, Republicans were probably meeting to discuss ways of strengthening the Populists—for example, by subsidizing Populist newspapers and speakers—to divert votes away from the Democrats.[35] In the end, Republicans carried the election in 1894: the only successful non-Republican candidate was a state legislator, a Democrat-Populist in the house. Tidball finished third in the race for governor.

While the 1894 returns from Colorado and Wyoming were disappointing, Idaho and Montana showed progress. The Idaho party had been picking up labor and farm support in 1893, in part because of the high-profile activities of the ten Populists in the legislature who pushed for measures such as greater regulation of rail and water rates and helped produce a law banning yellow dog contracts. Republicans accused the Populist lawmakers of scaring off eastern capital investors and showing the same dangerous tendencies as Colorado's Waite.

Reporting on the Populist convention in Shoshone County, a meeting controlled by the Knights of Labor and the miners' union, a reporter for a Republican paper took aim at one Adam Aulbach, who, he suggested, was typical of Populist leaders: "Upon taking the chair Mr. Aulbach delivered a characteristic speech, in which he dwelt upon the pure and holy purposes of the populist party with the same earnest eloquence displayed in years gone by in his appeals first in behalf of republican principles and later in support of democratic fallacies."[36] Two months later another Idaho Republican paper chimed in that the Populists were nothing more than a few political cranks and rejected office seekers who were good at calamity howling and willing to use whatever issue came along to gain office. The paper, however, considered the Populists to be dangerous because their success or even their appearance of electoral strength would frighten businessmen and dry up badly needed outside capital. Republican papers warned Democrats that by fusing with such a group, they risked the future of their own party, not to mention the future of the nation.[37] As in Colorado and elsewhere, another string in the argument against the Populists was that "[t]he people's party is not a 'silver' party as their Omaha platform would lead one to believe. Their 'howl' over the demonetization of silver is only made to deceive and blind the eyes of the voters to the true wishes of the party—the issuance of fiat money in the shape of 'greenbacks.' "[38] It was for this reason, one editor suggested, that Populists were opposed by the owners of silver mines.[39]

Idaho Populist party leaders looked on this attack as a sign that events, especially the hard times that had hit the state, were working in their direction. Seeing a marshaling of support, they rejected fusion with the Democrats. In October 1894 the editor of an Idaho labor-Populist paper noted that the party stood to do well with workers because they were fed up with Democrats and Republicans: "The determination of the working classes to abandon the ranks of the two dominant parties and to engage in an independent political movement or to join fortunes with the people's party, is now so generally expressed as to warrant the most serious consideration at the hands of all true friends of labor."[40]

The Populists wound up improving their position, jumping ahead of the Democrats, from whom they drew much of their new support, although failing to take a statewide office. Their candidate for governor in 1894 picked up 30 percent of the vote, finishing behind the successful Republican candidate.[41] Democrats in 1894 became the "third" party, picking up only 25 percent of the votes in the gubernatorial race. On the local level, the Populists captured nearly every office in Shoshone County where the Coeur d'Alene strike had taken place.[42] The party in Shoshone County had its base within the miners' union and the Knights of Labor. On the state level, Idaho Populists won fifteen seats in the state legislature. These Populists, who included Senator Edward Boyce from Shoshone County, made considerable noise in 1895 and 1897 while pushing for a wide range of reforms. They failed, however, to work out a governing coalition with the Democrats, and few of their measures saw the light of day. In Idaho, as elsewhere, the Populist legislators' frugality was apparent as they showed concern over the most minuscule budgetary matters, looking for ways to avoid waste and reduce state spending.[43]

In Montana, widespread unemployment provided the Populists with an opportunity for political advancement. They promoted free silver as an employment remedy and argued, with ample justification, that they were the only party truly dedicated to this cause. Attempting to draw upon the considerable anti-railroad sentiment in the state, they also condemned the use of federal troops in the Pullman strike. Along with the platform planks addressed to various groups, the Populists, with a bit of distortion, pointed with pride at their record in the state house in helping to produce laws favorable to labor, such as an eight-hour day for certain workers and restrictions on union-busting Pinkerton agents.

While the Populists put considerable effort into the campaign, as in 1892, they refused to take the one step essential to victory—fusing with the Democrats. Running alone, the best they could do under the most favorable economic conditions was what the party had done in Idaho—displace the Democrats as the opposition, or second, party to the Republicans. In the process, the party did improve its membership in the legislature—electing three members in the state senate and fourteen members in the house—but Republicans captured control of both bodies. In 1894 the party did well in Silver Bow County, home of Butte and a stronghold of the labor movement, and several other counties to the north.[44] The most prominent People's party candidate that year was thirty-nine-year-old Robert Burns Smith, who finished ahead of the Democrat but behind the Republican candidate in the race for U.S. Congress. Smith, a lawyer in Helena, had recently become a Populist, moving from the Democratic party because of the silver issue. He had been among the attorneys who had defended the 500 unemployed workers, discussed previously, most of whom were on strike against the Great Northern Railroad and had tried to join up with Coxey's army.[45]

In the remainder of the Mountain West, 1893–1894 brought new state or territorial Populist parties, few of which were very successful. In 1893 the decision of many Silver party members in the Nevada legislature to vote to abolish a state board that had raised railroad taxes lent additional credibility to the charge that this Populistic-sounding party was actually controlled by the railroads. While this did nothing to prevent the Silver party from sweeping the 1894 elections, the charge of railroad domination and the party's refusal to affiliate with the national Populist party did lead to the creation of the state's first genuine statewide Populist party.[46] The official platform of the People's party, however, was little different from that of the Silver party. The latter had turned rhetorically to the left to keep up with the changing public opinion caused by the unemployment problem and the Pullman strike.

The nationwide boycott against the Pullman Company, however, gave the somewhat feeble real Populist party something of a boost, making it a genuine working-class movement with discharged and blacklisted men at its core.[47] The Populists came up with nearly a full slate of candidates, headed by James C. Doughty as the party's pick for Congress. Doughty, one of the railroad strikers in 1894, was now a blacklisted engineer whose story had considerable appeal in railroad towns. The Silver party saw him taking votes away from their candidate, Francis Newlands. Hoping for this result, Republicans and the Gold Bug press did what they could to support Doughty, especially in the railroad towns where Newlands was his chief competitor.[48] Doughty, though, wound up neck to neck with the Republican candidate behind Newlands, the winner.

One of the "spellbinders" on behalf of the Nevada Populist ticket, R. A. Maynard, took considerable pride in Doughty's strong showing. Yet, looking back after turning to Socialism several years later, Maynard noted: "It was in this election that the foundations of my faith in the power of political 'reform' methods to secure relief were shaken. I was made heartsick at the sight of men, leaders in the strike a few months before, at the polls on election day working and voting for the success of the party whose ticket had been endorsed by the Southern Pacific Company. I had never heard at that time of class consciousness in the Socialist sense, but I could not understand how men could strike for a principle and then turn squarely about and refuse to give the same principle the endorsement of their votes."[49]

Utah, like Nevada, had experienced considerable economic disruption and a stirring of labor sentiment. The Populist party in Utah, which organized for the first time on a territorial level in Salt Lake City in the fall of 1893, adopted the Omaha party platform and the silver plank but came to life essentially as an urban-based party whose chief concern in this time of economic distress was furthering the interests of organized labor and the unemployed.[50] Its 1894 candidate for territorial delegate in Congress, H. L. Gaut, however, finished a weak third, drawing most of his support from Salt Lake City and Ogden—the places where the party was best organized.

Two individuals stood out among Utah's Populists, both of whom were committed to ending economic inequality and political injustice.[51] One was Warren Foster, who came to the territory in late 1894 from Kansas, where he had broken with the Republican party and launched a Populist newspaper. Foster reportedly gave the first speech on behalf of the People's party ever delivered in Salt Lake City and proceeded to establish the *Inter-Mountain Advocate* as a Populist outlet. The other influential leader was Henry W. Lawrence (1835–1924), who, years earlier, had been excommunicated by the Mormon Church for challenging its monopoly over the press and commercial matters. He had been a leader of the anti-Mormon Liberal party and had joined the free-silver movement before helping organize the Utah Populist party. In 1895, when Utahans elected the first set of officeholders for the state, Lawrence headed the ticket as the Populist candidate for governor, championing the eight-hour day, although he received only a handful of votes.

New Mexico Populists had a similar experience when it came to gathering votes. Organized for the first time on a territory-wide basis in 1894, New Mexico Populists announced that they were dedicated to statehood, to free silver, and to "purifying the public service and counteracting the influence of professional politicians."[52] They proposed to open the political system to all people "regardless of wealth or social station" and to govern with the people in mind, rather than "private ends." Party leaders added, "We believe that government can be so simplified and brought so close to the people, that much of its complicated machinery may be dispensed with and better results attained." Reflecting their desire to separate themselves from the violence-prone White Caps, the New Mexico Populists noted that "in the war between capital and labor, now but begun, our sympathies are with labor, but we believe that ballots are more effective than bullets, and that acts of lawlessness done by the supporters of any cause react to the hurt of that cause."[53]

At a sparsely attended assembly of thirteen delegates meeting in Albuquerque, New Mexico Populists endorsed a wide range of other programs but decided to pass on supporting woman suffrage.[54] County organizations adopted similar platforms. One of these denounced professional money changers, oppressive trusts, and corporate aggregations of capital. In this spirit it called for the "coinage of both silver and gold upon a basis of 16 to one for the American product, not only in justice to the western miner, and the people at large, but as a step toward restoration of the freedom from the moneyed influences which our fathers enjoyed before trusts and corporate aggregations of capital became possible."[55] Around the state there were reports that Populists had recruited well "from the better class of democrats."[56]

The territorial party nominated Theodore B. Mills for congressional delegate. Mills had served two terms in the territorial legislature as a People's party representative from San Juan County. His campaign stressed the great disparities in wealth between producers and capitalist nonproducers.[57] In 1894 he received just 1,800 votes, about 4 percent of the vote, in part because the free-silver issue had been somewhat neutralized during the campaign as politicians of all parties favored the cause. Most of his votes apparently came at the expense of the Democratic candidate for territorial delegate. The fact that the Democrat lost by more than 2,700 votes, though, suggests he would have lost even without Mills on the ballot. Mills carried only San Juan County, an agricultural county in the northwest part of the state. This was his home county and one that had been hard hit by the silver crisis, which reduced the ability of people in nearby Colorado silver camps to purchase the county's products.

Arizona Populists, meanwhile, came into the 1894 election with increased vigor and, given the changed economic conditions, somewhat more radical than they had been two years earlier. In the fall of 1894 the Populist party of Maricopa County (Phoenix), for example, proudly proclaimed that its success would bring "legislation in the interest of the masses instead of the classes" and many other benefits, including "a free people, free schools, free labor, free ballot and an honest count" and the "fostering of every legitimate industry and the abolishment of all manner of injurious combinations oppressive to labor."[58] The party also took care to point out to farmers that they had been robbed by the canal companies for years, and, to make things worse, they had been supporting the parties that allowed this wholesale robbery to take place. The solution: "Wake up you grangers. . . . Vote for the populist candidates for the Legislature."[59]

On the territorial level Arizona Populists made a surprisingly strong showing, having found a popular figure to head the ticket in the person of publisher and former sheriff Buckey O'Neill.[60] In an open letter to his opponents, O'Neill attacked the major parties as tools of "organized money" that "have been and are now, dividing the people into two classes—a pauper class, who are the laborers and producers, the workers in field and mine, and a moneyed aristocracy who are the drones and leaders in our body politic."[61] The Democrats, too, had moved to the left. There was a rumor that the Populists and Democrats would fuse behind O'Neill, but that never happened.[62]

Meanwhile, mainstream papers in Arizona, as elsewhere in the region, depicted the Populists as a threat to economic development and prosperity. One editor declared: "Opposition to the corporations is one of the cardinal principles of the People's Party. Their denunciation is entirely too sweeping, and serves to inflame an unreasonable prejudice. Corporations and aggregations of capital are necessary to the development and prosperity of our country and its industries, and without them the West would be a wilderness. The interests of capital and labor are mutual and they must remain dependent upon each other."[63] Some characterized the Populist party as "falling prey to the professional office hunter who is recruited from the ranks of other parties . . . men who have been rejected for office by the dominant parties . . . men who have sided with all the issues in politics and don't know today if they are on foot or horseback."[64] The territorial papers, though, made a relatively soft attack on O'Neill, a fellow newspaper man. Democratic papers were particularly easy on the Populist candidate. Said one Democratic editor: "Personally, he is dear to everyone who ever met him, for he has a magnetism that has attracted friends, wherever in the wide, wide world it has been his lot to abide. Populistically, we cannot but feel with sorrow that Buckey has got off somehow radically wrong. He will reform and become a good democrat in good season."[65]

In 1894 O'Neill surprised most observers by polling 22 percent of the vote in finishing a strong third behind the Democratic candidate John C. Herndon, who had 36 percent, and the Republican candidate N. O. Murphy, who garnered 42 percent of the vote. The mainstream press contended that the 14 percent of the vote received by another statewide Populist, G. W. Woy, was far more indicative of the strength of the new party. To the papers, Woy's third-place finish was a fitting rebuff to "a regular populistic demagogue who is full of the talk and blow of the man he aspires to pattern after, Waite, of Colorado."[66]

O'Neill, on the other hand, argued that the party did rather well under the most adverse conditions: "The party was young and unorganized; its members hardly known to one another in their own communities. It had no recognized leaders, neither had it a Territorial organization, while it had the vestige of a local organization in but three counties. In the matter of party publications— that most necessary adjunct to political warfare—it had but two weekly newspapers, while in its treasury there was a total dearth of funds—even for postage to circulate campaign literature—a condition doubly irksome on account of its candidates being men of small means."[67] O'Neill and Woy did unusually well in mining areas, where a class of industrial workers had emerged and employment conditions brought conflict and an interest in political reform.[68] More broadly, one reporter observed that the Arizona Populist party "largely voices the sentiments of people who are not wealthy and who have lost the hope of ever being so" and "of those who have suffered from the soulless grind of corporations."[69]

Overall, the events of 1893–1894 strengthened the organizational capacity of the Populist movement and pointed it in a somewhat more radical direction. Populists, though, did not do very well in elections, even under the most promising economic conditions. The party was wiped out in Colorado. The greatest progress was made in Montana and Idaho, but, because Populists ran alone, all that was accomplished was a rather hollow victory of making the Democratic party a third party. Democrats and Populists, whether they liked it or not, in many places were joined at the hip; one could not advance on its own, only at the expense of the other.

Free silver was of considerable importance to the Populist movement in much of the Mountain West in the early 1890s, giving the Populists a popular platform and one of their best "talking points." In some places, New Mexico, for example, the silver issue was dressed up as part of the broader anti-corporate program. For many Mountain West Populists, though, free silver was largely of value for its strategic purposes, that is, as a way of securing power so a broader reform program could be undertaken. Silver was a way of not only reaching out to the communities where it was produced but of appealing to farmers concerned about debt and tapping into feelings of resentment against easterners and the two major political parties. From the labor perspective, its chief value was as a way of increasing employment in the mining industry. Up to 1896, however, silver was only part of the Populist cause. In 1896 silver and fusion were to become the major focal points.

Davis Waite, Populist Governor of Colorado. Courtesy Colorado Historical Society, all rights reserved.

Captain Buckey O'Neill, Arizona Populist Leader, Courtesy of the Arizona Department of Library, Archives and Public Records.

Executive Board Photo, Western Federation of Miners, from Miners Magazine, July 1901. Ed Boyce is the middle first row and Bill Haywood is to his left.

Mother Jones, labor agitator in mining areas. Library of Congress.

Bill Haywood, Charles Moyer, and George Pettibone on the grounds of the Ada County Courthouse during Haywood's trial for murder of former governor Frank Steunenberg. Library of Congress.

Elizabeth Gurley Flynn, IWW organizer. Library of Congress.

CHAPTER FOUR

Fusion, Decline, Transition

In THE MID-1890s THE SILVER MOVEMENT CAUGHT FIRE nationally and became of even more importance in the Mountain West. Organizations such as the American Bimetallic Union, hordes of politicians led by young William Jennings Bryan of Nebraska, and scores of newspapers and magazines extolled the virtues of silver, as did William H. Harvey's *Coin's Financial School*, which spelled out the case for silver in simple terms for ordinary people.

As the silver issue became more salient, so too did the divisions within the Populist party between those who wanted to make it the central issue, because it was by far the party's most popular vote getter and the most likely key to electoral success, and those who wanted to advance the party's traditional anti-corporate program of which silver was only a part. Populists were also divided over a related issue of whether the party should fuse with other parties around the silver issue or retain its independence and go it alone. Central among those pushing for fusion were mining kings in Montana and other states who, after the

Panic of 1893, came to value fusion on the national as well as the state level as a way of promoting the silver issue.[1]

One faction, known as the middle-of-the-roaders or mid-roaders, was uncomfortable with silver as the major focus—they recognized its strategic value but were not true believers in the wisdom of the cause and were alarmed by the growing influence of non-Populist silverites within the party. They also opposed fusion with other parties around the silver issue, insisting that the party stay on course in the middle of the road as an independent force. Socialists including Eugene Debs were prominent among those in the middle-of-the-road faction. On the other side were those who wanted to win elections more than anything else. To do this, they argued, the party had to trim the Omaha platform down to one that highlighted the popular silver issue and combine forces with other parties committed to silver. In 1896 former Populist party presidential candidate James Weaver and national chair of the party Herman Taubeneck were prominent among those in the silver-fusionist faction.

Republicans set up the "battle of the standards," gold versus silver, by nominating William McKinley on a plank calling for the preservation of the existing gold standard. McKinley, aware of the fast-rising sentiment on the issue in the West, made some concessions on the silver issue, but they were not enough to satisfy western delegates to the Republican convention. Feeling rebuffed by the Republicans, twenty-one delegates from Nevada, Colorado, and Idaho followed the lead of Henry M. Teller of Colorado and bolted the convention. Said Teller during the debate: "This gold plank means ultimate distress and disaster to my followers, I cannot subscribe to it, and if adopted, I must, as an honest man, sever my connection with the political organization which makes that one of the main articles of faith."[2]

After the Democrats chose Bryan as their presidential nominee in July 1896, there was little the Populists, who met later, could do to come out ahead—they could either endorse Bryan and lose their independence or nominate someone else and jeopardize the election chances of a candidate who had adopted much of their platform. Silver-fusionists at the Populist convention did not breathe easily until the party officially nominated Bryan. Up to that point there had been considerable apprehension within their ranks that the middle-of the roaders would somehow get in the way of fusion and, as they saw it, ruin a strong chance for victory. Mid-roaders, led by Victor Berger, did, indeed, try to nominate Debs as the party's presidential candidate, but Debs refused to run.

Following a bitter internal fight, the Populists nominated Bryan and, in so doing, chose to place the silver issue at the center of the reform movement, much to the disgust of the mid-road faction. Populists went along with Bryan.

However, Bryan's Democratic running mate, Arthur Sewall, a wealthy eastern banker, was unacceptable to most Populists, and they nominated the fiery radical Thomas Watson of Georgia as their vice presidential candidate. Mountain West Populists concurred. As the People's party of Cochise County, Arizona, succinctly put it: "We approve and endorse the platform of the National People's Party adopted at St. Louis on July 23rd 1896 and most heartily endorse the nomination, by the convention, of W. J. Bryan and Thomas E. Watson for president and vice-president respectively, and fully approve the action of that convention in refusing to endorse the nomination of Arthur Sewall for vice-president."[3]

One of the mid-roaders who did not endorse Bryan or silver was Henry Demarest Lloyd, a Chicago journalist who wrote in muckraking style a damning indictment of trusts, particularly Standard Oil, in *Wealth against Commonwealth*, published in 1894. Echoing the views of many on the left, Lloyd called free silver "a step backward" and condemned it for diverting attention away from the monopoly problem.[4] In extending an invitation to Lloyd to speak at a Labor Day celebration in Butte, radical labor leader William Hogan also expressed his lack of enthusiasm over the silver issue, which he felt had become a "popular fixation" among workers as a miracle cure for all their economic woes. He hoped Lloyd would educate the workers on the need for more fundamental reform and the theme that "the only solution to the economic and social questions lies through the medium of the co-operative commonwealth."[5] Like others on the left, Lloyd had wanted to see the Populists nominate Debs. In 1896 Lloyd voted the Socialist Labor party (SLP) ticket.

For many on the left, the chief victim of the fusion experiment was not likely to be Bryan or the Democrats but the Populist party. Writing in August 1896, Socialist editor J. A. Wayland, for example, concluded: "There can be nothing clearer to me than the fact that the people's party has been swallowed up by the democratic party and while it may wiggle and try to get on its feet in a few states, it will never be, as an organization, a national factor in politics again. It has run its course, performed its mission and helped prepare the way for a party of scientific principles—the socialist party."[6] He believed that Socialism was inevitable and, indeed, was already "marching to certain success all over Europe."[7]

SLP leaders, sensing disaster for the Populists, looked forward to the 1896 election. During the party's 1896 July convention in New York City, Secretary Henry Kuhn read the report of the National Executive Committee, which happily predicted: "The People's Party will have the wind taken out of its sails by the silver development in the Democratic camp; it will be stripped of its Socialistic pretensions as soon as there is a chance to attain increased strength along the lines of its true character as a middle class movement; it will cease to stand in our way and hinder the growth of our party in Western States, where the allurements held out by Populist politicians served to give them quite a large following and from among the working class. The lines will be drawn much clearer and more distinct, and it will be easier for men to know on what side of the fence they really belong."[8] The SLP stood ready to pick up what it could of the wreckage of the Populist party, should this occur. The SLP also anxiously waited to make inroads in the labor movement. Daniel De Leon, failing in his efforts to infiltrate and control the Knights of Labor and the American Federation of Labor unions, began his own union organization, the Socialist Trades and Labor Alliance, in 1895.

Although he later regretted it, former Colorado governor Davis Waite accepted Bryan's nomination and the Democratic platform adopted at Chicago in 1896. Waite wrote: "For four years we of the People's party have battled against party ties and prejudice and our progress has been slow and toilsome. But Almighty God has breathed upon the waters. . . . Although I believe in more reforms than the Chicago convention has endorsed I shall vote for the electors who will support the presidential ticket that Bryan leads."[9] Not everyone was favorably impressed by Waite's endorsement of Bryan, perhaps least of all Bryan himself. Republicans looked forward to tying Bryan to the Populist Waite and suggesting that what they considered Colorado's hellish experience with Waite should make people think twice about voting for Bryan. In coming out for McKinley over Bryan, even though he favored Bryan's position on the silver question, Colorado senator Edward Wolcott, a Republican and a "Silver Senator," branded Bryan as a dangerous Populist and added, "For four years in Colorado we have been fighting Populism and Populists, that party is as unfit now as it has ever been to control the welfare of the people."[10]

Bryan borrowed freely from the Populists in the 1896 campaign—helping to bring their ideas into the mainstream of national politics—but he never referred to himself as the Populist candidate or mentioned the Populist platform, choosing instead to run as if he were exclusively the Democratic nominee. The slight was not lost on Mountain state Populists. The chair of the Colorado Populist party complained, "It irritates me . . . to hear Bryan constantly talking of Democracy and the Chicago platform. It makes me mad to hear him deny that he & his kind of Democrats are Populists as if there was a stigma attached to the name."[11] In truth, there may well have been a stigma attached to the name—a stigma that wound up hurting Bryan, despite his efforts to avoid identification as a Populist. Bryan, his biographer, political scientist Louis Koenig, noted, "paid the price of assuming the liabilities of the Populist caricature in the moderate political community. The Populist nomination gave Bryan a reputation for radicalism well beyond anything he deserved, and it especially imperiled his support in the East."[12] In 1896, in much of the country outside the Mountain West, Populism had become a bad thing, a label that should be avoided.

Bryan went down badly nationally in 1896. Although the Populist party stayed active for the next three presidential elections, sometimes fusing with the Democrats, it ceased to be an effective political force on a national basis. Looking over the ruins, Populist leader Ignatius Donnelly wrote in despair: "We had a splendid candidate and he had made a gigantic campaign; the elements of reform were fairly united; and the depression of business universal, and yet in spite of it all the bankrupt millions wanted to keep the yoke on their own necks!"[13] Socialists later expressed the same type of disappointment with voters and also puzzled about their behavior. How much of the workers' voting behavior reflected their true feelings, however, is unclear. In some places at least, employers forced workers to join pro-McKinley organizations and threatened to close down operations if Bryan were elected.[14] Populist activists also sensed the threat of losing their jobs. In Wyoming, for example, Henry Breitenstein turned down an offer to be a presidential elector for the Populists, reminding his colleagues that he worked for a great corporation and had a family to support and that such a position or a Populist nomination for any other office would put his job in jeopardy.[15]

With defeat, Populists began to move to other parties, particularly the Democratic party. Many Populists, however, also moved on to the SLP and other radical third parties, including the Social Democratic party led by Debs (the origin of this party is discussed in Chapter 5). At the end of 1896, Wayland—who had left Colorado two years earlier to help found an experimental Socialist settlement at Ruskin, Tennessee, in 1894—was rapidly developing a following for his *Appeal to Reason* among left-wing Populists disenchanted with their party. He was doing what he could to bring them to Socialism.

Overall, the idea of fusing with the Democrats may have been less divisive among Mountain West Populists than among Populists elsewhere in the country. In the Mountain West, changing party affiliations had never been a traumatic experience. Populist leaders in the area also seemed generally drawn to Bryan—he spoke their language, being a moralist who saw politics as a struggle between good and evil—and seemed relatively unconcerned about which party received credit for making necessary changes in public policy.[16] Too, for some Populists, fusion had at times proven useful in helping them share in government and patronage. Some Populists, finally, also agreed with mine owners' argument that fusion was essential in the interest of the silver cause. Yet, while Mountain West

Populists generally went along with fusion, the step was agonizing for at least some of its leaders and prompted more than a few middle-of-the-roaders to bolt the party.

In contrast to Waite's enthusiasm, several Colorado Populists viewed fusion and the approaching 1896 election with frustration and foreboding as to the future of their party. Writing to the SLP secretary shortly before the election, Edgar T. Tucker, secretary of the People's party in Leadville, Colorado, noted that many Populists were unhappy about the Bryan ticket. While Tucker expected the state to go to Bryan, he also expected that after the November election the Populist party would collapse because of its union with the Democrats and that "voters will begin to rearrange themselves and on Socialist lines." Tucker, in anticipation of this shift, volunteered to aid in organizing a section of the SLP in Leadville.[17] In Idaho fusionists had controlled the party in 1896, much to the disgust of Ed Boyce, who, like many other Shoshone County Populists, was a middle-of-the-roader who opposed the emphasis on silver. For Boyce, the free-silver movement did little more than promote the interests of the silver barons of the West who were bitter enemies of labor.[18]

In Montana, where the mining companies were particularly influential and sentiment was especially strong for silver in both the labor movement and public opinion, the Populist party had essentially already moved away from a multi-issue reform program in which anti-corporate themes were central and toward a more simplified silver offering even before Bryan came along. The party's initial stance was broadly anti-corporate. In February 1894, for example, *The Populist Tribune* in Montana informed its readers: "The initiative and referendum; free coinage of silver; government ownership of railroads, telegraphs, and the phone systems; a graduated income tax; postal savings banks; no government subsidies to private corporations; economical administration of public affairs; equal rights to all; special privileges to none. That's what we want."[19]

Silver advocates had no problem with the Populists' stand on silver, but many were frightened by what they perceived as the radicalism or impracticability of some of the party's other stands.[20] To attract this element, avoid the establishment of a competing independent Silver party, and improve their chances of electoral success, the Populists generally moved their program in a silver-only direction. By 1895, the official organ of the People's party of western Montana proudly announced: "The main thing for which Populism has contended is the free and unlimited coinage of silver. There are side issues, but silver is Populism and Populism is silver."[21] The party abandoned its resistance to fusion and joined with the Democrats on the state as well as the national level behind the silver issue in 1896. Meeting in convention in Helena on September 2, 1896, the

Populists sent a delegation to a meeting of Democrats in Missoula to work out an agreement. This gave Populists the power to fill the slots for governor, lieutenant governor, and secretary of state.

Wyoming Populists, having gotten nowhere by taking an independent route in 1894 after a successful fusion venture with the Democrats two years earlier, were also generally willing to work with the Democrats in 1896. Still, there was sharp disagreement among the delegates, reported to be only seventeen in number, who gathered at the state convention and debated the proper course of action.[22] Some middle-of-the-road Populists decided to run their own candidate for Congress and, refusing to endorse Bryan, put two anti-fusionist candidates for presidential electors on the ballot. The Republicans, anxious to divert votes away from the fusion candidates, gave covert aid to the independent campaigns. In the end, however, the independents attracted just a handful of votes and had little effect on the election outcome.

In Utah, Warren Foster initially warned of the danger of subordinating everything to the free-silver issue and opposed fusion. He changed his mind, however, after the Democrats had nominated Bryan and, in the process, other parts of the Populist platform. On July 17, 1896, he informed his readers: "To my utter astonishment, the democratic convention not only adopted a platform demanding the free and unlimited coinage of silver and gold at the ratio of 16 to one, independent of any other nation, but it also went farther along the lines of monetary reform and demanded the abolition of all banks of issue and favored the issuing of all paper money by the general government."[23] As an aside, he added: "We would like now to inform our democratic friends who have so recently swallowed so much of the Populist platform that the rest of it is just as good and fully as practical as the parts they have endorsed."[24] Foster pointed out that all this unpleasantness could have been avoided if the Populists had, as he and other Utah Populists demanded, held their convention before the Democrats held theirs: "Populists would feel quite differently now if it were the democrats endorsing them rather than they endorsing the democratic nominee."[25] He concluded that, while far from ideal, fusion was the most practical alternative. In the end, Foster's views prevailed, but not without a struggle.

Following the Populists' decision at their national convention to endorse Bryan, some Utah Populists, ignoring Foster's pleas, abandoned the party. Prominent among these was the chair of the Utah party, R. A. Hasbrouck, who resigned his position in protest. Taking the same route as Tucker did in Colorado—actually, he did it four days earlier—Hasbrouck wrote to Henry Kuhn, secretary of the SLP, in September 1896, offering to help form a SLP chapter in Salt Lake City. Hasbrouck noted that he had resigned as chair of the

People's party State Committee "the day that our national party organization turned us over to the tender mercies of the Democratic party." Hasbrouck added that many of the best workers within the ranks of the Utah People's party were now proclaiming themselves Socialists.[26]

Fusion had also been the order of the day in New Mexico and, for some offices, in Arizona. In New Mexico the push for silver was strong in 1895–1896, with both mining interests and farmers caught up in the frenzy. Territorial Populists, who were firm on the issue, felt they could dramatically increase their votes. Still, recognizing their slim chance of victory, they were far from reluctant to join forces. They initially chose L. Bradford Prince, a supposedly pro-silver Republican and former territorial governor and supreme court chief justice, as their candidate for congressional delegate. Populists, however, later found Prince a lukewarm candidate for their cause of free silver.[27] They rescinded his nomination and threw their support to the Democrat Harvey Butler Fergusson, known to friends as Harvey B. Fergusson, whose stand for silver could not be questioned. Fergusson was a transplanted southerner who, since coming to New Mexico, had developed a reputation as a great orator of the William Jennings Bryan variety. With considerable flamboyance and hyperbole, he came off sounding like the most fervent Populist possible in attacking the abuses of special interests. Drawing on his friendship with Bryan, Fergusson had encouraged the presidential-candidate-to-be to visit Albuquerque in 1895, where he delivered a well-attended and well-received speech.[28]

Populists around the territory had no problem with fusion and sang Bryan's and Fergusson's praises. Some leaders, though, let it be known to their members that the decision to fuse with the Democrats "was not taken without demanding and receiving some concessions from the Democratic party which we Populists regard as vital to the perpetuation of our cause. We have the assurance that we shall receive just and proper recognition on the Democratic county and legislative tickets and it was on these terms that we agreed to indorse Mr. Fergusson."[29]

The Bernalillo Populists endorsed not only Ferguson but the platform of the state Democratic party as well.[30] Populists here, as elsewhere in the territory, acted as an independent party only when it came to local offices. Fighting off an image of Populists as representing the lesser elements in society, they proudly announced that their ticket was composed of party members who were "well known, substantial citizens" in whose hands the county would be safe.[31]

Arizona Populists, meanwhile, chose to go it alone, once again nominating O'Neill for the congressional seat. Fusion, though, was the choice of some Populist local organizations, including the one in the labor stronghold of Gila County (Globe) in 1896. Here Populists joined Democrats and silverites to nominate a county ticket that included future governor and, like Fergusson, a "thunder stealer" from the left, George W.P. Hunt. Hunt at the time was running (successfully, it turned out) for a seat in the territorial legislature. A native of Missouri, Hunt had spent a few years prospecting for gold before settling in Globe in 1881. After several low-paid jobs, including as a mine mucker, he had become a successful businessman, the mayor of the city, and Gila County treasurer. The platform on which he ran in 1896 proudly declared: "The Populist, Silver, and Democratic Parties represent the best interest of the great mass of people, while the present Republican party stands for the plutocrats and the shylocks."[32]

When it came to votes for the fused presidential ticket, Mountain West Populists had nothing to complain about in 1896. Bryan, while going down nationally, dominated the Mountain West, receiving nearly 80 percent of the vote in Colorado, Idaho, Montana, Nevada, and Utah, which became a state in 1896. In Wyoming he gathered in about 52 percent of the vote compared with about 47 percent nationally. Yet, following the spurt in 1896, Populists began to flow into other parties, including Socialist ones. Many radicals began to leave the Populist party immediately after the 1896 fusion with the Democrats. The exodus grew in volume from 1898 to 1901.[33] Populist parties in some parts of the region held on for several years, but with diminished influence. Still, they had left a considerable impact on the radical movement.

Bryan's victory in the state was about all that went the Colorado Populists way in 1896 and, indeed, in any subsequent election. Colorado voters in 1896 opted for the gubernatorial candidate Alva Adams, sponsored by Democrats and Silver Republicans, rejecting both Morton Baily, who was supported by the Populists and the National Silver party (associated with the American Bimetallic Union), and Waite, who had the backing of the radical Populists. Waite received less than 2 percent of the vote. Most parties used Waiteism as a campaign issue. While steadily losing members, the Colorado Populist party did not die immediately after 1896. It worked out fusion arrangements with the Democrats and other parties in 1898 and 1900, which carried the state and gave Populists some offices and a share of the spoils. In 1902, however, the Democrats saw no reason to join with the Populists, and the party virtually disappeared.

Many of the radicals leaving the Colorado Populist party in the late 1890s and early 1900s found a home in either the SLP or the Social Democratic party (which became the Socialist party). These were competing organizations. In 1900 radical forces in Colorado were further splintered by the formation of a Labor party. The radically oriented Colorado Federation of Labor, however, decided not to cast its lot with any of these parties in 1900 and rallied behind a Democrat/Populist/Silver Republican fusion ticket. As part of their agreement to fuse with the Democrats and Silver Republicans in 1900, the Populists got to select the ticket's candidate for lieutenant governor. They chose David Coates, a longtime labor activist who had participated in the founding of the Colorado Federation of Labor and was its president in 1900. As publisher of the Socialist labor paper the *Colorado Chronicle* and president of the Colorado Federation of Labor, he had helped push the labor movement to the left. Coates, however, had chosen to work through the Populist party, even though he was a Socialist, seeing this as a more promising vehicle to power. In 1900 Coates wound up on the winning ticket along with James Orman, the Democratic party's choice for governor. Two years after being elected lieutenant governor, Coates officially joined the newly formed Socialist party. He could lay claim to being the nation's first Socialist governor, since he held that position in Colorado when Orman was absent from the state.

Bryan in 1896 narrowly carried Wyoming and would not likely have done so without capturing the bulk of the Populist vote. The Populist vote was also important in electing Democrat John Osborne to Congress. Beyond this, Republicans did well in most statewide races and won control of the state legislature. Wyoming Populists failed to make much of an impact in any election after 1896, although they kept trying at least on a token scale until 1916. Whatever thunder the party had was stolen by the Democrats. Some Populist leaders in Wyoming quickly moved on to Socialist activity. One was Lewis Cass Tidball, the Populist house speaker who commenced editing a Socialist paper in Sheridan, hoping to cultivate and channel discontent. Another Populist moving in that direction, as discussed later, was publisher F. W. Ott, a German immigrant who had come to the Populists via the Republican party.

Meanwhile, as radicals were leaving the Populist party, some were also filing reports of labor unrest in the state, although, to their distress, the unrest had not been accompanied by leftist political activity. In a letter to "Comrade Wayland" published in *Appeal to Reason* in June 1897, for example, one worker noted, "Here in Wyoming thousands of honest working men tramp up and down the state with the music of starvation; they go from place to place asking for crumbs of bread that are thrown away."[34] A month later the writer informed Wayland that he was now in Sherman, Wyoming, working in a gravel pit for starvation wages. He observed: "The laborers at this place seem to be dissatisfied, but they don't know of any remedy; they have no use for Socialism. They are waiting on the coming McKinley's prosperity. Where they want to look for prosperity is in the capitalists pockets, no where else."[35]

In 1896 Idaho Populists and Democrats combined to carry the state for Bryan and won several other offices as the People's Democratic party. This included a victory for James Gunn over Silver Republican William E. Borah for a seat in the U.S. House of Representatives. Populists also helped in 1896 to elect Frank Steunenberg governor. In addition, the fusionists took control of the state legislature where, after some complicated maneuvering, the lawmakers chose Populist Henry Heitfeld for the U.S. Senate. The Idaho party, however, torn by tensions between fusionists and non-fusionists, declined steadily after 1896. In 1898 it made public ownership of monopolies and direct legislation its key planks, hoping these issues would fill the role once played by silver. Divisions within the party, however, kept the Populists out of a Democratic–Silver Republican fusion that swept the state and put Steunenberg back in the governor's office. Running independent of any other party, the Populists managed to elect nine legislators, but the average Populist vote shrunk to around 14 percent. The last bastion of Populist strength was in Shoshone County, where the party won nearly all the county offices. The Populist situation in Shoshone County dramatically changed for the worse, however, as the party's political foes, Steunenberg now among them, took advantage of the industrial violence in the mines of Coeur d'Alene to oust the party from power. As in Colorado, although steadily declining in voter appeal, the party worked out a fusion arrangement with the Democrats and other parties in 1900, which carried the state and gave the Populists some offices and spoils. In 1902, however, the Democrats refused to work with the Populists, and the party soon disappeared. Many Populists, including Heitfeld, became Democrats, and some joined the Republicans. Others, drawn from the middle-of-the-roaders, became Socialists.

Running as part of the silver crusade behind Bryan in 1896 brought immediate gains for Montana Populists. Bryan's sweep of the state helped fusion candidates take control of the statehouse and all state offices, including that of governor, when Robert Burns Smith—the 1894 Populist nominee for Congress—coasted to victory. Following his election, however, Smith sounded like anything but a radical. Indeed, he told reporters: "No one need feel alarmed that anything very radical or anything sensational will transpire in my administration, if I can help it. Those persons who have been pretending to fear for the business interests of the state if I should be elected governor, were alarmists without cause."[36] Smith turned out to be at most a moderate, stressing economy in administration of the state's affairs. He had some interest in rail regulation and direct democracy but was unable to get even a modest reform program adopted. The 1897 session of the Montana legislature did little more than produce an eight-hour day for hoisting engineers and additional safety requirements for mine shafts. Some Populists were unhappy with the limited output and perhaps even more unhappy about the way Smith handled matters of state patronage—they accused him of favoring Democrats over Populists in making appointments. Smith was also criticized for backing away from the woman suffrage plank in the party's platform, put there through the efforts of Ella Knowles. Smith explained that as a "born and bred" southerner, he had seen the consequences of extending the franchise to a race unprepared for such privileges and responsibilities. He felt that women were not yet ready for the vote.[37]

In 1898 the Democrats, feeling they no longer needed the Montana Populists, went off on their own. Stung by this rebuff, the Populist editor of *The Silver Advocate* denounced the Democrats, charging that they would "not risk the contamination of a political union with a party of laboring people." Democrats, according to the editor, had asserted that the Populists "had no social standing on account of their membership being largely made up from the ranks of labor." The editor went on: "We will acknowledge that the populist party is very largely made up from the ranks of labor, and we are glad of it. If it were not so it would not be a people's party. It would be like the democratic party, a class party, operated by corporation lawyers and corporation satellites."[38] The Populists retaliated by fusing with the Silver Republicans. This action, in turn, prompted Governor Smith to drop his affiliation with the Populists and return to the Democratic party. The Populist-Silver candidates did poorly in 1898, but the Populists held on—albeit with diminishing effectiveness—into the 1900s.

As elsewhere, by the early 1900s many Montana Populists had returned to one of the two major parties. Others were attracted to the United Labor party and the Social Democratic party.[39] Within a few years many politicians changed stripes. In 1897, for example, Martin J. Elliot represented Silver Bow County in the state legislature as a Populist and in 1900 was running as a Social Democratic candidate for Congress. One of those who bolted from the Populists after they fused with the Democrats was James D. Graham, who moved to the Socialist Labor party and, later, to the Socialist party, of which he became secretary. In the early 1900s the Populist party in Montana was most active in Butte, where it joined several parties (Anti-trust, Democrats, Labor) in supporting F. Augustus Heinze in his struggle against Standard Oil's Amalgamated Copper Company. One newspaper caustically but accurately referred to the fusion ticket formed in Butte as the "Heinzeantiturstboltingdemocraticlaborpopulist ticket."[40] Only the Social Democratic party refused to become part of the union of reform forces.[41]

In 1896 Bryan and the fusion ticket won a massive victory in Utah, the state's first national election. Although Warren Foster was defeated in his bid for Congress, the Populists, running on an anti-corporate, pro-labor platform, won four seats in the state legislature (the Republicans won only two) and some local offices. The four Populist legislators proceeded to focus on labor and political reform issues.[42] Most Populist bills, such as those calling for a miners' hospital, the initiative and referendum, and an income tax and one eliminating the poll tax and capital punishment, went down or were weakened by amendments. Populists, however, did get through a measure creating a mechanics lien law and one providing for a state board of public works that would hire day laborers.[43]

In the fall of 1897 Foster attributed the Populists' failure to do better in Salt Lake City to a lack of party organization and to popular prejudices against the party caused by misrepresentations of its teachings by mainstream newspapers. He was happy to report, however, that the party was now "in better shape than ever before." He found growing enthusiasm for Populism among Utahans, as evidenced in well-attended Populist meetings. Foster concluded, "There are thousands in this city who are Populists and have been all the while, but had no idea that they were."[44] In 1898 Henry W. Lawrence and Foster dominated the state convention at Salt Lake City. Lawrence attacked the major parties for moving the bulk of the population to poverty and condemned monopolies. The party, though, continued to be bothered by the fusion question; several members favored joining forces with free-silver Republicans. Foster, apparently seeing Populism on the rise in the state, changed his 1896 position and stood against fusion. His side won, and the party put together a platform stressing direct legislation and the single tax. It drew only a handful of votes. In 1898 Foster joined the SLP and, four years later, became that party's candidate for justice of the state supreme court. Lawrence also moved in a radical direction as Populism faded, helping, along with other former Populists, to form Socialist organizations. Onetime People's party leader R. A. Hasbrouck followed up on his desire to join the SLP. He ran unsuccessfully for mayor of Salt Lake on the party's ticket in 1897.

In the rest of the region—Nevada, New Mexico, and Arizona—the Populists faded rather quickly, sending their supporters in a variety of directions, including to Socialist organizations. In the first of these, true Populists had been overwhelmed by the Populistic-sounding Silver party even before 1896. Below the presidential level, where Bryan won handily, the Nevada returns in 1896 went as one might have expected—the Silver Democrats won every office by large margins. The only ripple made by the Populist party was from James C. Doughty, who, in his second bid for Congress, picked up about 20 percent of the total vote, finishing just behind the winning Silver Democratic candidate Francis Newlands, while the Republican candidate ran third. In 1898, in a two-person race, the Populist candidate for representative in Congress, Thomas Wren, an ardent silverite who spent most of the campaign condemning the railroads, picked up 35 percent of the vote against Newlands. J. B. McCullough, the Populist gubernatorial candidate that year, received less than 1 percent of the vote in a four-way contest. By 1900 the Populist party had disappeared from the statewide ballot in Nevada. The Silver Democrats remained the dominant force in Nevada politics through the early 1900s. Socialist parties slowly emerged with the support of former Populists and the influx of miners into the state.[45]

New Mexico Democrat-Populist Fergusson campaigned in 1896 as a strong supporter of two principal causes: free silver and statehood for New Mexico. His opponent, Thomas Catron, was particularly concerned about the adverse impact of McKinley's stand on gold. He felt that miners were in favor of free silver and that their vote, as high as 3,000, could cost him the election.[46] With reformers united behind him, Fergusson defeated Catron, 18,947 to 17,017, doing particularly well among the increasingly frustrated dry farmers who settled the eastern part of the state in what were known as the "Little Texas" counties. Fusion in 1896 also produced victories on the local level in New Mexico. In San Juan County, for example, a stronghold of the type of agrarian Populism found in the Midwest, Populists took most county offices outright.[47]

Yet, while there were ample signs of life for Populist reform in New Mexico in 1896, two years later the movement in the state was all but dead. Fergusson was voted out of office, and a fusion ticket of Democrats and Republicans wrested control of San Juan County from the Populists. By 1902 about the only reminder of Populism's golden age in New Mexico was "Sockless" Jerry Simpson, the onetime Populist congressman from Kansas who had moved to New Mexico that year for health reasons. Simpson made a bid to become the Democratic territorial delegate to Congress in 1904 but failed to get the nomination, although he had considerable support in the more liberal southeastern portion of the territory.[48]

By the end of the nineteenth century the Fergusson Democrats had become the primary vehicle for the anti-corporate movement in New Mexico, although some insurgent and progressive Republicans had also begun to emerge. Ferguson was an ardent spokesperson. According to his son, the famous author of the same name, his father

> seldom bothered much with the details of local issues but his main theme
> was always clear and it was always the same—the struggle of the poor and
> the humble against their oppressors. He was a follower of William Jennings
> Bryan, the Trusts and Wall Street were the villains of his political drama,
> but he never tarried long in the prosaic present. His favorite theme was the
> French Revolution. He could seldom make a speech without bringing it in

and this obsession grew upon him with the years. . . . What he delivered was a dramatic recitation, sonorous and passionate. The strange thing about it was that by the time he got to the fall of the Bastille he would have a crowd of sheep-herders, who had never heard of the French Revolution, clapping and stamping on the floor.[49]

Overall, the son concluded, "It was the general implication of his remarks that unless the straight Democratic ticket was elected[,] something like the French Revolution was sure to happen in the long run."[50]

Arizona Populists, like their counterparts in New Mexico, placed great emphasis on statehood and free silver in 1896. The People's party of Maricopa County combined the two issues: "We urge the immediate admission of Arizona as a state and denounce as un-American the policy which has opposed its admission, simply because many of its citizens are the supporters of a financial system which does not find favor with the money-lenders and money traffickers of America and Europe."[51] In other counties the party hoped to gain power as a result of public disgust over local government corruption. For example, in Cochise County the Populist party took aim at the "system of extortion, peculation, jobbery, corruption and bribery" in county government and pledged that if any of its candidates were elected, "we promise to watch them and use our best endeavors to see that they serve the people faithfully and honestly without extortion, fraud or oppression, and that they do not degenerate into county ringsters, and plundering officials, and, if they should so degenerate we promise to be the first to expose them."[52] The Socialists, also often targeting corruption, made similar promises.

Populists in Arizona proudly supported Buckey O'Neill, running on just the People's party ticket, in his second try for a seat in Congress. During the campaign the Democratic territorial governor branded O'Neill as a demagogue and a charlatan who was falsely describing Arizona labor as an oppressed class. O'Neill retorted: "When you made this statement, did you know that today there are hundreds and hundreds of men in Arizona receiving but $4.50 per week and board in return for their labor—for six days of ten hours' work. Not coolies, nor the pauper labor of other lands, but men of our own flesh and blood, men of our own race and kind?"[53] O'Neill increased his percentage to 28 in 1896, although again finishing third in the race for territorial delegate. This time the winner was a Democrat, Mark Smith, who received 43 percent of the vote. Contemporaries viewed both O'Neill's percentage increase and Smith's victory to be the direct result of the Arizona Republican party's decision in the fall of 1896 to declare in favor of a single gold standard. Arizona Populists were most effective at capturing voters in mining communities.[54]

As elsewhere, the People's party disappeared in Arizona soon after the 1896 contest. A direct blow to the cause came with O'Neill's death while fighting in the Spanish-American War. Contemporary observers quickly predicted that the Populists had little chance without O'Neill and would fade away without the benefit of his name at the top of the ballot.[55] In 1898, party members tried to fuse with the Democrats and Silver Republicans.[56] These attempts failed, and the People's party soon became little more than a politically isolated small club. In 1898 the Democrats rode to victory under the banner of free silver and a highly Populistic-sounding program. The Democratic nominee was not only known as the "silver candidate" for Congress but also as the author of a platform that "advocates the cause of the people as against the shylocks who would subvert their personal ends by increasing the already heavy burden resting upon the tax-payers of the territory."[57] The same paper contended that the Democrats' victory would have been greater, but around 350 Populists in Maricopa County voted Republican out of pique because county Democrats had refused to fuse with the Populists.[58]

After the 1896 election, the Populist parties in the Mountain West began to slowly fade away. In the history of anti-corporate politics in the region, Populists had seldom been in a position to greatly impact public policy. The closest thing to a radical anti-corporate Populist takeover in the region, Waite's regime in Colorado, wound up with relatively mild accomplishments, even though its enemies successfully portrayed the regime as an extremist left-wing disaster. In Nevada a new statewide party came to power, which many contended only sounded Populistic and, indeed, may have been less liberal than the Democratic party it drove out of existence.[59] A more thoroughgoing, genuinely anti-corporate Populism appeared to have been thwarted by a conspiracy hatched by the railroads. In Montana the Populist governor was, at best, a moderate reformer. Some Populist legislators there, as elsewhere in the region, seemed no more reform-minded than non-Populist legislators.[60] Wyoming Populists swelled for a moment but did not come close to bringing down the Wyoming Stock Growers Association.

Populists throughout the region, however, were important agenda builders, softening up the public and major parties for reform. The Populists were among the first to call attention to adverse consequences of development on workers, farmers, and the operation of the political system; offer an explanation for the hardships evident in the region; and suggest solutions, such as the initiative and referendum, to these problems. During the 1890s state legislatures produced numerous reforms in regard to rail regulation, worker protection, campaigns and lobbying control, and other matters Populists had helped make popular and had helped push for inside legislative chambers. Populism also contained a radical element that frightened investors, mining companies, railroads, and community boosters.

Voting analysis suggests that Populist candidates had relatively strong support in mining communities.[61] Support in these places reflected, in part, the Populists' strong stand in favor of free silver and their concern over conditions of economic distress. Yet, the silver cause was supported by local Democrats and Republicans as well as the Populists; and a number of groups, including farmers, were in economical situations as bad as the miners, if not worse, but they did not vote for the Populists. Perhaps more directly related to Populist success was the party's appeal to the emerging class of industrial workers. The feelings tapped in mining areas appear to be less ones of economic distress than of class consciousness. In spite of their campaign efforts, Populists did not do particularly well with farmers or Mormon communities. Mormons may have felt particularly uncomfortable with a party such as the Populists that had a strong labor thrust. Populists' weakness in growing cities and towns may have rested in part on the pro-growth sentiment found in these places—predispositions encouraged by the economic elites in the settlements. Populists, to these people, in some direct or indirect fashion, threatened continued economic development.

Populists had aroused a new class of industrial workers, particularly in mining areas. At various times and places they were eager to dispel the image of the party as home to the struggling, less successful, working-class elements of society and, at other times, were defiantly proud of the fact. Throughout the region Populists paved the way for Socialists in building the agenda for anti-corporate reform, supplying leadership and an organizational base, and helping to arouse working people, especially unskilled workers. They also passed along lessons on what to avoid and look out for, particularly in regard to fusion. Populists had continually faced the difficult question of whether to align themselves with another party or go it alone. Socialists, in part because of how they read the Populist experience in 1896, decided to never consider the possibility of fusion. On the negative side, the Populists also stirred the corporate world and its allies in the media and government as to the dangers of radicalism. Opponents of Populism drew upon Colorado's experience with Waite to brand the movement as radical and put people on guard against anything that might be coming along the same line.

CHAPTER FIVE

Party Building

Bravery in the Face of Triumph

IN 1898, WARREN FOSTER SUMMED UP THE SITUATION as many radicals saw it: the Populist party "was born; it fused; it died; but its soul has gone to the better land of Socialism."[1] Eugene Debs concurred with this interpretation of events. He had campaigned for Bryan in 1896 but moved on after the election to Socialist activity. In June 1897 he formed an organization called Social Democracy of America (SDA) out of what was left of the American Railway Union (ARU). The new organization's chief emphasis was the creation of Socialist colonies in sparsely settled states such as Nevada and Idaho that would bring in workers, including those blacklisted as the result of the Pullman strike; take over existing governments; and establish cooperative regimes.

In 1898 Debs joined the Social Democratic party (SDP), created by a faction of the SDA led by Victor Berger. That year the SDP elected two of its members to the Massachusetts legislature and the first Socialist mayor in the country, John C. Chase, in Haverhill, Massachusetts. Chase, a twenty-eight-year-old clerk in a cooperative grocery store, took office along with three Socialist candidates for alderman and three for councilman. Like the many Socialists to follow him in the pursuit of municipal office, he downplayed revolutionary rhetoric and said he was going to focus on carrying out the principles in the local party platform that included public ownership of utilities, better distribution of tax burdens, more open government, the adoption of the initiative and referendum, and the creation of public works programs to help the unemployed.

The national party was less restrained. At the Social Democratic party's first national convention in Indianapolis in March 1900, delegates nominated Debs for president and Job Harriman of California for vice president. In reporting these developments, Debs went out of his way to make it clear: "The Social Democratic Party is not a reform party, but a revolutionary party. It does not propose to modify the competitive system, but [to] abolish it."[2] Leaders of the new party also saw themselves in partnership with organized labor: "The trades union movement and independent political action are the chief emancipating factors of the working class, the one representing its economic, the other its political wing, and both must co-operate to abolish the capitalistic system of production and distribution."[3] The party in 1900 had 4,500 members scattered among 226 branches in 32 states and territories.[4] Debs that year received about 87,000 votes for president. Although he had the strong support of the Western Federation of Miners (WFM), he had a mixed showing in the Mountain West, doing better than his national average in Montana and Utah but below that average in Colorado and Wyoming (the only four states where he was on the ballot; see Appendix, Table 2). The SDP faced the Socialist Labor party (SLP) in three of these states and outperformed the SLP in Montana and Utah. The SLP, however, was more of a force in Colorado, although not much of one; it outdrew the SDP by 714 to 684 votes that year.[5]

On July 29, 1901, around 125 Socialists attended the opening of the "Unity Convention" in Indianapolis, Indiana, the purpose of which was to further unite the various Socialist political organizations. The end result was a merger between SDP and a splinter group from the SLP and, through this, the creation of the Socialist party, also known as the Socialist Party of America. Leaders of the new party later claimed the party was actually born out of the Panic of 1893 and the ARU strike of 1894. It owed nothing to the SLP, "that ill-smelling organization."[6] Socialist party leaders, however, did recognize the historic role the Populists had played in leading "a genuine revolt at capitalistic control of the old parties." They also acknowledged the Populists as a source of many of the reforms that found their way into the Socialist party's platform and Populism as a movement in which many individuals first learned their Socialism.[7] In addition, Socialist party leaders remembered some of "the lessons" of the Populist experience, especially, as they saw it, the folly of fusing or even working with other political organizations.

From its beginning in 1901, the Socialist party was a divided one, both nationally and within many states and territories—including, as we will observe, the Mountain West. On the left in this division were members who focused on the revolutionary goals of Socialism, that is, hastening the end of the capitalistic system—a system they felt had outlived its usefulness—and establishing the cooperative commonwealth in its place. Leftists believed strongly in the class struggle and expected that class-conscious workers would soon rally behind the Socialist party in a spectacular national election, drive the capitalists from power, and usher in the new era. On the right were Socialists, sometimes called "constructive Socialists," who looked for more gradual changes in the economic system by rallying the middle class and even the rich, as well as workers, behind specific remedial reform objectives or immediate demands. Those on the right looked at those on the left as "reds" or "impossibilists" whose extremism threatened public acceptance of the party. Those on the left called those on the right "yellows" or "bourgeois reformers" and had nothing but contempt for "slowsocialism," or "Socialism on the installment plan," and reform politics. From the right came the notion that Socialists could and should work with or through established trade unions. From the left, on the other hand, came an emphasis on the solidarity of labor, skilled and unskilled, which needed to be organized on an industrial basis. Over time, many on the left became disdainful of electoral politics altogether and stressed direct action at the point of production on the industrial field to overthrow the capitalistic system.

At the Unity Convention in 1901, while delegates fought bitterly about nearly everything, they generally shared the goal of securing power through the ballot box. The party platform declared its aim of "conquering the powers of government and using them for the purpose of transforming the present system of private ownership of the means of production and distribution into collective ownership by the entire people." Socialists saw the problems facing the country and the world as rooted in the fact that the tools of production, once simple and owned by individual workers, had been replaced by a system in which capitalists owned the machines essential for production, and their ownership enabled them to control both the product and the workers. The platform expressed faith that economic conditions and the working class would ultimately bring the overthrow of the capitalistic system, but it was nevertheless essential that the Socialist party be proactive, that is, that the party "support all active efforts of the working class to better its condition and to elect Socialists to political offices, in order to facilitate the attainment of this end."[8]

The party's immediate demands, offered "as steps in the overthrow of capitalism and the establishment of the Co-operative Commonwealth," called for (1) collective ownership of all means of production, transportation, communication, and all other public utilities, as well as of all industries controlled by monopolies, trusts, and combines; (2) the progressive reduction in hours of labor and increases in wages (giving the worker a larger share in the product of labor); (3) state or national health, employment, and old age insurance; (4) a system of public industries; (5) free public education for all children up to age eighteen and state and municipal aid for books, clothing, and food; (6) "equal civil and political rights for men and women"; and (7) "the initiative and referendum, proportional representation and the right of recall of representatives by their constituents."[9]

Party leaders had to be happy with their prospects. Both unionism and Socialism—radicals viewed the two as part of the same movement—were on a rising tide. Membership in all types of unions had moved from 450,000 in 1897 to around 1.4 million in 1902.[10] The same period also brought a leftward shift in the union movement. Radicals delighted in the growth in the number of labor assemblies that pledged allegiance to the Socialist cause, supported Socialist party tickets, and sent delegates to Socialist conventions. They also pointed with pride to the increasing number of pro-Socialist articles in trade-union newspapers and in the frequency with which Socialist speakers were admitted to union meetings.[11]

According to a report prepared by the national secretary for the first meeting of the party's National Executive Committee in early 1902, the new Socialist party had close to 10,000 members and was still growing. It was also making solid contacts with trade unions, winning them to the cause of Socialism.[12] Party leaders were greatly encouraged by this progress. Success, to them, was inevitable and very close. They had great confidence in Socialism's immediate coming success not only in the United States but in many places around the world; they were, after all, part of an international movement. They were, on the other hand, anxious about being ready when the time came. Some feared growth might bring an invasion of opportunists eager to jump onboard and who, intentionally or unintentionally, would divert the party from its true course and send it the way of the Populists. Sounding such a warning, National Secretary William Mailly wrote to a Colorado party builder in 1903: "Our party is becoming so strong that charlatans and politicians are already casting longing glances at us. That, as you know, is a sign of strength, and it is also a note of warning. We must not permit the 'Leader[s]' to lead our movement onto the rocks as they did the Populist Party."[13] To some Socialist leaders, the party was on the way to a brilliant future, but it had to "be brave in the face of triumph" so it could fulfill its historic mission.[14]

The national party had wasted little time waiting to organize the nation, including the Mountain West, although in some places the new party was rather easily built from locals of the Social Democratic party. In the early 1900s the national Socialist party dispatched several organizers into the region, many of whom had a few choice words about the hardships of travel they encountered in the area. On a mission in the Mountain West in 1902, national organizer and the former Socialist mayor of Haverhill, Massachusetts, John C. Chase complained, for example, that he had "to ride all times of day and night and lay over at all kinds of places for hours, in order to make train connections. . . . To get to Silver City I was obliged to ride by team 50 miles over the low plains and mountains through sage brush and jack rabbits, and it was the most sandy and dusty ride that I ever experienced." Yet, Chase concluded, inconvenience "is a part of the life of an agitator and has to be met with a cheerful smile."[15]

After visiting Montana and Idaho, Chase was happy to report: "The population of these two states is made up of social rebels who have come from all parts of the country to the west in search for freedom from the oppression of capitalism in the East or in quest of fortune in the gold fields. They are therefore made up of freedom-loving whole-souled people who are not tied down by bigotry and ignorance and made cowardly by fear of losing a six dollar a week job."[16] As a consequence, Chase asserted, there was reason to hope "the western wealth producer will not allow himself to be subjected to the degrading and humiliating servitude of the eastern wage slave. He will strike a blow with the ballot that will not only prevent his enslavement but one that will strike the shackles from the limbs of his eastern brethren."[17]

National party officials were often excited about what they saw in the Mountain West, but they also often found themselves struggling just to keep up with developments. In much of the region Socialist party locals, or, at least, what appeared to be Socialist party locals (these required at least five members), sprang up spontaneously without national or even state party officials knowing anything about them. Because Mountain West states were often "unorganized"—that is, they lacked state or territorial organizations—Socialist locals had to get their charters directly from the national organization. Yet, many self-starting locals failed to establish contact. In June 1903, W. E. Clark, filling in for National Secretary William Mailly, complained to an Arizona party leader: "There are a great many items in the papers, especially the *Coming Nation* and the *Appeal,* concerning the organization of locals that we never hear anything much about. I do not understand why this is done, but quite frequently we read in a paper that a local has been organized in some unorganized state and we never receive any application for a charter at this office. Such locals are either mushroom organizations, or organized by people who do not understand socialism."[18]

National party officials had an additional problem in the early 1900s involving state organizations, including some in the Mountain West, that did not affiliate with the national organization or, if they did so, did not pay their dues.[19] Perhaps more troublesome from a national point of view was confusion over agitation. As one Socialist editor saw it: "States, locals and individuals, as well as the N.E.C. [National Executive Committee], have all been organizing lecture tours. The result has been a plethora of talent and depleted funds for lectures' expenses at some places and no agitation at all at others where it was perhaps most needed."[20] Adding to the confusion, national officials were getting requests, such as one from Sheridan, Wyoming, in 1903, from people they knew nothing about who wanted to be placed in the field as lecturers for the Socialist party. National officials politely rejected such requests.[21]

To give direction to something resembling a national movement, national party officials spent considerable time tracking down and officially establishing locals. Once this was accomplished, they worked, if necessary, to create or strengthen state or territorial organizations to reduce the flood of correspondence and requests for supplies coming from the locals to the national office and to improve overall coordination for national campaigns. Mailly and Clark, saw a large part of their job as encouraging locals to support state or territorial organizations.[22] They were also in the business of encouraging and advising state and local party builders and, sometimes, of trying to spur them into action. Generally, however, the national office tried to avoid interfering in the operation of state and local organizations, being especially reluctant to get pulled into the intra-party disputes it was frequently asked to resolve (although it sometimes did get involved).[23]

For their part, Socialist party organizations in the Mountain West sought assistance from the national secretary's office in the form of organizers, speakers, publications, and a variety of informational services. The amount of national assistance and, more broadly, the amount of attention from the national party seldom seemed to reach the level desired by Socialist leaders in the region.[24] Several state secretaries seemed to echo the message sent by Utah party leaders: "We urge the Utah membership to realize that they cannot and should not depend too much upon the National party for aid but should resolve and plan to maintain and build up the party in this state through their own efforts."[25] Some state parties wanted help from the national office but without national interference in their operations. They argued that because of the small populations in their states or territories, the national party stood a better chance of success and would be wise to concentrate its resources in these places. Others proudly announced that they could get along by themselves. Early on, for example, the Montana party took pride in carrying on "its propaganda and campaigns without asking [for] aid from the national organization and without solicitations for financial assistance from the party membership in other states."[26]

Socialist organizers could be found everywhere in the Mountain West during the early 1900s, sometimes acting on their own, sometimes on behalf of state organizations or the national party organization. They were hard at work at party building and trying to win elections. They went to cities, farm areas, and isolated mining camps. By all accounts, Socialists throughout the region were particularly strong within the union movement and, especially, in the labor movement that had taken hold in mining areas. Mining areas were prime targets of organizational work as Socialists sought to take advantage of tension-filled industrial conditions. They assumed that radical literature would be effective in mining camps because miners had not only the inclination but also the time, especially during strikes, to focus on the message. In many of these places the party received the endorsement of WFM or United Mine Workers leaders. Still, organizers for the unions as well as the party faced the determined opposition of mine owners. Socialists frequently had difficulty securing access to mining camps and were forced to do their recruiting among miners when they came into town.

Socialists, according to *Appeal to Reason*, made considerable progress in picking up former Populists.[27] One Populist who switched parties in 1900 was Henry B. Fay, the organizer for the People's party in Idaho, Montana, and other states in the party's Sixth Grand Division. In his resignation letter, Fay declared he was turning to the Socialist party and thereby going to immediately "wash from myself all old party and Populist 'tactics' and their patchwork of 'reform.'"[28] Many other Populists joined Fay. Still, as far as the new Socialist parties in the Mountain West were concerned, the conversion process in the early 1900s was anything but complete: they had to compete for several years not only with the remaining Populist forces but also with the older Socialist Labor party and a variety of other emerging left-leaning, labor-oriented parties. The rivalry was particularly intense between Debs's parties and the SLP. In Colorado, the SLP had a special appeal to miners. When the SLP was formed in Leadville in 1899, for example, most of the twenty or so founding members were also members of the Cloud City Miners Union. WFM leaders encouraged the miners to form the SLP local.[29] Some WFM leaders, however, such as D. C. Copley, a member of the WFM Executive Committee, chose instead to support Debs's Social Democratic party.

Throughout the region the new party also competed with the Democrats for the working-class vote. Taking a shot at Utah Democrats, Socialist A. B. Elder warned workers that voting for the Democratic party was not a step toward Socialism, indeed, not even for meaningful reform. Rather, he argued, the Democratic party "has always been a house divided against itself. It is composed of a conglomeration of disappointed politicians, panacea hatchers and political frauds, whose conflicting interests and opposite pursuits continually stir the party with internal dissension, rendering all efforts at reform futile."[30] Members of the emerging party also frequently fought among themselves.

Some of the most impressive early party efforts took place in Colorado. In 1901 around twenty people, with the help of national organizers, established Colorado's first Socialist party local in Denver.[31] Following this came rapid gains in organization in the city of Denver—where both "Big Bill" Haywood and Ed Boyce became members of the new party—and statewide, particularly in places where the WFM was active and the organization's *Miners Magazine* was circulated.[32] Party organizers in the state stood to gain from the endorsement of the Socialist party by the American Labor Union (discussed in Chapter 6) and WFM annual conventions in Denver in June 1902. Colorado Socialists, however, were fighting among themselves and largely failed to follow up on this momentum.[33]

Discord also characterized the party's first state convention, which convened in Colorado Springs on July 4, 1902. Lieutenant Governor David Coates was both one of the luminaries and one of the central objects of controversy at this meeting. Delegates wholeheartedly approved of Coates's action as acting governor in pardoning a Socialist convicted of a crime many on the left felt he had not committed, but a considerable storm swirled around whether Coates could be a member of the Socialist party and continue to hold office as lieutenant governor. The Colorado party's constitution declared: "No person holding an elective office or appointive office under any other political party shall be eligible to membership in the Socialist Party." Coates, elected to office on a Democrat-Populist ticket before officially declaring himself a Socialist, interpreted this controversy as a direct personal attack and hotly announced that he would not resign his state office even if it meant he could no longer belong to the Socialist party. Some delegates called Coates a "fakir and trickster" who hoped to ride the party to power and then turn it over to the Democrats.[34] A few days later, however, the convention resolved the Coates controversy by modifying its rule to allow Coates to both hold his office and stay in the party. Following a friendly visit from prominent Socialists headed by R. A. Southworth and Mrs. M. T. Maynard, Coates announced he was still a Socialist, although he was not going to run for any office.[35]

Although plagued by acrimony, the convention managed somehow to complete its official business. The forty or so delegates in attendance—the largest contingents were from Denver, Colorado Springs, and Cripple Creek, with the latter especially well represented—adopted a platform calling for no less than the complete overthrow of the capitalistic system and the establishment of a cooperative commonwealth. It also made it clear that this was a "no fusion, no compromise" party.[36]

Commenting on the new party while it was still at work, a mainstream newspaper editor gave it credit for making the transition from a pure propaganda party to a party with a large enough membership to have an impact on state politics. Still, the editor cautioned that the party was "aiming at an ideal condition that is probably impossible to attain because the cooperative commonwealth idea ignores human nature: people are selfish, quarrelsome, and will not long cooperate."[37] For the editor, "No more striking demonstration of this statement need be offered than the records of the proceedings of the convention of the Colorado Socialist party."[38] Another less-than-friendly reporter noted that the proceedings "were absolutely wild in their disregard for all parliamentary practice; and every available opportunity was taken for some enthusiast to get to his feet and harangue on some visionary doctrine, which would be vigorously applauded."[39] Delegates, the reporter observed, were caught up in "wild theories" and seemed unconcerned with practical questions of how to go about campaigning.

The convention produced a list of two possible candidates for each position for party members' consideration in a referendum vote. Party leaders hoped to nominate Ed Boyce of the WFM for governor. They believed "that his name alone, with no further effort on his part, will be a greater source of strength than that of any other eligible member of the party who may be willing to go about making speeches."[40] Boyce, although the favorite of party members, refused to accept the party's nomination, saying he needed a rest and wanted to take a year off before getting back into the battle for working people. It was for that reason, he said, that he had also refused to run again as president of the WFM.[41] In Boyce's place the central committee of the state party chose J. C. Provost, a plasterer from Cripple Creek in Teller County.

Colorado Socialists in 1902 set out to make a very strong campaign effort. Working from a base of 1,285 members organized into thirty-two locals, they sent speakers all over the state.[42] Members of the new party called themselves "the International Socialists," in part to distinguish their party from the SLP. The SLP also nominated a slate of candidates and wasted little time lambasting the new Socialist party, including its leaders such as Debs and Father Thomas

Hagerty.[43] Mainstream papers felt the SLP was unlikely to do well but that the Socialist party, described as the International party or Debs party, was likely to make an impact because of its backing by powerful labor leaders.[44] WFM leaders strongly backed the Socialist slate. Considerable support was also forthcoming from elsewhere within the union movement. Going beyond the customary demands for labor reform, delegates to the Colorado Federation of Labor's 1902 convention indicated sympathy with the new party by approving a resolution demanding "that the means of production and distribution shall be owned by the whole people" and recommending that affiliated unions undertake "the study and discussion of socialistic principles."[45]

The fact that the Socialists would even dare put forth a slate of candidates brought nasty comments from Democratic papers about Socialistic "rabble rousing." Socialists and WFM leaders dismissed this as the Democrats throwing their "sewer filth" on a party competing for the working-class vote.[46] Democrats, such as U.S. Senator Thomas Patterson, did indeed appear concerned about the threat from the Socialists. Patterson argued that the Democratic party was the unfailing friend of labor and that, while Socialists were no doubt concerned with the welfare of humanity, no party that stood for the abolition of the wage system had a chance of success.[47] Patterson also challenged the practicality of the Socialists' methods. To him, they were missing the boat by failing to support Democratic nominees. By not doing so, they were passing up the opportunity to bring badly needed labor reforms and, indeed, were putting the enemies of labor in office.[48]

In the 1902 general election, Socialists polled nearly 9,000 votes, about 5 percent of those cast. Some mainstream editors detected Populists swelling the vote for Socialist candidates.[49] For their part, Socialists complained that their vote total had been diminished by voter fraud and intimidation. One leader claimed that in Arapahoe County (Denver), "the democrats stole everything they could get their hands on. Many of our comrades were unable to cast their vote because democratic repeaters had come in and voted in their name."[50]

For the WFM, the 1902 election brought good news and bad news. The good news was that progress was made in the drive for an eight-hour day. Earlier, in 1899, the union had helped induce the Colorado legislature to adopt an eight-hour law for mine workers, but, in response to a suit initiated by mine owners, the state supreme court declared the law unconstitutional. Colorado voters came to the rescue in the 1902 general election by approving three-to-one a constitutional amendment authorizing the legislature to enact such a law. The bad news was that the union's endorsement of the Socialist ticket boomeranged because the votes the Socialists drew came largely from the Populist-Democratic fusion candidate. This diversion, in turn, helped give a narrow victory to Republican James H. Peabody, who was no friend of labor. Proving the point, Governor Peabody refused to push for eight-hour legislation. The Republican legislature, widely perceived as under the influence of mine owners, also failed to take action despite legislative leaders' campaign promises to do so. WFM president Charles H. Moyer summed up events: "The Fourteenth Colorado Legislature went into session pledged to the enactment of an eight-hour day. The representatives of the mill and smelter trusts went into session with them. The result was no law was passed."[51]

WFM officials and other labor leaders came out of the 1902 election not only unhappy with Peabody's election but also disappointed that the Socialist party candidates had not done better, especially in the mining areas. Part of the problem, some suggested, was that the Socialists had little to offer workers in terms of immediate relief and thus had little appeal to them. Reviewing the political situation in Colorado in 1903, the editor of *The Labor News*, the official paper of the Colorado Federation of Labor, declared: "Our Socialistic friends have put forth an industrial plan for curing the encroachments of organized money, but their methods of bringing reforms are so far in the sweet bye and as to afford no present relief. We must leave them out of our reckoning in this fight."[52]

Party change, however, was already under way in early 1903. The Denver local, with a predominately middle-class membership, turned right, deciding to get more involved in immediate issues. The Denver local also joined forces with a committee of prominent out-of-state Socialists called the "Social Crusade" in an effort to wrest control of the state party away from left-wingers based in the WFM. Right-wing Socialists toured the state for support, organizing new locals loyal to them in farm areas, and, in May 1903, they took control of the state committee. The right-wingers toned down their revolutionary talk.

Also making progress in the early 1900s was the Socialist party in Montana, which generally grew out of the Social Democratic party in the state. The latter came to life in Butte in May 1899, when twelve Socialists, most of whom were former Populists, met in an establishment known as Fox's restaurant and formed the state's first local.[53] Debs toured the state later that year and noted party organizational progress at Butte, Missoula, and other places. He concluded that "the miners and wage-workers generally of Montana are taking hold of our party and we shall have a thorough state organization for the campaign of 1900."[54] Debs was especially happy that the Montana Trades and Labor Council, at the urging of WFM president Ed Boyce, had decided to circulate literature for the Social Democratic party.[55] Debs further reported that the *Butte Labor Advocate*, under new management, had decided to stand behind the Social Democratic party, having given up on the older parties and their call for partial reforms that fell short of public ownership.[56] By January 1900 the Social Democrats had a statewide party organization headed by John N. Heldt of Helena as state secretary, which was built on six locals and around 100 members.[57] The party continued to grow, particularly in Butte, and by midyear it received an invitation from the Populists to merge with them and other reform forces in the upcoming election. Socialists turned down the invitation, preferring to keep their distance from other reformers.[58] Running alone, the Social Democratic party candidates picked up little more than 1 percent of the votes cast—Debs led the ticket as a presidential candidate, with 708 votes, and the party's choice for governor gathered in 505—while the Democratic-Populist fusion swept the state.[59] The vote, while small, was encouraging to party members.[60]

His tour through the state in 1902 led national organizer John Chase to conclude that the Montana Socialists were "weak on organizations as yet, but coming along all right." From what he could tell, "Socialism seems to have taken hold in the minds of all classes of people. I find it among the ranchers and herders as well as among the miners and other wage workers."[61] Still, the party appeared particularly labor-oriented, as had the Populist party before it. Montana Socialists, State Party Secretary P. J. Cooney wrote in 1902, had but one question when it came to measuring the value of any proposed policy: "How would it affect the condition of the working class?"[62]

The party's first convention lasted just five hours, much of which was consumed trying to find candidates willing to accept nominations for various offices. After a good deal of persuasion, a successful businessman from Helena, George Sproule, finally agreed to head the ticket as a candidate for Congress. The platform featured labor issues calling, for example, for an eight-hour day and anti-blacklisting legislation. Montana Socialists also enthusiastically passed a resolution against fusion with any other political party.[63] In August 1902 the Montana Federation of Labor, meeting in a convention at Livingston, all but officially endorsed Socialism and the Socialist party. Socialists also won two of the seven federation positions up for election.[64] Helping out with party building were national agitators such as the Reverend Ben Wilson, who addressed audiences in Anaconda and Butte in early September. According to a local report: "His [Wilson's] meetings were a great success. Halls were packed full in both these towns. The entire audience rose to their feet and with cheers pledged themselves to stand by the international working class party on election day. There are three points that he makes especially clear—the inevitability of Socialism, the folly of reform movements and the claim that Socialism has on all of us, on the moral and ethical side. He inspires his audience with a hatred and a horror of the present system, a belief in the possibility of and desire for a better system."[65]

The party's candidates in 1902 showed some strength in Silver Bow and a few other counties but generally lagged behind the competing, radical-sounding Labor party organized by F. Augustus Heinze, a mine owner who, until 1906, when he disposed of his mining interests in the state and moved to New York, was the dominant public figure in Butte. In the 1902 contest for representative to Congress the election went to Joseph M. Dixon, Republican, with 24,626 votes. Behind him came John M. Evans, Democrat, with 19,560 votes; Martin Dee, Labor party, 6,005 votes; and G. B. Sproule, Socialist, 3,131 votes. That same year, several candidates of an independent labor party running on a Socialist platform were elected to the state legislature. They were not members of the Socialist party, as that party's secretary quickly pointed out.[66] Some, however, publicly sided with the cause. Shortly after the 1902 election, one of them, John Morrissey from Deer Lodge County, noted, "I had the pleasure and honor of beating out several business men and superintendents of the Amalgamated Copper Co. for the legislature polling 1,330 votes, while the highest on any capitalistic ticket received 1,125." Morrissey, though, felt that in the future it was imperative that radicals not only talk about why Socialism was desirable but develop and distribute literature in several languages showing how it could be accomplished: "This I believe is the weak point of the Socialist which the sophist, the old party demagogues, are quick to take advantage of."[67]

According to a report from State Secretary George Willett in 1903, the movement was gaining strength. In a year's time, he noted, the number of locals had increased from six to thirty. Gains were particularly heavy in mining areas—especially in Butte in Silver Bow County, with more than 300 people, and Anaconda in Deer Lodge County—although farmers were also falling in line. Helping matters were five or six well-edited Socialist papers circulating around the state. Perhaps most encouraging were the Socialist victories in the spring 1903 municipal elections, capturing offices in places such as Butte and Red Lodge.[68]

Socialists in Montana and, indeed, throughout the country were particularly impressed with the party's capture of local offices, including that of mayor, in the company town of Anaconda in April 1903. One jubilant Montana Socialist reported: "We buried the old parties—the jackass and the elephant—after having 'killed them good' with cannon balls of an aroused public opinion, and, as we lowered their carcasses into the grave of political oblivion, and sealed them tight, the band played the Marseillaise, while the comrades shouted cheers of victory."[69] The *Anaconda Montana Standard* paid tribute to the Socialists following their victory: "The spokesmen of the Socialist party campaigned earnestly and in a manner worthy of unreserved commendation. They have expounded their views after the manner of earnest and intelligent men and they have not surrounded their improvised rostrums with hired shouters. They really represent the party in this campaign, which, in its political creed, is wide enough to offer proper party affiliation for every citizen of honest purpose who is not willing to ally himself either with the democratic or the republican party."[70] The incumbent Republican mayor was less gracious: he refused to turn over the office to John W. Frinke, the Socialist, and did so only after ordered by a court. Radicals were particularly impressed when the new Socialist assessor in that city proceeded to double the railroads' assessment and raise the assessment of Amalgamated Copper Company from $6 million to $16 million, "giving the money bags of that place a taste of the socialist platform worked into government."[71]

Looking back, James D. Graham, a prominent Montana Socialist, remembered: "As fine a lot of class conscious socialists as ever stood together were the boys of Anaconda, and they were aggressive and revolutionary too. Being afraid of nothing, they proceeded to carry out a socialist program."[72] This win, the first major party victory west of the Mississippi River, rested on the support of unions and immigrants working in the smelter.[73] In no time at all, however, Amalgamated struck back. It fired and blacklisted anyone it felt might be a Socialist or a Socialist sympathizer and, in the process, forced 1,200 people out of town. In 1904 the Socialists, with most of their supporters no longer in residence, were easily swept out of office. Anaconda later became known in the Socialist press as "The City of Whispers"—the epitome of a company-dominated community with no freedom of speech or thought and one where people, fearful of losing their jobs, dared not speak out.[74]

Socialists had also shown some strength in Butte in the 1903 municipal election, easily outdistancing the Labor party in this contest. Not long after that election, however, reports came out of Montana that many Socialists were being driven out of the Butte mines (and off the voter registration lists) through a system of blacklisting.[75] The Socialists also came under attack from P. A. O'Farrell, editor of the *Reveille*, Heinze's newspaper in Butte. O'Farrell set out to stem the rise of Socialist sentiment. With an eye on Butte's Irish Catholic vote, he charged that the Socialists were anti-church and anti-family (believers in free love), as well as a threat to property interests. The *Reveille* also complained that the Socialists were supported by Standard Oil in an effort to divide Butte's working-class vote.[76] At a later date, some Socialists acknowledged that the detested Amalgamated during this period was indeed funneling money into the Montana Socialist party, although not so much to divide the third-party vote as to strengthen the Socialists' ability to draw votes away from Democratic candidates.[77]

Traveling through Idaho in 1902, national organizer Chase found a better-working Socialist organization than the one in Montana and "some very fine, active, class-conscious workers who are doing much work and making many sacrifices for the cause."[78] As elsewhere in the Mountain West, Idaho Socialists were laying the groundwork by developing a following in mining areas. The Coeur d'Alene WFM mining locals, having begun independent political action with the Populist party in the 1890s, found it relatively easy to switch to the Socialists once the Populist party began to fade. Actively working in the Coeur d'Alene area in the early 1900s in an effort to link Socialism and unionism were organizers such as Vincent St. John, David C. Coates, and John Kelly—the latter a member of the Burke, Idaho, WFM local and the WFM Executive Committee.[79] Miners' locals in the various Coeur d'Alene mining district towns became an important element in the Idaho Socialist party's structure.

In the 1902 election, the first one in which Socialist party candidates appeared on the Idaho ballot, however, the party did not have the support of WFM locals. Nor did it receive any coverage in the regular press. One campaigner noted, "The daily papers ignored any mention of us. Silence as to what Socialists are doing is their policy."[80] Leading the Socialist ticket that year was John A. Davis, candidate for Congress, who polled only about 3 percent of the statewide vote and did only a little better in Shoshone County.[81] Many Idaho Socialists rejected the notion of fusion. Those gathered at the 1902 Socialist convention in Canyon County declared: "We are unalterably opposed to any kind of fusion or agreement with any political party and will regard every person claiming to be a Socialist, who advocates or proposes such fusion, as unworthy of our confidence as Socialists; and the County Executive Committee shall withdraw from the ticket the name of any nominee of this convention guilty of so doing."[82]

Going into 1903, correspondence coming into national party headquarters indicated that the state party was having trouble keeping track of the activities of locals and in putting reigns on loose cannon individuals—problems that would continue for several years.[83] Still, local party officials were optimistic. In a 1903 speech, for example, a state lecturer for the party, A. G. Miller, declared to an assembled group:

> The coming of socialism is not dependent upon the work of the propagandist—it must come, and in fact a great industrial change is now in process. We do not see it clearly because we are a part of it. The conditions existing are fast becoming intolerable. The exploitation of the producing classes is arousing the toilers all over the country. . . . The spacious and silly arguments of the capitalistic editors and politicians are wasted upon the workers who are beginning to use their own brains. True, some laborers are still engaged in

building gallows for themselves to be hanged upon . . . as is apparent by their continued voting the capitalistic party tickets. But they are beginning to get their eyes open.[84]

Chase did not visit Utah, where, a few years earlier, the roots of party organization had been laid by A. B. Elder, a lawyer living in Salt Lake City, who established the state's first local of the Social Democratic party and immediately, in his own words, sought out men and women willing to "sacrifice present popularity and position for the future good" for party work.[85] In 1900 he launched the *Utah Socialist* to solidify and further the movement in the state. That same year Elder accepted the party's nomination for a seat in Congress. According to a later report: "He stumped the state, and everywhere was met by large audiences. At the election which followed there [were] cast over 800 straight Socialist votes, which was a record-breaker for the time the party had been organized."[86] Among the demands in the party's platform in that election were making all appointive offices elective, adopting direct legislation, instituting state control and operation of all water canals, and spending more public money on schools.[87] Although Elder felt Debs would do well in Utah because of the support of railroad workers and miners, he wound up with only 717 votes in the state, less than 1 percent of the vote.

In the early 1900s the Utah party was well on its way toward the reputation of particularly "cursed by factionalism."[88] Outvoted by 512 to 67 at the party's first convention in 1902, delegates from six locals in Salt Lake City, representing the left wing, withdrew from the meeting. The dominant right-wing faction moved party headquarters from Salt Lake City to Murray, a small town. Later, the factions sent contesting national committee people to a meeting of the national group—Ida Crouch Hazlett represented the dominant group, Elder the smaller one in Salt Lake City. The right, which included Henry W. Lawrence and Kate Hilliard (a former member of the Populist National Committee from Utah whom Elder had proudly welcomed into the SDP), sought an open and broad party base that called for a list of reforms, including public ownership of industries controlled by monopolies, the initiative and referendum (endorsed by Utah voters in 1900), universal education, an eight-hour workday, equal rights for women, old age pensions, and a Populist-like money reform scheme. Writing for the left, Elder demanded "a strict adherence to the principles of the working-class movement as laid down by the national platform of the Socialist party of America." He warned against getting sidetracked by "middle-class reforms of money planks, old-age pensions and altruism." He insisted on maintaining an "uncompromising, international movement of the wage-slaves to forever abolish both big and little capitalists by abolishing the wage system."[89]

At one point Elder dropped out of active involvement in the party, denouncing the friction and telling reporters he had sacrificed much time and money for the cause and had done all he could be expected to do.[90] By the spring of 1902, however, he was back in the middle of things. Elder warned his comrades in April 1902 that they were involved in an unpopular and somewhat dangerous mission, especially where their own employment was concerned. He also quickly noted that history was on their side: "Deductions from historic facts and observation of the trend of events tell us unmistakably that a great social change is at hand. It is inevitable, it is close. We do not need to truckle for votes. They will fall in line."[91] In the meantime, he concluded, "what we do need is clean, clear, true Socialists, who will not be swerved from the straight path and who will know what to do when the hour strikes."[92]

Of particular concern to Elder was the possibility that the party organization was being taken over by nonbelievers or political opportunists posing as Socialists before it had the opportunity to perform its historic mission. He saw this development as the price of success: as Socialists gained voter support, the greater their appeal to those who would use the movement for their own ends. This opportunism, he concluded, had destroyed the Populist movement and could do the same to the Socialist movement. In the interest of purity, opportunists and traitors needed to be booted out. In the meantime, Elder made it clear, the party "reserved the right to exclude traitors and to keep its organization pure, firm and intact."[93]

The national committee, called upon to resolve the dispute, revoked the charter held by the right-wingers and sent George E. Boomer of Washington to reorganize all locals and call a state convention. Boomer called a convention for April 7, 1902, that was attended by twenty-two delegates from six locals from the Elder faction. They formed a state organization. The right-wingers objected to this action and on April 7, 1902, adopted a resolution denying "the right of the National Committee to invade the state of Utah for any purpose whatsoever." The resolution went on: "We claim the right of organizing our own state in our own way in conformity with the National Constitution" and "to conduct our own affairs as seem to us best suited to the local conditions existing in our own state." They warned that should they not receive a state charter, they would organize on their own.[94] In 1902 the two sides were able to agree on a ticket, but right-left battles continued to erupt. In 1903 left-winger W. H. Tawney was engaged in holy combat with party secretary E. S. Lund. Tawney accused Lund and his right-wing comrades of rank opportunism—trying to win votes by offering people such things as cheap car fares—and of trying to build a mass party by allowing just about anybody who wanted to join the party to do so rather than confining membership to those who were "true red-blooded members."[95]

Utah party factionalism included not only battles between the right and left but between people from different parts of the state and between Mormons and Gentiles (non-Mormons). Particularly volatile were issues concerning party offices and resources between the Salt Lake City Socialists and Socialists in the rest of the state.[96] The party appears to have also been split along religious lines, with Mormons and Gentiles in separate organizations. At the turn of the century as many as 40 percent of the Socialists active in Utah politics were Mormon.[97] The list of Mormon Socialists may have included some highly placed church leaders. To this point, Socialist papers cheerfully passed along an item from the mainstream press to the effect that Moses Thatcher, one of the twelve apostles of the Mormon Church, had discarded talk of harmonizing capital and labor as nonsensical and come out squarely for Socialism, although no mention was made of his membership in the party.[98] Many of the non-Mormon Socialists in Utah were actually anti-Mormon, viewing the Mormon Church as anti-labor and an authoritarian and reactionary obstacle to the advancement of Socialism.[99] The religious-based factions within the Utah Socialist party competed in Salt Lake City, with their own, largely antagonistic papers.

Reporting in 1903, State Secretary Lund identified the Mormon Church as the greatest obstacle to the growth of Socialism in the state. Still, he noted, the church had helped make the "cooperative idea" popular in Utah through its teachings; and, historically, cooperation had been practiced "as a matter of necessity, owing to the barren country and the poverty of the people." The Socialist movement in Utah, he went on to report, "has had its ups and downs common in the initial steps of a great revolutionary movement" but was now on its way to success. The party vote had swelled from 717 in 1900 to more than 3,000 in 1902. Presently, there were twenty-five locals, ranging from 6 to 50 members, in various parts of the state. Along with this were a healthy number of Socialist papers and strong growth in union membership.[100] Throughout the early 1900s the party enjoyed close and cordial relations with craft unions affiliated with the American Federation of Labor. In January 1902 the editor of the state federation's official newspaper in Utah estimated that over half of all union members in the state and over half of its subscribers were Socialists. Because of this, the editor felt, "it is only right that we should favor them at least as much as the Republican and Democratic dailies do and publish their news items and give them a fair hearing." At the time, the federation felt it had to remain officially nonpartisan.[101]

The party was best organized in the state's most densely populated areas and in mining regions, including, for a time, the coalfields of Carbon County where

Sunnyside, Clear Creek, Castle Gate, Winter Quarters, and Scofield comprised the major coal camps. In 1903 miners, many of them South Slavs, sought in vain to force concessions from their employers in these coalfields but were frustrated in this effort, finding that sheriffs, mayors, and other local politicians had sold their services to business interests. Out of frustration in trying to improve their economic status, some sought radical solutions to their problems.[102]

In Wyoming the Socialist party functioned as a vehicle through which several Populist politicians continued their quest for fundamental reform. One of these was Henry Breitenstein—railroad worker, member of the Knights of Labor and the American Railway Union, and Populist—who ran for governor in 1902 on the Socialist ticket. Another was Lewis Cass Tidball, the Populist candidate for governor in 1894 who, after the Populist party collapsed, joined the Socialists and edited a Socialist newspaper, *The Independent Press,* from Sheridan.[103]

Also among the party's early leaders was F. W. Ott, a German immigrant and an ambitious, complex person who moved from the Republican party to the Populist party to the Socialist party. In the early 1900s he was actively involved with labor unions and the Socialist party in Laramie, a local dominated by Germans. He also edited a Socialist newspaper and in 1906 ran as a Socialist candidate for justice of the peace. Ott, though, had a checkered past and fit the description of a Socialist not wanted by any other party: he had been caught, for instance, in Cheyenne trying to run off with band instruments and the receipts from a band concert he had organized and, later, in Laramie for attempting to blackmail a Republican congressional candidate.[104] A far more socially respected and prominent early Wyoming Socialist was Herman V. Groesbeck, a New York–born lawyer who moved to Wyoming in the early 1880s and, in 1890, was elected as a Republican to the Wyoming supreme court and later became chief justice. Losing a bid for reelection in 1896, he turned to local politics and his private law practice in Laramie. During the early 1900s Groesbeck joined the Socialist party and, at different times, was the party's unsuccessful nominee for governor and for a supreme court position.

The Socialist party of Wyoming first nominated candidates in 1902. Running a mostly symbolic campaign for governor, Breitenstein gathered in 552 votes (around 2 percent of the total). He received around 37 percent of his votes in Albany County, where several coal camps were located. Groesbeck, in a two-way contest with a Republican for a position on the state supreme court, picked up close to 5 percent of the vote. He also did particularly well in Albany County, getting 45 percent of his votes there. After the election Groesbeck wrote a cheerful letter to the editors of *Appeal to Reason,* crediting his fine showing to the influence that newspaper was having on Wyoming voters. He felt that much of his support came from "the great Appeal Army."[105]

In July 1903 National Secretary William Mailly wrote Ott that the party was sending an organizer to Wyoming to get the state organized before the next year.[106] Apparently impatient with the organization's sluggishness, Mailly wrote to J. T. Gates, secretary of the Wyoming party, a month later: "I will remind you of the fact that we have not heard from you since May 28th, and that we would like to know how your work is progressing, and especially if the office can assist you in any way toward perfecting your organization and so getting ready for the campaign of next year."[107] Although repeated requests to the national party for more help in organizing the area apparently went unheeded, party members were able for a time to support a Socialist newspaper—the records are unclear if it was Ott's or another—to help stimulate interest in Socialism and build electoral support. Still, little was heard from the Wyoming Socialists.

Socialist activity also appeared minimal in much of the remainder of the region. The national party heard little from Nevada Socialists; the state had a relatively weak Populist organization upon which to build and had yet to feel the impact of major mining activity. Socialists also did not appear well organized in New Mexico, although radicals such as thirty-seven-year-old Father Thomas Hagerty, who lived for a time in Las Vegas, New Mexico, could be found in various parts of the territory spreading propaganda. National organizers for the Socialist party, on the other hand, had set out on several occasions to more labor-friendly Arizona. On each trip they found an active interest in the new party.[108] Local Socialists already in the field also received pep talks from National Secretary Mailly. Writing to a Socialist activist in Globe, for example, he urged: "Keep up the fight. The time will soon come when it will not be dangerous to be known as a Socialist. Let us hear from you as often as you can and let the non Socialists hear from you twice to our once."[109] By the early 1900s Socialist organizations could be found throughout the territory. The party seemed particularly well organized in mining areas where the WFM was strong. Globe, a city where the WFM was well organized, was also a stronghold for the Socialist party in the state—many members of the city's Socialist club belonged to the WFM.[110] The party, though, was not ready for prime time. On the electoral level Socialists in Arizona, as elsewhere, began poorly. The Socialist candidate for Congress got on the ballot in only a few counties in 1902 and received just 510 votes.

Looking at the region as a whole in the early 1900s, one sees that organizations of the new Socialist party were strongest where the Populist movement had been the strongest, where the Social Democratic party provided building blocks, and where the WFM was active. Territorial status and, with this, the absence of presidential elections may have slowed party development. Still, the level of activity in the territories of New Mexico and Arizona differed; labor conditions growing out of Arizona's edge in mining activity seemingly gave the party in that territory an additional boost. Throughout the region, the problems Socialist parties would encounter in later years—disorganization, conflict over basic goals and tactics, competition from rival radical parties and the Democratic party, voter intimidation, the lack of press coverage, the hostility and power of mining corporations—had already surfaced. In Colorado the point had also been driven home that labor support of third parties could result in the worst possible outcome. Still, there was considerable optimism among Socialists in much of the region, built around the belief that their party was on the rise and victory was not far off.

CHAPTER SIX

Promoting the Miners' Agenda

IN THE LATE 1890S AND EARLY 1900S miners throughout the Mountain West sought solutions to various problems—low wages, long hours, unsafe working conditions—through political activity and by directly confronting mine owners on the industrial front. Using the vote to reward friends and punish enemies, they dominated local elections, turning governments in mining counties into miners' governments. In these places leading politicians and officeholders, including sheriffs and their deputies whose support came in handy during strike periods, were often members of the miners' union. Miners also had support for their political objectives at the state level through the representatives from mining communities elected to state legislatures. At one time or another, their demands had a prominent place in the planks of nearly all political parties in the Populist era. One found evidence of the miners' political muscle not only in their votes and the votes of their friends and neighbors in mining communities but also in the lobbying activities of mining union officials and the labor federations to which the miners' unions held membership, indeed, in which mining unions were often a dominant force.

In some cases the struggle was relatively easy. In the 1890s, for example, miners in Montana benefited greatly from the war between the Copper Kings Marcus Daly and William Andrews Clark for political supremacy in the state. Daly had good relations with the miners and smelter men he employed. He identified with his workers and kept them well paid. In return, he expected their undivided loyalty on election day in his struggle against Clark. Clark and, later, F. Augustus Heinze looked at their employees in a similar paternalistic manner. In the competition among the Copper Kings, workers gained a great deal in terms of material benefits without doing much at all. Mine owners, for example, as part of their political struggle, voluntarily implemented the eight-hour workday. In June 1900 mining independents Clark and Heinz, hoping to round up votes for a ticket opposed to Standard Oil's Amalgamated, announced they were immediately giving their miners an eight-hour workday at the prevailing $3.50 daily wage. Amalgamated did not immediately go along, thus wounding itself in the 1900 campaign, but the company eventually saw the light. As historian K. Ross Toole has noted, "The eight-hour day came to Montana mines not as the result of pressure exerted by militant labor, but as a ploy by Clark and Heinze to outwit Daly in the widening bid for the votes and support of laboring men."[1] To complete the process, in 1901 the Montana legislature passed an eight-hour-day law extending the protection to more workers, and in 1904 voters approved an amendment that placed the law in the state constitution.

Two unions pushed the agenda of miners in the Mountain West: the Western Federation of Miners (WFM) and the United Mine Workers (UMW). In the early 1900s the WFM was particularly strong in Colorado and Montana and modestly so in Arizona, Idaho, Nevada, and Utah. The WFM had little or no presence in Wyoming and New Mexico, but the UMW actively organized workers in the coalfields of these two states. The UMW was also active in the coalfields of Colorado and Utah. WFM leaders were generally more aggressive in organizing and more politically radical than leaders of the UMW's District 15, which covered Colorado, New Mexico, Utah, and Wyoming. Still, one can overstate the differences. The WFM engaged in a series of strikes around the turn of the twentieth century, but the UMW in 1901 and again in 1903 also waged intense and often violent campaigns to organize coal workers in the region. Both unions also shared radical tendencies. Although they were more apparent in the WFM, many Socialists could be found in UMW organizations in the region at the leadership as well as the general membership level.

The basic difference between the two organizations was the UMW national leaders' tendency to be more willing than WFM leaders to bargain with operators.[2] WFM leaders criticized UMW leader John Mitchell for being too cautious in his approach to mine owners and too eager to compromise the interests of the miners. Mitchell raised eyebrows among the more radical members by "shaking hands with the enemy" as a member of the National Civic Federation, an organization begun by the archenemy Mark Hanna. At the district level, UMW and WFM locals frequently shared political and economic outlooks. As far as the corporations were concerned, both were objectionable. Over the late 1890s and early 1900s, however, the WFM was the principal force behind the Socialist movement and the driving force for militant union activity in much of the region. Its impact in Colorado was of particular importance in setting the course of radical activity.

While the Populists were fading from the scene in the late 1890s, the WFM made a rapid transition. In its early years the union had focused on protecting the jobs of miners and other workers in and around mines and smelters; it refrained from making statements regarding the class struggle or Socialism. On July 7, 1896, it affiliated with the conservative American Federation of Labor (AFL), headed by Samuel Gompers. Starting in the late 1890s, however, the WFM became increasingly radicalized by employer and state resistance to labor demands and by the growing influence of Socialists within the organization. WFM leaders came to view themselves as heading something that was far more than a traditional labor organization. Rather, the WFM had become, in their eyes, the heart of a powerful working-class movement about to bring significant economic and political change.

Spearheading the change in direction was Ed Boyce, the former Populist senator from Shoshone County in the Idaho legislature who became president of the WFM in 1896, a position he held until 1902 when he was replaced by Charles Moyer. The WFM first became involved in a violent strike during Boyce's regime in Leadville, Colorado, in 1896–1897, where lead ore was mined in great quantities. Mine owners responded to a WFM local's demand for a uniform three dollar wage by closing down the mines and throwing over 2,000 miners out of work. When they reopened the mines, the owners did so with nonunion workers. The scabs, in turn, soon found themselves engaged in armed combat with union members. Following violence directed against strikebreakers, Governor Albert W. McIntire sent in troops to protect against interference in mine operations. Strikebreakers already in the area were sworn into the state militia and furnished with arms. Eugene Debs, at Boyce's request, went to Leadville and found "a state of hysteria" because of violent labor confrontations. He was met by a gang of thugs who warned him not to make any speeches. Debs did so anyway, staying with the miners for two months.[3] While the strike was still in progress, Boyce appealed to the AFL for moral and financial help. The strike had drained the WFM's resources. The AFL endorsed the strike but provided little financial assistance. Eventually, the miners, faced with military force, returned to work on the owners' terms.

At the WFM convention in 1897, Boyce, feeling that only force would win the West, came out in favor of the idea of arming union men, claiming "every union should have a rifle club."[4] He also suggested that the organization should think about purchasing its own mines as a way of giving workers the means of production. The idea of forming a rifle club was attractive to the rank and file— if the reports to mine owners from operatives working for the Thiel Detective Agency in Leadville can be believed[5]—but the WFM did not form such clubs. Nor did members act on the recommendation that the union buy its own mines. Under Boyce, however, in 1897 the WFM did sever its ties with the AFL, unhappy with its conservatism and, in particular, with the limited amount of attention and financial support it had received from the AFL in the Leadville strike. It proceeded, in 1898, to form the Western Labor Union (WLU) as an organization to compete with the AFL. Boyce, seeing Populism fading, also began edging the WFM toward an endorsement of Socialism and toward backing Socialist candidates such as Debs.

Meanwhile, growing frustration on the industrial front led the WFM under Boyce into a series of strikes, each of which resulted in violence and death, the calling out of the national guard, and the deportation of striking miners. One of the earliest and most significant of these strikes came in Idaho. In 1899 a violent strike broke out in the silver and lead mines of Coeur d'Alene after the Bunker Hill and Sullivan Mining Company resisted the demands of the miners' union affiliated with the WFM for union recognition and pay at union scale. On April 29, 1899, a mob, presumably made up of union men, dynamited the Bunker Hill concentrator at Wardner, killing at least one person. The governor at the time was Frank Steunenberg, first elected to that office in 1896 with 77 percent of the vote on a ticket in which Populists, Democrats, and Silver Republicans had combined their efforts. He had been reelected in 1898, although this time the Populists had been left out of the fusion ticket that swept the state.

Responding quickly to the events at Wardner and without consulting with the local Populist sheriff, Governor Steunenberg put the area under martial law and wired President William McKinley for the assistance of federal troops. McKinley complied, and the soldiers came in under the command of General Henry Clay Merriam who arrested 1,600 union men and their supporters, holding them in stockades without a trial. He later threw hundreds of them into bull-pens (in this case boxcars and a barn) the likes of which, Debs later remarked, were "to make decent devils blush with shame."[6] Several miners died under the harsh conditions. One mine union official, Paul Corcoran, was convicted—falsely, some claimed—for murder and sentenced to the penitentiary. The miners' union was crushed.

Most of the soldiers who went to Coeur d'Alene in 1899 were black. The idea behind this was that black soldiers would be less likely than white soldiers to view the striking white miners as fellow workers and, thus, to fraternize with them—something the military found had been a problem in previous interventions. Strikers and their supporters, not immune from the racial bigotry that characterized that time and place, were doubly outraged that the brutal treatment came from black soldiers. The radical press reprinted affidavits describing outrages committed against workers and their wives by military ruffians—including tales of black soldiers acting in a brutal way, beating and stabbing the prisoners and sexually assaulting white women whose husbands were in the bull-pen.[7]

Public sentiment in Idaho, however, turned against the strikers. W. E. Borah, who headed the prosecution of those arrested, considered himself a friend of labor but was appalled by the excesses of the WFM. To Borah, according to his biographer, political scientist Claudius O. Johnson, "murder was murder whether committed in the 'class struggle' or in accomplishing a robbery."[8] The immediate effects of these events on the Populist party in Coeur d'Alene were devastating. Many miners who also happened to be Populists fled the state.[9] Many other Populists, including prominent Shoshone County Populist party leaders and officeholders, were among those sent to the bull-pen. Through court proceedings the Populist sheriff and Populist members of the board of county commissioners were removed from office and replaced by county officials more acceptable to the mine owners. Many miners fled to other mining camps, including some in Canada, to avoid prosecution.

The 1899 Coeur d'Alene strike provoked an outrage that went well beyond concern for the Populists and miners of Shoshone County. Socialists like Debs wove the outrage into their speeches, and labor leaders throughout the nation rallied their members around the disaster. Radicals insisted that the mine owners blew up the concentrator at Wardner to create a crisis they could exploit so they could get rid of the union and the Populists. Union papers warned they had a score to settle with Steunenberg, and Debs, on tour in Montana, warned of "a day of reckoning for such a scoundrel as Steunenberg, the renegade governor, who violated every promise he made [to] the miners."[10] Debs insisted: "The Coeur d'Alene outrages are stirring this whole country to its depths. The barbarous treatment of the miners, the suffering of the families, the dastardly sentence of Paul Corcoran, all serve to arouse the working class to serious reflection, and the result will be that thousands who have heretofore voted for capitalism via the republican, democratic and populistic parties will in the campaign of 1900 support the Social Democratic Party."[11]

Still, Debs was well aware that much remained to be done in terms of consciousness raising and political mobilization within this group. While commenting on mining conditions generally, he pleaded in 1899: "Oh miners, will you not open your eyes, and will you not use your brains and see and think for yourselves? You have won no victories worthy of the name. You are slaves, every last one of you, the victims of the wage system, and as long as the mines you work are privately owned you will be robbed while at work and clubbed and shot like dogs when you quit."[12] Here we see Debs in his central quest of trying to arouse workers, to make them see that they were being victimized and imploring them to stand up like men in rebellion.

Boyce, too, expressed outrage over what had happened in Idaho and called for action on the political front. In 1899 he told delegates to the WFM convention that from here on the group must organize on behalf of building Socialism as well as union membership. As he saw it, "To accomplish any reform, we must take political action, not as individuals, but as an organization. We should write our own platform and stand by it."[13] It was also very important to the union leader that the WFM "inaugurate a system of propaganda of socialistic principles," which, in his opinion, was "the only true system of government."[14] Boyce went on to praise and endorse the Socialist Labor party (SLP).

To further the cause of radical labor, Boyce launched *The Miners Magazine* in January 1900. The purpose of the new publication, Boyce wrote in first issue, was to battle "the concentrated power of wealth" that was attempting to destroy the WFM and, thus, "reduce the members to a state of abject slavery from which they dare not offer a protest against their oppressors."[15] The enemy, Boyce added, "are banded together in combinations known as corporations, trusts and syndicates, that flourish by means of their financial influence in legislative halls and court chambers, whose doors are barred against the laboring people with glittering gold."[16] American laborers, he continued, were losing ground: "All the machinery of government is continuously in motion to crush them, whenever they make a stand for even a portion of their rights."[17] Beyond advocacy of the miners' cause, Boyce pledged, "We will at all times and under all conditions espouse the cause of the producing masses, regardless of religion, nationality or race, with the object of arousing them from the lethargy into which they have sunk, and which makes them willing to live in squalor, while their masters revel in the wealth stolen from [their] labor."[18]

Later that year, Boyce used the magazine to state his lack of confidence in the major political parties. He dismissed the Democrats as "devoid of all principle so far as government is concerned," adding that all they wanted to do was ride Bryan's coattails into office.[19] Saving much of his scorn for the Republicans, Boyce (or an editor writing on his behalf) said he would not even mention them "were it not for the fact that in our own ranks there are men so devoid of all reason and self-respect that they actually parade around with [the] brazenness of a cast iron statue wearing McKinley and Roosevelt buttons, as it were, to make a further display of their ignorance."[20] Any western miner who supported McKinley had to be labeled ignorant "after the persecution he has imposed upon their fellow craftsmen in Idaho for the past eighteen months, and maintains troops in the center of the mining district for the purpose of perpetuating a permit system." Boyce asked men of the mining region to remember the Wardner bull-pen when they voted. As for a choice of candidates, he noted that the Social Democratic party's (SDP's) Debs and Harriman came "nearer [to] representing the views of the Western Federation of Miners."[21] As the election neared, mining officials in some parts of the region complained that mine owners and their allies in government were trying to drive union members who were eligible out of the state so they could not vote.[22] Miners were drawn to the SLP as well as the SDP, and some contemplated forming a local labor party to pursue their objectives.

In 1901 Boyce's organization, considering itself "the most progressive labor organization in existence," put forth a political agenda calling for the eventual emancipation of labor and, in the short run, reforms such as a graduated tax on incomes and, in the belief that the system of legislative representatives was not working, the initiative and referendum to make laws. While committing itself to the "universal brotherhood of man," the organization also stated its opposition "to the expansion of our national boundaries for acquisition of territory populated by other than the Caucasian race."[23] When it came to immigration, "We view with alarm the possibilities of cheap labor that confront us by reason of the expiration of the Chinese Exclusion Act, and demand the enactment of a suitable law upon the statutes of the United States that will forever remove all Asiatic races from competition with the American workman and woman."[24] At the time, the WFM was largely made up of English-speaking workers and had conducted a virulent campaign against the employment of Mexican Americans as well as Chinese to build up membership.

By 1902 Boyce had apparently grown tired of the struggle and announced that he was not going to stand for reelection as president of the WFM that year. In the spring, however, he made one last effort to move workers into the Socialist camp during simultaneous conventions held in Denver by the WFM and the WLU. Boyce arranged a series of meetings for the delegates and, to further their radical education, lined up Debs, Father Thomas Hagerty, David Coates, and other like-minded Socialists to speak to them. At the first large meeting, 3,000 to 5,000 people poured into the Denver Coliseum to hear the speakers.[25] The delegates came in marching, accompanied by a band. Pictures of labor's heroes—Abraham Lincoln, John Peter Altgeld, and Davis H. Waite—hung on the wall behind the speakers' stand. Coates and Hagerty spoke briefly, advocating the program of the Socialist party. Debs, the principal speaker of the evening, went on for two hours telling the audience that it was time for working men to combine on the political and economic fields to use the ballot as a weapon: "It is criminal not to use it, or worse still, to use it to forge your fetters more securely."[26] He asked the audience to read and think about and dismiss whatever prejudices they had against Socialism: "You are told that it is a bad thing. Who says so? Trace the statement to its source and you will find that it is made by the man who lives [off] of your labor."[27] The movement, he noted, was worldwide and in five years "will have become so strong that it will be difficult to find a man in Denver who will not insist that he was the original Socialist. However, only those who stand by the movement now, when it is not considered respectable, will then be honored."[28]

During the week, similar messages were conveyed at a series of meetings, large and small. Debs and others also took on what they labeled the "eastern" labor movement, headed by the effete and reactionary AFL, which had been keeping workers out of politics and thus allowing the capitalists to pick the workers' pockets. They proposed a stronger WLU that would back the Socialist program and the Socialist party. In rebuttal, a representative of the AFL argued that the slow and conservative route to reform was likely to be far more effective and that, in the interest of unity, labor should work within the AFL rather than within a competing organization.

A few days later the Western Labor Union resolved to expand eastward to compete with the AFL and to change its name to the American Labor Union (ALU) to more properly describe its expanded jurisdiction. The convention also voted in favor of international Socialism and adopted the platform of the Socialist party as its political platform and program. While many Socialists were pleased with the party endorsement, many also opposed the ALU—as they had the WLU—on the grounds, as the AFL argued at the convention, that it fragmented the labor effort. Algie Simons, for example, argued in the *International Socialist Review* that the fight for Socialism should take place within the AFL and that the creation of the ALU would only play into the enemy's hands.[29] Wyoming

Socialist F. W. Ott, who had attended the Denver convention and worked for the changes made there, countered that all the members of the convention "saw the utter uselessness of trade unions without politics independent of present political parties" and recognized that Gompers would not easily budge on this issue unless something dramatic and extreme happened.[30] He suggested that the whole idea was to pressure Gompers into declaring for Socialism. Debs, too, came out in writing in defense of the action, criticizing the Socialist party for "turning its back upon the young, virile, class-conscious union movement of the West, and fawning at the feet of the 'pure and simple' movement of the East."[31]

Boyce in 1902 called on delegates to the WFM convention to also adopt the principles of Socialism and "sever our affiliations with those political parties who have legislated us into our present state of industrial bondage."[32] The delegates favored a more watered-down proposal that, nevertheless, put the WFM on record as advocating Socialism. Mountain West Socialists such as Ott, who "had many a hard battle and many a sleepless night" trying to win over delegates at both the WLU and WFM conventions, were ecstatic about the results and more than a little angry about the negative reaction of eastern Socialists.[33] A. B. Elder of Utah, who covered the conventions for *Appeal to Reason*, likewise applauded the actions, noting that they could only have happened in the West, where there was freedom from tradition and ancient superstition.[34] For Elder: "This means that the organizations will take up the active propaganda of Socialism, that speakers will be put in the field and funds advanced to carry the work on. With 120,000 organized forces added to its already growing number the Socialist party will be a mighty factor to be reckoned with in the next election. . . . Truly the Socialist Republic is not far away."[35] In November 1902 the WFM's *Miners Magazine* followed up by endorsing candidates—many affiliated with WFM locals—nominated by Socialist parties in Colorado, Montana, and other states for various offices.[36] Party functionaries felt the *Miners Magazine* was of considerable help in getting the party's message out to the miners.[37]

At the 1902 WFM convention, Boyce, showing his weariness and perhaps hoping to build the case for a sharp turn to the left, painted a somewhat overly dismal picture of the WFM's accomplishments. The organization, he declared, had, in fact, produced little in its battle for higher wages and a shorter workday. Its demands had been met by over fifty lockouts, which had been backed up by government forces used against the workers. Generally, he felt, "The relations between employer and employee are becoming more strained every day, as the trust magnates know they have nothing to fear from organized labor as it is now constituted, because it is without a policy and relies entirely upon public sympathy for its support in all contests to improve the laborer's condition."[38] As far as accomplishments were concerned, the overall picture was not as bleak as Boyce suggested; there had been a flurry of labor legislation in the region during the late 1890s and early 1900s on mine safety, blacklisting, payment of wages, working hours, and other issues.[39] There were, however, some danger signals and major disappointments, for example, on the eight-hour day. Some of the supposed political reforms had never actually materialized, prompting many to lose faith in the political process.

Boyce had happily reported at the WFM convention in 1899: "Through the untiring efforts of organized labor in Colorado, an eight-hour law, similar to the Utah eight-hour law, was passed by the Colorado Legislature. It was a grand victory for organized labor in that state and shows what laboring men can accomplish if properly organized. The mining corporations opposed the passage of the bill very bitterly, according to the words of senators upon the floor; they attempted to bribe legislators to vote against it."[40] This victory, however, was soon undone by a court decision. The WFM, as indicated in Chapter 5, became severely disappointed about its losses in regard to the eight-hour day and the election in 1902 of archenemy James H. Peabody as governor of Colorado, an outcome attributable in part to the WFM's endorsement of the Socialist party candidate.

In retrospect, however, the most damaging action affecting the WFM was its 1902 endorsement of Socialism. Looking back years later Guy E. Miller noted: "In 1902, at a convention of the Western Federation of Miners, eloquent speakers appeared before the convention advocating the endorsement of socialism by that body. The delegates were won to it in a moment of splendid enthusiasm; they did not represent the sentiments of the rank and file; the membership of the Western Federation of Miners has never been a Socialist body; the majority of them never have, but I want to tell you that it was sufficient to arouse and inflame the minds of the mine owners."[41] Indeed, mine owners became convinced, or so they publicly stated, that the WFM was setting out to establish dominance in Colorado, making it a Socialist stronghold from which the movement could spread into neighboring states. Out of fear, they organized into Mine Owners' Associations and readied for attack. Joining the fight against militant unionism were church leaders, businesspeople, and middle-class citizens who turned to such groups as Citizens' Alliances. Not long thereafter the new WFM president, Charles H. Moyer, a more conservative smelter man from South Dakota, found himself tied up in violent confrontations with the mine owners.

During the early 1900s radicals around the country kept their eyes on Colorado. An August 1903 *Appeal to Reason* editorial suggested what the radicals saw there:

"There is probably no state where the corporations are more powerful than in Colorado. The masters are in the saddle. Everything the people use, all the places where they can find employment, are in the hands of the corporations. Labor troubles are always on, as the masters grind their slaves down."[42] For many on the left, an arch-villain in the early 1900s was James H. Peabody, a business-friendly and law-and-order minded individual who mine owners and other business interests, working through the Republican party, were able to get elected as governor of Colorado. Peabody, a banker from Cañon City, naturally fell in with the Citizens' Alliance of Colorado, a new organization representing the views of around 30,000 business and professional people. He had no qualms about protecting the interests of the state's business and industrial leaders. He shared their values and their view that unions were neither necessary nor desirable. He aimed much of his wrath at union leaders. Peabody, as one historian has noted, "saw union officials as demonic leaders who advocated un-American concepts and utilized reprehensible methods in realizing socialistic objectives. To him they were an infamous 'inner circle' [from] whom the rank and file must be saved."[43]

With Peabody's help, the Colorado legislature in 1902 turned down the eight-hour law. This defeat, Guy E. Miller wrote, led organized labor to believe the "lawmakers were against them" and that "if they were to better their conditions they must take by organization that which they should have enjoyed by legislation."[44] With the apparent failure of political remedies, the WFM called a strike of 3,500 miners in the Cripple Creek, Colorado, gold-producing mining district for an eight-hour day for all miners. The strike lasted from August 10, 1903, to July 26, 1904. Owners, as usual, imported nonunion workers into the area, and striking workers tried to bar their entry. The striking miners were encouraged by the likes of WFM official Bill Haywood, who reminded them that the WFM "is the only friend you have against corporate oppression."[45] Turning to the mine owners, another of the strikers' supporters, Emma F. Langdon, warned: "The metalliferous miner of the West is a very different man from the Italian and Hungarian that used to be employed in the eastern coal mines. The most of them are American born. Those who have emigrated came from Germany, Sweden and Ireland. Many had been among those sturdy pioneers, who blazed away and made it possible to speak to the wilderness beyond the Rocky mountains as 'The Great West.' Such men are not easily subdued."[46]

During the early stages of the strike, things went well for the striking miners. The Cripple Creek Mining District, southwest of Denver, contained several small towns ranging from 12,000 to 15,000 people. Cripple Creek, the county seat of Teller County, was the largest of these towns. Also in the area were the communities of Victor, Independence, Goldfield, and Anaconda. The WFM was well organized in many of these communities and in the county as a whole. With the support of the county sheriff, a WFM member, the strikers drove off many scabs. On the other hand, many members of the business community lost little time moving to the side of the mining companies, joining Civil Alliances to maintain order and, at the behest of mine managers, departing from past practices by refusing to carry their customers on credit, thus increasing the financial pressure on those had gone out on strike. WFM President Moyer commented on this behavior with considerable bitterness:

> The lesson taught by the business element in the Cripple Creek district, the almost immediate withdrawing of all credit, the organizing of Citizens' Alliances, should be convincing evidence that the friendship of this class reaches no farther than the pocket book. It took the business man of the Cripple Creek district but a very short time to betray his true colors; always in favor of union wages because they brought more money to his till, like the non-union man in times of peace and the scab in times of trouble, ever willing to share the benefits secured by organized labor, yet at the first alarm that his profits might be affected or some union man whom he has robbed for years might ask for a dollar's credit, he cries 'The Cash System' but the same old profits.[47]

The WFM added to its opponents' consternation by establishing cooperative stores in the district. Ida Crouch Hazlett, at the time the state organizer for the Colorado Socialist party, reported from the scene that the cooperative stores did a flourishing business providing food and other necessities and were driving merchants associated with the Citizens' Alliance out of business. Still, she noted, "As always happens when the laboring men are getting the best of it, the capitalists desired an excuse for calling out the troops. Consequently, various accidents began to occur about the mines. Houses and mines were blown up, fires were set, lives were threatened, and everything [was] done to make it appear that a reign of terror was impending. The miners obtained satisfactory evidence that these things were done by the emissaries of the capitalists, but the capitalist press commenced a great outcry about the lawlessness of the strikers, and the Governor declared martial law in the strike district."[48]

Reacting to what they saw or depicted as acts of worker terrorism, mine owners evicted employees from their homes, employed thugs to assault strikers, and, following a dynamiting at a railroad station that killed thirteen nonunion members, asked Peabody to send in the militia to protect their properties. Peabody complied, sending in 1,000 men under the command of Adjutant General Sherman Bell, later described by Socialist writers as "one of the most depraved characters whom the western labor movement had ever encountered."[49] Bell proceeded to declare martial law in the strike district, dismiss the local (labor-friendly) police, and arrest workers and WFM officials, either putting them in various types of bull-pens or deporting them from the state. Nationally prominent Socialist Morris Hillquit later reported, "The strike was not broken, it was literally physically crushed."[50]

Emma F. Langdon, a witness to much of what went on in Cripple Creek, later wrote, "The district was in complete control of a mob, intoxicated with brutal power."[51] Langdon became a hero of the struggle by single-handedly keeping the pro-worker *Victor Record* alive and functioning after it had been suppressed by the militia and after her husband, a linotype operator, and others had been thrown in jail for opposing the use of the militia against the strikers. By the summer of 1904, though, the strike was broken. The mine owners followed up by blacklisting WFM members and reopening the mines with nonunion labor.

Mountain West Socialists competed in their condemnation of Peabody's Cripple Creek actions. The McCabe Socialist Club in Arizona, for example, acknowledged the "cry of anguish that arises from the scene of the reign of Peabodyism in Colorado" and denounced the "flagrant acts of injustice, perpetrated by a man in whose heart has died the last feeling of sympathy for his fellow-man."[52] Peabody, the Socialists continued, had used the military "to protect the few against the many," and the military regime in Cripple Creek had "been characterized by theft, murder, wanton destruction of property, false imprisonment and crowned by indignities heaped upon defenseless women and children."[53] Individual miners, too, if one can believe the reports of the detectives hired to spy on them, were stirred by the events. One miner in Jerome, Arizona, reportedly "said he considered it would be an honor to anyone who would blow up General Sherman Bell."[54] The Jerome Mining Union agreed to assess each member one day's pay to help miners in Cripple Creek. One member encouraging this action argued that "the strikers in Colorado were not only fighting their own battle but that of all union men; that if the Mine Owners in Colorado won out in this strike they would try to kill the unions all over the country and that in Jerome and Arizona they would try to reduce wages and increase the hours."[55] The Cripple Creek events came as further evidence to Mother Jones that Colorado belonged to the mining companies: "The governor was their agent. The militia under Bell did their bidding. Whenever the masters of the state told the governor to bark, he yelped for them like a mad hound. Whenever they told the military to bite, they bit."[56]

During the labor wars in Colorado, church leaders frequently joined mine owners and various employer associations in criticizing labor agitators. One critic, the Reverend J. H. Speer, pastor of the North Denver Presbyterian Church, for example, in one of his favorite speeches titled "The Agitator—A Man Not Wanted," warned workers that their worst enemy was not their employer but the unbalanced, agitating union leader and the saloon.[57] On this issue at least, he was joined by Bishop Nicholas C. Matz, head of the Roman Catholic Denver diocese. Matz was hostile to the WFM because of its militancy and the tendency of many of its leaders to endorse Socialism. He felt the tenets of Socialism violated church doctrine.[58] Debs, touring the strike-torn region in 1904, offered something of a rebuttal: "Socialists are called agitators even as Christ was. Socialist doctrines are similar to his teachings. If the mine owners of Colorado were on earth during his life they would have hated him and he would have been deported."[59]

While the Cripple Creek strike was in progress, coal miners in various parts of the state were also on strike for an eight-hour day, pay increases, and other changes. The strike involved UMW members from Colorado, Wyoming, Utah, and New Mexico, who were bunched together in the union's District 15. Meeting in Pueblo, Colorado, on September 23, 1903, delegates from the district had announced that the strike would take place on November 9 if operators did not meet their demands. Delegates at that meeting also adopted by a large majority a resolution endorsing Socialism. For mine owners in the area, the UMW seemed every bit as evil as the WFM, and they set out on a holy war against both organizations.[60]

When the mining companies failed to respond to union demands, a strike involving 22,000 miners took place as scheduled. Mother Jones came to Trinidad, Colorado, the strike headquarters, to help out in October 1903, along with other UMW organizers. The effort led by Jones and others in the coalfields of southern Colorado made considerable headway, but the strike throughout the district floundered. It never took hold in Wyoming or New Mexico; thus, little was done to reduce the overall production of coal. Operators continued to supply their customers and to make a profit in doing so. In Wyoming workers took a 10 percent raise and continued working. In New Mexico strike activity never got off the ground.

Especially upsetting to the strikers in southern Colorado was the decision of strikers in northern Colorado, on the recommendation of the national UMW leadership under John Mitchell, to accept a separate settlement with the operators. The settlement was also denounced by WFM leaders on the grounds that a statewide walkout of all miners was essential for victory in their battle in Cripple Creek. At this time local UMW officials were more often in agreement with the WFM as to goals and tactics than they were with the eastern UMW officials who controlled the strike.[61] Mother Jones and other Socialists in the organization opposed the settlement and openly denounced Mitchell and members of the executive board for recommending its approval. Meanwhile, the strike lingered on in the southern coalfields, marked by sharp charges and accusations (including an effort to destroy Mother Jones's reputation by linking her to a history of prostitution) and violence, most often directed at the strikers. Strike leaders had a difficult time providing food and shelter for the strikers and their families (who had been evicted from their company-owned homes shortly after the strike began). Financing the strike imposed a severe burden on the union.

In March 1904 Peabody ordered around 400 Colorado national guard troops into the southern coalfield to protect the coal miners' property from striking miners, declared martial law, and had strike leaders deported out of the state. Under Peabody's orders the militia, flashing bayonets, also deported Jones from the area. She, as we shall see later, moved on to Helper, Utah, where a related coal strike was in progress, but she was derailed by being quarantined because of her alleged contact with someone who had smallpox. Many of the miners forced out of Cripple Creek moved on to other states, most significantly Goldfield, Nevada, where they contributed to growing radicalism there.

Labor conflicts in Colorado dominated the headlines in the early 1900s. What happened there in mining areas, however, was mirrored in varying degrees in much of the rest of the region. Conditions, for example, were less than optimal in the coal mines opened by the Union Pacific Railroad in Rock Springs, Almy, and Hanna, Wyoming. In these places miners, many of whom were recent migrants to the country, lived in isolated places where the company owned virtually everything, including their homes. They worked long hours under dangerous conditions. In Hanna an underground mine exploded in 1903, killing 169 miners. By this time the UMW had established its first local at Dietz in the northern county of Sheridan and was working its way south. The Union Pacific resisted unionization and was able to minimize worker action by, among other things, mixing Asians with Asian-hating whites, thus keeping workers divided.[62]

In New Mexico, meanwhile, Gallup coal miners grumbled in 1901 about being cheated in weights (they, like coal miners elsewhere, were paid by the weight of the coal they produced) and the high prices at company stores. The complaints led 70 miners to join the UMW. The next day all of them were fired.[63] As elsewhere, there were disasters, such as the fire and violent explosion in the Dawson mine in 1903 that terrified 500 miners and left 3 dead.[64] Reports from WFM officials in Idaho during the same period painted the picture as ugly, especially in Wardner where labor, in an atmosphere dominated by the presence of federal troops and the continuance of martial law, was unable to do anything to prevent Standard Oil, owner of the Bunker Hill and Sullivan mines, from reducing wages or, as WFM officials saw it, to protect workers from unlawful treatment by "every hired thug and state official that comes along."[65]

Unionism flourished in Montana in the late 1890s, even while bloody labor wars were going on in other parts of the Mountain West for labor recognition. Problems in Montana, however, began to develop after 1899 when Standard Oil purchased Daly's Anaconda Company, turning it into a holding company called the Amalgamated Copper Company. Amalgamated proceeded to absorb other companies and related enterprises in the state, including William Clark's extensive holdings as well as the large Boston and Montana Company in Butte. Mine workers lost their bargaining power and, indeed, through a system of company infiltrators and spies, control over their union. Thus, while the WFM began moving to the left under Boyce, its first and most illustrious local in Butte, the Butte Miners' Union, was settling in on the right. To the horror of many in the radical labor movement, Butte Miners' Union officials in 1903 went so far as to accept an invitation from Theodore Roosevelt to join him for dinner in the White House.

In Utah the state legislature in 1896 implemented several labor-reform provisions in the state's new constitution, including an eight-hour day for workers in mines and smelters, along with several mine safety measures. Still, Utah coal miners had reason to complain about unusually low pay and unsafe conditions, the latter dramatically evidenced in a mine explosion in 1900 that claimed the lives of 200 workers.[66] Referring to the tragedy, a Socialist reporter noted: "Two Hundred miners, engaged in digging profits out of society and coal mines for some sleek, well-groomed masters living in Salt Lake, Utah, and London, England, far away from the hardships and dangers of the coal mines, were killed by an explosion of some kind in Scofield, Utah, the other day. To die for one's country is said to be glorious . . . but how glorious is it to die for a few Coal Barons?"[67] In spite of these conditions, UMW organizers had difficulty establishing strong unions in these places. The mining camps were filled with a variety of nationalities, and mining companies often played one ethnic group against another to prevent them from coming together in unions. The South Slav miners in the coalfields of Carbon County, Utah, constantly attempted to work with other ethnic groups to better their economic position and force concessions from their employers. They had little success. In the eyes of many South Slavs, radical solutions were needed because the political structure existed mainly to support their employers—the local police, the mayor, the governor—who would come to their rescue during strikes because they had sold their services just as workingmen were expected to sell their labor.[68]

One of labor's main targets, the Utah Fuel Company, regularly curtailed the activities of union organizers by, among other techniques, using its political influence to have union officials arrested on charges such as vagrancy or disturbing the peace. Law enforcement authorities were at the company's disposal and helped break a strike waged against it in 1903–1904. The miners, mostly Italians, walked out, demanding better hours and wages and recognition of the UMW. Forced out of their company housing, they set up a tent colony. Governor Heber M. Wells sent in troops and, after conferring with the president of the Utah Fuel Company, announced: "The only way I can see for the strike to be settled is either for the strikers to give up the union and surrender their certificates, go back to work, or else leave the country. As long as the present conditions exist, the troops will remain in the field, as it would be the utmost folly to recall them at this time."[69] The troops stayed in the striking area for several weeks, eventually breaking the strike.

The company blamed the strike on the ability of outside radical agitators to inflame the many foreign-born miners. One of those agitators was Mother Jones, who came to the strike area in Helper—a town in the middle of some of the major coalfields in Carbon County—after being deported from Colorado. Jones had barely begun to agitate—part of her message condemned the Mormon Church for being in league with the "thieving corporations"—when she was notified by health authorities that she had been exposed to smallpox and had to be isolated in a frame shack built for smallpox sufferers. Jones, convinced there was no smallpox anywhere in town, was spared this isolation after two Italian strikers set fire to the shack the night before she was scheduled to use it. Later, she was quarantined in a room an Italian family gave her, although she frequently broke the quarantine to address the striking workers.

Late in April 1904, reports that the Italians in the strikers' camp were about to engage in violence—indeed, some newspapers reported they had already amused themselves by holding up peaceful citizens on the highways, taking potshots at the armed guards of the Utah Fuel Company, and threatening to assault company officials—prompted the company to ask Governor Wells to send the militia back to the strike area. This time the governor, worried about reelection, hesitated.[70] The local sheriff, however, decided to take action and formed a posse of 40 men—mostly armed guards working for the company who were sworn in as deputy sheriffs—to clean out the strikers' camp. At dawn, with, as one paper noted, "the gallant sheriff well in the rear," the posse swooped down into the tent colony where the striking Italian miners were sleeping and took 120 into custody.[71] Mother Jones reported: "Between 4:30 and five o'clock in the morning I heard the tramp of feet on the road. I looked out of my smallpox window and saw about forty-five deputies. They descended upon the sleeping tent colony, dragged the miners out of their beds. . . . Not one law had these miners broken. The pitiful screams of the women and children would have penetrated Heaven."[72] Jones broke her quarantine and led a crowd of protesting women and children into Price, Utah, the county seat, where the prisoners were being held—some in a large, closely guarded warehouse because there was not enough room in the jail for them all. Authorities ordered her arrest for breaking her quarantine. An armed body of 100 miners, however, deterred a deputy sheriff from carrying out the order, and she took off for Salt Lake City to take her complaints to the governor and then went on to San Francisco where another set of strikers awaited her.

By the early 1900s twenty locals of the WFM had been formed in Arizona. Organizational efforts, though, often met with stiff resistance. In the southern Arizona town of Pearce, for example, a mine owner fired everyone who had joined the WFM local. In this case the owner, at least initially, passed up Mexican replacements and sent an agent into Mormon settlements in the territory to find nonunion men to take the place of the men he had fired.[73] By 1903 Arizona mining unions had made some progress in the territorial legislature on matters directly affecting their interests. In that year they successfully promoted a measure limiting underground work in the mines to no more than eight hours and another measure banning the practice of paying wages with tokens. The miners, though, failed to get approval of measures concerning blacklisting, mine inspection, and union labels. The eight-hour-day measure, moreover, stirred considerable conflict. Although the law prohibited a reduction in wages, some mine owners ignored this part of the law and cut pay to make up for the lost hours of work.

On June 1 around 3,500 miners, smelter men, and other workers in the Clifton, Morenci, and Metcalf mining area along the territory's eastern boundary went on strike after mining companies decided to reduce their pay to make up for the reduced hours. The strikers, mostly foreign-born (Mexican, Italian, and Slav), had their own organization; they stayed clear of the WFM, fearing it would demand the union wage—something mine owners would never give to foreign-born workers. The territorial governor considered the strike serious enough to justify sending the national guard and a law enforcement unit known as the Arizona Rangers into the district. Joining these forces were five troops of the U.S. Calvary sent to the area by order of President Roosevelt. Eventually, the strikers were restrained from interfering with the operation of the mines by court order. Eighteen strikers were later arrested on various charges. One of those convicted for inciting a riot and encouraging the strikers to blow up the town was W. H. Laustaunau (aka Laustenneau), later known as "Three Fingered Jack," who had been sent to the area by an anarchist labor organization in Chicago. Laustaunau was sent to prison in Yuma, Arizona, where, continuing with his chosen profession, he organized prisoner grievances committees and work strikes. He died there after failing in an escape effort in which he beat and nearly killed two prison officials.[74]

By the early 1900s, both the WFM and the UMW had moved to the left but were experiencing considerable difficulty on both the political and industrial fronts. Coal companies did all they could to resist the UMW organizing effort—using detectives to spy on workers, firing those who joined unions, and bringing in miners from other states who agreed in advance they would not join a union. Still, the 1901 strike brought some gains in regard to wages, hours, safety conditions, and, although less common, union recognition. In 1903, however, matters did not turn out as well. According to union estimates, coal companies blacklisted 6,000 of the 8,000 workers who had joined the union from 1900 to 1903.[75] The WFM had suffered setbacks in Arizona, Colorado, and Idaho, and its turn to the left had been rejected in Montana. Although most WFM members were probably not Socialists and perhaps only a relatively few members could be classified as revolutionaries, the organization's endorsement of the Socialist party in 1902 brought a concentrated attack against it—an attack waged through the press, the courts, hired gunmen, militiamen, and federal troops. The mining companies may well have reacted in a similar fashion to any threat to their economic well-being or to what they saw as their ownership prerogatives no matter what the source, but making Socialism the enemy broadened the stakes involved and helped rally other segments of society against the UMW as well as the WFM.

CHAPTER SEVEN

Party Progress

The 1904 Election

EUGENE DEBS, IN 1904, no doubt contributed to the success anxiety of many Socialist party members—the fear that growth would bring an influx of people who would divert the party from its mission. He did so by picking up 402,000 votes, almost five times as many as he had in 1900 (Appendix, Table 2). Right-wingers who dominated the national Socialist party could not help feeling they were on their way toward building a mass party that could compete with Democrats and Republicans and, on the local level, with the mushrooming number of municipal reform parties. To get things going they had added one immediate demand after another to the party platform. These steps were made over the vocal opposition of revolutionary leftists and prompted some on the left to drop out of active involvement with the party.

The right-left split in the national Socialist party boiled over in 1905 when leftists attempted to remove right-wing leader Victor Berger from the National Executive Committee (NEC). Berger's sin, as the left saw it, was in urging

Socialists in Milwaukee to vote for a Republican judicial candidate in the 1905 election. Wisconsin Socialists had decided not to nominate judicial candidates that year. Berger was accused of violating the national party constitution by supporting a "capitalistic candidate" for judicial office. The left pushed for and received a national referendum on whether Berger should be removed from the NEC. Before members had a chance to vote, however, the NEC itself acted, voting twenty-four to seventeen (with nine members not voting) to remove Berger from the committee. The decision was reversed, however, by the general membership vote (see Appendix, Table 7).

The Mountain West in 1904–1905 was something of an anomaly within the Socialist movement. It was a place where Debs and other Socialists did relatively well but also a place where party members tended to be somewhat to the left of their counterparts in other regions. Debs exceeded his national average in all six Mountain West states except Colorado, where the intense labor wars and demonstrated might of anti-radical forces depressed Socialist support. On the Berger issue, Mountain West members generally sided with the left: delegates to the NEC from Arizona, Idaho, Montana, Utah, and Wyoming voted for Berger's ouster; the member from Colorado (A. H. Floaten) voted against his removal. In the general membership vote that followed, members in the region as a whole were far more inclined to vote for Berger's removal than were Socialists nationally (61 percent to 47 percent, respectively), suggesting again a left-wing bent. A majority of members in all places except Idaho voted to oust Berger.[1]

Within the region the strength of the Socialist party was related in no small part to the strength of the Western Federation of Miners (WFM). In Colorado the WFM had been defeated, leading to a loss of potential Socialist supporters in mining communities. Some radically inclined miners left the state, taking up work and continuing the Socialist cause in places like Nevada. The Colorado Socialist party in 1904–1905 was struggling for its existence. It had been abandoned by the WFM, and other unions and party members spent much of their energy fighting among themselves. While the labor wars raged on in Colorado, keeping the Socialist party there in a constant state of agitation and serving as a harbinger of the future, party workers in much of the rest of the region showed promise. In spite of numerous obstacles, Socialists in Montana, Idaho, Utah, Arizona, and Nevada had reason to be optimistic about the future. The movement showed less vibrance in Wyoming and New Mexico, where the WFM was less well established.

In 1903 the Colorado party looked relatively strong. In the fall of that year, the right-wing faction that controlled the party could boast of having fifty-four locals around the state and 1,200 members.[2] Leftists, though, complained that the party had become a middle-class bastion where members were herded into the Denver Coliseum to hear expensive and ignorant right-wing speakers who would not entertain questions from the audience.[3] More to the point, they charged that the newly constituted state party had backed off from the cause of labor, its support of the striking miners in Cripple Creek falling far short of what was appropriate.[4] In retaliation, some leftist locals, including the one in Cripple Creek where miners were on strike, bolted the party.[5] Local police, alarmed by the rise of radicalism, showed little tolerance toward party members, whether on the right or the left. In Denver and other places, party workers spent considerable time in jail simply for taking to the street to spread the word about Socialism and the need for immediate reforms.[6]

Coming into the 1904 election, the Colorado Socialist party was prepared both to confront critics from the left wing of the party and to further risk antagonizing the powers that be by rallying to the side of labor and launching a major campaign against James H. Peabody, who was up for reelection that year. The WFM and organized labor, however, generally decided to look elsewhere for party help. They threw their support to Democrat Alva Adams, a former governor who condemned the Republican governor's use of the militia and martial law in labor disputes. In October 1904 John M. O'Neill, who had become editor of the WFM's *Miners Magazine* in 1901 after several years as a journalist in Colorado mining towns, declared, "The Republican party, during its two years of lawlessness in the state of Colorado, has shown beyond the question of a doubt, that it wears the collar of the Mine Owners' Association, the smelting trust and the Colorado Fuel and Iron Company."[7] For workers, O'Neill wrote, "the election of Peabody means the erection of more bull-pens in the state; more deportation trains, a further defiance of judicial tribunals and the complete annihilation of the legal rights of the great mass who are found in the avenues of manual toil."[8] Supporting Adams, the WFM concluded, was the only way to beat Peabody.

During the 1904 campaign the Colorado Mine Operators Association came out with a pamphlet known as the "Red Book" that offered an account of the WFM's "criminal record." One of the accusations made in the Red Book was that the WFM, "having formally and officially espoused the cause of the so-called Socialist party, is opposed to our present form of government and is aiming at its overthrow, together with the abrogation of the present constitution."[9] Responding to the charge, O'Neill wrote that it was "undeniably true" that the WFM formally and officially espoused the Socialist party. This, though, was something of which the organization had reason to be proud: "The Western Federation, by its endorsement of the Socialist party, sets the stamp of its approval upon the most comprehensive and scientific plan yet discovered for the further organization of society."[10]

O'Neill denied, however, that the WFM or Socialists in general were opposed to the present form of government or were determined to abrogate the present constitution. To the WFM's defenders, organized capitalists were the real revolutionaries because they trampled over virtually every right guaranteed by the constitution. The mine owners were also criminals who had killed hundreds, if not thousands, of innocent people using hired thugs and through mine disasters brought on by their culpable negligence and criminal greed. As for Peabody's frequent claim that he was not opposed to organized labor but only to the Socialistic WFM, O'Neill and others at the WFM asked the governor to explain why he had brutally cracked down on strikes in the coalfields led by the conservative United Mine Workers (UMW).[11]

Caught up in the middle of all this chaos was the state secretary of the Colorado Socialist party, J. W. Martin. Born in Pennsylvania in 1845, Martin was both a carpenter and an ordained minister by occupation. He was raised a Democrat but made the rounds: he became a Republican during the Civil War, then moved on to the Prohibitionists, the Populists, and the Democrats before settling on the Socialists. He came to Colorado in 1895 and supported Bryan the following year, but, objecting to the Democrat-Populist fusion in 1896, he dropped out of politics until 1899 when he joined the Socialist Labor party (SLP). From there he became a charter member of the Denver local of the Socialist party.

Contrary to the view of WFM leaders, Martin felt Peabody was speaking the truth when he declared it was not labor but the Socialists being singled out for attack. To Martin, the main targets of Peabody's attack had been "labor leaders who are known to be Socialists," while, at the same time, "those who are not Socialists have been immune from arrest, imprisonment, and deportation."[12] As the party leader saw it, the few hundred Socialists in the state were being opposed by the "political machine of capitalism, for it is plain that Gov. Peabody, a little country note shaver, would never undertake a crusade of such magnitude as the present war in Colorado unless inspired by powerful influences."[13]

Looking at the world around him in April 1904, Martin warned that Peabody and "the political machine of capitalism" had set out to destroy the party.[14] Labor unions, he feared, "in their blind rage," were likely to vote in the next election for the Democratic ticket "instead of doing the sensible thing, which would be to vote the Socialist ticket."[15] Martin contended that the party did not have to win office to be effective; just securing a large increase in the number of votes would frighten the powers that be into making changes. The party secretary believed, "Forty thousand votes for that ticket [the Socialists] would wring more concessions to labor than" anything the Democrats might do.[16] As for the condition of the party, the secretary concluded, "The Socialist party in Colorado is passing through a terrific struggle, but is not, by any means, discouraged. The greatest want now, is funds, and this is being supplied in part, by the kind assistance of comrades in other states who are sending donations to help the State Committee in its work. . . . The movement is well organized, and is a clear cut, class-conscious movement, and while Peabody's war on Socialism has almost destroyed a number of our locals, and caused us great financial loss and embarrassment, yet the spirit of the movement is unbroken."[17]

For the 1904 gubernatorial race, Colorado Socialists nominated A. H. Floaten, who had been deported from Telluride as a troublemaker during the labor disturbances there and who accepted the nomination from Richland County, Wisconsin, where he was working in a hay field. Floaten, then in his late forties, had left the country of his birth, Norway, at age fifteen and settled in Richland County where he held several jobs, including salesman, bookkeeper, and assistant postmaster. He became a successful merchant—thus, according to Socialist sources, once again dispelling the impression that Socialists were failures in life—and a Republican activist. In 1882 Floaten married Miss Octavia Thorpe, daughter of a prominent abolitionist.[18] He moved his family and business interests to Telluride in 1895, became an active supporter of Debs in 1896, and by the turn of the century was an active Socialist, motivated by concern over the conditions of labor he had seen in various places. In Telluride in 1902 he worked alongside Vincent St. John and Guy E. Miller for the Socialist ticket, which made such a strong showing—obtaining 30 percent of the county (San Miguel) vote for Miller—that the mine owners and their allies struck back. They arrested St. John, deported Miller, and subjected Floaten to a mob attack.[19]

In accepting the gubernatorial nomination, Floaten related: "I, with hundreds of others, are at present exiles from home and family." In reference to the mine owners of Telluride and "their hired thugs," he related:

> I have been arrested, put in jail, prosecuted and persecuted by these people. I have been boycotted to the extent that men who dared to trade with me have lost their jobs; I have had my home broken into at night, [been] beaten with guns and abused by vile and foul-mouthed thugs, torn, partly dressed and bleeding, from the side of my wife, who was driven from her bedroom and roughly handled, shipped out and told if I returned I would be hung. . . . Not satisfied with this, they have twice deported my brother, who was conducting the business in which we were both earning our living, so it became necessary for an adjustor to take charge of our store while we were out of our jobs.

> The charge against us was that we sold goods to members of the Western
> Federation of Miners.[20]

Floaten's woes continued into 1903 when, shortly after he was elected national committeeman, he was one of the Socialists arrested in Telluride for holding street meetings.[21]

Hoping to make some headway, the NEC of the Socialist party placed two national organizers at the disposal of the Colorado state party committee to work for a few weeks on campaign activities in 1904.[22] WFM leaders, however, remembering what had happened two years earlier, remained focused on making sure Peabody was not reelected. They abandoned Floaten and gave their support to Adams. The Federation of Labor also endorsed Adams, "seeming to think," in the opinion of a leading Colorado Socialist, "that a bull-pen with a democratic label on it would be less oppressive than the republican brand."[23] Debs, campaigning in the state in 1904, also criticized labor leaders who were encouraging workers to abandon the Socialist party's gubernatorial candidate.[24] Looking at the situation from Montana, a more practical-minded labor leader predicted in regard to Colorado workers, "The Colorado men have had all they want of republican administration tactics and naturally will support candidates most likely to win on opposing tickets."[25]

Labor emerged triumphant on election night, but two months after the election the state supreme court upheld claims that Adams had won through vote fraud and ordered that the office be given to Peabody. The decision, needless to say, was not well received on the left. Emma Langdon responded, "It is to the everlasting disgrace of Colorado and an object lesson of what little avail is the will of the people, when the corporations desire otherwise, that the choice of the people for governor, the Honorable Alva Adams, was unseated after having been elected by over [a] 10,000 plurality."[26] Adams himself added, "We have won the contempt of free men everywhere. By command of the corporations a usurper has been placed in the executive chair—a new record in political infamy has been made."[27] Under pressure, however, both parties reached an agreement whereby Peabody would resign immediately after taking office and allow the lieutenant governor, Jesse F. McDonald, to become governor.

After the election—which Adams won with labor support, only to have his victory overturned in court—some on the left continued to condemn the WFM leaders for failing to rally to the support of the Socialist party and for leading workers into the camp of the enemy.[28] The WFM responded through an editorial by John O'Neill in the December 1904 issue of *Miners Magazine*. O'Neill noted that the WFM had been largely responsible for the party's growth in Montana, Idaho, Utah, and other places in the Mountain West but that it had to take dramatic action to get rid of Peabody to restore constitutional order in the state. Now that this had been done, O'Neill assured, the WFM would once again support Colorado Socialists.[29]

Floaten was unmoved and unforgiving. He complained that labor union leaders had caused wage earners "to believe that by supporting the Democratic capitalist, Alva Adams, for governor, they would be rewarded, but just how was never explained. They were simply *fooled once more* by the political tricksters who control and manipulate elections in the interests of the ruling class."[30] Floaten went on to note, "After two years of war and turmoil Colorado is now at peace, but it is the peace of the Russians in Siberia, the Boers in the Transvaal and the Filipinos in the Philippine islands." The metalliferous miners, coal miners, and other union wage workers, he continued, had been "'benevolently assimilated' by the bayonets, the bull-pens, and finally have been chloroformed by the ballot, but the revolutionary feeling is still there and some of these days it will wake up and with a giant's strength overturn the temple built by the capitalists in Colorado."[31]

Debs in 1904 picked up 4,304 votes in Colorado, about 2 percent of the total cast, a poor showing compared with the 6 percent he received nationally. In explaining this, party leaders emphasized the movement of Socialist supporters out of mining areas—some through coercion by the mining companies—after strike activity began.[32] Still, many had hoped for more support, especially from the mining areas. Colorado Socialists did not altogether give up on labor, but the failure of the industrial wars to drive workers into the party's camp prompted some to shake their heads in puzzlement and one local Socialist to note, "It seems to require something more than persecution to make socialists."[33]

To compound the party's miseries, throughout 1904 and 1905 it continued to be torn apart by vicious battles between the right and the left. One participant observer was Henry Clay Darrah. Born in Ohio in 1841, Darrah lost an arm fighting in the Civil War and had been active in Iowa Republican party politics before turning Socialist and touring the country as an agitator and organizer. In February 1905 he wrote to a comrade, "I have done propaganda work in California, Arizona, Utah, Iowa, Minnesota, Missouri, and nowhere in all these states is there as little effort on the part of the membership to build up the party as in Colorado and so much effort expended in personal" infighting among members and locals.[34] In 1905 the left regained control of the Colorado state organization, but the future, once so promising, looked bleak.

While the above developments were unfolding in Colorado, Socialist parties in the remainder of the region faced their own particular problems, though some seemed to be making considerable progress. In Montana anti-corporate sentiment was brought to a head. There was no forceful putdown of striking miners. Corporate power, though, was demonstrated in a different manner. Rockefeller's Amalgamated Copper Company had a problem with F. Augustus Heinze, who gleefully stole from Amalgamated's mines in Silver Bow County by tunneling into them from his own properties. Amalgamated could do nothing about this because, by law, all mining litigation in the county had to be tried in courts that happened to be presided over by judges on Heinze's payroll. On October 23, 1903, Amalgamated shut down most of its mine, mill, and timber operations in the state, throwing around 20,000 people out of work. It announced that people would stay unemployed until the legislature and the governor agreed to a measure allowing a change in venue in civil suits involving mining disputes if one of the parties felt the judge was prejudiced or corrupt. The shutdown created such devastation and havoc that Governor Joseph K. Toole felt compelled to call a special session of the legislature in December. The legislature wasted no time giving Amalgamated what it wanted in the "fair trial" bill. Thereafter, Amalgamated ended its protracted lockout, and industrialized Montana went back to work. Observers noted that a corporation had easily humbled a "sovereign" state in the confrontation.[35]

Socialists condemned both Heinze and Amalgamated for the shutdown, while workers tended to take out most of their wrath against the once popular Heinze. In their minds, his "kept judges" were the prime cause of the problem. Not surprisingly, Heinze blamed Amalgamated, calling it "the greatest menace that any community could possibly have within its boundaries" and warning workers in a Butte audience that "[i]f they crush me today, they will crush you tomorrow. They will cut your wages and raise the tariff in the company stores on every bite you eat and every rag you wear. They will force you to dwell in Standard Oil houses while you live, and they will bury you in Standard Oil coffins when you die."[36]

Montana Socialists, in spite or perhaps in part because of this display of corporate power, were making progress. They continued, for example, to make inroads in the labor movement. In the fall of 1903, party leaders proudly announced, "The new president and a majority of the executive board of the Montana State Federation of Labor are Socialists."[37] At the same time, State Secretary P. J. Cooney reported the formation of several new locals, a new Socialist newspaper, and the party's virtual absorption of the Labor party.[38] National organizer M. W. Wilkins came to the state to further help the party. He toured the state from November 1903 through January 1904, visiting forty towns and making fifty speeches. He gave thirty-three of these speeches before party locals and the rest in recruiting drives. Wilkins noted, "A winter campaign in Montana is a trial to the nerves of an Organizer, to say the least."[39] The trip included enduring snowstorms, trains that did not arrive, long and bitterly cold trips in stages or open rigs, and an accident that left him with a broken rib and a broken arm. He felt, however, that progress was being made: "The general character of the Montana party membership is high and will make a strong movement."[40]

Statewide party membership grew from 100 members in 1900 to about 400 in 1904.[41] In 1904 the Montana Socialist party nominated a complete slate of candidates and, finding a popular issue, strongly endorsed the initiative and referendum. Direct legislation had been gaining in popularity since Amalgamated demonstrated its power, virtually shutting down the state in 1903 and forcing the legislature to do its bidding. Many looked on the initiative and referendum as a means of curbing the power of the copper magnates.[42]

In 1904 the party had the unusual experience of having several candidates fight for the gubernatorial nomination.[43] The winner, after two ballots, was George O'Malley of Butte. He campaigned throughout the state, accompanied at times by vice presidential candidate Benjamin Hanford. In October 1904 Debs also came through Montana. He later enthusiastically reported on his reception in Butte: "Ten thousand people tried to jam into the auditorium. The house and galleries were packed, all the aisles and stage were jammed—men and women sat on the edge of [the] stage and thousands had to be turned away unable to get in. . . . All Butte seemed to pour out and I want to tell you that in the two hours and ten minutes I spoke I put the straight and hot Socialist shot into them."[44] Going into the election, Socialists had the strong backing of the Montana Federation of Labor. They also had the predictable opposition of the SLP. At a Butte meeting open to all Socialists, the SLP candidate for president denounced Debs and his followers as "labor grafters" and "political knaves." The Debs people left the hall in the middle of the speech.[45]

The party wound up making a relatively strong showing, much of which came at the expense of the Democratic party with which the Populist, Labor, and Antitrust parties had joined forces.[46] Debs received 9 percent of the vote, compared with 3 percent nationally. The gains, however, were less impressive when it came to local elections. The Socialists captured some alderman seats in the coal mining town of Red Lodge, adding to the seats they had won there a year earlier. In Butte, by using the October 1903 shutdown as an issue, they had hoped to pick up some of the votes that had been going to Heinze's party in municipal elections, but the Heinze group continued to nominate candidates and, in prevailing, took away votes from Socialist candidates.[47] The party, though, was destined to make some breakthroughs in Butte. In 1904 it seemed like a party on the rise, building support with workers, cutting into the labor-Populist support that had rallied behind Heinze's antitrust coalition, and becoming somewhat of a threat to the Democratic party.

Following the November 1904 elections, the mainstream press commented on the Socialists' successes. On November 30, for example, an editorial writer for the *Bozeman Chronicle*, a Democratic paper, noted the "remarkable increase in the Socialist vote" and added that in the Montana election just concluded "it was big enough to have elected the entire democratic ticket had it been cast for the democratic candidates. . . . A very large per cent of this vote in Montana and elsewhere is drawn from the democratic party."[48] The editor warned: "It will pay the political student to keep his eye on the Socialist party. Sneering remarks about cranks and long-haired lunatics which constitute a major portion of the comment which one reads in the political press of the day about the Socialist party, will not reduce their numbers. They thrive on this sort of criticism. These people are in earnest. They believe in something and believe in it honestly. The spirit that characterizes the Socialist in his political action is a good deal like that which characterizes the salvation army in its religious and social action."[49] The editor also offered this commentary on the party's followers: "It is true that the great mass of their following comes from a class that is uneducated and untrained in logical thinking and [has] little knowledge of and acquaintance with the ethical, moral and economic forces that rule the world with a potency that statutes can never do, but it is also true that among their ranks are men of the widest education and culture, college professors, philanthropists, and men of practical experience in the business world."[50] Rather than meet the challenge presented by the Socialist party through a "style of cheap abuse and invective," as had characterized press coverage in Montana, "socialist propaganda demands from its antagonists serious consideration, courteous argument, and a strong appeal to common sense and reason."[51]

While the state had escaped violence on the industrial front, Ida Crouch Hazlett and other party leaders in 1904–1905 were concerned that the corporations were about to launch an attack on labor in Montana, much as they had done in Colorado. The Socialist party, she felt, had been of little use during the Colorado labor wars because it was riddled by factions—even, she noted, a revolt against the party in Cripple Creek itself—and workers had no confidence in it. This, she promised, would not be the case in Montana.[52] To head off trouble, party leaders adopted a "get tough" policy. Montana Socialists, for example, actively enforced the policy of nonaffiliation by suspending or expelling members who accepted endorsements for public office from, or participated in the convention of, another political party.[53] At the same time, in an effort to broaden its base, party leaders launched an extensive campaign of propaganda and organization in which speakers were sent to areas heretofore neglected.[54] Making the rounds, Hazlett had some disturbing encounters, such as one in a gold camp named Jardin, which she identified as under the control of a man named Ryan: "When I was there . . . everyone thought it was a miracle that I could even speak on the street in front of Ryan's hotel. The men sneaked out of the alleys and from behind buildings to listen like trembling and hunted robbers. I never saw the badge of fear so unmistakably impressed upon men. Out of probably seventy-five people, when I closed not one dared to stay for the collection or to buy any books, or to be seen talking to me, but slunk away into the night and their holes. I never had such an experience. . . . There was just one ray of light in the whole incident. The sweet-faced wife of the saloonkeeper, who was keeping the hotel, refused to take any pay for my staying there."[55] Overall, the party showed some progress in recruiting and party building, although these gains were soon mitigated by intra-party warfare.

The Idaho party, too, went through some rough periods and intense self-examination but seemed to be on an upsurge. In December 1903 the national secretary of the Socialist party issued a circular letter declaring that the Socialist movement in Idaho was disorganized and that national organizer M. W. Wilkins, on tour in the West, was going to look into matters in a few weeks. Meanwhile, G. Weston Wrigley, a newspaper person working in the Coeur d'Alene Mining District and a member of Local Wallace, the only Socialist organization in that district, reported that party membership had deteriorated largely because of labor blacklisting. Wrigley, a hard-nosed leftist, also contended that the Socialist party in the area had been infiltrated by strikebreakers, spotters, and Republican officeholders. Wrigley further noted with considerable disgust that "there were people in the party who felt the middle class should be considered equal to the working class." Despite all these shortcomings he felt "there is enough material at hand to build up a strong revolutionary Socialist party. The miners' unions are financially strong and their paper, the Idaho State Tribune, is now edited by ex–Lieutenant Governor [David C.] Coates of Colorado, who is in a position to be of great assistance to the Socialist movement."[56]

Wilkins, after touring the state, expressed a more negative view of workers in the Coeur d'Alene mining camps. He reported in April 1904:

> It must have taken a master effort on the part of the mining companies to get together so choice a lot of slaves. The spotter and fakir or spy abounds here. Men dare not open their mouths on political affairs for fear their working mate is a company sucker. There, too, we find the so-called "Industrial Union"

composed of men and masters—the latter dictating the policy thereof. My experience in these camps is the most disagreeable I have had since my field work of a year. But one thing is certain; if I have ever lacked anything in plain speaking before, I made it up in the Coeur d' Alene. The slavishness of those miners makes them contemptible.[57]

A few months later the *International Socialist Review* noted that Wilkins had been working in Idaho for six weeks on the campaign and was happy to report that the state was now quite well organized and should produce a good vote.[58] Debs helped out by campaigning in the state in 1904, speaking, for example, to an overflow crowd at the Masonic theater in Wallace in late September.

Wilkins's visit, improved organization, and the help of the miners' unions seemed to pay off in 1904, as the Idaho Socialist party replaced the People's party as the state's third party and pulled in about 7 percent of the vote for Debs at the head of the ticket. In Shoshone County, where the Coeur d'Alene Mining District was located, the Socialists garnered 13.3 percent of the vote, compared with 3.4 percent two years earlier. Socialists captured 23 percent of the vote in Burke. Burke Miners' Union president Vincent St. John, running as John W. Vincent, led the Socialist ticket for county offices but picked up only 9.2 percent of the vote. Many miners apparently preferred to support the major party out of power, the Democrats. Some, too, union leaders contended, wound up voting for Republican candidates because of concern for their jobs and intimidation by the mining companies.[59]

In Utah, Arizona, and Nevada, one also found promising signs. In Utah they emerged even though right-wingers and left-wingers in 1903 and 1904 continued to struggle for control of the state organization and of various locals. Those on the left focused much of their attack on right-winger Joseph Gilbert, a law-yer who had moved to Utah from Washington state, where he had also been a controversial figure in party affairs. Gilbert, a former Populist, was identified with the wing of the party that, if not pro-Mormon, at least appeared that way in an effort to get votes.[60] He headed the state's Liberal Socialist party in Salt Lake City, which, according to the left, "is almost exclusively composed of intel-lectuals or natural born leaders, the Moses, as it were[,] of the working class. The working class of Utah being in their estimation so hopelessly ignorant that they consider themselves the natural custodians of us."[61] Gilbert and his group competed with a left-wing group for the charter for Salt Lake Local but lost out in 1904. The state party that year had around 300 members in twenty-two locals.[62] In spite of all the turmoil, the Socialists helped produce 5,767 votes for Eugene Debs, around 6 percent of the total cast, a rather grand improvement over the 717 votes—less than 1 percent of the total vote—he received four years earlier (Appendix, Table 2). The party also did well in several local elections (see Chapter 11).

In Arizona during the summer of 1903, operatives from the Thiel Detective Agency, reporting to the United Verde Copper Company in Jerome, were particularly fascinated with the views and activities of Albert Ryan, head of the WFM local and, at the time, secretary of the state Socialist party. Ryan was trying to make Jerome the stronghold of unionism in the territory, but, from the operatives' reports, he was a man who would rather talk about Socialism than about unionism. One operative reported, "His idea seems to be to organize all the men and get them into the Union and then convert them to Socialism and have them cast their votes as such and in that way make Socialism and Unionism a political factor."[63] Ryan, according to the operatives, was more a Socialist than a unionist, someone who talked about Socialism at great length at every opportunity. One report to management described Ryan as "hard to get on intimate terms with" and someone who probably could not be "handled."[64]

Ryan reportedly complained about the lack of interest in Socialism among members of the union—he had to shell out funds from his own pocket to bring in Socialist speakers because members of the union did not take an interest in such activities and would not help pay expenses—and their lack of spunk compared with the miners in Cripple Creek.[65] The Arizona party under Ryan, however, made some inroads, building on its strength in mining areas but also making gains in farming areas. In some farming communities it threatened the domination of the Mormon Church.[66] Party organizations were active, for example, in the Mormon town of Safford where, according to a party paper of October 10, 1904, the "Safford local meets every Sunday at 4 o'clock and very few meetings pass without enrolling new names on the roster. This is an indication of the healthy growth of socialist sentiment in this county."[67]

The Arizona party had received just 510 votes in 1902, having been on the ballot in only a few counties. In 1904 it gathered 1,304 votes. By that time the party was better organized, and, although it still lacked a journal to advance its platform and candidates, it had begun to gain attention in the mainstream press. In August 1904 the *Arizona Daily Star* noted that the "Socialists held their convention in a quiet, unostentatious manner in Prescott," and their nominee for delegate for Congress was making a camp-to-camp and town-to-town canvas "without the blare of trumpets or the tom tom of drums." Rather, he was simply "going around and getting votes, and those who believe the socialist candidate won't cut any figure in the coming election must not be surprised if he would not be the last in the race, and in fact might be first. The socialists are in the field for business. They are in to make a record. They have organized their party to stay, and to work out some social and political problems neither of the old parties will recognize in their platforms. The socialists will make a strong showing this trip."[68] Reform-minded Democratic papers like the *Star* considered the Socialists a threat in part because they were identified with popular and, what seemed to progressive Democrats, "sound" ideas such as the initiative, referendum, and recall.[69]

The party in Nevada, meanwhile, although receiving little press coverage, also was beginning to grow, in large part because of the emergence of large mining operations in various parts of the state (for example, Tonopah, Goldfield, Rholite, Manhattan, and Ely) in the early 1900s, which eventually brought in tens of thousands of miners, a large percentage of whom had been born in foreign countries. Debs, drawing on such places, picked up about 8 percent of the state vote in 1904. Party officials happily reported that in that same year Socialists had elected a district attorney and a constable in Goldfield and competed well in other races. At the time, there were only two locals in the entire state.[70]

In Wyoming and New Mexico party advancement was less evident. In both places the UMW gave its tacit support to the party, and there was some support for party candidates in coal mining camps, but there is little indication of active party organizations. Wyoming cast 987 votes for Debs in 1904, about 3.5 percent of the total vote. In 1904 the New Mexico territory was still unorganized as far as the national party was concerned, and only a few locals, such as one in Albuquerque, were affiliated with the national party. Nevertheless, Debs's arrival in Albuquerque in the fall of 1904 on his way to a campaign stop in Los Angeles created a stir. New Mexico Socialists asked Debs to make a short speech during the scheduled twenty-minute stop. Problems with the engine turned the stop into an hours-long wait, allowing Debs to give a full speech to the crowd—a gathering Debs described as a mixture of "plutocrats and proletarians." W. P. Metcalf, a leader of the New Mexico party, reported: "Debs . . . spoke for nearly an hour from a baggage truck, while repairs were being made on the engine. Many of those present were old railroad men who were visibly affected at meeting their old comrade. The striking machinists are 'injuncted' from going on the station grounds, or they would have all been there. We presented him with a basket of native fruit and were awfully sorry to see the train move out."[71]

CHAPTER EIGHT

The WFM, Big Bill, and the Wobblies

Wᴿɪᴛɪɴɢ ɪɴ 1907, John Curtis Kennedy of the University of Chicago argued that trade unionism and Socialism were essentially the same movement. Trade unionists and Socialists, he argued, "hold to practically the same views and are seeking the same ends . . . it is only a question of time before trade-unionists in America will recognize this fact and lend their support to the Socialist party"— and, indeed, many were already doing so.[1] Even the American Federation of Labor (AFL) during this period was not as anti-Socialist and revolutionary as commonly supposed. Its step toward independent political action in 1906 led, in many cases, to closer working relations with Socialist parties. Socialists within the AFL and various trade unions had been working for this result. Still, the AFL had an ample number of critics from the left. Many Mountain westerners, especially the unskilled and semiskilled workers in and around mining areas, were impatient with what they saw as the slow-moving, conservative AFL. For radicals the craft unions, which the AFL prized, stood in the way of worker solidarity.

At the same time, the region's chief industrial union was having its own problems. Following the violent and unsuccessful confrontation with mine owners in Colorado, overall membership in the Western Federation of Miners (WFM) fell from around 28,000 in 1903 to 24,000 in 1904 and did not rebound to the 28,000 level until 1906. The major losses were in Colorado, and these were only partially offset by gains in Nevada. In Arizona, Utah, and Idaho, the union was maintaining its strength, neither gaining nor losing much. Membership drops in Colorado from 1903 to 1905 included declines from 800 to 185 in Telluride, 530 to 134 in Cripple Creek, 508 to 202 in Ouray, and 280 to 113 in Cloud City (Leadville).[2] The total number of locals in Colorado also declined in these years (see Appendix, Table 1).

The failure in Colorado convinced WFM leaders of one thing: the great struggle against giant corporations required a union of all working-class people, a role not even close to being filled by the American Labor Union. This union had picked up some affiliates but had not been successful in reaching the East or competing with the AFL, and it did not seem to have the potential to become a truly national organization. To accomplish this objective, the WFM took up leadership in a movement that led to the creation of the Industrial Workers of the World (IWW).

Gathered together at the founding convention of the IWW in Chicago during June and July 1905 was a familiar set of prominent radicals, including Bill Haywood, the black-bearded Father Thomas Hagerty, David Coates, Emma Langdon (who after Cripple Creek had moved to Denver, where she organized for the Socialist party), Guy E. Miller, Albert Ryan (from Jerome, Arizona), Mother Jones, Lucy Parsons (widow of one of the martyrs killed in the Haymarket riot), and Algie Simons, editor of the *International Socialist Review*. Eugene Debs and Daniel De Leon also attended, although the Socialist party and the Socialist Labor party (SLP) were not formally represented. De Leon brought several delegates from the party's trade union wing, the Socialist Trade and Labor Alliance.

WFM secretary-treasurer and Socialist William D. Haywood opened the first IWW convention in Chicago on June 27 by announcing: "This is the Continental Congress of the working class. We are here to confederate the workers of this country into a working class movement that shall have for its purpose the emancipation of the working class from the slave bondage of capitalism."[3] Haywood warned, "When the corporations and the capitalists understand that you are organized for the express purpose of placing the supervision of industry in the hands of those who do the work, you are going to be harassed and you are going to be subjected to every indignity and cruelty that their minds can invent."[4] Later in the proceedings, Algie Simons also warned that the effort to overthrow plutocracy meant that "all the cohorts of hell and capitalism" and the "powers of a prostituted press" would be used against them.[5]

Members of the new organization left Chicago with a show of unity, but the alliance they had forged was fragile. As with the Socialist party, within the IWW differences existed over the basic approach the union should take. Some, particularly those affiliated with the Socialist party and the SLP, saw value in an organization that heavily emphasized political activity. If he had his way, De Leon would have made the IWW an arm of the SLP. Debs and others with the Socialist party had different ideas as to with which party the new organization should be affiliated. A large number of delegates wanted the new organization to have nothing at all to do with political parties or elections. Many WFM members, fresh from bloody labor wars in which state and federal officials had lined up with employers, had concluded that trying to influence elections was a waste of time, that governors such as Waite were rare exceptions.[6] Speaking for this group at the founding convention, Father Hagerty declared, "The ballot box is simply a capitalist concession. Dropping pieces of paper into a hole in a box never did achieve emancipation for the working class, and to my thinking it never will achieve it."[7] Those opposed to political action favored direct attacks on employers at the point of production. At the end of the debate, as historian Melvin Dubofsky has noted, "[I]t would have taken an expert on medieval theology to define the IWW's position on political action."[8] The lack of a clear position on the issue was useful in that it kept both the political and anti-political (direct action) groups in the organization for the time being.

The organization began life by focusing on bread-and-butter labor issues in an effort to take over AFL affiliates. At the IWW's second convention in 1906, however, an insurgent faction led by De Leon, William E. Trautmann of the AFL brewers' union, and Vincent St. John took control of the organization. Those opposing this move, including the WFM delegates and many members of the Socialist party, withdrew from the convention en masse. With these groups gone, the IWW became a mix of De Leon's SLP and a group of unskilled and semiskilled workers largely from the West. Many of those in the second group were American-born migratory laborers who, deprived of the vote, had no interest in political action. A split over political versus direct action led to the expulsion of De Leon's political action Socialists two years later.

By 1906–1907 the radical movement was badly splintered. The WFM and IWW were becoming bitter enemies, differing in philosophy and competing for influence in mining camps. The IWW was unacceptable to the right-wingers who controlled the Socialist party nationally and in several Mountain West states. In return, Wobbly leaders contended in criticizing the right wing: "Socialism is not a bit of sentimentality. It is not a political nostrum compounded of equal parts of sighs and yearnings, brotherly love, golden rule, municipal ownership and an accidental vote. It is an economic system and requires an economic organization, educated and disciplined, as the primary force for its achievement."[9] Further fracturing the movement, the WFM, perhaps largely for strategic reasons, distanced itself from the Socialist party. In 1906, for example, a special WFM committee went to considerable lengths to make the point that the organization's mission was purely economic and one being pursued *without affiliation with any political party.*"[10] For all of this, the WFM continued to be left-leaning.

During the years 1905–1908 the WFM and the IWW were the principle noise-making unions in the region and stood out nationally in the eyes of many in their commitment to radicalism. Also attracting national attention were sensational events involving Bill Haywood—his arrest on a murder charge, his bid for office while in jail, his sensational trial—and labor disturbances in Nevada, Montana, and Arizona, all of which had implications for both the radical labor and Socialist party movements.

Speaking at the first IWW convention, Bill Haywood declared with considerable pride, "The capitalist class of this country fear[s] the Western Federation of Miners more than they do all the rest of the labor organizations in this country."[11] For many, confirmation of this point came on February 17, 1906, when Pinkerton agents, armed with extradition papers, arrested WFM officers Haywood and Charles H. Moyer and WFM business agent George A. Pettibone in Denver near WFM headquarters and rushed them by a special nonstop train—which radicals later called the "Kidnapper's Special"—to Boise, Idaho, to stand trial for the murder of former Idaho governor Frank Steunenberg. Steunenberg had been killed in Caldwell, Idaho, the previous December when he was blown apart by a bomb attached to his gatepost. There had been much bitterness among miners over his actions during the Coeur d'Alene strike in 1899, and, following the murder, attention immediately turned to the miners' union. Idaho authorities took action following the arrest of a drifter named Harry Orchard, who claimed the WFM officials were behind the murder. Ultimately, however, the effort to convict the officials failed, in part because the prosecution could not find anyone to corroborate Orchard's account.

Adding insult to injury, the three unconvicted prisoners spent much of the twenty-seven hours it took to make the journey from Denver to Boise (actually a record time) in a Pullman car.[12] Idaho officials initially put them on death row in the state penitentiary in the hope that conditions there would prompt at least one of them to crack. Later they were sent to a jail facility in Caldwell and then to the Ada County Jail in Boise. In March 1906 the defense was granted a change of venue for the trial from Caldwell, where Steunenberg had lived, to Boise. Meanwhile, the arrest, imprisonment, and pending trial of Haywood and the others riveted the attention of labor and Socialist leaders. Typical of the reaction from the left was a resolution put together by radicals in Goldfield, Nevada, that charged: "The outrageously conducted arrests and subsequent villainous persecution of the officers of the Western Federation of Miners are clearly parts of a subtle and deep-laid conspiracy, darkly concocted among the capitalistic vermin that infests the states of Idaho and Colorado and lays an immoral claim to the natural resources of these states, to destroy and disrupt the W.F.M., an organization which has proved itself an effective check to the rapacious greed of the exploiters of labor."[13]

From the left's perspective, the arrests were nothing more than a murderous conspiracy by the capitalistic class intended to destroy a strong labor union by brutal and illegal methods. An editorial in the *International Socialist Review* contended, "There is no question to-day but that capitalism is in the saddle and the fate of the three men in Idaho depends entirely upon whether those in control of the capitalist machinery of government decide that they will be less dangerous if dead than alive."[14] The root of the problem, suggested the review's editor, Algie Simons, on another occasion, was that the WFM, blessed with "a breadth of character and depth of outlook unknown to the average eastern trade union," had "recognized the truth of the socialist philosophy, and urged those truths upon their membership. This was the culminating crime that loosed all the bloodhounds of capitalism upon their track."[15] While absolving the WFM of responsibility for the murder, Simons conceded, as a way of illustrating Steunenberg's sins in Coeur d'Alene, "It may be possible that some man who had been brutally beaten or bayoneted by the bestialized Negro soldiery at that time, whose home was destroyed, or wife insulted, or who saw his comrades shot down like dogs because they had dared to be men, might have revenged himself upon the man who directed the conduct of these outrages."[16]

In Idaho the mainstream press charged that followers of Socialism, now displaying their outrage over the arrests, were simply the cat's paw of the WFM, which "stands for anarchy, pure and simple" and is "an outlaw organization of foreign laborers that has for its argument the one word, dynamite."[17] President Theodore Roosevelt joined in by referring to Haywood and Moyer as "undesirable citizens." This comment, the president later contended, was not intended to influence their trial; he had no opinion as to their guilt. At the same time, the president was of the opinion that the two individuals "stand as the representatives of those men who by their public utterances and manifestoes, by the utterances of the papers they control or inspire, and by the words and deeds of those associated with or subordinated to them, habitually appear as guilty of incitement to or apology for bloodshed and violence. If this does not constitute undesirable citizenship, then there can never be any undesirable citizens."[18]

Haywood's kidnapping, arrest, and pending trial were central themes of radical election activity in 1906. This was especially true in Colorado and Idaho. In the former, the Socialist party came up with an unusual form of protest. Coming to the floor of the Colorado party's convention in Denver on July 4, 1906, Secretary J. W. Martin made what to many was a startling announcement regarding the party's gubernatorial nomination:

> I do not rise to name a well-groomed business man nor a professional politician seeking graft. Nor do I name a labor leader who is dined and wined at Civic Federation banquets, or who hobnobs with Grover Cleveland, August Belmont or Theodore Roosevelt. But I rise to name a man who in executive ability is the peer of the best, and whose personal integrity is without stain. A man whose hands have been calloused by honest labor, and whose every heart throb is in sympathy with those who toil. A man who has never been praised by the capitalist press as "the greatest labor leader" in the world; but who, as a labor leader[,] has never betrayed his trust nor sold out a strike. A man who because of his loyalty to the working class has been struck down by a brutal soldiery on the streets of our city. And who, for that same loyalty was kidnapped by the command of the powers of capitalism and contrary to all legal forms and observances was carried to a distant state and thrown into a felon's cell, where for months he and his faithful comrades have waited, demanding in vain the speedy trial guaranteed to every citizen by our constitution and laws—Wm. D. Haywood, the prisoner in Caldwell jail.[19]

Later in his speech Martin noted with pleasure that "Haywood is not only hated, but feared by the capitalist class."[20]

At the time of his nomination, Haywood was in jail awaiting trial. His nomination by Colorado Socialists generated considerable comment, favorable and unfavorable, both inside and outside the state. An editorial in the left-wing *International Socialist Review* noted, "In nominating Comrade Haywood for governor, the socialists of Colorado have done one of those splendid things that sound the bugle call for action."[21] Milwaukee Socialists, on the other hand, protested the sending of campaign aid to Colorado, where they described the situation as "picturesque but unsubstantial."[22] Outside the movement, the less-than-friendly *Caldwell News* noted that, as a practical matter, Haywood's nomination was of little importance: "Even Colorado, with all its turbulent mining camp politics, is not in the least likely to elect as Governor a man who might be hanging from the gallows before he could take office."[23]

Socialists and labor leaders from around the country, contrary to the sentiment expressed by Milwaukee Socialists, joined the Colorado party in an effort to produce a large vote for Haywood as a way of protesting the trial, which they felt was part of a broader war on the WFM. A campaign fund of around $5,000 was raised, and three national organizers were sent to Colorado during the campaign.[24] Socialist insiders saw little possibility of a Haywood victory—the level of Socialist support, principally in Denver and a few mining camps, was not strong enough to give him a fighting chance—but noted that "the fight which is being put up is serving to attract attention and to educate the workers as never before."[25] Campaigning around Colorado, Guy E. Miller, the party's candidate for congressman at large, contended that the loud protest from the Socialists had already prevented a speedy verdict of death.[26]

Joining the Haywood campaign, Debs intoned, "Comrades of Colorado, the eyes of the century are upon you, and we know that you will do your duty and that the banner you have placed in Haywood's hands will be emblazoned with victory."[27] Another national figure, Ernest Untermann, noted more negatively that the working people of Colorado had the unfortunate habit of electing their worst enemies: "The question is: How long will the working people of Colorado try to reap figs from thistles? How long will they deliver themselves gagged and bound to the corporations? How long will they vote for injunctions, militia raids, kidnapping expeditions, deportations, murder plots and dynamite explosions?"[28]

In his acceptance speech, sent from the Ada County Jail, Boise, Idaho, on July 14, 1906, Haywood pulled few punches, seemingly refusing to adjust his views because of his upcoming trial. He declared: "The Socialist platform is the corner stone of industrial liberty. The program is clean, clear-cut, uncompromising. Principles cannot be arbitrated. Let the campaign slogan be, 'There is nothing to arbitrate.' The class struggle must go on as long as one eats the bread in the sweat of another man's face."[29] Haywood later gained fame as a direct actionist of the first order. In the 1906 campaign, however, he saw the value of political action. The candidate said: "The economic power of organized labor is determined by united political action. To win demands made on the industrial level, it is absolutely necessary to control the branches of government, as past experience shows every strike to have been lost through the interference of courts and militia."[30] Over the next few months Haywood personally directed his campaign from his prison cell, staying in touch with speakers working on his behalf and dictating the positions articulated. One reporter noted, "Haywood has waged a practical battle, along practical lines, for the accomplishment of practical results."[31] From July to October 1906 the campaign led to the addition of fifty Socialist locals in Colorado and an increase in the number of subscriptions to *Appeal to Reason* in the state, from 5,000 to 15,000.[32]

During the campaign, left-wing party leaders made it clear that they were in control; while the party offered immediate relief to workers in their struggle against mine owners, "it does so with the distinct understanding that it will stop short of nothing but the complete overthrow of the capitalistic system and the establishment of the cooperative commonwealth."[33] In promoting the party platform, leaders also reminded workers that every vote cast for the Socialists would help, even if the party fell short of capturing offices: "A large vote for the Socialist party, even though we should fail to elect our candidates, will compel the respect of the capitalist class, and secure concessions to the workers which they can never secure by voting the Democratic, Republican and Municipal Ownership tickets."[34]

Socialists working in Colorado in the fall of 1906 appeared to enjoy themselves, although they frequently ran afoul of the law. Around sixty were arrested while campaigning on the streets. The unlucky A. H. Floaten was arrested in Fort Collins, Colorado, for riding his bicycle on the sidewalk while distributing Haywood-Moyer leaflets. In some places Socialists felt compelled to organize in secret and to conduct agitations by stealth.[35] On the electoral level, all of this produced around 16,000 votes for Haywood—an improvement over the 4,000 votes the party had received two years earlier but hardly enough to make a dent in the race. Reformer Ben Lindsey, an anti-corporate candidate of the Independent Republicans, received 18,000 votes, finishing ahead of Haywood. The winner, Republican Henry Buchtel, received close to 93,000 votes.[36]

At the time of Haywood's arrest, the Idaho party was in poor shape. Statewide membership dropped from an average of 364 in 1904 to an average of 261 in 1905. State Secretary T. J. Coonrod wrote in early 1906, "Under the circumstances, with a state-organizer in the field a great part of the year, such a decrease is positively criminal . . . it is up to the membership to do a little housecleaning and see that the work is done properly."[37] Factionalism and a tendency to engage in personal revenge had also gotten in the way of party building. In one 1905 episode the Boise local brought charges against A. G. Miller that caused his suspension from the office of state organizer, but Miller was cleared of the charges by the state committee and, turning on his accusers, got the committee to revoke the charter of Local Boise and to bounce a fellow named Carter out of his national committeeman position. Only 89 party members of an estimated 300 bothered to vote to fill the vacant national committeeman position. In this election E. J. Riggs received 61 votes, defeating Vincent St. John (running as J. W. Vincent).[38]

Early in 1906, party officials in the Coeur d'Alene area boasted of large increases in party membership.[39] In August the state secretary proclaimed:

"Socialism in Idaho is going to reach the high-water mark this fall. Truth to tell, it is going to slop over the banks and spread out all over the state."[40] The Idaho Socialist party directly benefited in 1906 because the pending Haywood trial (he was to be tried first) had attracted several Socialist agitators, who lectured all over the state, and prompted Herman Titus to move his left-wing paper, *The Socialist*, to Caldwell from Toledo, Ohio, to give the workers' side of the story. Titus, born in Massachusetts, had been a Baptist minister for several years but resigned from the ministry, contending that the church had abandoned Jesus. He became a medical doctor, first in Newton, Massachusetts, and later in Seattle. Titus offered his paper's services in getting Idaho Socialists elected in 1906, declaring that because of the Haywood trial and the obvious failure of the Republican and Democratic parties on the matter, "the Socialist Party in Idaho faces the greatest opportunity ever offered a workingman's party in any state."[41] Titus, however, was a "by-the-book" Socialist and was angered by the apparent effort of the defense team and those going on trial to align Socialists with Democratic voters to defeat tough-minded Republican judge Frank J. Smith, who was scheduled to preside over the proceedings involving Haywood and the others. Titus later reported, "Comrade Moyer said to me, 'If your neck was in the noose, you would talk different.' "[42]

According to operative reports, around 400 people showed up in April 1906 to hear Dr. Titus speak on the subject of "Who Killed Steunenberg."[43] Titus had no doubt that Orchard was the murderer. As for motive: "My theory is, and I am an experienced physician of long years practice, that Orchard is a moral degenerate. His head shows it. Most men's two sides are alike, Orchard's are not. He was born a degenerate and cannot help it. He has a mania for killing people with explosives."[44] According to operatives in attendance, Titus's lengthy remarks, in which he linked Orchard's guilt to the fact that one of his ears was much higher than the other, made less of an impact with the audience than did David C. Coates, the chair of the meeting and the first speaker. Coates talked for an hour, roasting the Mine Owners' Association, saying that Governor Frank Gooding was their tool and that they were trying to break up the WFM. The operative noted, "Coates was frequently interrupted by applause. He was more radical than Titus and the audience applauded him more freely."[45]

The Idaho party, holding its 1906 convention on July 4 at Caldwell, nominated a card-carrying union man, Thomas F. Kelly, for governor and made the treatment of the WFM officials currently held in the Caldwell jail a major issue.[46] Kelly, a stonecutter, drew large and enthusiastic audiences in the Coeur d'Alene mining camps during the campaign.[47] Miners, however, were divided over whether to take their leaders' advice and vote for the Socialist or to support the

Democrat in their effort to oust Republican governor Frank Gooding, who had alienated much of the labor movement with his hard-line stance on the arrest and trial of Haywood, Moyer, and Pettibone—he had been quoted as asserting the three prisoners' guilt. Socialist party leaders in Idaho in 1906 acknowledged what those on the left could agree on—that the Republicans were a bad lot—but had a harder time promoting the theme adopted at their convention earlier in the year that "Democrats are only Republicans out of office."[48]

In 1906 party leaders in Shoshone County rejected Democratic leaders' offers to fuse with the Democrats in a joint effort to defeat the Republican party ticket, which was backed by the Mine Owners' Association. Like Socialists elsewhere, Idaho Socialist leaders cited the Populists' sad experience with fusion in 1896 as a reason for remaining independent. As the election neared, mining companies began to fire miners in the area who expressed support for the Democratic or Socialist parties and let it be known that more firings might take place after the election. Election board officials, it was rumored, would be more than willing to tell mining companies how individuals had voted if the Republicans failed to win.[49] Given the hostility of the mining companies, much of the activity of Socialists in the county took place off mining property. Two left-wing self-employed barbers, William Stache and David Pifer, who ran shops in Wallace, emerged as leaders of the local party in Shoshone County.[50] Undercover detectives working for the mining companies warned that Pifer in particular was a dangerous radical, very near an anarchist, who agitated at every possible chance. His shop, they reported, was "a bad hangout."[51]

Numerous Socialist speakers came to the Coeur d'Alene area in 1906, and Socialism was a regular topic at union meetings. In Wallace, however, some of the speakers experienced official harassment. The local sheriff, for example, ordered the street lights to be turned off in the middle of a street-corner speech by organizer Ida Crouch Hazlett—an event she later remarked upon with considerable venom before 150 people in the miners' hall.[52] The sheriff did the same thing to national organizer George H. Goebel of New Jersey, who, being prepared, proceeded to address a large crowd by torchlight.[53] Goebel, one of the organizers sent in by the national party, worked the northern end of Idaho—including the Coeur d'Alene, Wallace, and Wardner districts—and close to thirty towns in the four counties (Kootenai, Shoshone, Latah, and Nez Perce) where about half of the Socialist vote in the state had been cast in 1904. Montana secretary James Graham also sent Hazlett and other speakers to help out in this area.

In spite of all this activity and the excitement brought about by the Haywood trial, the Socialist Kelly fared poorly in his campaign for governor. Organized labor backed Gooding's Democratic opponent as the candidate most likely to turn the incumbent out of office. Many workers also appeared to have done so. Even so, Gooding emerged the winner. The top Socialist vote getter in 1906, the candidate for mine inspector, received only 7 percent of the statewide vote, 13 percent in Shoshone, and 21 percent in Burke.[54] On the positive side, in a victory for political action, Frank J. Smith, the tough Republican judge scheduled to hear the Haywood case, was turned out of office, defeated by a Democrat, Edgar L. Bryan, who appeared to have had considerable support from WFM members and Socialists. Bryan, though, had a conflict of interest and was replaced by Judge Fremont Wood as judge in the Haywood trial. Wood, age fifty, was a Republican but was generally regarded by both sides as fair-mined.[55]

Haywood's trial began a few months after the 1906 election. The radical press showed up, vowing to make sure the trial was a fair one.[56] Not surprisingly, radical reporters were not always received with open arms. The Socialist press reported that several of these journalists, including Ida Crouch Hazlett, now with the *Montana News*, "have been spat upon in the streets and hissed [at]." Others had trouble getting lodging, had their mail tampered with, and had to put up a fight to get into the courthouse where the trial was held.[57] Socialists also complained that prison authorities gave the regular press the right to interview Harry Orchard in his cell but denied that right to reporters for left-wing newspapers.

In the end, the jury came down on the side of Haywood. The editor of the conservative *Caldwell Tribune* gave considerable credit to the eloquence of Haywood's attorney, Clarence Darrow, who, the editor felt, captivated the jury. Darrow, in defending the WFM, had successfully put Steunenberg on trial for calling out the troops and the state on trial for excessive spending on Pinkerton services.[58] The editor concluded, though, "When The Tribune states that the people of Canyon county were disappointed in the recent decision in the Haywood case, the statement is drawing it mild, never were the people more disappointed."[59] On the other hand, a newspaper in Goldfield, Nevada, reported that around 1,500 miners celebrated the acquittal with speeches and a parade. One speaker cried, "What's the matter with undesirable citizens?" Another asked, "What shall we do to Roosevelt?"[60] Later, Pettibone was acquitted and charges against Moyer were dismissed. Bill Haywood, meanwhile, fresh from jail, made personal appearances around the region. One report from Idaho Falls stated: "The demonstration that met the Haywood train was a marvel. The machinists had the band out, and 5,000 people thronged the streets. It was a wonder where they all came from. Haywood was dragged from the car with Henrietta, the youngest girl, and mounted on a trunk where he made an inspiring speech of a few minutes' length. The coach was filled with flowers taken in to Mrs. Haywood."[61]

Even the most alienated and bitter radicals were forced to admit that the outcome of the trial could possibly be taken as evidence that the "system" was not entirely corrupt. Radicals had been greatly worried about whether Haywood could get a fair trial, especially considering where the trial was located. One radical had warned, "If you wanted to take a labor agitator to a place where you could murder him without local protest, no better spot in the country could be found than this region of Southern Idaho."[62] The verdict apparently came as a genuine surprise to Haywood and most of the radicals who had gathered in Idaho. A radical paper admitted that "everyone had guessed wrong" in sizing up the jury.[63] A headline in an IWW paper read "Haywood Acquitted by Honest Jury," leaving the impression that an "honest jury" was as newsworthy as the acquittal itself. The story also credited the judge as fair-minded.[64] Other radicals considered the verdict as evidence that Haywood had "been innocent to a sickening degree."[65]

Overall, though, the dominant theme in the radical press was that the working class, against all odds, had won an enormous victory and was eagerly looking forward to the next conflict. As a writer for the Socialist *Wilshire's* magazine proclaimed:

> We are mightily cheered and invigorated, we feel the power of the united millions of workingmen, we gird up our loins and joyously await the next conflict with baffled capitalism. We did not know our strength and our resources before the Idaho battle. Neither did the enemy. A draw seemed the best thing we could hope for in view of the complete capitalistic machinery that opposed us. They had unlimited wealth, the courts and the laws, a legion of spies and thugs, the newspapers, a poisoned local atmosphere, the approval of presidents, governors and all respectable people, yet they were unable to win. They tried to teach labor a lesson of terror, but they only succeeded in exposing the rottenness of the ruling class and in emboldening the nation's toilers to march on to final victory.[66]

The writer also ventured the belief that Haywood knew the Socialist party had stood behind him and would never forget his debt to that organization. In fact, while Haywood might not have forgotten, his relations with the Socialist party went rapidly downhill.

Other observers saw the arrest and trial as promoting class consciousness among trade unionists throughout the country.[67] Yet, while the trial stimulated a great deal of Socialist party activity, such as rallies to raise funds and arouse sympathy for the prisoners, the impact of this on votes for Socialist candidates was difficult to decipher. If nothing else, the trial may have provided the benefit of informing the public about, as the radicals saw it, the brutality of the class struggle and the "criminal career" of mine owners.[68] On the negative side, however, the trial had also produced a great deal of press coverage of the WFM and the IWW, which helped paint their members in the public eye as bloody revolutionaries. The episode also added to the tension within the WFM and the IWW, making some, such as Haywood, even more determined to overthrow the system through direct action and others, like Moyer, to tone down the revolutionary rhetoric and build more respectable unions.[69]

While the IWW and Haywood were making national news, the Socialist party in Nevada was starting to take root in the WFM and IWW locals found in mining areas. In 1906 the Nevada party's slate of state candidates consisted almost entirely of flaming revolutionaries who were IWW members. Harry Jardine, the party's candidate for Congress, fit that description. Making "the ownership of your own job" his central theme, he picked up about 9 percent of the votes cast—1,250 out of 14,000.[70] Goldfield, a booming mining camp of around 15,000 people in Esmeralda County (there were only 70,000 people in the state), was a particularly strong hotbed of radical activity. Socialists met at Goldfield for their first state party convention in 1906. The IWW, under the leadership of Vincent St. John, organized Goldfield from top to bottom in 1906–1907. Eager to replace the traditional craft unionism in the city with the IWW's idea of an industrial union, St. John began by organizing nearly all the "town workers"—dishwashers, engineers, stenographers, teamsters, and clerks—into a single IWW local. Later, the IWW took over and proceeded to dominate the WFM's Goldfield Local Union No. 220—at the time, the WFM existed nationally as the mining department of the IWW.

St. John boasted about labor's dominance over the town: "No committees were ever sent to any employers. The union adopted wage scales and regulated hours. The secretary posted the same on a bulletin board outside the union hall, and it was the LAW. The employers were forced to come and see the union committees."[71] Goldfield's IWW, on January 20, 1907, put on a radical display with a "Bloody Sunday" parade that both commemorated the massacre that followed the failed Russian Revolution of 1905 and protested the trial of Haywood in Idaho. Following the parade came a series of fiery speeches by St. John and others condemning capitalists in Nevada and in general. St. John promised, "We will sweep the capitalist class out of the life of this nation and then out of the whole world."[72]

The capitalists struck back, led by the mine owners. In the forefront was George Wingfield who, along with George S. Nixon, a U.S. senator from Nevada, headed the Goldfield Consolidated Mines Company, which had opened operations in 1906.[73] As in Colorado and Idaho, the mine owners pulled together in a Mine Owners' Association, formed alliances with state politicians, and ultimately were able to use troops to destroy the unions. Nevada also had its own Haywood trial. This involved union members and Socialists Morrie Preston and Joseph Smith who, in 1907, were accused and later convicted, on the basis of highly questionable evidence, of killing a restaurant owner during labor trouble. Mine owners tried to use the trial to convince the public that the unions represented a violent movement and should be eliminated.[74]

A little more than six months after the Preston-Smith trial, federal troops moved into Goldfield to put down a mining strike. In the mines the ostensible issues revolved around the owners' efforts to crack down on high grading, which had become a standard practice among miners of taking rich ore out of the mines for their own use. Miners "regarded stealing ore as a fringe benefit to which they were morally entitled" and resented the company's installation of change rooms to curb the practice.[75] Miners also became unhappy over being forced to accept scrip rather than cash because of a cash shortage following the October 1907 bank panic. Mine owners, intent on driving Socialists and radical labor out of the camp, refused to bargain with the Goldfield Miners' Union, closed down operations, and, on November 30, declared that the mines would remain closed until labor conditions could be settled to their satisfaction.

Soon thereafter, Governor John Sparks, acting on behalf of the mine owners, asked President Theodore Roosevelt to send troops into the area. Roosevelt did so on December 6. A contemporary nonradical observer noted: "There is talk of trouble, and a call for help is sent to the Governor. He sends in the United States regulars, who make camp over on the hill near us. They help the stores, saloons, and amusement places, and, as there is no trouble to quiet, have an easy time of it, skating at the rink, and getting drunk. But they were never arrogant with the miners, and I think they realized that having been ordered there was a mistake. Some of them did do a good turn by stealing provisions from the Government and selling them cheaply to the miners."[76]

Ultimately, though, the miners got the short end of the stick. With federal troops present as security against disorder, the mine owners announced they would reopen the mines on December 12 but that wages would be reduced and workers who wished to keep their jobs would have to sign an anti-union pledge card. When the mines reopened, very few miners reported for work, as most stood with the WFM, and owners were forced to begin recruitment drives in neighboring states. Reporting from Goldfield in January 1908 as a special correspondent for *The Socialist,* Ida Crouch Hazlett found everything was quiet. Lots of soldiers were living in comfortable quarters in a hotel, around sixty scabs were at work for Consolidated, and its vice president, George Wingfield, was in Salt Lake City trying to recruit more scabs.[77] Expressing her anger, Hazlett also reported: "Everything points to the fact that Governor Sparks was paid $50,000 for getting the troops in here. He is nothing but a drunken sot, as tough and disreputable as they make them, and nothing else could be expected."[78]

The record indicates that the governor had assured Roosevelt that violence in the camp justified the sending of troops. Roosevelt, however, later became suspicious that this was not the case—people in Goldfield seemed surprised to see the troops and wondered why they were there—and sent a commission to investigate conditions. The commission found that the sending of troops had not been warranted, indeed, that it had been requested for the sole purpose of helping mine owners get rid of a troublesome union. The president, in response, said the troops would have to be withdrawn, but the governor continued to insist that the situation in Goldfield was dangerous and blamed the lawless and anarchistic WFM for the turmoil. At the governor's request, the legislature passed a resolution asking that federal troops be kept in the area until the state had time to create its own military force.

The legislature proceeded to pass a bill that, as radicals saw it, brought "into being an irresponsible body of armed men"—in effect, "a body of legal thugs"—for the governor to use to club wage earners into submission.[79] The legislation, known as the State Police Bill, gave the governor control over an active police force of 31 men and a reserve force of 250 men, which he could use as he deemed appropriate. Radicals warned, "[I]n the control of such a man as Sparks has shown himself to be, this armed force of legalized guerillas can only become a weapon of revenge and oppression."[80] In February 1908, Nevada state police began replacing federal troops in Goldfield. Feeling secure, mine operators posted regulations at each mine declaring that they would not recognize unions and that no union representatives were allowed on the premises.[81]

The effect of all this was to eliminate the WFM and the IWW from the camp. Many miners left the area. Many who stayed dropped out of the unions. The few who continued as union members voted to end the strike on April 3, 1908. While the strike had not been accompanied by anything close to the level of violence that had characterized disturbances in Cripple Creek, when a settlement came, union labor at Goldfield was as thoroughly defeated as it had been at the Colorado camp.[82] With the defeat, the base of Socialist movement in Nevada moved north to the Reno area and toward a more moderate tone. For the IWW, the experience in Goldfield encouraged its members to think about concentrating more of their efforts on the more civilized and industrially developed eastern part of the country.

In December 1907 WFM president Moyer took note of troops going into Goldfield in stressing the need for independent political as well as industrial action—troop movement, he argued, would not have happened if labor had had a friend in Nevada's office of governor.[83] However, he was not anxious to write off working with direct actionists in the IWW. He went on record as saying that the WFM still believed in the principles of industrial unionism and was looking forward to the IWW conference in Chicago in hopes that the IWW could be reestablished "and emerge from its present state of disruption and uncertainty."[84]

Meanwhile, things were not going smoothly for the WFM. It faced an uphill struggle in several other places in addition to Nevada. Organizers, showing their frustration, put much of the blame for failure on the workers, although not forgetting to condemn the activities of employers and churches as well. Reporting from Leadville in April 1906, for example, Marion W. Moor wrote: "The chief obstacle to the organization of the English-speaking people of Leadville is their ignorance and cowardice. They are in constant fear of their jobs, though I found after careful investigation that not one man had been discharged in the past year on account of his membership in the union. A strong influence was brought to bear by the church on the Austrians, Italians, and other Latin races to refuse to join the union, and we have ample proof that the employers of Leadville gave a priest in the camp the sum of $2,000 for this purpose."[85]

At the time, relations between WFM officials and the conservative, if not corporate-dominated, Butte Miners' Union were strained, with Socialism part of the issue; many in the Butte union felt the national organization had ventured too far to the left. Leaders of the Butte union were also being challenged by Wobblies who, working from within, were attempting to develop an anti-company, pro-Socialist left wing. The decision of union leaders in 1906 to accept Amalgamated's offer of a token raise played into the hands of Wobblies and so greatly angered many rank-and-file union members that they threatened to go on strike, claiming the leaders had sold out to management. The company stymied this development by suspending all mine operations. In no time at all the entire move for a strike collapsed, and the company's men retained control of the union.

While the Wobblies and the WFM and, with them, the core of the Socialist party were being squashed in Nevada, the WFM, aided by Socialists, was spending considerable energy in Arizona in an effort to organize miners in Bisbee at the southern end of the state. A central target was the Copper Queen Consolidated Mining Company, owned by the Phelps-Dodge Company. Organizers were particularly upset with the intransigence of the company's local managers. One reported in 1906 that while Phelps-Dodge, "with offices in John street, New York, apparently does not care whether its mines are operated by union or non-union labor so long as dividends are forthcoming, there is a bunch of Copper Queen officials in Bisbee who imagine that every vice and iniquity in the universe emanates from the Socialist party and the Western Federation of Miners."[86] The chief obstacle to organization, however, was simply that Copper Queen had played it smart—it had paid its employees the union wage and strictly complied with the eight-hour law.[87] The company was also not above firing anyone suspected of favoring a union and did so in 1906 without hesitation.

The company was also openly hostile to Socialists. Still, the Bisbee local had some success in attracting miners to its meetings. In the spring of 1906, for example, it proudly reported it had held a successful "indignation meeting" out of which it raised funds for the Moyer-Haywood-Pettibone defense fund. The Socialists reported that they were surprised by the size of the turnout because "any one working for the 'good Copper Queen Company' will be discharged for even speaking to a Socialist on the street, let alone going to a Socialist meeting. But there are times when the wage workers throw all caution to the winds and express themselves openly and this was one of them."[88] The report concluded, "The meeting was a demonstration of the fact that the Copper Queen had not succeeded in driving all the union men out of Bisbee and also that the recent struggle here over the question of unionism instead of killing it, has kindled the spark until now it is liable to burst into flame at any moment, and when the next question comes up the issue will terminate successfully."[89] In 1906, however, the Bisbee miners voted against organization. That same year the Arizona Socialist party nominated Joseph D. Cannon, who had led the unsuccessful fight to organize Bisbee miners, as their candidate for delegate to Congress. With Cannon, the Socialist vote increased from 1,304 in 1904 to 2,078 in 1906, about 9 percent of the vote. Socialist candidates did best in places where miners were relatively numerous.[90]

The following year the Bisbee miners organized and struck for higher wages, but the strike failed. Reporting to the WFM convention in 1907, Cannon said the company would fire WFM members as fast as Cannon could recruit them. The union, he went on, constantly met the opposition of newspapers, tangled with Pinkerton spies, and ran the risk of violence. Cannon told the assembly, "It is a pretty hard proposition to be a union man when your life is at stake, when your job is at stake, and when your family is at stake."[91] Another delegate, P. C. Rawlings from the new Bisbee local, though, added with pride, "The words 'Western Federation of Miners' in Bisbee is a bugaboo that haunts the dreams of the corporate managers of that place."[92]

Following the 1907 conflicts in Bisbee and elsewhere in Arizona, employers launched what a leading labor official called "a ruthless campaign of blacklisting" against the workers who had participated in the strikes.[93] In Bisbee, Morenci,

and other camps, prospective workers were required to give detailed histories of their lives, in some cases of their families, as a precondition of employment. The end result of blacklisting was that miners who had joined the WFM were often forced to move from camp to camp to secure employment. A labor official described the process thus: "A union man would secure a few days' work, attend a union meeting and a detective would report him, with the result [that] he would soon be on the tramp again."[94]

Organized labor and the Socialist movement may have been growing hand in hand on a national basis, but the various unions and political elements within the radical movement in the Mountain West in the years 1905–1908 were, at best, in a fragile alliance, and progress on both the industrial and political fronts in terms of union organization and winning votes was limited. The kidnapping and trial of WFM officials provided a rallying point. Radicals were one in calling attention to this outrage and in condemning what had happened. Cracks in the movement, however, were also apparent as the WFM backed away from both the Socialist party and the IWW, even though the latter was largely its own creation. Within the Socialist movement, midwestern and eastern Socialists were less than enthusiastic over the attention given to radicals like Haywood. While Socialists had a measure of success in using the arrests and trial of the WFM officials to build class consciousness and the ranks of radical organizations, this seemed not to have added appreciably to the votes for Socialist candidates. Haywood's candidacy gave a boost to the Colorado party but not enough to result in anything close to victory, leaving some to ponder if there was any Socialist who could win an election. In Idaho, where the arrests and trial had spurred considerable Socialist activity, the attention of labor and many workers was focused on getting rid of a hostile Republican governor, and they rallied behind a Democratic candidate rather than the Socialist candidate as the best way to achieve that goal.

On the industrial front, as the Nevada events indicated, the federal and state governments continued to demonstrate a willingness to come down on the side of mine owners. Indeed, in 1906 the governor of Arizona went so far as to send troops, around 250 Arizona Rangers, into Mexico where they were sworn in by the governor of Sonora as Mexican volunteers and used to help put down a 1906 strike against the American-based Consolidated Copper Company. The crushed strike had been led by Mexican and American Wobblies and the WFM in protest over the low wages paid to Mexican workers. Corporate resistance in Montana was built around capturing the mining union, a less violent but equally effective tactic. Even with all this, however, there was considerable enthusiasm among radicals in the region as the nation approached the 1908 election.

Ida Crouch Hazlett, Socialist editor and organizer. Photograph courtesy of the World Museum of Mining. Copyright World Museum of Mining.

Joe Cannon, Arizona labor and Socialist leader. Courtesy
Arizona State University Libraries.

A. Grant Miller, Nevada Socialist leader. Courtesy of Anne Ward.

Mayor Duncan of Butte. Photograph courtesy of the World Museum of Mining. Copyright World Museum of Mining.

*W.C. Tharp, Socialist in New Mexico state legisla-
ture. Photo: Nerw Mexico Blue Book, 1915.*

Ruins of Ludlow Colony, Trinidad, Colorado. Library of Congress.

Butte Miners Union Hall Riot. Photograph courtesy of the World Museum of Mining. Copyright World Museum of Mining.

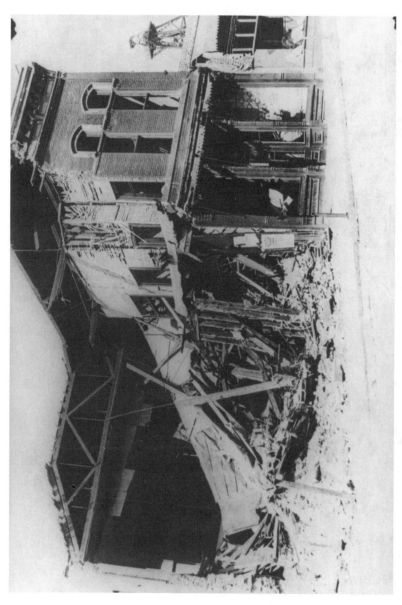

Butte Miners Union Hall after blast. Photograph courtesy of the World Museum of Mining. Copyright World Museum of Mining.

Butte Court House during martial law period, 1914. Photograph courtesy of the World Museum of Mining. Copyright World Museum of Mining.

Taking Applications for Membership in the WFM, during strike in Morenci, Arizona, 1915-1916. Courtesy Henry S. McCluskey Photographs, Arizona Collection, Arizona State University Libraries.

Picketing at Morenci during strike, 1915–1916. Courtesy Henry S. McCluskey Photographs, Arizona Collection, Arizona State University Libraries.

Picketing at Morenci during strike 1915–1916. Courtesy Henry S. McCluskey Photographs, Arizona Collection, Arizona State University Libraries.

CHAPTER NINE

The Red Special, Elections, and Free Speech

Delegates from the Mountain West took advantage of the opportunity to make their views known on a variety of topics during debates at the 1908 Socialist party convention. Some joined in the debate over relations with trade unions, often, but not always, coming down on the side of those opposed to forming stronger ties with such organizations. Said delegate Joseph D. Cannon of Arizona: "There are two kinds of unionism and both of them cannot be right . . . one is class unionism and the other is craft unionism. . . . Let us endorse the class form of unionism."[1] A. Grant Miller of Nevada, though, did not want the party to take a stand either for or against trade unions, while Ida Crouch Hazlett made an impassioned argument for strengthening relations with trade unions, lest they slip away from the revolutionary movement.[2]

The solidarity of Mountain West Socialists was more apparent on various issues with a regional bent. They were, for example, as one in criticizing their eastern comrades such as Morris Hillquit for being, as Guy E. Miller of Colorado put it, at best, "lukewarm friends" of the Western Federation of Miners (WFM).[3] They were also in agreement on what to do about Asian immigration, another western problem easterners knew or cared little about. A. Grant Miller argued that Orientals were different from other immigrants; they were not coming to stay but just to make money and leave. He warned that "if you want to emasculate the labor movement in the west, just stand for the immigration of all these people from the orient, if you please, and you will do it, and you will satisfy the capitalist masters of the Union."[4] Delegate Ernest Untermann from Idaho, a well-known Socialist writer, evoked considerable applause with this convoluted declaration: "I believe in the brotherhood of man, regardless of races, but I do not believe in extending that brotherhood to my brothers of other races. I am determined that my race shall be supreme in this country and in the world."[5] Untermann later linked Asian immigration to the production of a large army of transient white unemployed workers known as blanket stiffs, who, having no settled abode, had lost the franchise, rejected political action, and moved from the Socialist party into the Industrial Workers of the World (IWW)—an organization that was a millstone around the party's neck.[6]

Delegates to the 1908 Socialist party convention from all regions of the country continued to be divided over the wisdom of making immediate demands, but they came out of their deliberations with a compromise platform that allowed everyone, whether right or left, to think they controlled the party.[7] Once again the party nominated Eugene Debs for president, and he set out to educate the American people. He took aim at the party's political enemies, among whom Samuel Gompers drew intensified scorn for abandoning the American Federation of Labor's (AFL's) established policy of nonpolitical intervention by endorsing the Democrat candidate Bryan. In 1908 Debs toured the country on the "Red Special" train, which consisted of four cars carrying several dozen people, including musicians as well as party workers. Around 15,000 subscribers paid for the cost of the train campaign. Sometimes addressing crowds from the train, sometimes getting off the train and holding rallies at various venues, Debs spoke from six to ten times a day for sixty-five straight days to an estimated 800,000 people. Within a few months the enthusiasm aroused by the campaign helped boost party membership from 30,000 to 46,000.[8]

Enthusiastic crowds greeted Debs as the Red Special chugged its way through various parts of the Mountain West. Among those onboard with Debs and his managers for at least part of the trip was A. H. Floaten of Colorado, whose job was to hand out literature. Anticipating a great demand, Socialists had filled the baggage car to the brim with reading material for distribution. They were not disappointed at the size of the crowds. In Missoula, Montana, the Red Special came in six hours late but, nevertheless, was greeted by a crowd estimated by friendly observers to number about 6,000 people. A writer brought along to report on events later wrote: "We are never likely to forget the man with the red flag. It was about as big as he could manage; but there was a look in his eyes and in his moustache that boded ill for any man rash enough to touch that flag."[9] Lewis J. Duncan, destined for a tumultuous political career in Montana politics, reported that Debs spoke from the rear platform and "[a]s the train pulled out a cheering crowd of working men ran after it, clinging to the railing and climbing up to seize the outstretched hands of their champion and to bid him God-speed."[10]

Debs also energized the party faithful in Wallace, Idaho. Arriving about an hour late on a cold and disagreeable September morning, he was greeted by a crowd of 800 people. Later, he spoke to many more at a ballpark, reminding them of Bryan's limitations.[11] As the train chugged into Nevada, a Republican paper referred to Debs and the other Socialists with him as "preachers of the doctrine of discontent."[12] Damning with faint praise, the editor continued: "As an entertainer Mr. Debs is a success. As a presenter of convincing arguments he seemed to be a little shy. Yet with his pleasing personality one can understand how it has been possible for him to maintain his position in the hearts and minds of the habitually discontented [for] so long."[13] On at least one stop in Nevada (and probably on most of them throughout the tour) Debs remarked: "There is no difference between the Republican and Democratic parties. . . . The Republican party has all the big capitalists and the Democratic party all the little capitalists. It don't make any difference to you whether you are eaten by an alligator or by ten thousand mosquitoes."[14]

Debs reportedly had a great meeting in Denver, but he and his fellow passengers were disappointed at the conditions in Leadville. The onboard writer reported: "Unemployment we found to be a chronic state of things, and the busiest places seemed to be the saloons and the flaunting redlight district. It made one's heart sick. There was very good reason for the flaring motto that smote me between the eyes when I entered the newspaper office—'Smile, damn you!'—for everybody, even in the open-air meeting that we had, at a corner where the four winds met, seemed unutterably miserable. Before Gene got through with his speech he had kindled a few sparks in the hearts of his hearers—but Leadville was a sad experience."[15] Going through Glenwood Springs, Colorado, Debs received a bunch of flowers from a little girl; a photo of the event found its way into Socialist publications. The train was late when it reached Utah, and, as might have been expected, there was a squabble between rival locals—one in Ogden, the other in Salt Lake City—over when and where he should speak.

Socialist party officials in the various Mountain states in 1908, as always, were officially optimistic coming into the election. Most could point to some evidence of increased interest in the party, particularly when it came to party membership. Yet, the pickup in votes, if any, generally turned out to be less than spectacular. Prior to the election, the party secretary in Colorado hedged in explaining that he expected the party to do better than in 1904 but not as well as in 1906 when Haywood was the party's nominee for governor. Said Secretary Lewis E. Floaten: "This year we have nominated H. C. Darrah, an old soldier, for Governor, a man who is not identified with any labor organization and who is not known outside the Socialist party. Our campaign fund will be *very* small and the vote that we poll in 1908 can be depended on to be a strictly class-conscious Socialist vote. We have but one organizer in the field."[16] The party vote did severely dip from 1906 when Haywood headed the state ticket and gathered 16,000 votes. In comparing the party vote in the 1904 presidential year to that in 1908, however, we find an increase from 4,959 to 6,400, from 1.8 percent of the vote to 3.0 percent of the vote (see Appendix, Table 2). The state party organization also appeared to be in very good shape. On May 1, 1908, the state party had forty-four locals in good standing. This total included three Finnish locals in Denver, Leadville, and Telluride and separate locals for German, Jewish, and Scandinavian Socialists in Denver.[17]

In Wyoming, meanwhile, the party appeared to be gaining strength with the emergence of organized labor in the state, particularly in the coal mining areas. By 1907 the United Mine Workers (UMW), persisting in the face of company opposition, represented nearly all of Wyoming's coal miners and had negotiated an eight-hour day in the coal industry. Under the union contract, Wyoming coal miners had some of the highest coal mining wages in the country.[18] Miners had also achieved some legislative victories, for example, laws limiting companies' ability to pay their employees in scrip or coupons redeemable only at company stores.

Ida Crouch Hazlett reported in 1907: "For its population, Wyoming has added more members to organized labor than any other state in the union this year. Towns and camps all over the state that had no unions at the beginning of the year are now thoroughly organized. Those acquainted with the local situation say that with the advent of the organization of labor the socialist sentiment sprang up all around and socialist buttons which were never seen, suddenly sprang into sight. The socialist sentiment was lying dormant and with the advent of organization it suddenly sprang into activity."[19] To help cultivate this sentiment, Socialists in Rock Springs brought in speakers like Hazlett to speak in the UMW hall. The UMW gave its tacit approval to the party.

The Wyoming Socialist party in 1908 held what mainstream newspapers called a well-attended statewide convention in Rock Springs, with representatives from Sheridan, Evanston, Kemmerer, and Laramie among those in attendance.[20] According to the notes of one of the participants, "The convention was double in number to that of two years ago, and was very enthusiastic. Miss Anna Maley, National Organizer[,] was present and made an address at night."[21] Wyoming Socialists adopted a platform that called for several labor measures, including employers' liability, eight-hour laws, sickness and accident insurance, the employment of convict labor, and worker immigration. The labor platform also demanded that coal mine inspectors be elected only by miners. Along with the labor items was a call for direct legislation and measures to protect small owners and users of water from encroachment by land and water monopolies.

In the fall Debs picked up strength, getting 4.6 percent of the vote compared with 3.5 percent in 1904. James Morgan of Sheridan, the Socialist candidate for Congress, did even better by pulling in 6.6 percent of the vote. The party polled about 14 percent of the vote in Sweetwater County (Rock Springs). Much of the vote for both candidates came from coal mining areas where the party's labor planks, especially the eight-hour day and improved mine inspections, were popular. Mainstream newspapers, seeing the party as a reform party built around modest labor issues, were willing to give the Socialists some publicity and report on their activities.[22]

Doing fieldwork in southern Idaho in 1907, Hazlett—who like Debs years later was scheduled for Burley but did not make the trip, this time because the town was experiencing a smallpox epidemic and public meetings were prohibited—was encouraged by the reception she received and the potential Socialist vote.[23] Yet, she was appalled to discover that there was virtually no organization in the state and almost no Socialist literature was being distributed.[24] As always, she had triumphs and disappointments in her travels—she received an unexpectedly warm response in some farm areas but also encountered miners whom she felt were afraid of their own shadows as well as a brass band that, with the encouragement of the police, tried to drown her out while she was speaking.[25] The following spring (1907), David C. Coates was the party's candidate for mayor of Wallace, the "Queen City" of the Coeur d'Alenes, that year. Miners were a minority; most of the 3,000 living there were tied to businesses that depended on mine operations. Coates wound up with only about 7 percent of the vote.[26]

Idaho Socialists, though, seemed well prepared for the 1908 election. In October 1908 state party secretary Thomas J. Coonrod reported that the organization was greatly strengthened and that the dues-paying membership had almost doubled since January, to more than 800 people.[27] About a third of these members were in Shoshone County.[28] The party, however, was also showing signs of strength in other counties.[29] In one of these counties, Socialists meeting in convention encountered the wrath of local citizens by taking down the United States flag from over the building in which they met and replacing it with the red flag of Socialism. In the interest of peace, the Socialists backed down and restored the American flag.[30] At other times, the party came out on top. In the summer of 1908, a prominent Socialist-bashing Republican orator got into trouble when it became know that he had deserted his wife and children in Coeur d'Alene, leaving them in virtual poverty. The Socialist party press duly reported this development and noted that the individual in question had long opposed Socialism on the grounds that it "would break up the home."[31]

Debs wound up with 6.5 percent of the Idaho vote. Ernest Untermann, running for governor, also received a little more than 6 percent of the vote. As in the past, the total was likely suppressed by mine owner threats that their employees would lose their jobs if they voted "wrong" (for a Democrat or a Socialist). For the general public, the owners made it known that if the wrong candidates won, the mines would shut down, throwing everyone out of work.[32] Although the Socialists showed little real progress in picking up votes—their percentage of the total in the 1908 presidential race was a little less than that in 1904—Idaho party officials said they were pleased. They announced that the campaign of 1908 "was undoubtedly the best ever conducted by the Socialist party of Idaho, and on the whole, eminently satisfactory. The vote for our candidate was a splendid showing. The increases of membership of [the] party gratifying and financial support [as] good as could be expected."[33] After the 1908 election, leaders of the miners' union locals of Coeur d'Alene continued their effort to popularize Socialist ideas. They brought in radicals from around the country for speaking engagements. On June 27, 1909, Big Bill Haywood came to Wallace for that purpose. Unfortunately, Big Bill arrived in such an advanced state of intoxication that he could not speak.[34]

Following the election, Idaho party leaders also made much of the inroads they had made with farmers in the region, lightly touching a vein of support enjoyed by the Populists. The *Appeal to Reason* was happy to publish such testimonials, including this letter from an Idaho farmer: "We farmers have long been called the only independent workers. We are skinned buying and selling and get skinned by as many trusts as any class on earth. I voted for the Socialist ticket in 1908 for it seems the only reasonable party before the working people."[35] Another farmer from Idaho explained his conversion to Socialism: "I have made the change because I see that the farmer has the same relation to economics as any other laboring man or producer. Most everything we raise, we have to sell for what is offered us or not sell it at all, let it rot or give it away. When it comes to buying we will have to pay what is asked or do without. So where is the difference. Are we not exactly in the same boat as other workers? . . . Socialism is the only thing that can give equality of opportunity."[36]

In Montana, meanwhile, the state Socialist party gained visibility and perhaps a few followers by championing the initiative and referendum as a means of curbing corporate control of the legislature. Some of the rewards the party might have received from its association with these popular reforms, however, may have been lost when it opposed the direct legislation measure that reached the ballot in 1906 and was overwhelmingly approved by voters. Socialists opposed the measure because it exempted appropriation bills and constitutional amendments from its provisions. At any rate, the party received only its customary 9 percent of the vote in the contest for the U.S. House of Representatives in 1906.[37]

With the help of an energetic membership drive, membership in the Montana party more than doubled, from 400 in 1904 to about 800 in 1908.[38] Because of corporate pressure and the dismal prospects of winning, however, the party was having trouble finding candidates. At the national convention of the Socialist party in 1908, Montana delegate George H. Ambrose reported in reference to Butte, "The amalgamated companies have such control on the town that if a man accepts a nomination on the Socialist ticket it is equivalent to losing his job."[39] Another problem in Montana, according to Ida Crouch Hazlett at the same meeting, was the infiltration of Socialist locals by IWW types who advocated direct action instead of political action. Certain persons, she contended, "have pointed with scorn to our members who are advocating the political party and have called them maniacs . . . saying that we will get nothing by the ballot and nothing can be achieved by the ballot."[40]

While all the elements were not in perfect accord, the party's growth coincided with the growth of the IWW and anti-company sentiment within the Butte Miners' Union and the public at large. In 1908 the party did as well as or better than any other Socialist party in the region. Debs led the ticket with 5,920 votes, most of which came from Silver Bow County. Debs's percentage of the vote (8.9), though, was down a little from 1904. The party managed to offer a full slate of candidates for state offices, and they picked up around 8 percent of the vote, enough in all but one case to deprive the winning candidate of 50 percent of the vote. While party leaders had reason to hope for the future as far as the electorate was concerned, soon after the 1908 election conflict within the Montana party over the conduct of party affairs and control of the *Montana News* produced an intense factionalism that nearly destroyed the party.

The Nevada party probably had more momentum than any other party in the region in 1908. Following the crushing of the IWW and WFM in Goldfield in 1907, it underwent considerable change, moving away from the influence of radical labor to a more conservative and politically sophisticated stance that enhanced its appeal to middle-class voters. The party lost a dedicated cadre of radical organizers in Goldfield following the collapse, under the pressure of federal troops sent in by a duped Teddy Roosevelt.[41] Filling the void, however, was the emergence of new leadership, best represented by Reno attorney A. Grant Miller who, earlier in his career, had worked for a time as a miner and been a member of the Knights of Labor. Miller, born on a farm in Kent County, Michigan, the son of a minister, came to Nevada in 1907 at age forty seeking a healthier climate. According to historians Sally Zanjani and Guy Louis Rocha, Miller "became the most popular Socialist ever to contend on the Nevada ballot" and "almost made Socialism respectable."[42]

The newly reorganized party could still count on votes from Goldfield and Tonopah, but the core of the party moved north to the Reno-Sparks area where one found more conservative craft unions, trade alliances, and railroad brotherhoods.[43] Several locals, under the influence of the IWW, advocated direct action rather than political action.[44] The party as a whole, however, was controlled by more moderate, politically inclined forces. The Nevada Socialist platform of 1908, adopted by a convention meeting at Sparks in July of that year, played down the revolutionary rhetoric and asked for such reforms as direct democracy, equal suffrage, and free textbooks for students.[45]

While preparing for the 1908 campaign, Lora Harris, state secretary of the Nevada party, told a Socialist audience, "Your vote may not bring immediate Socialism, but little by little we are gaining, and the time is not far distant when you will be proud to say that you voted a straight Socialist ticket in 1908."[46] The party had been adding a considerable number of members. At the same time, though, party leaders claimed they were cautious about who could join. The party press proudly pointed out that party membership was not that easy to secure: "The method of organizing the Socialist party is distinctly different from that followed by any other party in the world. Not withstanding the fact that it is a political organization, every man who becomes a member must be a man of standing and must be vouched for before he can obtain a membership card in the party."[47] The party press was also proud of the fact that it was part of a movement that was making a difference by pushing the older parties into accepting reforms: "They endorse, for instance, the initiative and referendum and right of recall only because the Socialist party has so far educated the people on the principles of government that they now demand the enactment of the measures and the old parties are beginning to adopt them because they think they have to and not because they want to."[48]

In early 1908, radicals saw the possibility of good things happening in Nevada. *The Socialist* declared that "wage slaves" were in the majority in the state and could well produce a Socialist victory in the fall. The publication's editor, Herman Titus, called on the Western Federation of Miners to help make this a reality.[49] Debs ran relatively strong in 1908, receiving 9 percent of the vote compared with only about 3 percent nationally. A. A. Hibbard picked up 2,772 votes for a seat on the Board of Regents of the state university, coming in last in the contest but doing better than any other Socialist on the ticket; Debs's most popular elector received 2,103 votes.[50]

Utah, New Mexico, and Arizona gave radicals little to be excited about in 1906 and 1908, although even in these places the Haywood saga and Debs's campaign stimulated interest in the cause. Utah Socialists demonstrated that a party could make progress, at least as far as membership was concerned, in spite of intense intra-party conflict. After a fierce struggle, right-wingers gained control, only to come under heavy fire from the left in 1906 for backing certain candidates of the anti-Mormon American party. The leftists concluded: "In fact, in Utah there is no Socialist Party. It has committed suicide. It has fused, amalgamated, lost its separate existence, become a base alloy, is no longer Socialist. The fundamental law of Party Existence, without which there can be no party, is 'No Compromise, No Fusion.'"[51] Some Utah Socialists were pushing for a movement that, on the political front, would be a power broker, shifting its support to any party that would promise the best results for the working class while, at the same time, organizing on the economic field under the IWW banner.

The Utah party, in spite of the internal friction, grew from around 300 members in twenty-two locals in 1904 to 1,300 members in forty-seven locals in 1908. With more than his share of optimism, State Secretary Joseph MacLaulan reported in October 1908, "This year even our opponents grant the probability of our reaching 17,000" votes.[52] The estimate fell far short. Indeed, while membership was up, the party vote was down. Debs had picked up 5,767 votes in 1904, 5.7 percent of the total. In 1908 he received only 4,890 votes, 4.5 percent of the total (Appendix, Table 2). In the race for governor in 1908, Socialist V. R. Bohman trailed the pack, picking up 3,936 votes. In front of him was John A. Street, a candidate of the American party, the choice of 11,404 voters.[53]

In New Mexico the election returns were even more dismal. Socialist W. P. Metcalf made a bid for the seat of territorial delegate and picked up 211 votes in 1906, which looked good only when compared with the 162 votes he had gathered in 1904. Metcalf was probably in better humor in 1908—running again for

Congress, he moved to a more respectable 1,056 votes. When he was not running, Metcalf engaged in activities such as debating with a congressional minister over whether Jesus would advocate Socialism if he were alive today—Metcalf took the affirmative, the minister argued that Jesus would not teach the Communism he had espoused 1,900 years ago.[54] During the early 1900s the future of the party was being shaped in a positive fashion by the continued migration of home-steaders and dry farmers from Oklahoma and Texas into the eastern part of the state—a migration that would lead to some Socialist victories.

Arizona party leaders were also disappointed; this was another case where party growth had not been accompanied by increased voter support. From 1904 to 1908 the number of locals in the state increased from fifteen to twenty-seven.[55] Among the more active locals was one in the town of Safford in Graham County, where there was a large Mormon population. Mormons, however, were not looked upon by Socialists as likely recruits. Writing from Safford in 1907, one Arizona Socialist noted:

> I am a member in good standing in the Church of Jesus Christ of Latter Day Saints and among a few workers in that organization who comprehend the class struggle and are fighting and working for the education of our people along these lines. But so effectually [have] the great money kings done their work of deception among the people that even the Church of Christ is [permeated] with its [pernicious] doctrines. The Idea being that those who have the ability to corner the worlds wealth and appropriate it to themselves are entitled to it even though it means the enslavement of the masses and the destruction of humanity. Thus you will see that the battle is before us.[56]

Still, party leaders were optimistic. With the 1908 elections in mind, the former editor of the Socialistic *Graham County Advocate*, also president of the WFM local in Clifton, Arizona, declared that the Republican party was under the thumb of the "master class" and the Democratic party was headed by a particu-larly evil bunch of reform demagogues out to hoodwink the workers.[57] Under these parties, the editor concluded, the country had succumbed to rule "by an oligarchy of wealth as cruel and vicious as ever wasted the wealth of the past."[58] The editor believed the future belonged to the Socialist party as the means by which a united working class would "redeem our beloved country and be the first in all the world to erect the banner of true democracy."[59] In 1908, however, the party slumped, receiving only 1,912 votes in the territory.

In spite of the strong effort made by Socialist campaigners, the national results in 1908 were disappointing (see Appendix, Table 2). Debs wound up receiving 420,000 votes that year, only slightly better than the 402,000 he had received in

1904. Looking at percentages, he actually did worse, receiving 2.8 percent of the vote in 1908 compared with 3.0 percent in 1904. The Mountain West had done more than its share, although even there Debs did not do as well as he had in 1904. Debs's percentage of the vote in 1908 was higher in all six Mountain West states—Arizona and New Mexico were still territories—than in the nation as a whole. The percentage of votes for Debs in 1908 was highest in Nevada and Montana—both at 8.6 percent—followed by Idaho, Wyoming, Utah, and Colorado. In the Mountain West as in much of the nation, the AFL's endorsement of the Democratic candidate may have hurt the Socialist vote.

Members of the party's left wing, as represented on the editorial page of the *International Socialist Review,* saw the vote in Colorado and Idaho as particularly gratifying because it proved their point: the party in both states had stayed on message, stressing the class struggle and saying little about immediate demands, and by doing so did better than right-wing parties in other states that had offered watered-down Socialist programs.[60] To the left, the gains in these states represented a victory for those "who think it is more important to awaken the wage-workers to the fact that it is to their interest to destroy the whole capitalist system, [rather] than to agitate for municipal ownership, scientific reforestation and tax reforms."[61] In addition to staying focused on the major general objective, the left praised the party for taking on the fight of the WFM against organized capital.[62] As far as electoral success is concerned, the case made by the left was somewhat weak. There were strong showings in left-wing Colorado and Idaho, but there were equally if not more impressive gains for Socialist parties in other Mountain states, some of which highlighted modest immediate demands. In 1908 Nevada stood out as a rapidly growing but right-of-center party. The reform-sounding Wyoming party had also done relatively well.

The Mountain West as a whole in 1908–1909 looked unusually strong for Socialism when one considers voting patterns, party membership figures, and subscribers to the radical newspaper *Appeal to Reason* (see Appendix, Table 5). Controlling for population differences, in 1909 average party membership in the region was more than three times the national average, and the subscription rate to the newspaper was more than twice as high as the national average. Within the region, though, variation on the different measures, including voting returns, indicated differences in the extent of party success. In Nevada, a state with only 82,000 people, one of every 39 people voted for the party, one of every 54 persons had a subscription to the *Appeal,* and one of every 341 people belonged to the party. Wyoming had an even better membership ratio, but for some reason this was not accompanied by a high level of votes. New Mexico had a relatively large number of subscribers to the *Appeal,* but that did little for the party in terms of either voter or membership support. The party seemed not to be connecting with a potential base. In New Mexico there were 2,526 subscribers, 1,056 voters, and 175 members. In Nevada, with about a fourth New Mexico's population, there were around 1,500 subscribers, 2,000 voters, and 240 members (see Appendix, Tables 3, 4, and 5).

Making her own evaluation, the officious and ever-critical Ida Crouch Hazlett declared in the summer of 1909 that because of the lack of organizing work, the movement was practically at a standstill in Colorado, Utah, Idaho, and Wyoming. Hazlett wrote: "This alarming lethargy is so deep-seated that the State Secretaries complain that half the time they get neither responses nor reports from the Local Secretaries, and it is almost impossible to make it satisfactory for a speaker. Speakers say that they are met with countless complaints of party lack of interest, trifling locals, disputes, lack of attention to halls, advertising and entertainment of speakers, and that local members instead of realizing their own shortcomings say that the National Organization should take up the local work."[63] Hazlett, in setting the course of proper conduct for her readers, also made it clear that Socialists must not engage in fusion, compromise, or political trading. These, she noted "caused the death of the populist, union labor and greenback party, and it will kill any party, even the Socialist. No true Socialist will dally with the enemy, our path is clear and we must lean neither to the right or the left and any defaulters must be treated as spies and traitors to the working class."[64] Along with adhering to the fundamental principles of Socialism, without collusion or compromise, Hazlett told her comrades they must remember that "the Socialist movement is a labor movement or it is nothing."[65]

In the summer of 1909, however, the exclusive labor focus of the party nationally had been brought into question by a vote of the membership in favor of two amendments to the party constitution that had the effect of guaranteeing small farmers that their properties would not be confiscated under Socialism. The left denounced the move as a miserable vote-catching plank that, in effect, turned the Socialist party into a Populist party.[66] The issue had been hashed out at the party convention in 1908. Delegates shunned the idea that the party should make a special appeal to small farmers, but the vote of the membership reversed this decision. During the debate Joseph Cannon from Arizona had argued against the proposed changes, contending that "the public ownership of all machinery and land is one of the things for which the Socialist party is working" and that to exempt farmland was "nothing more nor less than political expediency."[67] Among the few places where the propositions failed to get a majority vote of party members were Cannon's Arizona and, ironically, farmer-rich New Mexico. In several parts of the Mountain West, Idaho as an example, party officials had already attempted to reach out to farmers and were making considerable progress.

On the labor front, much of the news in 1908–1909 concerned the IWW. Ideological differences with the IWW leadership over direct action tactics prompted the WFM in 1908 to withdraw from the organization it had helped create. Problems between the two organizations had escalated after the Goldfield strike, the failure of which the WFM blamed on hostility in the community toward the IWW unions. To some WFM leaders, the IWW had become a "millstone around the neck" of the WFM. At the 1908 convention IWW direct action radicals—among whom were a bunch of delegates from the West, known as the "Overalls Brigade," who had tramped their way to the convention on freight trains—forced out the De Leon Socialists and thus ended their flirtation with politics. With this ouster, the IWW came under the direction of Vincent St. John, onetime WFM and Socialist party leader. As general organizer from 1908 to 1915, St. John headed an organization that wanted little or nothing to do with politics and emphasized conducting the war on capitalism directly on the industrial front. In 1908 Bill Haywood, having fallen out with Charles Moyer, also shifted his allegiance from the WFM to the IWW and soon became one of its most celebrated spokespersons.

The IWW under St. John and Haywood turned its attention to militant industrial organization as it tried to organize the unorganized, many of whom had no interest in political action because they were transients who could not vote. The revolutionary doctrine articulated by St. John left little room for political action. As St. John saw it, "The only value that political activity has to the working class is from the standpoint of agitation and education—its educational merit consists solely in proving to the workers its utter inefficiency to curb the power of the ruling class and therefore forces the workers to rely on the organization of their class in the industries."[68] To its critics, including right-wing Socialists, the IWW, having dismissed political activity, became little more than an organization of anarchists, bums, and dynamiters.[69]

The debacle in Goldfield encouraged the IWW to look to the industrially developed East in recruiting members, the argument being that Eastern workers were less mobile and, thus, better material for stable organizations.[70] Yet, while the IWW did turn eastward for a time, the organization's presence was still felt in the West as it organized migratory farmworkers and loggers, adding recruits of all nationalities and races—including Asians—and skill levels, and engaged in free-speech fights in western cities.

By the end of the decade, the IWW was making itself known in various places around the region. In the spring of 1909 Wobblies reportedly picked up ten to forty new members a week in the city of Phoenix alone; there "the low-priced wage slave" reportedly was taking to the organization like "a duck to water."[71] In Globe, Arizona, at about the same time, a sheriff arrested three Wobblies bearing an IWW banner in celebration of May Day, ostensibly for their own protection. A member of the Press Committee of Globe Local, IWW, recalled:

> [W]e started with a procession, bearing a banner of the I.W.W., a beautiful blood-red banner of silk, having emblazoned upon it our three stars of hope: "Education, Organization, Agitation," when lo and behold, our patriotic sheriff immediately got busy and arrested the three banner bearers, fellow workers Bell, Oleson and Jardine, and threw them into jail without warrant, law, justice or reason. The sheriff attempted to excuse his action by stating that if he had allowed us to parade with a red banner that we would be attacked, rotten-egged and maybe manhandled, etc. Upon being asked why he did not arrest those who were going to start the riot, he did not answer and we have received no answer yet.[72]

The Wobblies had little good to say about anyone in Globe, including the workers. The latter, according to the Press Committee, had "degenerated into organic jobites" whose work had destroyed "their initiative, independence and thought." Their jobs had mentally castrated them, creating eunuchs who "leaned on Jesus."[73]

In 1909 the IWW began to attract attention nationally by conducting "free-speech" campaigns for the right to agitate and recruit members on city streets. Hoping to catch the attention of migrants who gathered in cities between jobs, agitators took to the streets to preach class struggle, blast the practices of labor agents, or "sharks," who recruited and commonly exploited those looking for work, and to seek new members. Having little access to workers at job sites, they had little choice but to wait until the workers came to town. Their free-speech movement had less to do with standing for the abstract principle of free speech than with ensuring that they could do their work in the one place where it was possible to do so and where it could be done with the greatest effectiveness.

The soapbox deliveries of IWW and other agitators upset business interests who, because of their political standing, had no difficulty getting cities to ban street speaking. In 1909 the city council of Missoula, Montana, responding to business concerns about IWW street agitation, was one of the first to make such activity illegal. The Wobblies responded by increasing their agitation, sending hundreds of members into the city to join those already there. Elizabeth Gurley Flynn, at the time just nineteen, was among the small group of IWW agitators originally sent to Missoula. She later noted: "We sent out a call to 'all foot-loose rebels to come at once to defend the Bill of Rights.' A steady stream of IWW members began to flock in by freight cars—on top, inside, and below. As soon as one speaker was arrested, another took his place."[74] Arrests began to pile up, overflowing the jails, and city officials found themselves hard-pressed to support the extra police and jail costs being generated by trying to enforce the law. The sheriff arrested Flynn and, after clubbing him, her husband, J. A. Jones, on the charge of "inciting to riot."[75]

The Montana Socialist party and its official organ, *The Montana Socialist*, and the Montana WFM locals, including the large Butte Miners' Union No. 1, joined the chorus of those condemning the arrests. Several Socialists went to jail to "uphold the natural right to talk," while others gave funds to support the demonstrators.[76] Frustrated about the costs, the city council repealed the speaking ban and freed the arrested Wobblies. Flynn and Jones reported from the scene in October 1909: "The I.W.W. in Missoula, Mont., has practically won its fight for free speech, as we are now speaking on the streets without being molested. We didn't appeal to justice but the taxpayers felt the pressure on their pocketbooks and capitulated. About 40 members have seen the inside of the Missoula jails during the last two weeks, giving this town a forcible example of the motto, 'An injury to one is an injury to all.'"[77] The IWW found the practice of nonresistance to arrest an effective direct action technique it did not hesitate to use again. After Missoula, the IWW went on to conduct around thirty free-speech campaigns, including a major one in Spokane in 1910.

CHAPTER TEN

Thunder Stealing, Respect, and Relevance

By THE SECOND DECADE of the twentieth century the image of the Socialist movement in the Mountain West, thanks in part to press coverage of violent labor wars and the emergence of the Wobblies, took on the character of wild-eyed, rough-and-ready, bent-on-destruction radicalism. This was not only a public view but a view held by many in the party. A study by Robert F. Hoxie of the University of Chicago, based on reports supplied by around 600 party workers in various states and localities in 1910, for example, led him to conclude that the Mountain West was home to a particularly intense form of Socialism. He found strong mine worker unions, a class-conscious Socialism, and a Socialist party that rested "very largely on the support of men with European blood in their veins."[1] Hoxie, though, also suggested that something other than nativity was involved by noting that the "special type of Socialist victory at mining centers in otherwise unaffected territory leads to the thought that there is something in the working environment of these miners which makes them think in different terms from those about them and gives them a different outlook on life and society."[2]

Whatever the reasons for the type of radicalism found in the Mountain West, right-wingers from the East who controlled the national party were often condescending toward the unschooled, rough-and-tumble, revolutionary-minded Mountain West radicals who showed up at national meetings.[3] They probably also grew impatient hearing about their western comrades' concerns, such as Oriental immigration. In this connection, W. L. O'Neill of Wyoming, at the National Socialist Congress in 1910, took up where other western Socialists had left off two years earlier in condemning Orientals for displacing white men as laborers and lowering the standard of living. O'Neill declared that white workers were caught up in a struggle for existence and, to make it sound like a less uniquely western problem, warned: "The orientals are coming in such hordes that they will not only flood the west but they will flood the east in a short time."[4]

Mountain West Socialists who participated in national party affairs tended to side with the minority left wing, although they were not of one mind on issues concerning political action versus direct action and relations with craft unions and the American Federation of Labor (AFL). What we often find in the Mountain West around the time Hoxie and others examined the movement are groups of Socialists who were trying to build viable party organizations by establishing strong ties to trade unions and, by veering sharply to the right, were attempting to cultivate voting support not only among the workers but among the middle class as well. Contrary to the inclinations of those on the left, many were also looking for victories on the local level, and in that pursuit they enjoyed a surprisingly large number of successes (see Chapter 11). Rather than being engaged in revolutionary pursuits, scores of Socialists were trying to resolve the multitude of practical problems emerging on a daily basis in trying to run a city. Others were trying to influence the development of state legislation or the writing of state constitutions. Their problem was not so much that they were not relevant but that the ideas they promoted, such as the initiative, referendum, and recall, when proven popular, were being stolen by others.

With this in mind, Guy E. Miller told his comrades from around the country in 1908 that the party must get involved in the issues of the day and that, by doing so, it could accomplish a great deal. By taking stands and entering campaigns, he argued, the party could bring about reforms such as reducing mining accidents and eliminating child labor. These things would happen, Miller argued, not because the party was likely to capture lots of offices but because the party, by campaigning and gathering votes, would continue to put the fear of God into the capitalist class: "Don't we know that the capitalists as we march steadily on are going to grant more and more of the demands of the Socialist Party? Let us agree definitely [on] what we want, for remember, what we want now we are soon going to get."[5]

Writing in 1910, A. Grant Miller noted that the problem facing Socialists in Nevada and elsewhere was not that they were out of touch: "In quite personal conversations it soon transpires that nearly every man you meet believes in Socialism to some degree."[6] Much more of a problem, as he saw it, was that potential supporters were reluctant to vote for Socialist candidates because they felt the candidates could not win and they would be wasting their votes.[7] Miller was also aware that major parties, especially Democrats, were hurting the cause by stealing Socialist ideas, although, he quickly noted, the "thunder stealers" for the capitalist parties "will first steal those things that harm the 'interests' the least, those things that they will be able to manipulate in such fashion as not to harm them at all."[8] With a bit of bravado he declared that while the capitalistic parties "might steal the socialist's thunder, they could not steal the socialist's lightning."[9]

Most often the thieves were Democrats, but Socialists also had to worry about Republican "insurgents" who had broken away from the "standpatters." According to a popular definition of the time, "A Standpatter is a Republican who has stopped and can't start; an Insurgent is a Republican who has started and can't stop." Since 1900, thunder stealers around the Mountain West had not only stolen Socialist ideas but had also enacted much of what the Socialists had demanded into law. Colorado lawmakers, for example, made a variety of Progressive reforms during the administration of Democrat John F. Shafroth, who the voters elected governor in 1908 and reelected in 1910. Among the major accomplishments during these years were changes providing for the initiative and referendum, primary elections, and regulations regarding registration and campaign finance. For working people, Progressives provided hour protections for children and women and people in dangerous occupations, more factory and coal mine inspections, and legislation to handle labor disputes.

Insurgent Republicans led by Edward P. Costigan generally supported the Shafroth program but hoped to make the state Republican party the major vehicle for Progressivism. On the other hand, as historian Carl Ubbelohde and colleagues once noted, conservative Democrats and standpatter Republicans saw the Colorado reformers as "potentially dangerous people." They "viewed with alarm or horror the suggestion that the state power be extended into so many aspects of man's activities. Such regulation and regimentation, they believed, would ultimately sap the individual's initiative; it was perilously close to, if not identical with, the plans and programs of Socialists." They also feared these measures would drive away eastern investors.[10]

Socialists could do little about having the ideas they were trying to promote become the property of other parties. There was little they could do but stay the course, to continue competing with ideas and hope for the best. With this in mind, right-wingers regained control of the Colorado Socialist party in 1910 and offered a long list of reforms. They declared that their party was "no longer a mere propaganda club" but a real political party eager to cope with short-term problems as well as long-term goals.[11] Thus, "As a political party it must meet the vital questions of the day as they arise. While it must never lose sight of the ultimate goal, the collective ownership of production and distribution, yet it must take a reasonable position on minor questions as they arise."[12] While becoming outwardly more respectable and relevant, the party was still cursed by conflict. One brawl involved a charge by one W. B. Dillon, who later surfaced in New Mexico, that A. H. Floaten was a do-nothing state secretary more interested in his salary than in anything else and who, moreover, had broken the rules by accepting the railway company's offer of a free pass. Veteran Socialist W. P. Collins came to Floaten's defense, calling Dillon a malicious liar who was making these charges out of spite because the secretary had refused to give him a fixed salary to go on a speaking tour. As far as Collins was concerned, the secretary had made the right decision because the last time the party sent Dillon out, he "stayed nearly one whole week in one place and got up a meeting, and only succeeded in raising about $20.00. On the trip he left the party in debt over $30.00."[13]

Around the same time, Wyoming Socialists also struggled with an emerging crop of thunder-stealing Progressive reformers. Joseph M. Carey was the major headache. Carey identified with the insurgent Republicans but ran for governor as a Democrat in 1910 after being passed over by the Republicans. The platform Carey insisted upon as part of his agreement with the Democrats called for a host of reforms the Socialists and the Populists before them had helped make popular—for example, direct democracy, a direct primary law, and an eight-hour day for women and children. During his 1910 campaign Carey declared, "It is high time, for her own protection, that Wyoming should take her stand with the Progressive movement that is everywhere seen and felt in the American Union."[14] Carey directed much of his wrath at the entrenched political machine run by old-guard Republican politicians, a small band of men who "have prostituted office and the property of the state for their personal, political and financial gain."[15]

Coming into the state in 1910 to help the struggling Socialist party, national organizer Anna Maley was outraged when the police in Kemmerer denied her the right to discuss Socialism at street meetings. In a letter of protest to a local paper she pointed out that "our party [the Socialist party] is the largest political party of legitimacy in the world, numbering from ten to fifteen millions of voters, and more than double this number of followers" and explained that her purpose in Kemmerer was "to discuss the possibilities for establishing free industrial institutions, fine free libraries, and those things that make for the physical, moral, and intellectual uplift of the people."[16] The irony was, "I was forbidden the right to do so by those who make no protest against the actual existence of the fourteen saloons and two brothels, which poison the lives of men and women alike, within the borders of your town."[17]

Maley later reported in an article based on her visit that the Wyoming party in 1910 was still drawing much of its support from coal mining towns such as Hanna, which had around 1,300 people. Most of the miners there belonged to the United Mine Workers (UMW) (at the time Paul Paulsen, a leading UMW official, was state secretary of the Socialist party). Finnish miners formed the backbone of both the union and Socialist party activity in Hanna. In 1910 Finns in Hanna, women as well as men, grouped together in a Socialist local of 275 people.[18] Hanna, though, was a hard-luck place. In 1908 an explosion in the same mine that had exploded in 1903 killed 59 men, including miners and several people who attempted to rescue them. Most of the victims were Finns. In response to this disaster and, indirectly, in part to the prodding of Socialists, the Wyoming legislature in 1909 approved measures advocated by the Socialists in regard to the state coal inspectors' office and the eight-hour day for coal miners.[19]

In addition to coal camps around the state, the party was very visible in Rock Springs, sponsoring lecture courses and holding conventions in Finn Hall. Ida Crouch Hazlett was among the popular speakers. On November 5, 1910, Eugene Debs spoke at the Union Opera House in Rock Springs under the auspices of the Socialist party there. In the November contest with Carey and Republican W. E. Mullen for governor in 1910, the Socialist candidate, W. W. Patterson, received 1,605 votes of 37,926 cast, about 4 percent of the total. Carey may well have drawn some Socialist votes.[20] The Socialists had continued to press for labor-related legislation to improve working conditions, and they continued to do relatively well in coal camps. In these places the party received considerable press coverage and had the tacit backing of the UMW.[21]

While Carey was leading Wyoming into an era of Progressive reform on the state level—although he was more focused on righting the political system than on bringing about economic reform—and thus was stealing at least some of the Socialists' thunder, similar developments were taking place in Idaho. There, as historian F. Ross Peterson has noted, "It did not matter whether the individual politician was a Republican, Democrat, or a Progressive, for the first fifteen years of the twentieth century, progressivism was key to Idaho political success."[22] There, too, national Socialist leaders like Anna Maley and Debs pitched in. In 1910 Debs lectured in various parts of Idaho. While working in the small town of Nampa, he heard a rumor that Frank Steunenberg's sons were out to get him should he venture into Boise. Debs shrugged it off, saying he was doing God's work and, besides, he was guarded by fifteen sturdy farmers.[23] The payoff for the party was only minimal success when it came to statewide offices—the party's candidate for governor received just over 5,000 votes in 1910, about 6 percent of the total and a slightly smaller percentage than in 1908—but was considerably more successful in electing local officials (see Chapter 11).[24]

In 1910 evidence of the Progressive tide could also be found in Montana, Utah, and Nevada, although the outpouring of reform in these places was a few years away. In Montana the party suffered not as much from thunder stealing as from internal bickering. It soon recovered, however, and began to show significant signs of life. Utah was able to minimize bickering and build a moderate respectability-seeking and office-seeking party organization. A similar organization was emerging in Nevada, a state where Socialists saw considerable promise.

Writing in October 1909, Montana Socialist leader James D. Graham sadly noted: "A year ago our dues paying membership was at the 1,500 mark and our vote was almost 10 per cent in the state. We were rapidly growing, broadening out and becoming a factor in politics to be reckoned with. The old party campaign could no longer ignore us. In municipal elections in different cities of the state our vote ran eighteen, twenty and twenty-four percent. . . . Today we have no organization, no state secretary, no party, no socialists filling the office of mayor in any city . . . all we have is a few socialist constables and one justice of the peace."[25] To Graham, the deteriorating state of affairs was a result not of a lack of interest in Socialism but of the success of corporate spies and disrupters within the Montana party. A more complete explanation would have given weight to an intense internal feud involving control of the party newspaper—a battle that resulted in a defeat for Graham and his ally Ida Crouch Hazlett, who was discharged as editor and later expelled from the party. After the battle, the state party in 1910 was left with only about 200 dues-paying members.

At this low point, Lewis J. Duncan came to the party's rescue. Duncan, called "the Eugene V. Debs of Montana," was born in St. Louis and raised in Quincy, Illinois, where he became a lawyer and, later, a Unitarian minister. He moved to Butte in 1902 to help organize the Unitarian Church in that city and soon became an active Socialist, ardently defending the WFM leaders on trial in

Idaho and offering anarchist Emma Goldman the use of his church to stage a rally after the city of Butte had declined to allow her to use the public halls. His political activities cost him his job. Writing to a friend in August 1910, Duncan said, "People with means and especially people with capitalistic minds, whether they have means or not, would not support my preaching."[26]

Duncan became secretary of the state Socialist party in the spring of 1910, a position that paid him seventy-five dollars a month. He went to work and in no time brought the membership up to a thousand people, scattered around in forty to fifty locals. He saw much of the party-building problem to be one of imposing greater control over the locals. He complained about the parochialism of the individual locals, especially the difficulty of bringing them into a coordinated statewide campaign. As he saw it, the comrades who ran the locals "do not have any appreciation of, or sense of loyalty to, the party as a world embracing organization and movement. They only see and feel the little local interests, and these loom up out of all proportion to their real value and significance."[27]

For Duncan, the nub of the problem was getting the locals to collect dues: "If our local secretaries were diligent about keeping after delinquent members, and getting the dues collected every month, things would be different; but to expect this of local secretaries is as utopian as anything that Moore or Bacon or Bellamy ever dreamed. About one third of our membership is in bad standing all the time."[28] He also complained about getting mixed up in "petty little fusses" in the locals and about incompetent local secretaries who could not keep their accounts straight.[29] Duncan, though, did an incredible job of getting the party in shape and leading it to some remarkable victories at the local level, including his own election as mayor of Butte in 1911.

The Utah party, although still cursed by conflict, was also building up an image of respectability. In 1910 the party was nearing its height and, despite some hard-nosed leaders and organizational rigidities, was an organization that offered a moderate reform program, enjoyed the support of large segments of organized labor, had an active press, and attracted support not only from workers but also from intellectuals, educators, clergymen, small businessmen, and farmers. It even had a brass band. The party was not filled with outcasts on the fringes of society and foreigners committed to violence and revolutionary change. Most Socialist party members were white, male, native-born Americans who held a variety of occupations, including professional positions. Close to half of the members were Mormons. The party, in short, appealed to a cross-section of Utahans.[30] The state party enjoyed the backing of the Federation of Labor. Utah unions supported the party through trough publications and propaganda leagues. The party, in turn, supported the labor movement in a variety of ways.

Socialists, for example, got involved in strike activities, helped raise funds for striking workers, and held labor rallies.[31]

In Nevada, meanwhile, A. Grant Miller and other Socialists were also hard at work trying to build a respectable reform-minded party that would appeal to the middle class as well as workers and farmers. Taking stock in December 1910, Miller claimed the level of the Socialist vote in Nevada was best indicated by the votes the party had received a month earlier for regent of the university. This amounted to about 16 percent of the vote, as compared with 8 percent of the vote for the same office in 1908.[32] Miller himself had been the Socialist candidate for the U.S. House of Representatives in 1910 and managed to attract 12 percent of the vote, probably taking enough votes away from the Democratic candidate to toss the election to the Republican opponent. Indeed, Democrats charged that Republicans had been behind Miller's candidacy for the very purpose of throwing the election to the Republican. Miller shrugged this off and suggested that the Socialist vote would have been even larger in 1910 had it not been for the departure of many Socialists from the state. Many of these were miners who went elsewhere looking for work. Others were railroad workers sympathetic to the party who, according to Miller, were fired by the Southern Pacific simply because they were Socialists.[33] Still, Miller felt, the party did fairly well in the absence of an extensive campaign—he made speeches in only three counties—and considering that the party had only thirteen locals in the entire state. In 1910 an enemy-to-be Republican, Tasker Oddie, defeated the Democrat Denver S. Dickerson for governor. The Socialist candidate, Henry F. Gegax, picked up 1,393 votes, cutting into Dickerson's total and contributing to his defeat.

The party's platform in 1910 covered the Socialist agenda by calling for woman suffrage, direct democracy, industrial compensation for injured workers, abolition of the death penalty, and provision of free textbooks and medical services for schoolchildren. With Nevada specifically in mind, it called for the abolition of the detested state police force, the strengthening of labor laws regarding wages, and laws protecting the secrecy of the ballot. The party also wanted to reduce the length of the residency requirement to ten days to accommodate the waves of itinerant workers coming into various parts of the state.[34]

Matters looked relatively positive for Nevada Socialists, but party members were nevertheless conscious of the overall unpopularity of being identified as Socialists. For example, in explaining why she did not want her name on the Executive Committee of the Equal Rights Cause in Nevada, A. A. Hibbard wrote to Professor Jeanne Wier in late January 1911: "I am a prominent worker in the Socialist party . . . as both of the old parties are afraid of the rapid growth of the Socialist party, it would lose the cause of suffrage many votes if it was seen that a Socialist was on that committee. The Socialist party is already pledged to equal suffrage however and anything I can do for the cause I will gladly do," although, she noted, only in a quiet way.[35] This view of Socialist unpopularity was shared by non-Socialist suffragists like Anne Martin, who pointed out that Socialist support for suffrage did not imply a reciprocal response from women.[36] One suffragist, writing in 1912, declared that a Socialist agitator brought in to speak on behalf of the movement had hurt the cause by focusing instead on the merits of Socialism.[37]

Socialists in New Mexico and Arizona also fought for a place within the tide of Progressive-era politics as they tried to influence a series of events in 1910 and 1911 involving statehood. The major task facing politicians in both states was coming up with a constitution that would be acceptable to Congress and President William Taft. The latter had issued a warning to constitution makers in both places not to put forth anything like what had been done in Oklahoma, with its call for the initiative, referendum, and recall. Socialist newspapers complained that the president had acted in an imperial fashion, as though he was speaking to the "peasants and workmen of his vast dominions."[38] The National Executive Committee of the Socialist party attempted to be of service by drafting a model constitution Taft would never live with and circulating it through the party organizations in the two states.

New Mexico Socialists tried, but they had little, if any, influence on the shaping of what turned out to be a relatively conservative document framed in Santa Fe by a predominately Republican convention. Only one of the 100 delegates chosen to the convention was identified in the press as a Socialist, and he ran as a Democrat. That delegate was Green B. Patterson from Chaves County. Born in Texas and a longtime member of the Farmers' Alliance, Patterson had been in Chaves County since 1906 as a county lecturer and organizer for the Farmers' Union. At the convention, he reportedly succeeded only in offending the other delegates. To get rid of him, someone at the convention, perhaps thinking of what had been done to Mother Jones in Utah, notified the Santa Fe health authorities that Patterson had been exposed to smallpox. As a consequence, he was placed in quarantine during the period of incubation. Whether he actually had been exposed is an open question.[39]

In another county, Luna, in southern New Mexico, it looked for a time as though Democrat John N. Upton, a prominent rancher, would have competition from Socialist S. Lindauer, a clothing merchant, for a seat as delegate to the constitutional convention. The Deming Local No. 11 of the Socialist party ran a newspaper advertisement that said Socialism "stands for social justice, for a direct primary law, for the initiative, referendum and recall, for an eight-hour work day, for an employers' liability law, for a bank guaranty law, for an inheritance and income tax law, for an Australian ballot law, for physical valuation of railroads, for municipal ownership of public utilities. If you prefer these measures vote for the Socialist candidate to the Constitutional Convention."[40] More than anything else, Lindauer—like other Socialists in the state—pushed for the initiative, referendum, and recall. After the Democrats had decided to also endorse these devices of direct democracy, Lindauer pulled out of the race, and the local Socialist party threw its support to Upton.

Noting all this, one editor charged, "The democrats[,] not being satisfied at adopting the socialists' platform, are pulling themselves into the saddle with their 'initiative and referendum' friends and are expecting to ride to victory."[41] The strategy was not a bad one—it had actually worked in Arizona—but it failed to give the Democrats the edge in New Mexico. The Socialists, though, had shown some strength. They helped Upton get elected. In the territory as a whole, they had their own tickets in ten of the twenty-six counties, and together their candidates polled around 1,600 votes; two years earlier they had polled only a little more than 1,000 in the entire territory. In dry-farming Roosevelt County along the eastern border, the party came within 101 votes of electing a delegate outright.[42]

During the convention, the thunder-stealing former Populist-Democrat Harvey B. Fergusson led a small group known as the "irreconcilables" because of their demand for a constitution built around Progressive principles. Fergusson was described by one of his fellow delegates as the "most eloquent and ablest defender of the rights of common people" among those assembled.[43] Another delegate described him as an average-sized, rather stooped sixty-year-old whose eyes had the "expression of a thinker with a soul" and who was determined to do what he could to protect the poor and neglected from the greedy, rich corporate interests that controlled the convention.[44]

While the convention was at work, the territorial Socialist party adopted this motion: "Resolved. That we use our voice and vote against ratifying the proposed constitution unless it contains the following provisions: First—The right of free speech, free press and the right of assemblage; second the initiative, the referendum, and the recall."[45] The convention, under the control of conservative Republicans, produced a document that President Taft found most satisfactory and that Fergusson and other Socialists urged New Mexico voters to reject. They were unsuccessful in this effort.

Much of the debate in New Mexico, as in Arizona, was over the value of the initiative, referendum, and recall. The New Mexico convention rejected outright the initiative and recall and provided for only a limited referendum, a far cry from what the Socialists demanded. Eight Democrats refused to sign the constitution. In addition to Fergusson, the list included Green B. Patterson and Upton. In the state's first election in 1911, Progressive forces rallied to elect Fergusson to Congress and Democrat William C. McDonald governor, although McDonald had to contend with a legislature controlled by old-guard Republicans. The Progressive Democrats, like the Socialists, were particularly strong in the "Little Texas" dry-farming counties—Chaves, Eddy, Quay, Roosevelt, and Curry—along the eastern border.[46] In 1911 the Socialists put up a state ticket and a ticket in several counties.[47] The *New Mexico Blue Book* for 1915 shows the Socialist candidate for governor in 1911 getting 1,787 votes and the Socialist candidate for secretary of state receiving 2,026 votes, the most of any Socialist candidate in the state in that election. Socialists on the whole, however, averaged only about 3 percent of the votes cast. New Mexico, meanwhile, enjoyed a Progressive burst in 1911–1912, passing some thunder-stealing reform legislation. With the prodding of John L. Lewis, representing the AFL, the state may have moved to avoid future labor strife by enacting measures relating to mine inspection, blacklisting, and regulation of hours. These measures established New Mexico as a mildly pro-union state.[48]

The radical forces in Arizona had a considerably greater impact on the development of the state constitution, although they violated party norms by participating in a new political organization. On July 11, 1910, several Socialists and labor officials from around the territory attended a meeting in Phoenix called by W. E. Stewart, secretary of the Bisbee Miners' Union, to draw up a platform of general provisions they wished to see in the new state constitution. Delegates elected J. C. Provost, a Socialist who had been active with the Colorado party, chair of the convention. Among the twenty-seven items recommended for inclusion in the new constitution were the initiative, referendum, and recall (the very first item), woman suffrage, the right of the state to engage in industrial pursuits, protections against labor injunctions, and an employer liability law.[49] Many of these objectives had, according to a prominent Socialist in attendance, been taken from the immediate demands of the Socialist national platform.[50] On the second day of their meeting the delegates decided to form a Labor party that would not only pursue these demands but would attempt to get its own members elected to the constitutional convention.

Progressive Democrats, led by George W.P. Hunt, were frightened by the prospect of this competition for delegate seats. They had been depending on the labor vote. To keep workers onboard, they agreed to support the Laborites' demands in exchange for the latters' support of the Progressive Democratic ticket. With this support, the Progressive Democrats won control of the constitutional convention and went on to formulate one of the nation's most progressive state constitutions, although it failed to provide for some of the reforms suggested by the Labor party, with woman suffrage a prominent example.[51] As a member of the territorial legislature, Hunt had acquired a pro-labor image, for example, introducing legislation to end the presence of armed bodies of Pinkerton men and the practice of blacklisting. He also was noted for his advocacy of Progressive reforms, particularly the initiative, referendum, and recall. Hunt's image as "the father of the Initiative and Referendum in Arizona" was looked upon by his supporters as putting him in a good position to become governor.[52]

In 1911 WFM executives expressed their pride in having had an impact on the Arizona constitution. The WFM had responded to the Labor party's request for help during the campaign by donating $1,000 and had joined in the campaign for "direct legislation popular government." It was proud to report: "The net result of our efforts is a constitution more liberal and progressive than the constitution of any other state in the Union."[53] The emergence of the Labor party in Arizona, however, almost destroyed the state Socialist party, from which it drew much of its leadership and support.[54] In the fall of 1910 a leading Arizona Socialist complained: "Two years ago we had between two and three thousand votes in Arizona. I doubt if we have more than two and three hundred this year, so well have these traitors done their work."[55] In 1910, shortly before the Labor party emerged, the Arizona Socialist party had close to 600 dues-paying members scattered across the territory in twenty locals. Defections to the Laborites reduced the Socialist party membership to fewer than 100 and the number of locals down to three. Six locals were eventually expelled from the Socialist party for participating in the creation of the rival political organization.[56]

Joseph D. Cannon, organizer and executive board member of the WFM and the Arizona Socialist party's nominee for Congress in 1906 and 1908, was a driving force behind the Labor party and took much of the blame from his comrades for the havoc it caused the Socialists. In defense of his actions, Cannon argued that the last territorial legislature had taken the Socialists out of the race for delegates to the constitutional convention by raising the cost of nominating candidates beyond the level the party could afford. This forced party members who wanted to influence the constitution to use other means.[57] Cannon also took pride in helping to create what he felt was "the best state constitution in any of the states," particularly because of its commitment to direct democracy, although he thought it fell short of the ideal Socialist constitution.[58] Arizona Socialist leaders, on the other hand, were bitter about "the betrayal of the party by one who had been its most trusted and honored exponent for years," and, while conceding that the Labor party's bluff may have indirectly influenced the new constitution, they argued that the years of agitation by the local Socialist party and the circulation of the model constitution prepared by the national Socialist party also indirectly impacted that document.[59]

Mainstream Socialists gave considerable credit to the sentiment stirred up by the "wide circulation of a constitution made by Morris Hillquit," although the extent to which lawmakers were exposed to and influenced by the Socialist model is unclear.[60] We do know that members of the Labor party actively lobbied the delegates at the constitutional convention. Radicals also took it upon themselves to give the delegates various types of reading material. Socialist and WFM member Ernest Lebel (aka "Liebel" and "St. Lebel") reported: "We sent copies of the Appeal [to Reason] to the delegates at the constitutional convention. It was quite a spectacle from the galleries watching these fifty-two men absorbing the news that the Socialist vote had doubled in the United States in two years, and in some instances quadrupled, and increased 1,000 percent."[61] Lebel noted that the editor of the local Republican newspaper mentioned the incident, calling the *Appeal* a "journal of discontent [and] extreme radicalism which falls hardly short of anarchy."[62] He added that the Republican newspapers were going to try to defeat the constitution, but "we Socialists are ready to fight for its acceptance and then use the 'direct legislation' powers to get everything else we want."[63]

In spite of all the turmoil caused by the Labor party episode, by November 1911 the party had grown back to 500 members in twenty-seven locals. It nominated a full slate of candidates, headed by P. W. Galentine, a miner from Globe, as its candidate for governor in the state's first election that month. Galentine declared that "our constitution represents the political desires of a majority of the people of Arizona, who have been educated by the continuous propaganda of the Socialist party."[64] He was particularly proud of the direct democracy provision. Socialist papers suggested that he would do well because "the workers of Arizona are as progressive in their ideas of government as those of any state in the union."[65] The party invited Mayor Duncan of Butte to campaign on behalf of the party, although there is no record that he did so. Galentine received 1,247 votes, far behind Hunt and his Republican opponent, Judge Edward Wells. The latter, identified in newspapers as the candidate of the Phelps-Dodge Company, had agreed to run to prevent the state from being captured by Socialists.[66] During the campaign Republican editors warned: "Vote for Judge Wells, and if he is elected governor, we will have a sane, sound, safe, and sensible administration of state affairs; an administration void of wildeyed 'isms,' and other bunc schemes that are used by demagogues solely to catch the sucker vote. Don't allow your-selves to be buncoed into supporting 'isms,' but keep on the right side by casting your vote for Ed. W. Wells for governor of our new state."[67] Some WFM locals endorsed the Democratic party in 1911, with George W.P. Hunt at its head, much to the disgust of the more radical WFM leaders.[68] During the campaign, Democrats urged leaders of left-leaning unions to support Hunt. Writing to the head of the Jerome Miners' Union, one argued, "Would George W.P. Hunt be any better [a] man if he was a socialist? I claim he would not."[69]

After the election Hunt received congratulations from Lebel. He wrote from New York "hurrah for Arizona" and said he had known all along that Hunt would win, although he and others associated with the Labor party could not claim any credit for his election: "All we did was to tell the people the TRUTH about the situation and to voice our faith in the integrity of your motives."[70] Lebel continued: "While I have not always thought you quite clear on the socio-economic phases of our present political evolution I have still felt that at heart you were and are FOR THE PEOPLE ALL THE TIME."[71] Lebel said he was a Socialist, although not a wild-eyed revolutionary one, who felt Hunt was about to usher in a new era on the road toward a cooperative commonwealth, a "peaceful culmi-nation of this inevitable change from privately owned means of production for PROFIT to publicly owned means of production for USE."[72] He ended by calling on Hunt to push for the Labor party reforms that had not yet been enacted: "These measures MUST become laws before Arizona is REALLY free from the capitalistic tyranny which has reduced States like Pennsylvania to a condition worse than slavery."[73] In control of the new state after 1911, the Progressive Democrats, under Hunt's leadership, worked to live up to such high expectations by pushing through a wide variety of thunder-stealing changes. Throughout his career as governor, Hunt drew considerable support from the same groups the Socialists were trying to attract.[74]

CHAPTER ELEVEN

Going Local

Water and Sewer Socialism

IN 1911 THE MUNICIPAL PLATFORM of the Socialist party in Great Falls, Montana, promised municipal workers an eight-hour day at union scale, free water for widows making a living doing laundry work, free legal advice from the city attorney to members of the working class, and municipal ownership of the electric power, gas, and street railway companies. Also included in the platform was a call for "a municipal owned and controlled ice plant, coal yard, loan office, hospital, dance hall, sanitary department, and free employment office."[1] A year later the Socialist party in Prescott, Arizona, sought votes in the upcoming city elections with a similar program when it came to municipal ownership and also called for such steps as more economical administration of the city's finances (the city was deep in debt), greater equalization of taxation and water rates, an ordinance closing down all saloons in the city on Sundays, and greater enforcement of laws against prostitution.[2] As was typical of Socialist parties around the country at the time, the party also called for the initiative, referendum, and recall—the popular package of direct democracy that Socialists claimed as their own. In pressing their credentials, Prescott Socialists made a point of noting that "the Socialist Party is the largest political organization in the world. It is international in scope. The International Socialist Party has locals and branches in every country in the world. Affiliated with the locals and branches are more than thirty million men and women working heart and soul together toward the realization of an ideal."[3]

Socialists often ran for office simply to educate the voters, not expecting to win. In running for office on the local level, however, to the surprise of nearly everyone they sometimes won. On the aggregate level, the number of surprises is greater than one might imagine: the Socialist party secured dozens of victories in local contests throughout the Mountain West from 1910 to 1912, particularly in the spring of 1911.[4]

As noted in regard to Anaconda, Montana (see Chapter 5), Socialist parties had enjoyed isolated local victories prior to this time, but municipal triumphs became more common toward the end of the first decade of the twentieth century, when the party's strength was reaching its peak. Victories—most evident in Colorado, Utah, Idaho, and Montana—sometimes came by riding a protest vote against corruption in local government and incompetent local administration.

Colorado Socialists enjoyed a particularly pleasing triumph in Victor, the scene of fierce fighting between the Western Federation of Miners and mine owners in the years 1904–1908, by capturing the office of mayor and four other offices in the spring of 1911. The mayor, J. B. Bitterly, took pride in making "sound business decisions" to get the city of around 4,000 people out from under a debt of more than $500,000. In response to citizen complaints about the weight of coal and other commodities, he installed a municipal scale to ensure that people would get the correct weight on their purchases. The mayor also improved sanitary conditions in the city, thereby reducing the amount of sickness, and he would have pursued other reforms had it not been for a lack of funds.[5]

Colorado Socialists also won local offices in Coal Creek in 1910–1911 and a number of local offices, including that of mayor, in Grand Junction in 1909. In regard to the latter, a Socialist newspaper in 1912 reported that the small town of Grand Junction was one of the richest towns on the Western Slope and that some time ago it had become a Socialist town "from Mayor to Dog catcher" and been so successful that the people had continued to elect Socialists to office. The paper further reported that the city "expects to own and operate the first municipal coal mine in the United States. . . . It already owns and operates one of the largest and most successful water systems in the inter-mountain west." The city was also thinking about taking over "the now privately owned electric light, gas, and ice plant" and street railway.[6]

In 1911 Socialists in Utah captured thirty-three offices in ten communities around the state.[7] That level of accomplishment caught the eye of national party activists.[8] One of those elected was Henry W. Lawrence, retired merchant, to the city commission in Salt Lake City. According to party sources, the party also held offices in Bingham, Cedar City, Eureka, Mammoth, Monroe, Murray, and Tintic. In Murray and some other localities the full Socialist ticket had been elected in the spring of 1911. The newly elected Socialist officials were so numerous that they began thinking about forming an association to keep in touch and keep informed.

Socialists, as historians John McCormick and John Sillito have demonstrated, were particularly well entrenched in Eureka, a mining town of around 3,500 people southwest of Salt Lake City. Voters there elected Socialist Andrew Mitchell, a non-practicing Mormon carpenter, mayor in 1907 and again in 1911.[9] The party began offering candidates for local office in 1903 and steadily built up its percentage of the vote, moving up to second just behind the Republicans in 1905, before scoring its first success in 1907. The party had control of the five-member city council in the years 1912–1914. Two of the Socialist members were Mormon miners, a rare combination. Examination of the local membership book of 300 names also reveals that most members were married males and had skilled or semiskilled jobs, mostly as miners. The range of occupations, though, was diverse; among the party's ranks were a Baptist minister, a first-grade teacher, and the owner of a local pool hall. About 40 percent of the members were Mormons and about 60 percent were native-born, the others coming mostly from Britain, Western Europe, or Scandinavia. Once in office, as McCormick and Sillito described, the Socialists set out to "provide good, clean, capable administration of city affairs" and, in the process, to show that there was no merit to the view "of socialists as either dangerous troublemakers seeking to pit one class against another or irresponsible, impractical dreamers who, though, perhaps well meaning, had little patience or ability to deal with the problems of the real world."[10]

Local Socialist officials in Eureka spent the bulk of their time taking up less-than-revolutionary matters involving the running of the city. They focused on issues involving public health and safety, constructing a sewer system, establishing municipal collection of garbage, paving roads—and paying union wage for all city work. They also ventured into the moral realm by strictly enforcing city ordinances banning the sale of liquor on Sundays and prohibiting gambling.[11] The national party proudly announced these accomplishments, plus the fact that with the Socialists in charge, "Gunmen were refused to capitalists during strike trouble and the first Pinkerton detective caught in town was arrested on the charge of carrying concealed weapons and fined $75."[12]

Idaho Socialists, with the help of national organizers like Anna Maley, joined their colleagues from around the region in the quest for local office. In Nampa, Maley's visit in July 1910 led to the creation of a local of 16 people, 14 men and 2 women. After a large rally the following February, the party could count 180 members and decided to nominate a candidate (one Jesse Gardner, a photographer) for mayor and several city council candidates. The ticket was not well received by the local paper, which stressed what it depicted as a strong link between the Socialist party and the dangerous Industrial Workers of the World (IWW).[13]

The party fell short, though, getting just 40 percent of the vote. Two years later it was able to elect one of its members to the city council.[14] In the spring of 1911 the Socialists managed to win offices in several Idaho towns—Orifino, Reubens, and Stites among them.

The greatest triumph, though, came on April 4, 1911, when Socialists took control of Coeur d'Alene City in Kootenai County. On that date voters chose Socialist Dr. John T. Wood mayor and four Socialists for the city council. They also elected a Socialist police judge, city clerk, engineer, and treasurer.[15] With the mayor voting in the case of a tie, the Socialists had a 5-4 majority in the council. Wood, an energetic campaigner, received 43 percent of the vote, coming in ahead of his two opponents. In the only two-way matchup, the Socialist candidate for city treasurer defeated the pro-business Citizens' party candidate 799 to 725. The Socialist party had around 200 members in the city.

During the campaign the Socialists had promised an equitable distribution of city services to various parts of the city and solutions to the problems of a rapidly growing area—Coeur d'Alene had grown from a small village of fewer than 500 people in 1900 to a crowded town of more than 7,000 in 1910—particularly in regard to sewage disposal, garbage collection, and water quality. Wood was highly regarded even by an opposition paper, the *Coeur d'Alene Evening Press*. The newspaper's editor acknowledged that Wood was "one of the city's most estimable men" and that his platform was not all that radical: "a plea is made for union day labor, adequate provision for public health and safety, and the assurance of a businesslike administration."[16] The editor continued, "It is not the harm that Dr. Wood as a mayor might do if elected, as he would doubtless make a capable executive; it is not the ideas advanced in his platform, as they are for the most part excellent. But the danger consists in the inference that will certainly be drawn by the prospective citizens at a distance."[17] The editor dreaded "the unenviable advertising the city will get throughout the country as a socialist stronghold. Property owners and business men cannot afford the notoriety."[18]

Shortly after the Socialist victory—one that surprised everyone, including the Socialist candidates—Anna Maley arrived in town. She told a gathering of party members that the Socialist city administration could accomplish much in terms of reform, just as the Socialist administration had done in Milwaukee, Wisconsin, but that the real revolutionary work awaited the party's takeover of the state and nation, a development she expected in 1916 or 1920 if present trends continued.[19] Maley also noted that there were likely to be "misunderstandings" between the local Socialist organization and the newly elected Socialist officials:

> The socialist organization may not always promptly perceive the practical
> difficulties with which the elected candidates must cope. These officials,
> on the other hand, will not appreciate the anxiety of those who have given
> years of bitter struggle to the building of our organization even to its present
> imperfect stage. They will know that not only in Coeur d'Alene, but all over
> the world, the socialists will jealously watch their experiment and that we
> will jubilate with them as their policies show forth the fidelity to the splendid
> slogan of our class, "Workers of the world unite! You have only your chains
> to lose; you have a world to gain!"[20]

The Coeur d'Alene Socialist party went to considerable lengths to hold its elected officials accountable. Each candidate had taken a pre-election vow to remain true to the party's platform should he secure election. To help ensure that this pledge was honored, each candidate was also required to file a signed resignation from office with the party secretary that would be submitted if party members, by majority vote, decided the pledge had been broken.[21] Shortly after the election, the local party declared it would make a decision on all important matters coming before the city council by majority vote, with each party member having one vote. The Socialist mayor and councilmen were, according to party leaders, bound by these decisions; should they vote otherwise, they faced removal from office. Several members of the Socialist local believed they would personally have an active role in running the city. They felt this was only right because the people, through the election, had decided to experiment with a Socialist government and that the party, rather than the mayor, would be held responsible by the voters for whatever happened or failed to happen.[22]

Wood, however, rejected party members' efforts to dictate policy, saying he was a servant of the people, not of a particular party, and that the party was no more than one source of advice. Following a dispute over the selection of the police chief, the local voted to submit Wood's resignation through one of the Socialist city council members, but the Socialists on the council split two to two over accepting the resignation and non-Socialists on the council uniformly supported Wood's retention. Wood declared that he was "proud of being a socialist" but would not resign from office. The Socialist local responded by requesting that Wood appear "before a meeting of the local to 'show cause why he should not be expelled.'" He was charged with violation of both the state and national constitutions of the Socialist party. Specific infractions in the indictment against Wood were the refusal to comply with priorities voted by the local and an attempt to organize a new Socialist branch made up of his supporters. Wood was expelled from Coeur d'Alene's Socialist party on July 28, 1911, by a unanimous committee vote. He completed his two-year term, however, pushing for reform measures along with the four Socialist city council members.[23]

In Montana in 1911, Socialist parties enjoyed some success in local elections in Basin, Helena, Lewistown, and Miles City, but the greatest victory in the state and, indeed, in the region was in Butte. On April 3, 1911, Lewis J. Duncan became mayor. Elected along with Duncan were several other city officials, a municipal triumph heralded by Socialists as a case in which the workers of Butte "put men of their own kind into office."[24] Of the eight Socialists elected, five were miners. Duncan listed his occupation as "Agitator." The successful candidates were inspired in part by the Socialists' control of Milwaukee, Wisconsin, a year earlier. They borrowed from their Milwaukee comrades a municipal program built around the promise of honest and efficient local government and improved living conditions, all of which were badly needed in this city of 40,000. The hard core of the Socialist vote came from working-class neighborhoods.[25]

Duncan won with a plurality of the votes, slipping ahead of the Democratic and Republican candidates. He credited his victory to reaction against antilabor laws passed by the state legislature the previous winter—laws, he felt, that opened the eyes of the laboring class to the true nature of the major parties, with the result that the Socialist candidates in Butte received nearly unanimous support from organized labor.[26] Duncan confided to a fellow believer: "It was the labor vote that carried us into power this time and it can do it every time if we can retain the confidence of the workers. This situation is going to result in a clear class alignment in future political fights—organized labor with the socialists on one side and the Amalgamated with the old political machines on the other side."[27]

Butte's Irish, fundamentally a working-class group, were not onboard as Socialists, in part because of the stand of the Catholic Church. At the time, they constituted about one-fourth of the population but only about 10 percent of the members of the English-speaking Socialist local in Butte.[28] In the 1911 municipal election, however, many apparently broke with the Democratic party and swung to Duncan.[29] An important component of that support was that of the Butte Miners' Union. Duncan and others also gave credit for their victory to "some of the old time reds of Butte who" had initiated and distributed a propaganda sheet throughout the city on his behalf.[30] Duncan also deserves part of the credit for the victory because, as state secretary of the Socialist party, he had built up the strength of the party in Butte, making it a much more effective campaign vehicle.

In explaining the outcome, the mainstream press gave much emphasis to the low status of Butte's city government—the city, financially bankrupt and facing major health and sanitation problems at election time, had not been well run and had been plagued by graft and corruption under both Republican and Democratic administrations. Reviewing conditions in Butte, the non-Socialist *Montana Lookout* concluded, "The tremendous majority given to the candidates of the Socialist ticket signified Butte's return to civic consciousness, rather than Butte's conversion to Socialist principles."[31] As the paper saw it, the respectable people of the city had simply risen up in rebellion and were willing to give the Socialists a try. Mary Stevens Carroll, a writer growing up in Butte at the time, also saw the Socialists as coming to power on the failure of previous administrations—a failure evidenced in the refusal of banks to cash city warrants and in a variety of health and sanitation problems.[32]

The Socialist press, as might be expected, offered a more positive view of Duncan's victory: "The Socialist victory last spring was by no means the result of the sudden rising of public indignation in revolt against rotten politics that the capitalistic newspapers would like to have it appear. It was the legitimate outcome of a long, hard, forceful, never-ceasing campaign to bring the working class of Butte to a class consciousness that would make them see that their interests are the interests and purposes of the Socialist party."[33] Socialist intellectuals and activists seized upon the victory to illustrate that hard work and suffering will be rewarded and that, in the end, the cause will win out. Soon after the election one observer wrote in the *International Socialist Review*: "For years persecution has been the lot of the radicals in the mines of Butte. For them this victory is doubly sweet. Taught by experience that it is but folly to expect appreciation from the workers for their efforts, they have labored on and trusted to the future. They knew the time must come when conditions would force the workers to pay heed. It has come sooner than expected. The laws of evolution have been silently, but none the less surely at work."[34] A few months later another national organizer wrote: "In 1905 I spoke to the Socialist local of Butte. It contained about forty members and was not considered seriously by the powers that were. In 1912 I had the pleasure of meeting the Socialist mayor, councilmen and other municipal officials. May we dare to conclude that the progress of [the] working class in Butte is an indication of its general development throughout the country?"[35]

Not all Montana Socialists, though, were particularly pleased by Duncan's success (he had some enemies within the party) or about the general idea of putting resources into efforts to secure local offices. An editorial in the *Montana News* pointed out that municipalities in Montana lacked home rule, and, as a consequence, local officials could not do much: "If the Socialists elected every city official in Montana from Mayor to dog pelter, these officials could do very little in carrying out the Socialist program, except giving a good administration and municipalizing the water system, and the majority of Montana cities already own their own water system."[36] As the editor saw it, for Socialists in city councils to do much to change the social system, state laws would have to be changed. For this reason, if no other, it made greater sense to "concentrate our efforts to electing men to the legislature from a number of counties instead of attempting to capture a few cities."[37] Other Socialists were concerned about "water and sewer" Socialism at the local level taking the focus off revolutionary goals and miring the party in trivia.

Mayor-elect Duncan, aware of this concern, informed readers of the left-wing *International Socialist Review*: "The Butte Socialists are all revolutionists; not mere reformers or parlor Socialists. We realize fully that, under capitalism and capitalistic laws, little more can be accomplished than superficial reforms. But our realization of that fact does not mean we are content to stop at that point. We are as determinedly revolutionary in office as we were before getting political power, and we hold mere political success very cheaply."[38] At the same time, however, Duncan contended that it was important to show the world that his Socialist administration could successfully confront the "practical problems of city administration" and "that working men can run a city government as well as 'business' men."[39] Privately, he wrote to a supporter: "I think you must realize that at the present time the eyes of the comrades throughout Montana and indeed throughout the United States are centered upon this administration. We simply got to make good."[40] What Duncan eventually offered Butte residents was a scaled-down version of the model employed by the Socialists in Milwaukee.[41] Building upon a moderate program that he hoped would appeal to the middle class as well as the working class, Duncan planned to carry the fight for Socialism to the state level.[42]

When it came time to make appointments, Duncan was careful to clear his choices with members of the city's Socialist party, a problem that plagued the Socialist administration in Coeur d'Alene. Writing to a party member in that city on May 12, 1911, Duncan noted: "In Butte every appointee was brought to the consideration of the city central committee before the nominations were made to the city council and I made no recommendations to the city in the matter of appointive officers until my nominees had been approved by the comrades; this seemed not only just to the party but also a wise tactic to prevent such wrangles as are bound to follow upon political success in a party that has not been disciplined to political responsibilities."[43] Duncan, however, like Mayor Wood, later differed with party officials over some of his appointees and refused to allow party officials or a vote of the party membership to dictate his appointments. He wound up facing a rebellion within his own Socialist local, which, having been captured by the IWW, threatened to recall him and the five Socialist aldermen from office—something that might have happened had not the state party stepped in.

Not surprisingly, Duncan provoked the determined opposition of mining company officials. The 1911 victory, as historian David M. Emmons has noted, undoubtedly increased Amalgamated's "fear that the principles of capitalism were not universally cherished in Butte."[44] Duncan showed his stripes by attempting to extend the city's boundaries to include Amalgamated's mines, a move that would have led to increased taxes on the company and brought an end to an arrangement whereby the sheriff empowered the company's mine guards by making them deputy sheriffs.[45] With the council controlled by members from the old parties, the attack on the company fizzled out. Duncan, meanwhile, concentrated on reducing the city's debt, eliminating graft, improving the streets, enforcing liquor laws, and improving sanitary conditions in red-light districts.[46] In regard to prostitution, word spread that Duncan was promoting a plan that would make prostitutes wear a uniform when they appeared on the streets so they could be identified by others as fallen women; this, Duncan declared, was a false rumor circulated to discredit him.

As a sign of voter approval, the Socialists did well in the April 1912 Butte municipal elections, gaining one alderman against a fusion ticket of Democrats and Republicans. According to the radical press, the Socialists did well even though "the Anaconda Copper Mining company used all its power against the Socialists as also did the church and the red-light saloon interests."[47] In March, Amalgamated had fired as many Socialist miners and smelter workers as it could, hoping to drive them out of town before the election. In the end, it got rid of 500 Socialists, mostly Finns, for simply being Socialists. The company-dominated union did not even protest the firings. Mayor Duncan, however, kept many of the fired miners in Butte through the 1912 elections by finding them jobs on city street-cleaning crews.[48] Still, by holding the Socialist gains to one alderman,

Duncan's opponents deprived him of a council on which the Socialists were in the majority. Moreover, as political scientist Jerry Calvert has noted, "[T]he mining companies had sent workers a clear message that it was risky to openly support the Socialist Party."[49]

Mary Stevens Carroll remembered Duncan as a well-educated, "courtly dignified white-haired gentleman of the old school" who had a relatively peaceful and effective first term in office.[50] His election, however, did stir things up a bit by attracting radicals to the city. The mayor helped draw class lines and advance Socialism among the people by bringing in a steady stream of Socialist speakers from all over the country and circulating an unusually large amount of Socialist literature throughout the city. The editor of the *International Socialist Review* wrote in May 1913, "We in this office can testify that during the last two years Butte has circulated more scientific Socialist books in proportion to its population than any other city in the United States. Industrialist speakers from all over the country have found a hearty welcome and big audience in Butte."[51] On June 13, 1911, the thirty-third anniversary of the Butte Miners' Union, the city had a monster parade of around 10,000 people, 6,000 of whom were members of the Miners' Union. Big Bill Haywood was the honored guest and gave a rousing speech at an outdoor rally.[52]

Duncan generally earned high marks from non-Socialists as well as Socialists for cleaning up the town and helping lift it out of bankruptcy.[53] The left-wing *Inter-Mountain Worker*, in 1913, proudly reported: "The socialist administration of Butte, Montana, has issued a compiled statement showing that this year $300,000 worth of public work is being done, or is contracted for. Sidewalks are being built in the working class districts, where before people traveled in the mud, and sewage [is being] provided for the working class section. This work is all being done under the direction of the Socialist city engineer and by home labor. Three years ago Butte was a bankrupt city. Today its credit is as good as any city in the nation."[54] As a sign of public approval, in the spring of 1913 Duncan won reelection, securing a majority of the votes over a "citizens" ticket backed by the two major parties. Along with his victory came a victory for several other Socialist candidates.

While some municipal triumphs did turn sour, with Duncan's a case in point (see Chapter 13), in 1910–1912 Socialists in the area could and did take considerable pride in what they had accomplished. They had to overcome an image of radicalism that made local boosters nervous about the consequences of their winning and the efforts of Democrats and Republicans, sometimes combined under some other party label such as the Citizens' or Taxpayers' party, to defeat them. Yet, often by playing off the obvious failures of Democratic or Republican regimes, Socialists came to power with a modest reform-minded program tailored to local conditions that made them look considerably less than revolutionary in intent. They commonly stood for municipal ownership of utilities; improved roads, water, and sewer systems; more honest, economical, and efficient government; and more morally uplifting policies involving drinking, gambling, and prostitution. In emphasizing these elements of "good local government," they sounded much like the Populists.

The prostitution problem seems to have been unusually severe in the Mountain West, one that caught the eye of Socialists throughout the region. In Salt Lake City, Utah, Socialists referred with considerable disgust to the crowding of prostitutes into a restricted district called the "stockade" located near the railroad yards in the ugliest part of town.[55] In Prescott, Arizona, Socialists labeled a similar district the "City of the Dead." In their call for controlling the problem, party leaders made it clear to voters:

> We have no word of condemnation for the women who have been driven by economic causes inseparable from our modern civilization to seek their bread in the oldest profession in the world. Even you, in your support of a system of society which placed them there[,] are more to blame than they. . . . Socialists will tell you that no man or woman is naturally bad or vicious except as environment, false teaching or no-teaching has made them so. Socialists would defy you to find a single woman in your City of the Dead who is there because she loves that life. She is there, because the hand of modern civilization, most uncivilized, has crushed her to that place, or because someone makes a profit from her shame. Her landlord who rents the house in which she dwells, the vendor of liquor, everyone with whom she comes in contact, takes their profits from her. You will not end the traffic by an attack upon the woman. Nationally you will not be able to end the traffic until at least every working woman may have a fair day's wage for a fair day's work.[56]

Socialists in power often sought to do what they could to control the problem, although, as in Duncan's case, they ran the risk of radicals seeing them as too severe in their proposed remedies.

The more practical-minded Socialists had no difficulty with the party entering municipal elections and focusing on everyday problems of concern to people in a particular locality, although, as in Montana, some party officials wondered if scarce resources might be better used elsewhere. Had they spent less time on municipal issues and more time on the problems of the industrial workforce, they may have done much better with immigrant workers.[57] Revolutionary Socialists worried about the reform emphasis of municipal Socialism and sneered at the reformers for offering little more than "sewer Socialism." Socialists on the right, however, saw control over local government as valuable in providing an opportunity for the party to show the electorate that Socialists could be trusted and could do a good job of governing. Taking over cities also gave the party a chance to educate citizens on Socialist principles, build a showcase for Socialism, and, on a more practical level, secure a source of employment for party members and supporters. For the more practical-minded, public jobs also came in very handy as a way of keeping supporters such as unemployed miners around so they could vote in the next election. With success at the local level, however, as illustrated in Idaho and Montana, came the problem of making sure successful candidates stayed loyal to the party and its campaign pledges—a problem that also occasionally popped up in relations between the party organization and state legislators.

In the historical context, the triumph of Socialists in local elections in 1910–1912 demonstrated that the Socialist party could be relied upon to provide responsible public servants who could be trusted to do the job of running the government in an orderly and efficient manner. This accomplishment helped set the stage for the party's great surge in the November 1912 general elections.

CHAPTER TWELVE

The Rising and Falling Tide

Condition of the Parties

Fʀᴏᴍ 1910 ᴛᴏ 1912, the fortunes of the Socialist party on the national level took a sudden leap forward. Membership swelled from 58,000 to 113,000 during the period, and the party reached what turned out to be its peak with the electorate in 1912 when Eugene Debs polled more than 900,000 votes, about 6 percent of the votes cast, for the presidential office. By 1912 the party could also boast that it had sent two members to Congress and had enjoyed several triumphs at the state and local levels, including more than seventy mayors running largely on municipal reform issues.[1]

The national party coming into the 1912 election had beefed up its staff and service capacity. The national office grew from a place where the national secretary had one or two assistants to one where the secretary had more than a dozen full-time employees.[2] The national party also launched the Lyceum Lecture Circuit, a nationwide system of lecture courses featuring Socialist speakers. In addition, in August 1912 the national office initiated a publication called

The Party Builder, providing information on the Lyceum program and other party developments and activities.

Less satisfying for the Socialists, but also a testament to their impact, was the fact that by 1912 many of the proposals they had long sponsored were being included in other party programs. Socialists were particularly hostile to the thunder-stealing Progressive (Bull Moose) party, formed in 1912 to promote Theodore Roosevelt's candidacy. Among the items in its national platform were direct legislation, woman suffrage, corrupt practices acts, and a host of labor reforms—including the eight-hour day—that Socialists had carried over from Populist days. When informed by reporters that some observers had labeled Roosevelt Socialistic, Debs snapped: "I resent the imputation. We would not take him into the party."[3] Debs argued that Roosevelt was, in fact, nothing more than a tool of the capitalists, trying to head off fundamental change by stealing from the Socialists' party platform.

Debs worried that Roosevelt and, to a lesser extent, the Democratic nominee Woodrow Wilson would siphon off Socialist votes, especially those of the more conservative "parlor Socialists." Debs and other Socialists also took aim at Wilson, depicting him as a staid creation of university life who "could not stir up a hungry lion with a red-hot poker."[4] Occasionally, Socialist candidates even took shots at the Prohibition party—describing it, for example, as a party that "can only see poverty when there is a beer sign in sight."[5] Throughout the 1912 campaign, however, Debs concentrated much of his fire on Roosevelt. Debs also heavily emphasized education and the need for the masses to think for themselves rather than rely on leaders. As he pointed out to an assembly of supporters in the mining center of Bisbee, "It would do no good for me to lead you to the promised land—Roosevelt would only come along and lead you out again."[6]

Throughout the Mountain West, Socialists competed with Bull Moose Progressives for the third-party vote, each tapping a different audience. In Arizona, for example, Socialists did particularly well in mining areas and in places where there was strong support for a host of anti-corporate reforms. Progressives, on the other hand, did best among transplanted midwesterners in rather conservative farming areas and in places where interest in reform meant little more than prohibition.[7] A similar portrait of Progressive party supporters appeared in other states in the Mountain West.[8] After 1912 the Progressive party rapidly declined in the area, and Bull Moosers moved on, although largely to the Democratic party rather than back to the Republican party.[9]

Along with the threat of the Progressive party, Socialist party leaders worried about the emergence of the farm-based Non-Partisan League (NPL). This organization came to life in North Dakota in 1910 after the legislature failed to follow up on a voter-approved referendum authorizing the state to construct a terminal grain elevator. A former organizer for the Socialist party, Arthur C. Townley, headed the new organization and built a league program that was avowedly Socialistic. The NPL called for state ownership of various enterprises, such as terminal elevators and flour mills, and other benefits of particular interest to farmers. Townley regularly spoke in terms of the class struggle and condemned business interests. Townley, though, rejected the third-party route as unproductive and, as an alternative, advised his followers to capture the machinery of one of the major parties as a means of winning elections and eventually turning the league's program into law. In 1912 a report by John Spargo to the National Executive Committee (NEC) noted that the list of organizers of the NPL "reads like a list of present and past members of the Socialist party."[10] Spargo looked upon the NPL as a menace to the Socialist party generally and as a particular threat—already beginning to materialize—in states such as Colorado, Idaho, and Montana, where, if unabated, agrarian and industrial radicals might end up in separate and rival organizations.[11]

In 1912 Socialists fought not only with Republicans, Democrats, Progressives, Prohibitionists, and Non-Partisans but, as always, with each other. The principal rift was between the left and right wings of the party, and often at the center of the controversy was the Industrial Workers of the World (IWW), which had become the most feared labor organization in the United States. Bill Haywood had taken a new interest in the increasingly radical organization and in 1911 began to travel the country serving the IWW as well as the Socialist party. In a speech given in New York in December 1911, he made it clear that he was a rebel who favored the overthrow of the capitalist system, by force if necessary. He declared that there was nothing wrong with a little sabotage in the right place and at the right time and was proud of the fact that he was not a law-abiding citizen. Haywood claimed no Socialist could be a good citizen, since by definition he or she was dedicated to overthrowing the system.[12]

Other IWW leaders followed Haywood in shunning politics and emphasizing direct action techniques on the industrial front, such as strikes, slowdowns, and sabotage, toward the broader goal of replacing the present system with a society run by labor through one big union. The IWW's extreme direct action tactics aroused the fear of many Americans, creating, as economists Harry A. Mills and Royal E. Montgomery noted, an image of "a mysterious, incalculable force, likely to appear any time and work destruction."[13] Fear of the IWW increased after its substantial 1912 victory in leading a strike by around 25,000 workers in Lawrence, Massachusetts, although it failed not long after in leading a strike among silk workers in Paterson, New Jersey. Coming into the 1912 election, Socialist party leaders saw a bright future for the party if they could just dump the IWW—it had gotten in the way of the party's ability to focus on the political fight, made it difficult to form ties with the American Federation of Labor (AFL), and, because of its violent image, threatened the radical cause.

While 250 delegates were gathering for the opening day of the Socialist party's national convention in Indianapolis in May 1912, conservative party leaders told reporters they were going to demand that the convention denounce the IWW and its violent direct action principles. "The Socialist party," Victor Berger declared, "cannot afford to continue to be embroiled with this riotous organization."[14] To right-wingers, led by Morris Hillquit and Berger, the IWW stood in the way of building a respectable Socialist party that sought power both by working within the AFL and through conventional political means.

During the convention a direct attack on IWW types came in the form of a proposed amendment to the party's constitution, Article 2, Section 6, which stipulated: "Any member of the party who opposes political action or advocates crime, sabotage or other methods of violence as a weapon of the working class to aid in its emancipation shall be expelled from membership in the party." The motion sailed through the 1912 convention, but leftists successfully petitioned to have the matter settled by a vote of the entire membership. Conservatives claimed they welcomed this vote, confidently predicting that the membership was on their side and that the vote would further drive home the point that the Socialist party stood squarely against violence in the emancipation of the working class.[15] When the vote came, more than 75 percent of members voting approved the anti-sabotage amendment.

Haywood, however, continued to speak out in favor of sabotage and direct action. Conservatives reacted by initiating a campaign to have Haywood removed from the NEC. Haywood, the right argued, had put the party in a situation of "constant necessity of explanation and apology" and, by his open advocacy of sabotage, had violated the newly adopted provision in the party constitution.[16] In a national referendum, 2 of every 3 of the 23,000 party members voting approved recalling Haywood from the NEC. The ouster may have prompted many of the more radical types to leave the party, particularly hurting membership levels of state and local parties in the Mountain West. By one estimate, the party as a whole lost between 30,000 and 40,000 workers in 1913, largely because of the policy changes directed against the IWW and Haywood.[17] By another count, between 1912 and 1918 the party lost almost 23,000 members, many as a result of this fight.[18] Among others ousted for similar activity was David Coates, who at the time was living in Spokane. Although perhaps slightly more to the left, the attitudes of Socialist party leaders in the Mountain West regarding the IWW differed little from those of national party leaders on the Haywood question—tensions between Wobblies and Socialists in several places, including Butte, were at a high level. Relations grew worse after the party's expulsion of Haywood.

Meanwhile, even though Debs did better than ever, many radicals in the Mountain West and elsewhere were disappointed by the 1912 election returns. Some had expected much more and blamed Theodore Roosevelt, who gathered more than 4 million votes, for cutting the size of Debs's vote.[19] There was also considerable debate among radicals over the motives of the 900,000 people who did vote for Debs and, related to this, over bringing these people into the party. One line of thought was that they were not so much voting for Socialism or even for Debs as they were protesting the other parties. Debs, on the other hand, saw them as clear-cut Socialist votes from dedicated revolutionary Socialists.[20] Those who shared Debs's assumption that the people who voted for him were voting for Socialism saw the possibility of adding a large number of party members (see Appendix, Table 6). They were struck, however, by the party's apparent unwillingness or inability to do so. The editor of *Miners Magazine* complained, "We pour money into propaganda in an increasing stream, win over multitudes of voters and then fail to follow up our work by getting our voters into the party."[21] Some argued that the country was still filled with Socialists but that they preferred to operate as "individual bushwhackers" because they saw no value in joining a Socialist party organization.[22] Thus, it was up to the party to give members activities that made membership worthwhile and gave them a feeling of accomplishment they could not get on their own. Just what those activities were and whether the party should move in that direction, however, were matters of considerable debate. Indeed, not only did the party fail to bring in new members, it rapidly lost old members because, as noted earlier, of the IWW split. Within a year the loss of dues-paying members forced it to suspend publications such as *The Party Builder* because of a lack of funds.

On the campaign trail in 1912, the former Socialist mayor of Milwaukee, Emil Seidel, running as his party's vice presidential candidate, told an audience in Missoula that fifteen or twenty years ago Socialists had received a far less positive response than he and Debs were now receiving: "Then those who were bold enough to make a socialist speech very often had to clean their clothes of stale eggs or decaying vegetables. They don't throw eggs any more." The vice presidential candidate, in good humor, admitted that this may have had less to do with an increase in the stature of Socialist candidates than with the increased cost of living, making eggs—even rotten ones—far too expensive to throw away.

In a more mellow tone, one reflecting the uphill struggle the party was facing, Seidel remarked, "If we as a party are never able to do anything else we have at least succeeded in arousing the people to the great social evils which beset them and have suggested a remedy for their correction. If we never do anything else this much has been well worthwhile."[23] The party press noted: "Seidel is becoming so well known that he is detected everywhere and approached by many who are interested in Socialism and anxious to know more about it. This is especially true of the traveling men who make [up] a large part of the cargo of every train traveling the Rocky mountain and Pacific coast states."[24]

Seidel teamed up in 1912 with other national campaign orators such as George H. Goebel and Walter I. Millard and the Socialist mayor of Berkeley, California, J. Stitt Wilson.[25] Also campaigning in the Mountain West was Caroline A. Lowe—Canadian-born, former schoolteacher, and ardent suffrage worker as well as a Socialist. According to a party source: "Miss Lowe's method of converting people to Socialism is ingenious and shows a high grade of individuality. When she meets a non-Socialist, she transfixes him with her gaze, points the index finger of her right hand at the pupil of his left eye, and imperiously seethes the word: 'Listen!' He listens. And she never lets the poor devil go until he promises to be a good Socialist."[26]

Socialists in the Mountain West, like Socialists elsewhere, were swept up in the excitement of the 1912 election. They made gains in much of the region, sometimes causing conservative forces considerable alarm. A backlash caused by the Socialists' success helped bring them back down to earth by 1913. They looked inward, spending much of their time fighting among themselves and pondering problems of organization and support.

In Colorado the party's gains were less spectacular than those in much of the region: Socialist party candidates received about 6 percent of the vote, although they did considerably better in mining communities and old Populist strongholds.[27] Shortly after the 1912 election a fight broke out when members of the Denver branch took aim at State Secretary A. H. Floaten. An old issue seems to have resurfaced: that Floaten had sold out to the railroad companies by accepting free railway passes. In reporting on the story, *The Miners Magazine* intoned, "Socialists do not believe that passes from railway corporations to a state secretary are to be taken as proofs of his loyalty to the principles of socialism."[28] Party leaders were also concerned about the loss of membership after the election—from 1912 to 1913 membership dropped from 1,976 to 1,030—and they began to consider ways of retooling the organization so it was something more than one centered around elections and offered enough social and intellectual activities to maintain member interest when there was no election.[29]

Socialists in neighboring Wyoming had a similar electoral experience in 1912–1913. Debs picked up 6.5 percent of the vote. Herman Groesbeck did a little better, picking up 7 percent in his campaign for a seat on the state supreme court. Going through Rock Springs in 1912, Seidel reported that hundreds of miners had come out to hear him and were very enthusiastic.[30] Returns suggest relatively high levels of support in mining areas. From a growth perspective, however, the future did not look particularly bright. Wyoming remained a state where Socialists attracted relatively few voters beyond their membership base. The party had 685 members, a relatively large number when we account for population, but it only attracted 2,760 votes for the ticket (see Appendix, Table 6).

In most of the remaining states in the region, the election results were more impressive. Montana Socialists were in a good mood going into the 1912 election because of the apparent success of Mayor Lewis Duncan's regime in Butte. The voters of Montana gave Debs close to 14 percent of the vote, compared with around 9 percent four years earlier. Duncan ran as the Socialist candidate for governor and received more votes than Debs, the only Socialist to do so. Socialist candidates throughout the state in 1912, though, generally trailed far behind Progressive party candidates as the third-party choice. They also suffered some hostility. In Butte, for example, election day was marred by a riot. According to an IWW source, a ruffian mob, "filled with patriotism and cheap whiskey" and led by an "insane woman," set things off when they attacked a crowd of Socialists waiting for election returns.[31] Buoyed by successes at the polls in municipal elections, membership in the Montana Socialist party increased from a low of 200 in 1910 to more than 1,600 in 1912 (about a quarter of whom were in Butte), before dropping back a little in 1913. The party remained strong with miners but had made gains with farmers. Indeed, according to one estimate, 40 percent of the party membership in 1913 was composed of farmers or people in small farming communities.[32] The party, though, had severe competition for this vote from the NPL.

The Socialist vote in Idaho in 1912 rose as high as 14 percent for some candidates. Debs got over 11 percent of the vote that year. The party drew much of its support from the Democratic party.[33] In relatively revolutionary-minded Shoshone County the party suffered from the national party's attack on the left wing, especially Haywood's expulsion, but still received 16 percent of the vote. Outside the mining areas the Idaho party, like the Montana party, aimed for and apparently tapped into some of the discontent among farmers.[34] In 1912 the party also took a stab at increasing the women's vote. Party leaders later concluded, though, that the addition of women to the electorate had little effect on the Socialist vote.[35]

Overall, however, the Idaho party was relatively healthy in 1912, with, as State Secretary I. F. Stewart reported, around 1,800 members in 120 locals.[36] Following the 1912 election, the editor of an Idaho paper backing the Progressive party concluded, "The Socialists have come to be an important figure to be reckoned [with] within Idaho politics." He warned that supporting the Progressive party was the only way to arrest the drift toward Socialism.[37] Also concerned about Socialist success, conservative forces began a counter-education campaign. Following the lead of conservatives in other parts of the country, they brought noted anti-Socialist lecturer David Goldstein of Boston to talk about "Socialism in Its Relation to Religion and to the Christian Family." Speaking to a Boise audience, Goldstein contended, among other things, that the Socialist party stood for free love and atheism. Contrary to what Socialists believed, said Goldstein, Christ "was not an agitator, a rebel, nor the waver of a red flag." Socialists in his audience interrupted him throughout the evening, often hissing at his statements. After the meeting some followed Goldstein down the street, yelling at him.[38] The enthusiasm evident in Idaho in 1912 largely disappeared the following year, as membership dropped from 1,667 to 818 (Appendix, Table 3).

Leaders of the national Socialist party felt that Nevada, a state with about 20,000 voters scattered over 100,000 square miles, could be carried for Debs and sent dozens of prominent Socialist speakers and hundreds of thousands of pieces of literature to the state in 1912. Rallies were held in places like Tonopah, where a large Socialist audience gathered at the Nevada Theater to hear J. Stitt Wilson and a variety of local leaders who occupied seats on a stage profusely decorated with American flags and pictures of Debs, Seidel, and Abraham Lincoln.[39] Party leaders boasted of thirty-seven locals and 1,042 members who represented every county in the state.[40] To some extent the Socialist campaign in Nevada had been furthered by Governor Tasker Oddie. Oddie, elected in 1910, continued his predecessors' push for reform in regard to railroad assessment and other matters but helped keep radicalism alive by alienating labor through the use of troops. He backed workmen's compensation legislation and favored basic safety laws but had no sympathy for labor and strike activity, especially when conducted by foreign miners. His decision to use troops and the state police in the fall of 1912 against striking Greek Western Federation of Miners members at Ely and McGill apparently inflamed workers and helped the Socialist ticket.[41]

In November Debs wound up with 17 percent of the Nevada vote, his best showing in the nation.[42] He received over 30 percent of the vote in Nye County, the state's mining center where Manhattan, Round Mountain, and Tonopah were located. The Socialist vote in Tonopah in 1912 increased from 159 four years earlier to 508 and was larger than that for any other party—Democrat,

Republican, or Progressive.[43] In 1912 Harry Dunseath, a native of England who had held a variety of occupations including prospector and Wells Fargo stage driver, was elected police judge in Tonopah. He soon became famous throughout the state in his capacity as coroner for blaming mine operators for the many mining deaths and injuries. As the Socialists saw it, he "made it too expensive for the mines to kill and injure their employees."[44] With continued organizing efforts, Nevada Socialists suffered less of a letdown than Socialists in 1913, and, indeed, the party seemed well on its way toward forcing a fusion with the Democrats similar to the earlier Silver-Democratic merger that had dominated state politics.[45]

To some extent, the Nevada party had succeeded in rallying several groups— among which miners, railway workers, and reclamation-land farmers stood out—behind a moderate multifaceted reform program.[46] More negatively, one of their opponents, U.S. Senator Key Pittman, wrote in reference to the Nevada Socialists: "That party is not seeking reform; it is simply seeking power."[47] If so, it seemed to be moving in the right direction.

In Utah, the euphoric feelings resulting from the 1912 elections were short-lived. Party secretary P. J. Holt reported in April 1912 that the party had experienced a growth in average membership from 263 in 1910 to 611 in 1911 and, with the aid of a full-time organizer, was giving out a lot of literature and sending speakers everywhere. He also noted that the party had added a newspaper at Helper, Utah, and was planning to establish a chain of newspapers under central management throughout the state. Holt declared, "The general condition of the party in this state is excellent." He went on: "As to how many votes we will get, that is immaterial. What we want is organization and education. Nor do we expect to have a perfect organization composed of angels, but rather to spread the propaganda to every nook and corner in the state and let the internal development of intelligent membership follow. To that end we will discourage all possibilities of factionalities and sometimes brush technicalities to one side for the sake of unity."[48]

In a sharp departure from the past, solidarity seemed to catch on among the various Utah Socialist locals as they pulled together through the state party to make a major effort to get the Socialist message out to the voters. Coming into the 1912 election, national organizer J. L. Engdahl reported that Socialists were carving out a foothold among Mormons in Utah; some Mormon elders were even serving on the Executive Committee of the Utah party. The party too, he noted, had picked up additional support among miners, particularly in Bingham Canyon where an industrial struggle had led to increased worker solidarity (Chapter 13), and had showed evidence of strength in several recent local elections.[49]

With the continued support of organized labor, the Utah Socialist candidate for governor that year, a medical doctor, Frank McHugh, received nearly 8 percent of the vote (compared with 4.5 percent in 1908), running just slightly behind Debs. Debs received 8,899 votes, also around 8 percent of the vote. Socialist Murray E. King did better, getting 8,971 votes, 8.7 percent of the total, in his bid for the state's only seat in the U.S. House of Representatives, just edging out the Progressive candidate for third place. Newspapers, including the church-friendly *Deseret News*, congratulated the Socialists on their improved showing.[50]

Yet, while 1912 was encouraging, a year later party membership had dropped from 1,667 to 818. For many, the atmosphere had become more repressive. Reporting on the situation in 1913, a party leader declared: "Here in Utah Capitalism is supreme. Socialist speakers are denied the use of public buildings. To be a Socialist in a Utah coal camp is to be jobless if a miner; if you are a rancher it means your products will be boycotted."[51] In 1913 the party still had the support of the Utah Federation of Labor.[52] After 1913, however, the federation discontinued its endorsement in an effort to enhance its ability to work with candidates of the major parties. Utah radicals continued to be at each others' throats. Even Christian Socialist Bishop Franklin Spencer Spaulding got caught up in the turmoil, booed in 1913 by Wobblies in the audience for a speech he gave at Socialist party headquarters in Salt Lake City after saying it was wrong to favor direct action over political action.[53]

The 1912 presidential election in New Mexico and Arizona was exciting because it was the first national election in those places. In June 1912, New Mexico state secretary Lurlyne Layne noted that the party was still small in number—around 400 members in fifty locals scattered throughout the state—but, as she saw it, it was filled with people "who have no idea what the word quit means."[54] Still, New Mexico had organizational problems. Many of the locals were composed of farmers scattered over a large land area, a situation that made it difficult to arrange meetings. In those places counties were used as the basic organizational unit, with local branches as needed.[55] To bring the scattered Socialists together, the party sponsored several encampments and brought in lecturers such as Kate Richards O'Hare and P. G. Zimmerman from Texas for these events. Along with miners and farmers, there were indications that the party had hidden support among workers on the Santa Fe Railroad. One "John Doe" letter writer disclosed: "I have worked on the New Mexico division of the Santa Fe for some time, and know personally many good socialists, both among the organized and the unorganized workers. . . . As a rule the unorganized employees on the Santa Fe and especially if they have a family to support, keep their views on politics and unionism very much to themselves, for there is no telling when you might be talking to a 'spotter' on the Santa Fe."[56]

In 1912 the New Mexico party nearly doubled its percentage of the vote over 1911, from around 3 percent to 6 percent. In its first real burst into the limelight in 1911–1912, the party continued to do particularly well in the southeastern part of the state. One of the party's future leaders, W. C. Tharp, came from that area. He had moved to the town of St. Vrain in Curry County in the early 1900s as a schoolteacher and later established what in 1912 was the only Socialist paper in the state, *The St. Vrain Journal*. State Secretary Layne declared: "W.C. Tharp is a full-fledged Revolutionary Socialist, whose editorials give forth no uncertain sounds, and his paper deserves the enthusiastic support of all Socialists in New Mexico."[57]

By early 1912 the party's national committeeman for Arizona was happy to report that most of the comrades who had been "deceived by the self-seeking leaders" of the Labor party "had come back into the fold."[58] The party and locals around the state were also throwing themselves into various causes, sometimes with surprising effectiveness. Arizona Socialists, for example, showed political muscle in a matter involving Socialist Miss Emma Hiatt, a schoolmistress in the Prescott Groom Creek District. On January 3, 1912, the county superintendent of schools, C. W. Persons, sent this directive to Miss Hiatt: "I hereby order you to cease singing socialist songs, to stop all political talk and teaching which includes your talks on economies, in your school work, and to remove all red flags from the school building where you are teaching. Complaint has come to me that the law was being violated in this respect and upon investigation I find same to be true."[59] Persons put Hiatt's salary on hold until she made the changes. Socialists protested that all she had done was to have students sing "songs whose burden was the brotherhood of man." They also said she was not responsible for the red flag; it was left on the building by Socialists who had recently used the schoolhouse as a meeting place. Hiatt asked to have her salary reinstated, but Persons refused. Persons, a Republican, had gained his position through an appointment and was planning to seek election to a full term. Socialists considered nominating Hiatt to run against Persons for the office. As perhaps intended, the threat frightened the Democrats, who had their eye on capturing the position. To head off a candidacy that would drain votes from their candidate, the Democrats nominated a candidate friendly to Hiatt who made it clear that, as far as he was concerned, "she could teach her children what she liked."[60] The Democrat was elected, Hiatt was retained as a teacher, and, for a time at least, her students sang Socialist songs.

In January 1912 members of the regenerated party were deeply involved in the creation of the Arizona Federation of Labor, which grew out of a Phoenix convention attended by delegates from forty unions. Presiding over the convention was E. B. Simanton, a miner from Globe and candidate for the U.S. Senate on the Arizona Socialist party ticket. While the organization's constitution did not endorse the Socialist party, it had endorsed Socialism with the adoption of a clause in the preamble: "We demand the enactment of laws establishing the collective ownership by the people of all means of production and distribution."[61] Throughout the early 1910s, ties were strong between the Arizona Socialist party and the Arizona Federation of Labor. Socialists were especially strong in the union movement in mining areas scattered around the state.[62] Yet the mining camps were not a safe haven. In 1912 W. S. Bradford, secretary of the Arizona party, noted, "In a number of the larger camps to be known as an active Socialist is equivalent to prompt dismissal."[63]

The first presidential election in the state, and the candidacy of Eugene Debs, who carried his campaign to Arizona in 1912, greatly stimulated Arizona Socialists. Party workers campaigned enthusiastically on Debs's behalf throughout the state. They also campaigned for A. Charles Smith of Douglas, candidate for Congress, described as a "fluent talker and gentleman" in the mainstream press.[64] As the Socialist campaigners saw it, they were educating the voters rather than saying whatever was necessary to secure votes. They assumed that once the people became informed about the Socialist program, the party would not have to worry about getting votes.[65]

Debs received 13 percent of the Arizona presidential vote in 1912, easily doubling the party's previous high and outdistancing William Howard Taft. The Socialist candidate for the House of Representatives, the only other office up for election in 1912, did equally well, suggesting a level of party support that went beyond support for Debs. Following this burst of strength, Arizona Socialists saw themselves in the mainstream of reform and witnessed a "rising tide of socialism" in the state.[66] Indeed, the possibility of this happening was noted in the mainstream press. Both Democratic and Republican editors called attention to the threat of Socialism and offered their parties as the only safe alternative. As far as Progressive Democrats were concerned, the best way to head off the rising tide was to purge their ranks of reactionaries and provide needed reforms.[67] To some extent, this was done. Over the next several years the strength of the Socialist party was undoubtedly reduced by the appeal of the Progressive wing of the Democratic party. Several prominent Socialists became Democrats, and a number of Socialists appeared to have registered Democratic to vote in that party's primary for candidates such as George W.P. Hunt.

Socialist leaders were clearly no match for the highly visible Hunt in competing for the votes of left-wing workers. Hunt spoke their language. For example, in a speech delivered before a very enthusiastic crowd in Bisbee on July 4, 1913—a speech printed in its entirety in *Miners Magazine*—Hunt spoke out against the privileged classes' attempts to rule and exploit the masses and the evils of "greed backed by power." He referred also to the "grinding oppression of the masses" in the modern industrial system and demanded "that labor, which possesses all wealth and makes possible every comfort of life . . . have a greater share of what it creates, and that privilege shall no longer be permitted to seize as much of the profits as its greed dictates." Hunt called for "Progressive democracy," which to him meant

> that this country, its institutions, its resources and its rewards for industry belong to the people whose labor makes them possible. Progressive politics is the faithful application of Thomas Jefferson's equal rights to all and special privileges to none. . . . Progressive politics aims to make industry bring comforts for the homes of the working multitude, as it does now in an unequal degree for the homes of the privilege[d]. . . . Progressive politics challenges the theory that privilege and monopoly make whatever prosperity we enjoy, and insists that fair and equal prosperity for all is the only sure safeguard of a free government.[68]

Working largely below the radar screen, Socialists in Arizona continued to be engaged in a variety of activities. In 1913, for example, Socialists in Phoenix threw themselves into a number of issues growing out of a strike against the Phoenix Street Railway Company, owned by outsiders living in Los Angeles who, according to the Socialist press, were abusing their workers and "extracting every cent possible from the people of Phoenix and giving back as little as possible in the way of service."[69] Workers in this conflict locked horns with professional strikebreakers brought in from the Thiel Detective Agency of Los Angeles. Socialists pushed not only for terms favorable to the workers but also for a city takeover of the transit system.

At around the same time, the editors of *The Arizona Socialist Bulletin* stated one of their major purposes: "We voice the protest of the oppressed who have no medium by means of which they can express their protest and no avenue for securing redress for their wrongs."[70] They followed up by expressing outrage over a variety of matters, including the brutality of Southern Pacific Railroad detectives in their handling of nomadic workers. Socialist editors also demanded the abolition of capital punishment, a movement that, at the time, was gaining momentum in the state. Seeing this as another struggle in the class war, the editors pointed out: "No murderer of any substantial means has ever been legally hung in Arizona. Only murderers who are poor are hung in Arizona."[71] The Arizona crusade to abolish the death penalty also caught the eye of Eugene

Debs, who observed in 1913: "The people of Arizona have shown themselves to be so progressive and so entirely abreast of the enlightened spirit of the times in so many other matters that I feel safe in predicting that she will follow the lead of other progressive states and blot this insufferable stigma from her fame."[72]

Along with all this activity, Arizona Socialists still found time to fight among themselves, as suggested by an item in the July 11, 1913, issue of *The Arizona Socialist Bulletin*: "Local Yuma has changed its meeting night to Tuesday, and last night was a hummer. Our late secretary, Comrade Matilda C. Milton, resigned a week ago and Comrade Beverford was elected to succeed her. His elevation to the position stirred up all of his fighting blood and he looked around for someone to devour, and in the absence of scabs and capitalists he jumped on Comrade Teufert. For a while it looked bad for Teufert, but the local took his side of the case and handed one to Beverford. . . . If the enemy will not accommodate us we will have to scrap among ourselves just to keep in practice."[73]

In 1912 the Mountain West continued to be a region where the Socialist party did relatively well. While Debs received 6 percent of the vote nationally, he received 11 percent of the vote in Idaho, 13 percent in Arizona and Montana, and nearly 17 percent in Nevada. In Colorado, Utah, and Wyoming Debs also received a higher percentage of the vote than he received nationally, and he came close to the national average in New Mexico. Debs ran ahead of Taft in Arizona and Nevada (Appendix, Table 2). Mountain West Socialists had also made above-average use of the Lyceum Lecture Circuit in 1912. When total state population was considered, in 1912 Nevada ranked first, Arizona second, Idaho fourth, Montana sixth, Colorado seventh, Utah eighth, and Wyoming thirteenth among the states in the use of the speakers. Only New Mexico had not gotten involved.[74]

On the whole, in the Mountain West during this period, Socialists appeared not only relatively numerous and active but a little farther to the left than the party as a whole, although not as much as one might expect and not consistently within the region. The vote on the anti-sabotage amendment at the 1912 national convention provides a rough indicator of where Mountain West Socialist leaders stood in the left-right debate of 1912–1913 and of the divisions among them. A motion supported by the left and opposed by the right to strike the amendment went down 191 to 90, about 68 to 32 percent. Of the 21 delegates from the Mountain West voting on the question, 9 were in favor and 12 were opposed, a division of about 57 to 43 percent. Although a majority of Mountain West delegates rejected the left's position, they were more supportive of that position than the delegates as a whole. Yet, the various Mountain West delegations did not see eye to eye. All 5 of the Montana delegates voted with the left, while all 5 Colorado delegates took the right wing's side and voted against the motion. The only other delegation supporting the motion, by a 2 to 1 vote, was Wyoming. The Arizona delegation was evenly split, and delegates in Nevada and New Mexico sided with the right. In Idaho the delegation was split 3 to 1 for the right.[75]

A better, although far from perfect, indicator of left-right sentiment in the area is provided by the membership vote on Haywood's removal from the National Executive Committee. Nationwide, around 23,000 Socialists voted, including those whose votes came in after the official cutoff date. This amounted to roughly 20 percent of the party's members. On this vote, a majority of members from the Mountain West voted for Haywood's removal, but Haywood still did better in that region than he did nationally. In the Mountain West, 48 percent of members opposed his removal, while only 33 percent did so nationally. Within the region, though, we again find considerable division. Haywood's supporters were in the majority in Montana, Nevada, and Utah—the percentage of support for Haywood in Montana trailed only that in Texas—but a majority of members in each of the other five states, including Colorado, where he had been the party's gubernatorial candidate, favored his ouster from the NEC (see Appendix, Table 8).

Soon after the 1912 election, Mountain West party leaders became concerned about membership. Two questions were raised: how to attract those who had supported the party's candidates in 1912 and how to keep the members the party had. Nationally, party members could account for only 13 percent of the votes going to Debs. In the Mountain West, the percentage was not much higher, although it varied from 9 percent in Utah to 25 percent in Wyoming (see Appendix, Table 6). Still, the size of Debs's vote raised tantalizing possibilities of membership growth in each of the states. On the other hand, the second problem—how to retain membership levels—became more pressing. Between 1912 and 1913, party membership in the region fell from 8,364 to 5,792—a loss of 2,572 members, or 31 percent of the membership. Nevada and Wyoming had made small gains in membership, but the losses were large elsewhere in the region, particularly in Colorado and Idaho, where membership dropped around 50 percent (Appendix, Table 3). A number of ideas were advanced, including upgrading meetings, doing a better job of educating members as to the party's historic role, introducing members to more speakers, or giving them activities between elections. Some entrepreneurial types, much to the dismay of their more revolutionary colleagues, thought of offering inducements such as prizes to bring in new members.

Several parties in the area also made strenuous efforts to recruit female members. Among the most successful of these was Nevada, where, according to a 1914 survey, women made up about 33 percent of the party's membership. In Nevada, a special propaganda effort had been made to recruit women.[76] The survey also found the percentage of female members at 13 for Arizona, 10 each for Idaho and Montana, and 5 for Wyoming—figures for Colorado, Utah, and New Mexico were not available. Although the survey was incomplete, the percentage of women party members in the region appeared to compare favorably with percentages in other regions.[77] In Wyoming the party secretary reported that several women wanted to run for office as Socialists, but relatively few wanted to be party members—the number of women candidates equaled the number of male candidates on the Socialist ticket, but there were fewer women than men in the party organization.[78] Socialists also noted that Idaho was one of the woman suffrage states and that women were actively involved in Socialist activities.[79] Still, there were limits to female participation. Anna Maley, who spent much time and energy in the region in 1911 trying to recruit women into the Socialist party, noted: "The women of Idaho and Utah vote, I am told, but so far as I can observe, they are passive political factors. The same deadly conservative influences which hamper our unenfranchised sisters operate here. The women with whom I have contact are housemothers chiefly. They are not active breadwinners. The church, the lodge, the cradle and the kitchen absorb them."[80]

Some advocated organized participation in initiative campaigns as a useful outlet and a way of keeping members. Said one activist in Arizona, "By concentrating our campaign upon certain initiative measures we avoid a campaign of personalities and we inaugurate a 'Do Something' policy for our organization which will be to our everlasting credit and benefit."[81] For some Socialists, doing something meaningful through the organization also required more flexibility when it came to the policy of nonalignment. In arguing for more flexibility, exasperated Colorado Socialist Mila Tupper Maynard acknowledged in 1910 that "often our essential principles force us to stand in isolation," but she went on to argue that this was not always the case and that when Socialists could join in fellowship "with our neighbors we should be glad to do so. Prejudices against us are tremendous at best; why add to them when not essential?"[82] Maynard, speaking to her colleagues at a national assembly, cited the refusal of Socialists in Denver to join in a cooperative campaign with other groups to secure direct democracy and other reforms, simply because doing so involved working with others, as an example of a more general fear among Socialists "of agreeing with our neighbors on anything."[83] She concluded: "This spirit is all wrong. We should be glad to work in common cause where we can fully endorse a measure and where no organic or political affiliation is required."[84] Most Socialist leaders in the Mountain West, however, continued to insist on the lesson learned from Populism: that the party must retain its purity when it came to affiliation with others, as well as when it came to membership in the party.

Another thing party leaders in the area agreed on was the lack of funds at their disposal. Party leaders constantly bemoaned the financial condition of their organizations. Coming into the election season, they commonly encountered special financial problems such as finding funds to pay the fees necessary to place their candidates on the ballot—those fees were set by lawmakers representing the major parties, and they seemed to increase with the increases in Socialist votes.[85] Some asked for aid from the national party, arguing that because of the small size of their states, the chances of winning were greater. Party leaders, though, did not want national interference in their operations. Within the states, issues of control often revolved around party newspapers. State parties that could afford them had their own official newspapers. In some places the party owned the state's only Socialist paper, thus augmenting its control over the movement and the message it was attempting to get across. Indeed, some organizers saw having such a monopoly to be at the core of state party strength. Many appeared to concur with the view of an Arizona party leader that "[t]he party is in its childhood until it can control its own propaganda organs."[86] Arizona, in 1913, was one of the states where the party owned and controlled the only Socialist paper in the state. A survey conducted by the national party that year found more chaotic situations elsewhere. In Utah, for example, there was no party-owned newspaper, but the state had two highly competitive and contentious privately owned Socialist papers.[87] Colorado had a party-owned paper but also four privately owned ones, including one from a group that had recently left the party.[88]

Over the years, Socialist newspapers in the region came and went with considerable speed, but in several states at any given time the Socialists were without any paper. The Socialists made up for some of this loss through their allies in the union press. The mainstream press, for the most part, felt the best way to deal with the Socialists was to ignore them and "let them get their own publicity." Much of the publicity coming from the mainstream, often corporate-owned, press was negative, stressing the radical side of Socialism and labor unions and the violent industrial conflicts with which they were associated. Several events of this type were to occur over the period 1914–1916, the popular coverage of which helped set back the movement.

CHAPTER THIRTEEN

Pitching the Battle

Ludlow, Hill, Duncan, and Hunt

RADICALS IN 1913 STILL THOUGHT FONDLY of two major forces working toward the same end in the Mountain West: "As the Socialist party stands for the eman-cipation of the working class on the political field so the Western Federation [of Miners; WFM] and the United Mine Workers [UMW] stand for the complete abolition of wage slavery on the economic field."[1] Relations among Socialist par-ties, the WFM, and the UMW were close, although there were bumps along the road that showed up during intense labor disputes. Relations between the WFM and UMW had soured after the WFM joined the Industrial Workers of the World (IWW), but the UMW paved the way for the WFM's reentry into the American Federation of Labor (AFL) in 1911. The UMW, the AFL's largest union, threatened to secede if the WFM was denied reentry. Both mining unions had many Socialists among their ranks, some of whom were in leadership posi-tions and hoped to use their influence to turn the AFL in a leftward direction. Both unions and Socialist party activists in much of the country had a common irritant in the IWW. For mainstream Socialists trying to build a mass-based political party, the less they or anyone else heard from the troublemaking Wobblies, the happier they were. The IWW dismissed political action and, when it came to action on the industrial front, liked to tell miners that the WFM, in joining the AFL, had "lined up with the reactionists as one of the main bulwarks of the capitalist system." It was, as a consequence, no longer a revolutionary force and had lost whatever ability or desire it had to win strikes.[2]

The WFM at the time of its reentry into the AFL was still leftward leaning and willing to engage in industrial conflict in Arizona (with the help of Governor George Hunt) and other places, even moving to defend the rights of "non-American" workers it had previously neglected. As for the other miners' union, the *Appeal to Reason* happily reported in February 1909 that the UMW convention had adopted a resolution introduced by Frank J. Hayes, Adolph Germer, and James Lord, among others, that called for "public ownership and operation and the democratic management of all those means of production and exchange that are collectively used" and demanded "that every man or woman willing and able to work can have free access to the means of life and get the full social value of what they produce."[3] Going into the 1910s the UMW was an organization in which Socialists had considerable influence and was in a restless and bold mood. It made some dramatic moves in the Mountain West, particularly in Colorado where events led to tragedy at the mining camp of Ludlow.[4]

The IWW showed up in various places in the Mountain West. Members like Frank Little continued to engage in free-speech battles. In this regard an IWW publication in March 1913 noted: "The boys in Denver have been returning to jail as soon as released, thus keeping up the fight until reinforcements arrive. Those who have fought so far are of many nationalities, and so show clearly the solidifying power of the One Big Union."[5] Another report a few months later read, "Things are beginning to move in this dead burg of Denver—the best lighted cemetery in the world. Since the settlement of the free speech fight extensive agitation has been carried on with splendid results."[6] Some of the more dramatic cases involving the IWW concerned the murder of Joe Hill in Utah and complex relations with the Socialist party and the WFM in Butte, which produced more violence and the entry of the state militia.

In 1913–1915, developments involving the activities of the miners' unions, along with the IWW, captured most of the attention in the Mountain West and, indeed, given the violence and dramatic turnabouts, considerable notice in the nation as a whole. Colorado during this period continued to be plagued by labor problems—most dramatically in the coalfields where labor agitators, including the eighty-two-year-old Mother Jones, did what they could to make life as difficult as possible for John D. Rockefeller. Developments began in the spring of 1910 when the UMW initiated strikes in the coalfields of northern Colorado to force owners to bargain with the union. Later, realizing it would also have to shut down coal operations in the south to have any effect on the market and thus, on the companies, the union sent organizers to the southern coalfields, largely in Huerfano and Las Animas counties. The operation was a clandestine one; organizers posed not only as ordinary miners but also as house painters, peddlers, and religious personages.[7] Still, they did not go unnoticed by the mining companies. LaMont Montgomery Bowers, an agent for Rockefeller who kept an eye on the Colorado situation, reported to headquarters in 1912 that the men working for Rockefeller's Colorado Fuel and Iron Company (CFI) were well paid and housed and seemed content but that union agitators were constantly "dogging [at] their heels" and that "we are always fearful of strikes . . . we can never tell when trouble will come."[8]

By September 1913 the visible phase of the organizational effort took over, as organizer John R. Lawson and Socialists Frank J. Hayes, Adolph Germer, and Mother Jones, fresh from a similar conflict in West Virginia, began openly agitating and directing strike activity around Trinidad against the CFI and two other firms. Their major demand was recognition of the UMW as the miners' bargaining agent. Without this, whatever concessions were won from the company in a moment of weakness might be taken back. The mining executives refused even to confer with the miners. The miners went on strike in late September, and sixty-six people were killed before it was over.

As miners walked off the job, mine operators brought in trainloads of nonunion labor, mostly immigrants, using armored railroad cars. They also looked to the Baldwin-Felts Detective Agency, which had dealt harshly with a miners' strike in West Virginia, for additional men to protect strikebreakers and mining property. Sheriffs in the strike areas owed their jobs to the coal companies. Accordingly, they welcomed the incoming gunmen and gave them commissions as deputy sheriffs. The deputies rounded up and arrested dozens of striking miners for interfering with the hiring of strikebreakers. Mine managers responded to the strike by evicting miners and their families from the company-owned housing. In anticipation of this move, however, the UMW had shipped in tents from West Virginia and, when the crisis came, relocated miners and their families into tent colonies on property rented by the union. The largest of these was in Ludlow, eighteen miles north of Trinidad. Others were located at Walsenburg, Rugby, Aguilar, Forbes, Suffield, and Sopris.

Following some gun battles between the mine guards and the strikers, Governor Elias Ammons, in late October 1913, ordered the Colorado national guard, around 800 strong under General John Chase, into the southern Colorado coalfields. Rockefeller associates and prominent business leaders in the state apparently had been able to "reeducate" Ammons, a Democrat elected with labor support.[9] Upton Sinclair later described Ammons as a kindly man, "in intellectual caliber fitted for the duties of a Sunday school superintendent in a small village," the type of person corporations deliberately select for leadership so they do not have to worry about anything.[10]

Reporting from the field, UMW organizer Adolph Germer, a Socialist who later became national secretary of the party, wrote to the national office on November 30, 1913: "General Chase has finally succeeded in putting his pet idea, the court martial[,] into operation. He says it is only for the purpose of investigating offenses. . . . He has ordered the wholesale arrest of strikers, especially the Greeks. The militia is operating with the same evident hostility against the strikers as under Peabody. The soldiers are now performing the same duties at the expense of the state that were formerly performed by the mine guards at the expense of the coal companies."[11] Colorado Socialist leader George N. Falconer used the episode to illustrate the fact that the capitalist government, whether under Republicans or Democrats, "is nothing but a business man's committee."[12] The party chief also referred to Colorado as "the land of big mountains and puny statesmen; a land possessing an invigorating climate, and as ugly a bunch of raw, crude, insincere, brutal political huxters [sic] as ever crawled from some dark corner to cut down their unsuspicious prey, and lots of them attend church regularly."[13]

One of the guard's first objectives was to get Mother Jones out of the strike area. The militia, known in Socialist circles as Ammons's "dogs of war," accomplished this in January 1914 by escorting Jones out of Trinidad. Around 150 guardsmen greeted her attempt to return to Trinidad a month later by locking her up in a San Rafael hospital facility converted into a military prison. She was held incommunicado for nine weeks. According to Jones's diary: "Outside my window a guard walked up and down, up and down day and night, day and night, his bayonet flashing in the sun. 'Lads,' I said to the two silent chaps at the door, 'the great Standard Oil is certainly afraid of an old woman!' They grinned."[14] The *New York Call* chipped in with the thought that Mother Jones had achieved a new type of American citizenship: "a military prisoner in time of peace."[15]

On January 22 the troops received more bad press when Chase led a charge of mounted guardsmen, swinging their rifles, into a crowd of women and children parading in the streets of Trinidad demanding Mother Jones's release. The general's anger may have been fueled by the smirks on the faces of some of the demonstrators who had seen him fall off his horse earlier in the proceedings. For his part, Chase said the parade had gotten out of hand and that the demonstrators had to be forcibly put down and dispersed. He further saw the parade as an attempt by labor radicals to use women to cause disorder and further their ends: "They adopted as a device the plan of hiding behind their women's skirts, believing, as was indeed the case, that it would be more embarrassing for the military to deal with women than with men."[16] As for Mother Jones, the general concluded that she seemed "to have in an exceptional degree the faculty of stirring up and inciting the more ignorant and criminally disposed to deeds of violence and crime. . . . I confidently believe that most of the murders and other acts of violent crime committed in the strike region have been inspired by this woman's incendiary utterances."[17] He also noted that some of the strike leaders told him Jones's ability to arouse the workers in the early stages of a strike made her invaluable as an organizer but that she inevitably turned out to be an embarrassment to strike leaders in the later stages, particularly when they were trying to work out a compromise or an adjustment. Mother Jones, it seemed, marched to the sound of her own drummer, often much to the annoyance of strike leaders.[18]

A few months later the national office of the UMW responded to Jones's plight with a wire to President Woodrow Wilson: "Federal intervention sorely is needed in Colorado. We can ill afford to talk about protecting rights of American citizens in Mexico as long as a woman 80 years old can be confined in prison by military authorities without any charge placed against her, denied trial and refused bond, her friends prohibited from communication with her."[19] Chase, hearing about this message, sent a telegram to Wilson stating that there was no need for federal intervention because Colorado military authorities could handle the situation in the southern coalfields. Chase, whose men had razed the Forbes tent colony a few days earlier, said he was going to keep 450 men on duty in the southern coalfields and that no reductions could be made at the time.[20]

Socialist party leader Falconer, meanwhile, had accepted an invitation from the Trinidad Socialist local to spend a few days among the miners in the strike zone. Falconer reported that he was so well received by the striking miners that he ran out of literature. Everywhere he and other agitators went, though, they ran into soldiers, and in one place they were arrested and taken to military headquarters. The chief obstacle to the mission, however, was the reluctance of UMW officials to allow Socialist agitators to do their work. Falconer reported: "The Socialists of Denver tried hard to get out a 20,000[-run] edition of their party paper, *The Colorado Worker*, devoted to the strike exclusively, but owing to a cancellation of 8,000 which were to go to the strike zone only about 13,000 were printed. Someone inside the union didn't want Socialist papers to be read by the miners."[21] The problem, he concluded, was that union organizers were afraid of Socialists or Socialist propaganda coming into strike areas because they felt it only antagonized businessmen and made strikes more difficult to settle.[22]

Falconer nevertheless conducted meetings and handed out working-class Socialist propaganda in Trinidad, Starkville, Aguilar, and Ludlow. Of the latter he noted: "Ludlow is unique in the annals of industrial warfare. Over 500 miners and their families are housed in tents on land-leased by the Miners' union. Here they eat and drink with an ever watchful eye on their enemy, the armed soldiery, camped a few rods to the right of them. What a sight! Workers on one side; the armed Hessians of capitalism on the other, each watching and fearing the other!"[23] The Ludlow colony of more than a thousand men, women, and children offered a diverse cultural mix—Italians, Greeks, Eastern Europeans, and Mexicans, whose first languages were not English, existed alongside an English-speaking–only minority. Living together under considerable hardship and danger in the tent colony, however, brought an unusual level of community solidarity. Falconer was delighted with the response to his efforts in Ludlow: "A splendid meeting was held in the big tent, and a quantity of anti-military literature distributed. The men were very hungry for something to read."[24]

A few months after Falconer's visit, the tension he had found in Ludlow erupted into violence. In what is commonly known as "the Ludlow Massacre," on April 20, 1914, the troops sent into the area went out of control. In an attempt to force the striking miners and their families to vacate their tents and remove themselves from company property, they fired on the tent colony throughout the day. The strikers fired back (some say they fired first) but ran out of ammunition late in the afternoon. At dusk the troops set fire to the tents in which striking miners and their families were housed, causing the deaths of two women and eleven children. Some reports had it that the victims had been burned to death or suffocated in a pit inside the largest tent, which the strikers had dug to shield their children from possible gunfire from the militia. Others, including Ella Reeve Bloor, a Socialist who was in the area agitating among the miners, contended that the children were killed by indiscriminate shooting by the soldiers on bridges before they had a chance to fight their way out of the blazing tent.[25] One of the women who survived left two dead children in the pit. Years later her husband remembered: "I was in the hills with the other men. We had our rifles. We saw the flames in the colony. My wife and children were down there. I could do nothing."[26] Along with these deaths, five miners and one militiaman were killed in the battle.

The tragedy gave rise to several days of armed rebellion by the strikers and their families, who fought a small war with militia detachments and company guards. While some claimed the mining community was filled with unpatriotic, bloodthirsty radicals, scholar Priscilla Long views the situation differently: "Colorado coal miners and their wives were neither revolutionaries nor radicals. They believed in democracy, and equated America with democratic values. Before Ludlow they had patriotically raised and lowered the American flag morning and night. They had begun all union meetings by singing the national anthem."[27] After the massacre, however, many lost control and went on a rampage.

In late April the continuing violence prompted Democratic state senator Helen Ring Robinson to lead a thousand or so outraged women to Governor Ammons's office in Denver. The women conducted a three-hour sit-in to pressure the governor into requesting President Wilson to send federal troops into the strike area. The governor made the request, and Wilson sent 1,590 federal troops. Coming into one camp, Major W. A. Holbrook of the Fifth United States Calvary urged 200 strikers to disarm and give their guns to the federal authorities. Holbrook warned:

> When the United States speaks it is a matter of serious moment. The President of the United States must be obeyed. We have soldiers and officers here to see that his command is obeyed. We do not want to, nor do we intend to shoot you men. Killing is a terrible thing, but if we must do it, then we will. . . . We have nothing to do with the operators and we have nothing to do with the union. We are representatives of President Wilson who has told me he is extremely desirous of restoring order and peace among you. I have come here to see that his command is obeyed. . . . I have the most friendly feeling for you men, but I insist kindly, now that you give up your arms.[28]

Sending the troops eventually led to the removal of the militia, the closing of the saloons, and general disarmament.

Socialists did what they could to call attention to these events. Writing in the *International Socialist Review* in June 1914, Vincent St. John concluded, "The massacre of striking miners, their wives and children, at Ludlow, Colo., by the hired gunmen and state militia of the coal operators has served to emphasize the fact that the workers have no rights that the employers respect."[29] After viewing the scene of the tragedy, Socialist writer Upton Sinclair reported: "I have come home with my nostrils full of powder smoke and the scent of burning flesh; my ears full of the screams of murdered women and children. What I have seen has made me admit for the first time in my life the possibility that the social revolution in America may be one of physical force."[30] In July, Mother Jones announced to a mass meeting in New York City that she was going back to Colorado, a place where babies "were sacrificed in order to protect Standard Oil dividends." Jones also declared: "The President will have to see to it that the mines are taken away from the Rockefellers! These mines belong to the people! This strike is going on until we break the back of the great capitalist machine in Colorado."[31]

Socialist editor Frank Bohn also made a trip to Colorado, where he was mobbed and pelted with eggs by a well-dressed crowd at an open-air meeting in Boulder as he gave the Socialists' view of the Ludlow affair. Bohn concluded: "Insofar as there is a local 'public sentiment' in Colorado it is but an outpouring of the soul of real estate. . . . All the towns people seem to want is eastern investors, tourists and settlers. They 'are venomous against the strikers' because they 'injured the name of Colorado back East.' That is the secret of the whole aftermath of Ludlow. It was excused, covered up—forgotten. . . . Such is the middle class in Colorado—a greedy, gambling lot of money-grubbers, nine-tenths of them failures—who would stop at nothing in the game of getting rich quick."[32]

From the other side, the mine owners told Congress that the bloody conflict had been inaugurated by the miners' union. The operators' brief went on: "Instead of a strike this controversy is an armed insurrection against the sovereign authority of the State of Colorado, conceived, planned, financed, managed, and directed by the officers and leaders of the United Mine Workers of America, inaugurated more than a year ago and pursued with a persistency and villainy most insidious and reprehensible. . . . If the strikers are as earnest in their wish to settle the strike as they are active in the circulation of stories of sensational episodes, the difficulty could not continue for even a brief period longer."[33]

Women of the camps, especially immigrants from Italy, came to life during the Ludlow strike. For many, this was the first time they had joined men in dealing with the outside world. Inspired by Mother Jones and others, women often took the lead in cursing and attacking the scabs and the military. Jones urged women to encourage or shame men into fighting but also to stand up and fight on their own. She further recognized that women had a certain immunity from violence, which made it all the more difficult for company guards and troops to deal with them.[34]

In the fall of 1914, some of the women in the strikers' colony in Ludlow picketed at the train depot, hoping to head off scabs coming into the area for jobs. Federal troops tried to break up the picket. One picketer, Socialist Helen Schloss, reported: "The soldiers surrounded us like a pack of hounds, and tried to remove us from the platform. But alas, they were mistaken, they thought perhaps we would be so frightened that we would run back to the tent colony. But we did not move. One husky solider grabbed me and dragged me from the platform, and I had a toss and tumble with him. Mrs. Dominiske took hold of a post and stuck to it with all her strength. Mrs. Baratolotti had her faced slapped."[35] Schloss, while proud of the women's resolve, felt compelled to add that life was not that good for the small group of radicals remaining in the area: "The Socialists here are having a hard fight to make ends meet. We have no money and not many workers, and we appeal to the Socialists of this country to aid this weak district. The Socialists are a pack of undesirables here."[36]

In August 1914 Schloss and other members of the Las Animas County (Trinidad) Local of the Socialist party formed a committee to recall a judge who had kept dozens of striking miners in jail for several months, holding them illegally as "military prisoners" without bail. They received the support of Mother Jones and *Appeal to Reason* in their effort to combat what they considered a bankrupt system of justice.[37] Several strikers were indicted for the murder of militiamen and mine guards. Not a single mine guard or militiaman was indicted on any grounds.[38] Lawyer Edward P. Costigan, a Progressive leader in the state, was able to win an acquittal for some of the indicted defendants. Among those convicted was UMW leader John R. Lawson for shooting and killing a deputy sheriff during a confrontation between strikers and mine guards in 1913. Authorities arrested Lawson in April 1915, and the following month a jury in Trinidad found him guilty as charged and he was sentenced to life in prison. Socialists contended that the trial was a mockery, his conviction based on perjured testimony and jury intimidation. Lawson appealed to the Colorado state supreme court, which in June 1917 reversed the judgment and set him free.

The strike officially ended in December 1914, with the UMW, short of funds and having lost confidence in District 15 officials, writing off Colorado as a lost cause. The union gained nothing for its efforts. It withdrew from the fields, and union miners were permanently replaced by nonunion miners. Showing no affection for the defeated union, one Colorado Socialist party activist predicted: "The United Mine Workers of America is afflicted with the creeping paralysis and another year will see it relegated to oblivion. There are many United Mine Workers in Colorado who will hesitate a long time before repeating the experience of 1913–1914, with only starvation awaiting them at the finish."[39] The Colorado legislature, in an effort to head off future strikes, enacted a law requiring a thirty-day cooling-off period before strikes could begin and created an Industrial Commission to oversee labor-management conflicts. The legislature also passed legislation giving workers insurance against accidents or death. For its part, in an effort to improve its image, the Colorado Fuel and Iron Company instituted a plan of employee representation known as the "Rockefeller Plan," which critics described as a thinly disguised company union. To Socialists, such reforms could be written off as "benevolent feudalism."

Republican George A. Carlson easily won the Colorado governorship in 1914 by running on a law-and-order platform in the wake of the Ludlow disaster and by championing the call for prohibition; a constitutional amendment to this effect was approved by voters in the same election. Costigan, the Progressive candidate, was hurt by having represented the Ludlow miners and having become one of the principal attorneys for the UMW. Back in the summer, one of his campaign advisers had cautioned that "at this time anything that savors of an affiliation with Socialism does us lots of hurt."[40] Costigan, he said, needed votes from the conservative union-hating rural areas. He risked alienating conservatives by appealing to "the dissatisfied element" and overdoing radicalism.[41]

Colorado Socialists, meanwhile, directed their wrath at labor leaders, the UMW in particular, and the miners in general. One angry Colorado party activist questioned why Socialists should give a damn if labor leaders in that state such as John Lawson were being carried off to jail when none of them had shown the slightest inclination to support the party. Indeed, he pointed out, "There is not one 'labor leader' in Colorado that I know of who would not stick his right hand in a fire and burn it off clear up to the elbow before he would vote a Socialist ballot."[42] Another declared, "The Socialists are the only friends that labor has, and yet when election time has come the strikers have joined forces with the business element, the church people and the scabs—all of whom had literally stood over them day and night with drawn guns—and fought the Socialists with all the fury of beasts."[43]

While these events were unfolding in Colorado, Utah faced labor problems of its own. Conditions in the coalfields of Carbon County may have been as bad as, if not worse than, those in Colorado or West Virginia, but, thanks in part to an elaborate spy system concocted by the principal company in the area, Utah Fuel, there was relatively little union activity.[44] The same, however, could not be said about Bingham Canyon, twenty-five miles from Salt Lake City, where, rather than dig down in a mine, workers employed by the Utah Copper Company, owned by Daniel J. Guggenheim, and other companies were removing the top of a mountain in search of copper. The open-pit miners were unskilled "new immigrants" from Greece and Italy. Many of them joined the Bingham Canyon Mining Union, a WFM local, which had its fair share of Socialists, and pressed the Americans who led the local to call a strike to improve conditions. National leaders such as Moyer did not favor a strike, but the union went on strike anyway on September 18, 1912. The strike involved 4,000 to 6,000 workers from twenty-four nationality groups—an act of solidarity that Socialists found impressive—and featured workers' demands for union recognition, improved compensation, and ending the profiting of labor agents, particularly Leon Skliris who recruited unskilled Greek labor for the Utah Copper Company.[45]

Mine owners responded by bringing in Japanese and Mexican labor to fill the jobs (ending all talk about worker solidarity) and armed gunmen to protect the nonunion workers and the mining property.[46] The workers, however, were equally prepared for war. The IWW's *The Industrial Worker* related on September 26, 1912: "According to reports the miners have bought up all the automatic revolvers and ammunition in Salt Lake City and nearby towns, while the mining companies have secured high power rifles for the company guards. Much firing has already taken place. Governor Spry has notified the strikers that should they attack the men who are sent in to scab, the militia will be called out. . . . Three hundred deputy sheriffs are guarding the property of the company and a clash is feared as feeling is high."[47] Clashes between the strikers on one side and strikebreakers and deputies on the other eventually resulted in two deaths. After nearly a year, the strikers gave in and went back to work without achieving union recognition by the company, although they had forced Skliris to resign his position as Greek labor agent.

By the time of the Bingham strike, the IWW had made its presence known in Utah. This happened every day on the streets of Salt Lake City because of the presence of a man named John Houland, who hopped around with the aid of an "industrial leg"—a rod in place of a missing left leg—selling copies of *The Industrial Worker* and other radical papers.[48] Wobbly unions also met regularly in the city. In October 1912, for example, the Local 69 of the IWW held a rousing meeting in the Socialist hall downtown in which speakers focused on problems in the southern lumber camps. As was customary, the meeting closed with the singing of revolutionary songs. In reporting on the meeting, the IWW Local Press Committee noted: "The wage slaves in the Mormon stronghold are getting pared loose from their ancient superstitions, handed down to them by the prophets of the faith. Typical of all religions, the statute of the chief prophet in Salt Lake has its back toward the Temple and its hand outstretched toward the bank."[49]

In 1913 the IWW led an unsuccessful strike against the Utah Construction Company, after which it launched a free-speech campaign in Salt Lake City. At about this time, Joe Hill (aka Joe Hillstrom) came to Salt Lake City. Hill—a native of Sweden—immigrated to the United States in 1902, joined the IWW in 1910, and soon became famous as an IWW organizer and songwriter. He was heading east from California when he decided to stop off in Utah to do some mining. He found work of this nature in Park City in the Salt Lake area. He was later arrested and found guilty of killing a grocer during a 1914 holdup in Salt Lake City. On the evening of the murder Hill went to Frank McHugh, a medical doctor in Murray who, as noted earlier, had been the Utah Socialist party's nominee for governor in 1912, to treat gunshot wounds in his chest. Hill knew McHugh, and some suspect he went to McHugh thinking that as a fellow Socialist he would be sympathetic and not report the incident to the police. If so, he must have been disappointed. After learning about the murders and the fact that one of the two masked holdup men had been wounded, McHugh informed the police that he had treated Hill. At the time there was considerable tension between Socialists and Wobblies in Utah, which may have influenced McHugh's decision to tip off the police.

Radicals and all types of people in the Mountain West and around the nation, believing Hill had been framed and convicted because he was a Wobbly, deluged Utah's Governor William Spry with letters and telegrams on Hill's behalf. Socialists condemned Utah's "capitalistic courts" and demanded Hill's release.[50] Officials of Tonopah Miners' Union of the WFM declared Hill had been convicted "on the flimsiest kind of circumstantial evidence" by a jury biased against the IWW. Hill's execution, the officials warned, would "put a blot on the record of the State of Utah that the lapse of a thousand years cannot remove."[51] The Socialist party local in Ogden, Utah, was among several Socialist locals in the region to protest Hill's conviction and ask the governor to spare Hill's life: "We submit to you that there is a general impression in Utah, that this man did not have a fair trial, and that there is no doubt but that the fact that he had made himself obnoxious to a certain class thru his affiliation with the I.W.W. organization made it easier to convict him. In a large number of states, capital punishment has been abolished. Utah has not taken this advanced step, but it is in the power of the pardoning board to give this man the benefit of ALL DOUBT by commuting his sentence."[52]

Radicals claimed Hill was the victim of a campaign against labor conducted by the Utah Copper Company, the Utah Construction Company, and the Church of Latter Day Saints (the Mormons). Despite an international protest by the Swedish government and President Wilson's intervention, Spry held fast and Hill was executed by a firing squad on November 19, 1915. Hill's wish "not to be found dead in the state of Utah" was honored, and his body was shipped to Chicago for cremation. He became a well-known martyr to labor's cause. His statement "Don't mourn, organize!" became a rallying cry for workers throughout the nation.

Wobblies also had a troublesome time in Montana. They organized a Propaganda League in Butte that distributed literature throughout the district. On several levels the Wobblies had good relations with the Socialist party. Many Wobblies were also members of local party chapters, and Wobblies and their sympathizers regularly voted the Socialist ticket. The Butte party local reciprocated by strongly defending the IWW and the industrial union idea. Local party and IWW organizations, moreover, were united in their criticism of the Butte Miners' Union (BMU) as a corrupt and conservative organization, alien to the interests of workers.

On the other hand, Montana Wobblies and Socialists, like their counterparts on the national level, fundamentally disagreed over the value of political action. Ties between the two were further strained in 1912 as the national Socialist party, hoping to move more into the political mainstream, began to distance itself from the IWW and became a harsh critic of that organization. In Butte the strain was increased as Wobblies began complaining about pursuing Socialism through municipal reform—reform, they felt, was moving too slowly under Mayor Lewis J. Duncan, and many suspected it would not likely lead to much of anything of a revolutionary nature in any event. IWW members, particularly the Finns among them, also felt Duncan had been unfair to them in making appointments to city positions. Duncan had initially lost the fight within the party over his appointments—some of his selections were rejected by both the Butte party's central committee and a membership vote—but he defied those actions and declared he was not going to give jobs to IWW members in the manner dictated by the party. Charging that the Wobblies had infiltrated and taken over the Butte party, he asked the state central committee to revoke the local's charter as a way of eliminating the direct actionists. This was accomplished, causing a loss of about 400 members, including many Finns and union activists.[53] The party, though, was reconstituted in short order, with the Finns reinstated on the promise that they would follow party rules.

The Finns still harbored several grievances. They were angry about Duncan's attitude toward them and, being leftists, about the national party's recall of Haywood. Many also had an ax to grind against the BMU. Many remembered that they could not persuade members of that union to stand up for the hundreds of Finns fired by Anaconda in March 1912. The BMU strike committee recommended strike action to restore these jobs—it would have been the first strike ever called by the union—but a majority of the members rejected that suggestion. Apparently, even some or many of the 2,000 Socialists in the union refused to help the fired workers.

Many miners in the Butte local were unhappy about the failure of the union to protect the fired workers and also about a "rustling card" system imposed in 1914 by Amalgamated—a system that allowed the company to screen troublemakers by requiring miners to secure what, in effect, were work permits before they could seek employment at one of the company's mines. Dissidents, urged on by the IWW, claimed that a reactionary, company-controlled faction had gained control of the Butte Miners Union—replacing union officers, mostly Socialists, who had taken positions with the city after Duncan became mayor. They felt the union had made an unfair contract with the mining companies, complained about misconduct in the election of union officials, and were angry about the continuing assessment of wages to help Michigan strikers, even after the strike had been called off. The rumor spread among miners that the assessments were not going to strikers but were being pocketed by union officials. Under these conditions, many miners, especially those who lost their jobs in 1912 and those caught up by the radical economic ideas promoted by the IWW, had little difficulty believing that the WFM, while costing them much in dues and special assessments, was of little or no economic value to them and, indeed, was run by corrupt, company-controlled reactionaries adverse to their interests. Finnish miners were prominent among the rebels.[54] Discontented miners took their complaints to WFM headquarters but received no help.

On June 13, 1914, rebellious miners took out their frustration by attacking WFM officials who were leading a parade in Butte honoring Miners' Union Day.[55] A mob pulled the officials off the horses they were riding. The following day a mob took off toward the Miners Union Hall, tearing the hall apart in a search for records and money. Mayor Duncan was out of town, but the acting mayor, Frank Curran, rushed to the scene and from a second-story window urged the crowd to go home. All he got for his effort was a shove out the window and, after the fall, a broken arm and dislocated ankle. The rebels quickly formed a new union, the Butte Mine Workers' Union, which was independent of the WFM and led by prominent Wobblies.

Duncan returned to the city on June 15. He conferred with city officials, the governor, and the attorney general and concluded that bringing in the militia would just make matters worse. A few days later WFM president Charles Moyer came to town to try to patch things up with the rebellious miners. He called a meeting at the Miners Union Hall for the evening of June 23, which was attended by a hundred or so WFM loyalists. During the meeting an exchange of gunfire broke out between the miners inside the hall and the crowd gathered in front of the hall, and an innocent bystander was killed. By some accounts, including Duncan's, one of Moyer's followers started the shooting from inside the hall. At any rate, some men in the street crowd went off in search of dynamite with which to blow Moyer and his followers out of the building. By the time they returned, Moyer and eleven of his followers had escaped and were on their way out of town by automobile. The rioting miners allowed everyone else who had attended the meeting to leave the hall. They then proceeded to blow up the building.

Duncan had earlier checked out the meeting and, finding everything peaceful, left for his office, leaving behind a contingent of police in case trouble broke out. On his way to the office he heard the first shot and saw the crowd falling back from in front of the hall. He later testified: "Between ten and eleven the dynamiting began and I was worried I tell you. I didn't know how to handle that situation. I called on the governor myself, told him the dynamiting had begun, that it seemed to be directed against the hall, that as near as I could find out, it was an act of reprisal on the part of the people outside against the Miners' Union because the opening of the assault that night had come from inside the hall."[56] Still, Duncan saw no need to ask the governor to send in the militia. The dynamiting continued until about 1:30 A.M., and Duncan left his office at around 2:00.

Over the next few days, the WFM blamed the IWW for the dynamiting, but Duncan was inclined to dismiss this charge, contending that the WFM had invited the action itself by alienating miners who had been on the job in Butte for years and were loyal union members. The Socialist party also blamed Moyer for trying to put the old company-led union back in power. The AFL and Anaconda, on the other hand, joined the WFM in blaming the IWW. Others blamed private detectives working for Anaconda who had apparently infiltrated some or all of the organizations involved—the WFM union, the new union, and the IWW—to keep track of the company's employees and foment trouble, acting as agents-provocateurs in an effort to destroy the union movement.[57]

The mayor stayed in Butte after the riot and was in his office on July 3 when, in a bizarre episode, he was attacked and stabbed three times about the shoulders and neck by Eric Lantala, head of the Finnish branch of the Socialist party in Butte. The mayor fought back, drew a pistol, and fatally shot his attacker in the abdomen. Duncan, not seriously hurt, had been expecting trouble and had a revolver within reach because of threats by the city's radical element of a physical attack on him. Lantala had demanded that the mayor deport Frank Aaltonen, a journalist who supported the WFM and opposed the IWW, on the grounds that he was a menace to the community. Duncan said he did not have the authority to do so. Lantala had tried to convince Duncan to change his mind and attacked him after he refused.[58]

Duncan, under fire from Wobbly extremists, also incurred the wrath of the WFM, which accused him of being in cahoots with the IWW and of making a false charge that Moyer had asked the governor to send troops to Butte. At the WFM convention on July 25, 1914, delegates approved a vote of censure against Duncan, along with a demand directed at the Socialist party that it expel him from membership if he failed to retract his statement regarding Moyer. Moyer joined the discussion, remarking, "I don't care what you do as to the Socialist Party, whether you ask that they expel this miserable, slimy whelp, or not—it matters not to me. If this convention brands him as a liar, I am satisfied."[59] At other points in the convention, Duncan, the onetime hero of the Socialist party, was referred to as a "long-haired freak."[60] The statement was met with applause. Others at the convention tied Duncan to the archenemy, the IWW. If nothing else, many delegates were probably not happy that Duncan had stood by and done nothing to prevent the destruction of the Miners Union Hall.

On September 1, 1914, the state militia, under the command of Major D. J. Donahue, came to Butte. This followed the dynamiting by miners of a company shack where rustling cards were issued. Bill Haywood recounted the subsequent events: "Times were lively in Butte during the reign of Major Donahue and his soldier boys. The writ of habeas corpus was suspended. The press was censored, one paper, the 'Montana Socialist,' was closed down. Public speaking was forbidden and members of the I.W.W were deported or sentenced to jail for minor infractions—one for speaking on the street corner, another for singing a song."[61] Amalgamated, taking advantage of the situation, declared Butte an open shop and said it would no longer deal with unions. Those with a record of being agitators or voting incorrectly could not get a rustling card issued by Anaconda's employment bureau, which was needed to secure employment. The same was true for those with a record of complaining about working conditions.

The Montana Socialists' state convention in Helena in September 1914 protested "the establishment of military rule and censorship of the press during the mine war" and demanded that Governor Samuel V. Stewart make a "personal and impartial investigation of the Butte situation." Should he refuse to do so, he stood "as a willing party to brutal conspiracy to intimidate and enslave the people of Silver Bow County, in the interest of the Amalgamated Copper Company."[62] Going the other direction, what was called a "Vigilance Committee," composed largely of leading businessmen, pushed for impeachment proceedings against Mayor Duncan and Sheriff Tim Driscoll. Both men were impeached, tried in a civil court, and removed from office for neglect and inefficiency in discharging their duties during the riots. Following his impeachment Duncan told a reporter, "My scalp is in the wigwam of the Anaconda Copper Mining Company."[63]

In addition to the explosive situation in Butte, WFM leaders in August 1914 were concerned about their failure to gain a firm foothold in Arizona. The WFM had virtually no influence in that state, even though around 30,000 people there were working in and around the mines, mills, and smelters and should have been part of the union.[64] Some indication of the problems the WFM faced in Arizona is found in a letter from a local union secretary named John Striegel to WFM organizer Ernest Mills, written on August 2, 1914, from Humboldt, Arizona. In the letter, Striegel resigned as secretary of the local union. The local, he reported, was in debt, unable even to pay the $214 he was owed in back salary. He had been borrowing money from members to keep things going—and to put in a hardwood floor in the union building—but there were only a few members left and they refused to put more money into the organization. More important to Striegel, he had been fired twice in the last five months by corporate managers when they learned that he was with the union. The same thing had happened to other workers in the area. He had a family to support and was going to have to quit the union to get work.[65]

In early 1915 the WFM took part in a strike in Miami, Arizona, a town of 1,500 people near Globe, of mostly Anglo-Irish skilled workers who protested a wage cut. This turned out to be a peaceful strike, supported by town merchants and devoid of strikebreakers. Governor George Hunt conducted negotiations because the operators refused to deal with any union. The strike concluded within two weeks when the strikers agreed to a sliding wage scale tied to the price of copper.

A strike in Arizona's Clifton-Morenci copper-producing districts in the fall of 1915, however, proved far more difficult. WFM agents, headed by Guy E. Miller, entered these longtime unorganized districts, where a majority of the miners were Hispanic, in the summer of 1915. At that time the price for copper was low, and owners had recently cut wages. Salaries in the Clifton-Morenci districts were the lowest of any mining camps in Arizona. To compound the problem for Hispanic miners, they received considerably less pay than others for the same work.[66] Mine owners defended the practices and fiercely resisted the WFM's attempt to organize and represent the workers. Miller reported to President Charles Moyer in July that the "Mexicans are alive and enthused throughout Arizona, if the sentiment can be crystallized into organization it will mean much."[67]

On September 11, 1915, around 5,000 unskilled and semiskilled mine workers, 90 percent of whom were Hispanic, went on strike to secure higher wages and union (WFM) representation. According to the conservative press, a reign of terror took place as authorities stood by while members dragged strikebreakers out of their beds: "Threats of lynching, abuse and curses heaped upon men and their families at every turn caused many to leave."[68] Managers of the involved companies also fled, telegramming Hunt from Lordsburg, New Mexico, that they had done so because they feared their presence in Clifton might trigger violence. They asked Hunt to rid the area of WFM organizers and to follow a course of action such as the one taken by Governor Elias Ammons of Colorado in the coalfield strikes.[69] Hunt, however, by his words and actions concerning the strike, won the applause of organized labor. He made it clear that he was sympathetic to the workers and their demands. More important, unlike other governors of his time, he ordered the national guard into the area to protect those who were on strike and to prevent strikebreakers from entering the camps. Hunt was well aware of what had happened in Colorado and was anxious to avoid another Ludlow situation. Feeling the mining company officials were more likely than the Hispanic workers to incite violence, he made it clear that he would not tolerate the importation of hired thugs and gunmen in the guise of strikebreakers into the district.[70]

National as well as local labor leaders praised Hunt for his actions at Clifton-Morenci. James Lord, president of the Mining Department, AFL, lauded him for his "fearless and humane attitude" in avoiding what could have been another massacre and placed Hunt on the same level as the "immortal [John Peter] Altgeld" as one of the greatest governors of all time.[71] Praise was also forthcoming from Mother Jones, who had been in the state assisting in the organization of miners. She later helped campaign for Hunt's reelection.[72] On the negative side, Hunt enthusiasts quickly pointed out that he had also created some powerful enemies.[73]

The copper companies did indeed respond with alarm to the demonstration of labor's strength during the fall strikes, and they banded together in opposition to both labor and Hunt. Mining companies gained control over an increasing number of newspapers and used them to lambaste Hunt for siding with the radicals and, in the context of the European war, unpatriotic worker demands. The fact that most of the striking miners were Hispanic made Hunt, to some of his critics, a traitor to his own people. One paper complained: "The speech made by Governor Hunt in Clifton recently was wholly inflammatory in effect. He caused the strikers to spit in the face of good citizens by telling them that they were as good as anyone."[74] Mining companies circulated a petition asking for Hunt's recall from office on the basis that he "has deliberately attempted to foment and encourage class hatreds and divisions" and "that by a program of unconcealed and deliberate catering to the most radical elements, he has created a condition approaching anarchy in certain sections of the state."[75]

The Arizona Socialist party, meanwhile, took pride in the fact that Guy E. Miller, who had general charge of the strike, and his assistants, Guiterez De Lara of Los Angeles and George Powell of Miami, Arizona, were Socialists. Party leaders said they had made no attempt to "divide the strikers on politics," but they did conduct "considerable quiet propaganda" such as distributing Socialist papers. These, they thought, were well received because the strikers had considerable time to read, talk, and think. The party expected a victorious outcome to bring it increased support in Clifton, especially among the Spanish-speaking workers.[76]

Whatever benefits awaited the party, the WFM came out of the 1915 experience in Clifton-Morenci in a weakened position. To many, the strike underlined what had been becoming apparent: the failure of the union to make much, if any, progress in organizing the industry. Members also complained about the heavy assessments levied on them by WFM locals, much of which was used to support a long and expensive strike in Michigan. In 1916 there were frequent calls for "new blood" in the organization at the leadership level. Moyer survived a challenge, but the organization, hoping to get a new start and to shed whatever association it had in the public's mind with the IWW, in July 1916 renamed itself the International Union of Mine, Mill, and Smelter Workers.

CHAPTER FOURTEEN

Slipping, But Holding On

In the Legislature

IN 1914 NATIONAL SOCIALIST PARTY LEADERS thought they had a winning issue by becoming the only party attempting to keep the United States out of the European war. The party took a clear-cut antiwar position and by September of that year had distributed hundreds of thousands of antiwar leaflets and called upon the 6,000 or so locals to stage mass meetings and pass resolutions against the war.[1] Whatever the net effect of this effort, the party, by its own calculations, gathered in only about 595,000 votes in 1914, 10,000 fewer than it had in the previous non–presidential election year of 1910.[2] Within the party there were also the beginnings of a pro-German and anti-German division, a divide that would become more serious in later years.

Eugene Debs maintained a high profile in the Mountain West in 1915–1916. His 1915 "Pacific Coast Tour" took him to Montana, Nevada, Utah, Idaho, and Colorado. He took another western trip in 1916 that included several of these states again, along with New Mexico and Arizona. In 1916, however, he was not the party's nominee for president. That honor went to Allan Benson, a journalist from Yonkers, New York, who was far less colorful or charismatic than Debs. Opening his campaign at a meeting in the Bronx, the quiet speaker failed to excite the crowd, and many left before he had finished his speech. Joseph D. Cannon, former Arizona Socialist and Western Federation of Miners (WFM) organizer who had moved to New York, also spoke at the meeting and seemed to capture more attention with his claim that Pancho Villa's raid on Columbus, New Mexico, on March 9, 1916, was the product of a plot by American millionaires. Seeking to promote their own interests, the millionaires, according to Cannon, had hired Villa to lead the raid in an effort to provoke the United States into taking over the northern states of Mexico.[3]

Benson campaigned against U.S. involvement in the European war. Woodrow Wilson, however, took the same position. Socialist candidates were not only preempted on the war issue but were hurt, according to some reports, by their adoption of the ban on sabotage and the defection of Haywood supporters after his ouster.[4] Dues-paying membership fell from around 125,000 in 1912 to 65,000 in 1916. Some on the right suggested, however, that the party lost out not so much among leftists as among more conservative members upset by the "rule or ruin" campaign launched by the left after the ban was approved. Benson, for example, argued that "by persistent wrangling and quarreling at party meetings," the syndicalists "discouraged and disgusted enough Socialists to bring the dues paying membership down to 65,000 where it was at the beginning of the 1916 campaign."[5] According to the 1916 standard-bearer, they also drove members away "by foisting anarchist ideas upon the country as Socialist ideas."[6]

In 1916 Benson received only 600,000 votes, about 3 percent of the total. For the first time in its history, the party failed to increase its number of votes since the last presidential election. Its share of the total vote in 1916 was about half what it had been in 1912 (Appendix, Table 2). Within the party, leftists took some pleasure in the failure. To them, it reflected the inability of the right-wing leadership to move the party ahead. Under the right wing, according to the left, the party had lost the revolutionary fervor that had propelled its rise.[7]

Although Socialists in the Mountain West region did as well as or better than Socialists in any other region of the country in the 1914 and 1916 presidential elections, they were generally slipping. Thunder stealing continued unabated, and whatever hope Socialists had of being rescued by woman suffrage seemed to fizzle out, even though Socialists had promoted this cause. In 1914–1916 they enjoyed an occasional victory on the local level and, although rarely, in a state legislature.

In much of the Mountain West there was little in the 1914 or 1916 election results for Socialists to get excited about. In Colorado, for example, the party dropped to about 6 percent of the vote in 1914 and to about 3 percent in 1916.[8] The Wyoming party, meanwhile, virtually disappeared from the electoral picture in 1916. Benson received only 2.8 percent of the vote there, his worst performance in the Mountain West states, picking up a handful of votes from the coal camps (Appendix, Table 2). In Utah, leaders kept a stiff upper lip in spite of continued disappointments. In mid-October 1914 state organizer C. T. Stoney reported to his comrades as part of his plea for money to carry on the struggle: "The work throughout the state is perfectly satisfactory, considering the odds against which we are fighting. The sentiment is getting strong, and it is only a matter of time, and that a very short time, until we will see our efforts crowned with success. Keep your nerve, and you will be rewarded for every effort you put forward."[9] Things did not improve, however. In 1914 party candidates for the two congressional seats got 4.7 percent of the vote in one district and 5.3 percent of the vote in the other, compared with 8.7 percent for the single seat in 1912.[10] In 1915 Stoney continued giving pep talks and reminding party members: "By assuming an unpopular cause, you become great. Let your greatness be achieved in a struggle for the masses of the people. Let this be the supreme effort."[11] Stoney also promised: "Socialism will take over the government. It will take it peaceably. Not by strife and bloodshed. But by the ballot."[12] In 1916, though, Socialist Frank McHugh picked up just 3 percent of the vote in his bid for Utah governor, about the same as received by Socialist presidential candidate Alan Benson and other Socialists on the ballot.

Also falling into the 3 percent level of support was the New Mexico party. Much of the effort of putting the state's party in order and conducting campaigns was in the hands of Secretary A. James McDonald, an attorney in Clayton. In 1914 veteran Socialist W. P. Metcalf vouched for McDonald, describing him as a "Roman Catholic but an ardent socialist."[13] McDonald, who took the job as secretary that year, had little patience with Socialists who urged the industrial over the craft form or who argued that Socialism and Catholicity were in conflict. He felt that the image of Socialists as anti–craft union and anti-Catholic was making it difficult to build the party in New Mexico. He had a long-term goal of enlisting Hispanics in the party. As party secretary he was particularly anxious to get hold of a Socialist newspaper written in Spanish (but one that did not use controversial religious, anti-Catholic rhetoric) that he could circulate in New Mexico—for him, Hispanics were a large untapped source of members.[14] In early 1916 McDonald reported to the editor of the *International Socialist Review* that he was making progress in getting a Spanish Socialist weekly paper off the ground.

Said McDonald, "I believe the reaching of the native Spanish-speaking people is the most important single item of work that we can lay out for ourselves, and I bespeak for our Spanish paper your heartiest support."[15] Other secretaries after him also shared this goal but, like McDonald, found it difficult to raise enough money to put together a Spanish newspaper or even bring in Spanish-speaking organizers.[16]

While McDonald was pursuing this agenda, his state executive committee struggled with the problem of what to do about lagging membership. Some members proposed that the state party offer a prize to the local with the most effective recruitment campaign. Other members found little value in the idea. As McDonald reported, "One member opposed it because one ought not to be paid to become a worker for the party, and another because of the tendency to bring in as members persons who probably would not have any clear idea of socialism and would drop out, the reaction hurting worse than if they never had become members."[17] On the electoral level the party struggled along. N. A. Wells, the Socialist party candidate for governor in 1916, received 3.2 percent of the vote, although he did better in the eastern counties: he got 6.2 percent of the vote in Chaves, 5.1 in Eddy, 10.0 in Quay, 10.1 in Roosevelt, and 18.4 in Curry counties. Benson, the presidential nominee, picked up about 3 percent of the vote statewide.[18]

In the remaining states of the region—Idaho, Montana, Nevada, and Arizona—Socialists did a little better with voters in 1914–1916, exceptionally so in the case of Nevada. In Idaho the party was somewhat reinvigorated by turning left, while elsewhere parties did about as well by staying to the right. In Arizona the party was engaged in a losing battle with thunder-stealing Democrats but retained enough support to act as a spoiler.

In 1914 the Idaho party took a left turn and eliminated reform measures, under the name of "Immediate Demands," from the platform. The result, proponents of the change announced, was a platform that "stands out [as] clear-cut, concise and revolutionary, containing nothing which the old parties will care to steal."[19] Candidates running for governor and U.S. Congress that year put out a campaign book that, along with the revolutionary message, declared: "The Working class in most places in Idaho is about at the last ditch. They all know they must have a 'change' or be counted out."[20] The candidates made a point of mentioning that back in April "the Militia of the state of Colorado shot, beat, clubbed, and burned in most brutal fashion not only men but defenseless women and innocent children because these strikers were demanding their rights."[21]

Although their message was often dire, the candidates at times seemed to enjoy themselves. The highlight of the 1914 campaign was an automobile tour covering every section of the state. As described in the Socialist press:

The party consists of four. C. F. Fields, Canyon County Secretary, is driving the car; L. A. Coblentz, candidate for Governor, deals with state issues; A. B. Clark, candidate for Congress[,] deals with national issues, and I. F. Stewart, State Secretary[,] furnishes music and entertainment and an explanation of the organized Socialist Movement. They are making from two to five stops per day and are greeted everywhere with crowded houses. The most intense interest has been shown at all times. Where an evening meeting has been arranged they drive to [the] center of the main corner about five o'clock and Comrade Stewart plays a bugle call and "The Marseillaise" on the cornet. This draws the attention of everyone on the street. Then Comrade Clark announces through the megaphone that the car belongs to the party, that no railroad or banker contributed toward it, that Socialism is the only movement of today that promises actual relief to the workers, calls attention to the place of meeting, etc. They then proceed all over town repeating the performance every few blocks. By such and similar means they have drawn packed houses even in places where no Socialist sentiment has been shown.[22]

During the campaign the candidates made much of the party's system for selecting candidates (through a vote of the entire membership), financing campaigns (funds from workers only), and recalling Socialists who happened to get elected if they betrayed the wishes of voters.[23] In the end, the 1914 candidates received 8 percent of the vote. Two years later Idaho Socialists picked up just 6 percent for Benson, compared with 12 percent for Debs four years earlier.[24] Although losing strength overall, the party seemed to be doing better than ever in farming districts, but the Non-Partisan League (NPL) was also organizing in these areas and posed a potential threat.

As an indicator of the insignificance of the immediate demands debate, Montana Socialists in 1914–1916 stayed to the right in offering a variety of reforms and had a similar experience to the one in left-leaning Idaho in terms of vote catching. In 1914 Lewis Duncan appeared relatively strong, finishing far ahead of Progressive party candidates in the race for two at-large seats in the U.S. House of Representatives. Duncan led the ticket, getting around 15 percent of the vote. In a pamphlet published by the state as an information guide for voters, party officials wrote, "Lewis J. Duncan, candidate for U.S. Congress[,] needs no other introduction than to say that he was twice elected mayor of Butte, and gave such good service that the corporations have had him impeached."[25] In 1914 Socialists in Montana did relatively well in Silver Bow (where they captured some legislative seats) and also drew support from farmers in the northeastern part of the state, especially the Scandinavians in Sheridan County.

As in Idaho, however, party leaders were well aware that the NPL was planning to cut into this rural following. Indeed, the party's *Montana Socialist* warned its readers in 1915 that "something sinister is growing in North Dakota, very close to the heart of the Socialist movement there," headed by Socialists or former Socialists who were organizing hard-pressed farmers. The paper continued:

> This sinister thing goes under the name of the "Non-Partisan Political Organization League." It is something which the Socialists of Montana, especially those in the rural districts of this state, should be on their guard against. It is not in any sense a revolutionary or even a clear cut organization, according to reliable information at our hand; but a mere opportunistic, reformatory halfbaked compromising political organization, the purpose of which is to divide the farmer vote for the purpose of securing some immediate advantages of no greater or more fundamental significance than a few belated laws that merely touch the surface of the problems that confront the farmers.[26]

Continuing to blast the NPL as well as the capitalists, Montana Socialists nominated candidates for all state offices in 1916 and generally got about 6 percent of the vote—Duncan was again the top vote getter, gathering about 6.5 percent of the vote in his quest for governor.[27] A year earlier Butte Socialists had gone into the 1915 city campaign hoping to hold on to municipal offices. They advanced the theme: "Socialists have given the cleanest and best administration Butte has ever known. Why change?"[28] The voters, however, found reasons to do so, and the Socialists lost control of Butte to the Democrats. As noted later, the party largely blamed newly enfranchised women voters for this outcome. Election outcomes in 1915 and 1916 were generally disappointing for Butte Socialists. Writing about this period, political scientist Jerry Calvert noted, "In Butte, the Socialists' faith in political action was tried, sorely tested, and ultimately found wanting."[29]

Nevada Socialists went into the 1914 election feeling they had reason to be optimistic because there were only 20,000 voters in the state and most were wage-working miners who moved around from mining camp to mining camp. Thomas M. Fagan, Nevada party secretary, contended: "They are among the most independent of the working class. They are the most favorable material to bring the message of Socialism to, because only those with initiative and personal resources are found where the jobs are so precarious and so far apart."[30]

To reach the ballot, the secretary reported, party members struggled mightily to raise outrageous filing fees: "It costs the Socialist party of Nevada over $10 per member of the party to file complete county and state tickets. Over $9,000 for filing fees alone for less than 1,000 members to pay." Members, though, were "contributing far in excess of their means, because they recognize the hour to strike has arrived and they are making every sacrifice of time and money to grasp the critical moment of opportunity."[31]

In 1914 the party nominated A. Grant Miller for a seat in the U.S. Senate. Miller's party biography read: "Recognized by all as one of the leading lawyers of the state and easily the foremost trial lawyer in the state, he might have been rich if he had sided with the exploiters, but has preferred the other course and has never expressed any regret at his choice."[32] During the campaign, Miller and other Socialist candidates were particularly well received in the mining areas of Nye County, although in Tonopah Socialists and the Industrial Workers of the World were accused of being behind the dynamiting of the anti-radical *Tonopah Bonanza,* a charge the radicals denied.[33] In 1914 Miller received 20 percent of the vote for a seat in the United States Senate, cutting into the vote for the Democrat Francis Newlands, who barely held on to win. In Nye County Miller received 37 percent of the vote, and the Socialists reelected Justice Harry Dunseath.[34]

In preparing for the 1916 election, State Secretary Justus Taylor saw victory on the horizon but also noted problems in campaigning and organization because of the state's small population—"Nevada has a population that would not make a good first class city if they were all bunched together"—which was widely scattered over a very large land area. The secretary reported that high costs of travel meant that "we cannot meet together in conventions" and that "each local is practically an isolated unit."[35] Hoping to overcome the difficulties in putting a campaign together over the state's 100,000 square miles, the party asked for national party assistance. Taylor felt compelled to explain, "We have a fighting organization that up to this year has never called upon the outside for help!"[36]

The national party, impressed by what the Nevadans had been able to accomplish, decided to pour resources into another attempt by Miller to gain a U.S. Senate seat. Miller's campaign generated considerable enthusiasm among Socialists, both in the state and nationally. He polled an impressive 29 percent of the vote against Democrat Key Pittman in the Senate race. Still, the national party must have been disappointed—it had made the election of Miller one of its leading priorities. Statewide, Benson received 9.2 percent of the vote, the highest in the region and second only to Oklahoma in the nation.[37]

In Arizona, meanwhile, the thunder-stealing George W.P. Hunt easily won another term as governor in 1914. The Socialist candidate, J. R. Barnett, finished fourth in this contest behind the Republican and Progressive party candidates, with 5.8 percent of the vote. Hunt undoubtedly cut into Barnett's vote. Bert Davis, president of the Arizona Federation of Labor, one of many officers in that organization who was an active Socialist, ran on the Socialist ticket that year for a seat in the U.S. Senate and did better than Barnett, picking up 7.4 percent of the vote in a four-way contest, although again finishing last. Socialists claimed the

party vote was generally diminished by the larger-than-usual pre-election shut-down of mines and other industries.[38] In August 1914 Arizona State Secretary Alice Eddy reported: "We hear from every side reports of the larger mines laying off hundreds of men and cutting the wages of those who remain. By election time there may be few, if any, voters in the mining camps."[39]

Socialist party leaders generally saw Arizona as leaning to the left under the leadership of Hunt, who was running for reelection in 1916. Writing in October 1916, the editor of a Phoenix-based Socialist paper noted, "We must recognize the fact that the dominant political thought in Arizona is not reactionary, that it is in fact progressive and even radical."[40] Arizona Socialists were also aware that the dominant Hunt Democrats were stealing their thunder, which had a great deal to do with their meager showing at the polls. Because of this, party leaders felt compelled to declare that "Gov. Hunt is not a Socialist. Were Gov. Hunt a Socialist he would not only have taken the stand he did in the Miami, Ray and Clifton strikes, but he would have done much more to protect and advance the interests of the workers in Arizona."[41] Socialists also expressed disgust over how easily workers were being bought off. One discouraged Socialist leader com-plained, "Socialists are used to advocating what workers want, or claim they want, and then seeing the said workers throw fits of joy on the rare occasions when some member of the old parties reluctantly concedes [to] the workers the right to stay on the earth, and rush to their support, ignoring the Socialists."[42] Socialist party leaders called upon workers to favor Hunt's Socialist opponent for governor in the 1916 election. Some leaders, though, seemed deeply torn. One declared: "As state committeeman from Gila county I will quarrel with no Socialist for supporting Governor Hunt by voting for him at the next election. But for my own part, I am going to vote to preserve the consistency and stabil-ity and integrity of the Socialist Party. Why? Because I know that no kind of 'ism' that is inseparable from an individual can survive to attain the co-operative commonwealth."[43]

Arizona Socialist party leaders found themselves not only losing votes to labor Democratic candidates like Hunt but also losing some of their most prom-inent members to the Democratic party. Socialist party newspapers occasionally commented on the career developments of former comrades who had taken this route. The Arizona Socialist Bulletin of October 11, 1916, for example, reported: "Our former Comrade, Lester B. Doane, who ran for nomination for state sena-tor on the Democratic ticket, was turned down so hard that the fall was almost audible. He received fewer votes by several hundred than his nearest competitor, which can be taken as proof that the Democratic voters want in addition to good men, good democrats, as well. Mr. Doane's faux pas does not seem to discourage others, however, as Mr. L. W. Wyman has just been elected Secretary-Treasurer of the Gila County Democratic something or other and is trying to do his former political friends as much damage as possible."[44]

The 1916 general election brought Hunt face-to-face with Republican Thomas E. Campbell, who, two years earlier, had won election to the State Tax Commission. Supported by an organization of relatively young workers (average age thirty-seven) and money raised by the "hundred club" (composed of those who contributed $100 or more to defeat Hunt), Campbell toured the state with the slogans "Good Government versus Huntism, Industrial Peace Versus Wobblyism" and "Tax Payers versus Tax Eaters." On the first count, Campbell won the election by a vote of 27,976 to 27,946, but after lengthy recounts and court decisions Hunt emerged the victor by 43 votes. Hunt's friends argued that the Socialists, by putting up a gubernatorial candidate, had cost Hunt around 2,000 votes in 1916. Although there were only an estimated 700 "red card" Socialists in the state in 1916, they allegedly were able to convince 1,400 American Federationists to support Peter T. Robinson, the Socialist candidate.[45] In 1916 Arizona Socialists nearly played the role of spoiler. Hunt, it appeared, had been hurt not only by the Socialists' ability to retain the loyalty of many workers but also by the fact that in moving to the left to attract the radical labor vote, he also alienated conservatives in his own party and, on balance, probably lost more than he gained with the general electorate.

The Socialist vote in Arizona fell off in 1916, as it did nationally. Benson picked up 5.5 percent of the vote, compared with Debs's 12 percent four years earlier. On the other hand, average party membership in 1916 was 549, up from 441 in 1915. Included among twenty or so locals around the state were Spanish locals in Clifton and Metcalf, a Finnish local in Miami, and a Slavic local in Globe.[46] To the conservative forces, Socialism, Hunt, and the Wobblies—the three were combined in their thinking—were a force to be dealt with, and in no uncertain terms.

In 1914–1916 Socialists continued to be supportive of woman suffrage, although many had doubts about what suffrage meant for party support; as it turned out, they had reason to be apprehensive. Socialist women from small towns in mining areas—miners' wives, teachers, and other professionals—played prominent roles in the movement.[47] So, too, did women as national agitators who came to the area. Fearful of public reaction, however, state suffrage leaders distanced themselves from national spokespeople who coupled their call for suffrage with a call for Socialism. Often local Socialists were asked, or volunteered, to work behind the scenes to avoid discrediting the suffrage cause by associating it with radicalism.

There was no doubt, however, where the Socialist party stood on the issue. In New Mexico in 1914, for example, the party proudly declared: "The Socialist Party, based on universal democracy, industrial as well as political, holds that true democracy cannot be attained so long as women are denied the ballot. In every test by which we may measure the fitness of citizens to participate in governmental affairs, and especially in intelligence which is the prime qualification, women are the equals of men and therefore qualified to vote. They are the mothers and teachers of the race, tax payers, and in many other ways bearers of the burdens imposed by civil government and are therefore entitled to vote as a matter of right."[48]

Nevada Socialists were equally committed to the woman suffrage cause, although they had no illusions as to how this would benefit their party or program. The party's manifesto read: "We hold this truth to be self-evident, that all mankind (male and female) were created with equal rights." On the other hand, party leaders also noted: "We are fully aware that the granting of suffrage to women will retard as a matter of time, the success of the socialist principle of economic justice, for the reason that women have not been trained in political and economic life except to a slight degree comparatively and they have not felt the full force of the evils in capitalism to the extent that men have, and therefore will be slower to realize the great need of socialism; but the Socialist Party, standing for natural rights, never hesitates on such grounds."[49]

In the November 1914 election, Nevada voters extended suffrage to women. Suffragist leaders had been inclined to play down Socialists' involvement in the cause, and after the election they did not, at least publicly, attach much significance to Socialist support for the measure. In fact, though, a good many Socialists may have worked for equal suffrage; and the Socialist vote, as reflected in mining camps, may have been instrumental in its passage.[50]

Nevada Socialists followed up on the 1914 election with an effort to bring women into the party and to win over the female vote.[51] In early 1916 the party created a "Woman's Propaganda Department" to conduct an active campaign among women.[52] Debs declared that the newly enfranchised women of Nevada "are going to vote the Socialist ticket almost unanimously" because they "realize that they owe their enfranchisement practically to the activity and agitation of the Socialists alone. Not another party in the state has put forth so much effort, so much money and such devoted energy toward the enfranchisement of the women as did the Socialists. And the women have not forgotten."[53] On the other hand, Nevada governor Emmet D. Boyle assured a reporter for an eastern paper: "The women of the state have taken an active and intelligent interest in all public questions. They have shown no tendency toward revolutionary methods in government."[54] How the addition of women to the electorate affected the outcome in Nevada in 1916 is unclear. Empirical research from Arizona on elections during the same period, however, suggests that the addition of women voters did not work to the advantage of the Socialists or to anti-corporate reform measures on the ballot.[55]

Colorado Socialists, drawing upon past experiences in their state, voiced their concern about women voters. Writing in 1914 prior to the election, Emma F. Langdon, Colorado state secretary, suggested that the major problem presented by suffrage extension was that women allied with the capitalist class were more likely than wives of workers to vote: "[O]ur so-called aristocrats in this state are always on hand [on] election day, while the poor workers' wives are too busy trying to solve the bread problem but in the wrong way."[56] Writing in a national radical journal two years later, another Colorado Socialist, State Secretary Jennie A. McGehe, reminded her comrades around the nation that several years back politicians had used the women's vote to defeat the Populist governor and friend of labor Davis Waite and warned about the danger of "untrained and unenlightened" women voters.[57]

Montana Socialists also worked hard for woman suffrage and apparently had high hopes of receiving substantial support from women, who were just entering into the electorate as a result of the adoption of an equal suffrage amendment by voters in 1914.[58] They had long endorsed equal suffrage and were happy do so again at their state convention in September 1914.[59] In 1915, however, Socialists lost control of Butte to the Democrats and blamed women voters in part for their defeat. A Socialist editor declared, "The majority of the voters of Butte, and particularly the newly enfranchised women voters, have spit upon the hand that helped them, and in a frenzy of unreason and blind folly have slapped the face of their faithful servant and protector, the Socialist party, and discharged that servant to re-engage the one who brought upon their municipal household debt, dishonor, disease and death."[60]

The 1914–1916 period had some bright spots for the radical cause in the Mountain West. Although Butte was lost, Socialists could point to a scattering of victories on the local level. In April 1914, for example, Socialist M. R. Jones, a double amputee and former railroad worker and state secretary of the New Mexico party, was elected town clerk in Clayton, New Mexico.[61] That same year George Lindsay, a businessman, wrote national party headquarters that the unexpected had happened and he, "a poor socialist," had been elected county commissioner for the newly created county of Duchesne, Utah. When the votes were counted, he felt he would be the only Socialist in office, which bothered him:

"The Socialists in this new county will come to me to do all that I possibly can do to advance the interests of our party by passing or at least introducing Socialist measures for the governing of the county, and I must have some help as I realize my own weakness." In asking for information and advice, he noted, "My aim is to promote the influence of our party, and I have no personal aims whatever." He said he just wanted help to protect the people from having the government give away franchises and other benefits "to the hungry corporations."[62]

The Arizona party in the early 1910s enjoyed some local victories, although the Socialist winners were not always received with open arms. In Miami, Arizona, for example, three non-Socialist members of the city council refused to meet with the two Socialists elected to that body in 1915 until they were legally compelled to do so.[63] In some cities, mobs disrupted Socialist street meetings and threatened Socialists with deportation.[64] On the other hand, in Nevada in 1916 Socialist Harry Dunseath was reelected justice of the peace in Tonopah, and William H. Thomas, a butcher, became the Socialist sheriff of Nye County. During the campaign one Nevada Socialist noted, "We sure need all the Socialist sheriffs we can get, as they come in very handy during strike periods."[65]

Socialists in 1914–1916 elected state legislators in Idaho, Montana, Nevada, New Mexico, and Utah. Most of the time, though, there were only one or two Socialists in the legislative bodies in which they served. Some of these lawmakers expressed concern that the party would be judged on the basis of their performance alone and wished for more Socialist legislators to help carry the burden.[66] They were not entirely alone, however, as they received some assistance from national party headquarters as well as a good deal of advice and direction from their state parties. State party leaders were anxious to have successful candidates stay loyal to the party and its campaign pledges. The national party tried to help the legislators any way it could and to publicize their achievements. It served, on request from individual legislators, as a clearinghouse, sending bills introduced by Socialists in one state (often Wisconsin) to Socialist legislators in other states. It also developed a Socialist legislative program for use throughout the nation and encouraged its implementation.[67] Along with pursuing party-approved measures, Socialists saw a large part of their job as one of blowing the whistle on legislation they deemed detrimental.[68]

One of the few Idaho Socialists elected to state office was Earl W. Bowman, a poet and prose writer who served in the state senate from Adams County on the western border. Bowman reported to the national office in 1915 that he had been treated well by other legislators and had spent much of his time speaking to various organizations.[69] He also hosted a reception for Eugene Debs that was attended by most of the legislators who, according to Bowman "were delighted" with Debs.[70] Bowman, the only Socialist in the body, on one occasion took the floor and said: "Mr. President, I am the ultimate minority of this body. I have caucused with myself for some time as to just how I would cast my vote on this occasion."[71]

Bowman gained considerable publicity by pushing for an emergency employment act that required county commissioners to provide work for those seeking employment. The bill cleared the senate and passed the house with only one dissenting vote. Bowman, enjoying the moment, told national party leaders, "I ventured all my energy on the passage of this bill . . . it was a fight—a heart breaking, nerve wracking, killing fight but eventually I got the thing before them in such a way that they hardly dared to vote against it. Strong republican and democratic members of the House of Representatives spoke for the measure and declared that if this bill were Socialism that they were 'proud to be called Socialists.' "[72] In an interview with the *Idaho Statesman*, Bowman made it clear, however, that he was not, as might be expected from a Socialist, acting out of softer sentiments: "My emergency employment bill is not a charity measure. It is a cold-blooded business proposition. There is no maudlin sentiment in it. I am simply tired of dividing what I earn with a lot of other people who are as able to work as I, and hope the legislature, by making this bill a law, will put it up to the man who is out of a job to go to work and feed himself. I need what few dollars I earn to feed my own family—let the other fellow feed his."[73] After reading the interview in which Bowman made this statement, the mayor of Ontario, a town in eastern Oregon, wrote to the *Statesman* that if Bowman was a "Socialist, he "was a Socialist with a vengeance."[74] Socialists around the country, though, cited Bowman's accomplishment as an illustration of "the tremendous swing of public sentiment toward Socialist methods" of meeting the unemployment problem.[75]

On the state level the Nevada party showed some strength, putting several of its members in the legislature. The state party, moreover, appeared unusually involved in developing state legislative policy and making sure Socialist legislators toed the party line. Nevada Socialist legislators, in accordance with party rules, agreed to meet daily and to be united in their actions. They also agreed not to engage in political compromise or horse trading or to get mixed up "in trivial affairs of capitalistic organization and procedure." Other ironclad rules to guide their behavior were "hard work, eternal vigilance in pushing working class legislation and in fighting all action against the working class"; and "absolute loyalty and obedience to the Socialist Party of Nevada, of the United States, and of the world."[76] One Socialist legislator was expelled from the party for, among other things, ignoring party policy by voting against an amendment providing for woman suffrage and working with Democrats in a battle over the speakership.[77]

Nevada legislators took their duties seriously but also delighted in making corporate interests uncomfortable. Socialist M. J. Scanlan, serving in the state senate, got into a position where he could ruffle feathers by becoming, with the backing of the Railroad Brotherhoods, a member of the Committee on Labor. Scanlan later reported, "Being a member of this committee gave me an opportunity to quiz the corporation lobbyists, which was not to their liking and after the first week or so they never came near the Labor Committee but contented themselves with buttonholing the members outside the committee meetings."[78] Scanlan, a Massachusetts native, had taken up mining in Tonopah in 1906 and become president of the WFM local. In the legislature he took an interest in mine safety, workmen's compensation, direct democracy, and reforms to provide poor people with equal access to the courts. One of his few triumphs was a bill requiring the state mine inspector to post a notice concerning the safety condition of each mine at a conspicuous place at its entrance. More commonly, legislation introduced by Scanlan and other Socialists was "unceremoniously killed."[79] In 1913 Nevada Socialists introduced thirty-three bills and resolutions in the legislature and had four bills enacted. Socialists noted that in the 1914–1915 session, "[T]he state police force was increased—in the interest of 'free government'—to provide better facilities for shooting down strikers."[80] The legislature, as Scanlan saw it, was dominated by lobbyists for the mine operators, Southern Pacific Railroad, and Cattlemen's Association.

During the second decade of the twentieth century, only a few Socialists captured seats in the Montana state legislature. At any given time they were so few in number that they were not in a position to accomplish much. In 1914 Charles H. Conner, the only Socialist in the legislature, reported to the national party that his "heaviest work was in the exposure of the true meaning of certain bills introduced by other members."[81] Only one of the five measures he introduced— a measure requiring the reporting of information on cases of tuberculosis in copper mines and smelters—made it through the process.[82] All in all, though, Conner was rather upbeat about the ability of Socialists, himself included, to at least build the policy agenda for reform: "There is no doubt in the minds of the Socialists of Montana but what the advocacy of their principles in the campaign [has] driven the old parties to more advanced legislation. Several old party members are openly advocating the government ownership of transportation lines. The Socialist propaganda among the agricultural parts of the state [has] resulted in fairly wide spread demands for state flour milling. I think it only a question of time until we gain that point in the industrial world."[83] In regard to direct legislation, Conner reported to the national party: "I worked hard to build up a sentiment in favor of initiating laws by people, and it is rapidly gaining ground. The Butte, Helena and other locals have sown the seed in the industrial centers and the farmers here and there through the state have taken up the cause."[84]

In 1915 two Butte Socialists—Alexander Mackel, an attorney, and Leslie Bechtel, a Presbyterian minister—working closely with their party, attempted to make their presence known in the state house. The Socialist press reported: "The attitudes of the socialist members of [the] house are a revelation to many people. They expected to see introduced a lot of destructive, free-love, home wrecking legislation. Instead of that on every moral question the Socialists have stood on the side of the sanctity of the home, the protection of the youth of the state, the welfare of the common people."[85] Still, the paper was forced to admit that "four weeks have been sufficient to prove that the best way to kill a bill is to have the two Socialist members support it, and to get a bill through it is only necessary to whisper that the Socialists are opposed."[86] Initially, following party instructions, Mackel and Bechtel had planned to introduce legislation supportive of each plank in the Socialist platform. They abandoned this approach after several pieces of legislation they introduced went nowhere. Among the measures supported by the Socialists were ones to facilitate voting—for example, making a legal half-holiday on election day to encourage workers to vote and making it possible for traveling men and railroad men to vote by mail. Also high on the list were labor bills, such as preventing companies from employing gunmen.[87] The two men failed on these efforts. They were, however, able to defeat a bill that would have required voters to state their party affiliations, a measure they felt was intended to detect and punish Socialist supporters.[88]

Also doing what he could to further the cause was the lone Socialist in the Utah state legislature, J. Alex Bevan, who, like his counterparts elsewhere, saw a large part of his job as one of blowing the whistle on legislation he deemed detrimental. In some cases the defensive action was effective. Bevan, for example, blew the whistle on an attempt to weaken the eight-hour law and, working with the WFM, stymied the effort.[89] Bevan was eager to be more proactive and asked the national party for assistance in preparing legislation.[90] Most of the bills he introduced, however, went nowhere—failing, party sources asserted, simply because they were introduced by a Socialist.[91] Meanwhile, the legislature went on a reform binge under the leadership of Governor Simon Bamberger, elected in 1916. The victory of Bamberger, a wealthy businessman, ended twenty years of Republican rule. Bamberger was the state's first Democratic and first non-Mormon governor; he was Jewish. In 1917 what became known as the most liberal legislature in the state's history guaranteed labor the right to organize, passed a workmen's compensation law, and created an industrial commission. Along with these reforms came a public utilities commission, a corrupt practices act, and improvements in education and public health, among others. Bevan was still in the legislature and was no doubt delighted to see some of the measures he had long sponsored receive a more favorable response.

The major victory for the New Mexico party in 1914 was the election of W. C. Tharp, a former schoolteacher and newspaper editor from Curry County, to the state legislature. In commenting on his victory Tharp noted: "In the recent election I got 178 Socialist votes and 212 that would be either old party or independent voters except for a possible few that are socialists only when there is a chance for victory. There are some few who will vote for a man on our ticket if there is a chance to elect and vote for their second choice when there is not thought to be a chance to elect our man. There are a few of this kind here."[92] Tharp suggested that his Democratic opponent had been hurt by being a Catholic and a member of the Knights of Columbus. He let it be known that "while I am not prejudiced against any man because of his religious views I am opposed to a K. of C. and I feel that the Catholic Hierarchy is a bitter foe to all advanced ideas that are Democratic."[93] A less-than-friendly newspaper editor noted that Tharp had won by just 86 votes and that many felt that by electing a Socialist, "a blot has been placed upon the fair name of Curry county."[94] From the Democrats' point of view, not all was lost. Wrote one party strategist to newly elected governor William C. McDonald, "Although Curry county has elected a socialist, on a straight socialist ticket to the legislature, he is pledged to support your program for low salaries, taxation measures etc. I do not know what he will do but think he will be found with us on every occasion when the veto override is involved."[95]

Heading to his new job, Tharp said he planned to pursue a Socialist agenda but felt it would be best to start off slowly because he was going to have to deal "with a hard bunch" in the legislature.[96] He asked the national secretary for examples of bills ranging from inheritance taxes to mine inspection so he could phrase his own bills. Tharp explained that he found drafting legislation the hardest part of the job—he knew what bills he wanted but was not experienced enough to draw them up.[97] Tharp made similar requests for aid from the state party, although he did not always receive an enthusiastic response. For example, party secretary A. James McDonald, an attorney in Clayton, reported to members of the state committee in 1915: "Now I want to co-operate with Comrade Tharp as far and as thoroughly as possible, for he needs all the assistance that the state committee can give him, and especially he needs the assistance of someone with legal training. I believe, however, that it will be well for him to adopt and strictly adhere to the policy of 'safety first'; in other words to be sure he is right and then go ahead, and not until then."[98]

McDonald suggested that Tharp was being reckless in his choice of measures to introduce and that the members had to "bear in mind that the Socialist Party of New Mexico will get the brunt of the criticism if Comrade Tharp introduces a bill which for any reason turns out to be a freak."[99] In the legislature, Tharp generally seems to have been cast adrift among partisan forces—his own party called upon him to implement the legislative program outlined in the state party platform.[100] Tharp wanted to sit in as an observer in both the Republican and Democratic caucuses.[101] Under his picture in the official 1915 *New Mexico Bluebook,* Tharp, the only Socialist in the chamber, was identified as the Socialist floor leader.[102]

The official records do not reveal any Socialist victories for state legislative seats in the Arizona legislature in 1911–1912. There were, however, Democrats in that body who at one time identified with the Socialist party or were identified as Socialists in the party or the mainstream press. One of these men, A. A. Worsley, was identified in the popular press in 1906 as a "socialist orator of marked ability."[103] He became a Democratic state senator from Pima County and a champion of labor legislation in that body. Before arriving in Arizona in 1904, Worsley had been a candidate of the Labor and Populist ticket for governor of Wisconsin and an activist in the Single Tax Club and the Direct Legislation League. Worsley as a legislator not only championed labor causes but also encouraged the state and local governments in Arizona to engage in industrial pursuits: "Arizona is what we make it. . . . Why should not Arizona build a sawmill and convert her vast pine forests into lumber and thus put the lumber trust out of the state? Why should not Arizona build dams and power plants and convert all the dormant power in her great streams into [a] living, active force for the use of her own? Why should not Arizona convert her vast coal fields into electric energy and transmit it all over the country for the people's use and profit?"[104] Thus inspired, the Hunt Democrats set out on a very ambitious reform program. Wrote one of his critics, "Governor Hunt has not interposed an objection to any fad, fancy, or new stunt in the way of freak legislation proposed by the most violent of agitators."[105] Several reforms—including many having to do with labor but also including woman suffrage, prohibition, and capital punishment—came though the initiative process, itself the product of the reform effort in the state. Socialists were very much involved in churning reforms though the initiative process, a procedure they had long advocated.[106]

While Progressives in Arizona continued to have a champion in Hunt, a similar role was played by Governor Joseph Carey in Wyoming, although historian

T. A. Larson has noted: "In comparison with other Progressive leaders, Carey was primarily interested in reforms designed to purify the political system, secondarily in humanitarian reforms, and scarcely at all in reforms calculated to circumscribe big business."[107] Working with a Republican legislature that included a few friendly fellow insurgents, Carey was able to secure a direct primary and some limits on campaign expenditures. A majority of voters supported his proposal for the initiative and referendum, but the vote total was too low to meet the requirements of the law. Carey again asked for some reforms in 1913 but got little from the legislature, which was under the control of the faction loyal to Carey's enemy F. E. Warren. All in all, though, given the circumstances, Carey's accomplishments were noteworthy.[108] In 1914, reform continued with the election of Democrat John B. Kendrick as governor. Kendrick was able to secure more reforms from the Republican legislature in areas such as workmen's compensation and public utilities regulation.

George W.P. Hunt, Arizona governor. Courtesy of Arizona Department of Library, Archives and Public Records.

Loading cars during the deportation of suspected Wobblies at Bisbee, Arizona, July 12, 1917. Courtesy of the Arizona Department of Library, Archives and Public Records.

Train filled with deportees leaving for New Mexico, July 12, 1917. Courtesy of the Arizona Department of Library, Archives and Public Records.

Eugene Debs as he stepped from the Atlanta prison on Christmas day, 1921. Photo: Library of Congress.

CHAPTER FIFTEEN

War and Repression

The Law of Necessity

T HE SOCIALISTS' ANTI-MILITARISM presented little problem for presidential candidate Allan Benson in 1916; after all, Wilson swept the West on the peace issue. From 1914 to 1917 American Socialists could oppose the war in Europe without opposing their own government and thus opening themselves to the charge of siding with the enemy. Matters changed after April 6, 1917, the day the United States entered World War I. The Socialist party moved quickly, holding a National Emergency Convention in St. Louis, Missouri, on April 7–14, at which delegates—including fifteen from the Mountain West—adopted an antiwar proclamation later overwhelmingly ratified by the party membership. The St. Louis Anti-War Proclamation and Program stated: "The Socialist Party of the United States in the present grave crisis solemnly re-affirms its allegiance to the principle of internationalism and working-class solidarity the world over, and proclaims its unalterable opposition to the war just declared by the Government of the United States."[1] The party also pledged its opposition to conscription and censorship.

Membership records indicate that the party did not immediately suffer from its antiwar stand—indeed, membership increased from 67,788 in April to 81,172 in June 1917.[2] However, as popular support for the war grew, party leaders' unwillingness to change their anti-miltarism stand hurt the cause. The party's stand, commonly interpreted as unpatriotic, if not pro-German, prompted many members to abandon the party. Among the more prominent of these were Upton Sinclair, John Spargo, and the 1916 presidential nominee, Allan Benson. Benson's resignation in July 1918 nearly completed the exodus. Benson declared that he had disagreed with the party's stand for some time but had delayed resigning in hopes that the party would change its policy. For Benson, "[N]othing worse could happen to the world than to be placed under the heel of German imperialism."[3] Benson felt the Socialist party was not pro-German, in the sense of being in favor of a German victory, but it did have among its ranks some foreign-born leaders who "cannot get the American point of view. All nations look alike to them. . . . They cannot feel what Americans feel."[4] The crucial error, according to Benson, was that "a few men in the party, who should have known better, have accepted the false doctrine that a workingman can have no country, and, therefore, that it is immaterial to him whether the country in which he lives, if it be at war, shall be defeated or not."[5]

Socialists who remained in the party became subject to considerable harassment by federal, state, and local authorities. As the war progressed, party newspapers were censored and put out of business by the post office, party offices and meetings were raided, and party officials were threatened with jail for obstructing the draft or engaging in other seditious activities. Some, including Eugene Debs, were sentenced to prison for violating the federal Espionage Act, passed in June 1917. Matters got even worse in terms of repression after the Bolshevik Revolution on November 7, 1917. By the end of the decade the national party had established a Prison Comfort Club to send food and clothing and letters of comfort to political prisoners in Leavenworth and other prisons around the country.

Nationally prominent Socialists came to the Mountain West during the war to stir up opposition to U.S. involvement. In 1917 Socialist Kate Richards O'Hare held antiwar rallies on several occasions at party gatherings in southwestern Idaho.[6] O'Hare also found her way to Globe, Arizona, where, according to a special agent for military intelligence, on June 6, 1917, she wooed a crowd of around 1,000 people with an unpatriotic message—although, the agent unhappily reported, not one that would land her in jail. O'Hare, the agent wrote,

> is a smart socialist, a good talker, and can stir up the mind of a sluggish
> thinker in double-quick time by her suggestive manner of speaking. The

most disappointing part of this meeting to me was that a great proportion of the crowd seemed to be in sympathy with the views she expressed. When a crowd of this size will stand up for over two hours and listen to the kind of talk this woman made, and applaud as this body of people did, it convinces me that they were hearing the message they believed in. I worked through the crowd many times, and also had other people go through it, and it was alarming the number of champions this woman seemed to have. It was a much more enthusiastic crowd than attended the meetings held to encourage patriotism. . . . I secured a stenographer to take down this speech, but as there was no statement which could be construed as seditious it was not transcribed. It might be proper to state that this woman is of no help to this country at this particular time, as her style is to get seditious thoughts and seditious statements to her hearers by reflection—or on the bounce, perhaps would be a better way of expressing it.[7]

O'Hare escaped harassment on this occasion. Others, however, were not so lucky. Throughout the Mountain West, citizens acted through organizations known by such titles as loyalty leagues, home guards, national defense committees, and safety committees to track down draft evaders, saboteurs, and war critics. Several states passed syndicalism laws that made mere membership in any organization hostile to the government a crime. Many radicals went to jail on various changes such as handing out antiwar pamphlets and urging men to resist the draft. Some were taken from their homes and even killed. War brought rough sledding not only for Socialist parties but also for the Non-Partisan League (NPL) and especially for the Industrial Workers of the World (IWW). The IWW became a much-hated symbol of radicalism and dissent. The mainstream press constantly accused the Wobblies of being allied with the German war effort—the IWW, to some, stood for "Imperial Wilhelm's Warriors." Bill Haywood recalled that in 1917: "An extremely bitter stream of publicity had been started by the press, charging the I.W.W. with receiving vast sums of German gold. It was said that we intended to poison the canned goods used by the army, and that we were responsible for the spread of the hoof and mouth disease that was raging and had killed great herds of cattle."[8] Many IWW leaders were convicted under federal or state laws and sentenced to prison.

Support for the war effort and for drives to root out war resisters appeared throughout the Mountain West region, although the slacker rate was generally higher there than in the rest of the country—especially in Arizona and Nevada where mining radicalism was still relatively strong and where, consequently, the population contained a relatively large number of radicals (see Appendix, Table 9). In Wyoming, lawmakers resolved in favor of conscription before Congress had acted on it and commended President Woodrow Wilson for severing ties with Germany.[9] Many citizens felt there were German spies in the state. German Americans, labor leaders, and Socialists were immediately suspected, and various groups went in search of them. Colorado citizens and politicians were also eager to track down subversives at home. Among the targets was Governor John C. Gunter, who got in trouble for appointing a German American to the State Council of Defense—for which the media labeled him pro-German and effectively ended his career. Also forced to alter his career was Paul Jones, Episcopal bishop of Utah, whose opposition to the war and support of Socialism (he was a party member) became so controversial that he was forced to leave his position.[10]

In Idaho, home guards, patriotic leagues, and protective associations took the law into their own hands to root out subversives. People were arrested for advising persons not to register or for merely defending the IWW. Many suspected German Americans of subversion or disloyalty. The suspicion extended even to the German-born governor Moses Alexander, who was criticized for not taking greater action to protect reservoirs, railroad centers, and electrical power plants from enemy agents. Alexander also had some trouble because he refused to dismiss a Socialist draft board member.[11] Idahoans apparently believed Germans, working through the Wobblies, were behind a loggers' strike in the summer of 1917. Governor Alexander visited the strike area and tried, without success, to get the lumberjacks to go back to work. The lumber trust reacted by leading a successful effort for the passage of a criminal syndicalism law, intended to be used primarily against the Wobblies. The act made it illegal to advocate sabotage as a means of industrial or political reform. Even handing out IWW leaflets fell into the category of sabotage. Throughout the summer and fall of 1917 Idaho sheriffs raided IWW halls, swooping up literature and correspondence and making arrests on charges of criminal syndicalism. In the St. Maries fairgrounds forty Wobblies were held in a hastily constructed stockade. Home guards thereafter took it upon themselves to regularly visit Idaho lumber camps in search of Wobblies they could round up.[12]

In New Mexico, U.S. Senator-elect A. A. Jones told reporters in February 1917, "There may be pacifists somewhere in this country, but there are none in New Mexico that I know of."[13] Yet, although New Mexico officials took pride in New Mexicans' willingness to support the war, they were also on the lookout for slackers and war resisters. Typical of the warnings was one sent to three suspected war resisters on August 13, 1917, by the New Mexico Guadalupe County Council of Defense: "It has been brought to the notice of the Guadalupe County Council of Defense, recently appointed by the Governor of New Mexico, that you have uttered remarks entirely unbecoming to a person enjoying the Liberty and Protection of the United States and we wish to impress upon you, most emphatically, that such conduct will at no time be tolerated within the United States. This information comes to us through a very reliable source, and should we have such complaint made against you the second time, we will be obliged to apply such remedy as is necessary to counteract seditious conduct, and we are acting under orders given us by the Governor of the State of New Mexico."[14] Authorities followed up by arresting a man for making "false statements concerning the cause of war."[15]

Prior to the war, New Mexico had been somewhat quiet on the labor front, having generally been spared the mining conflicts that occurred elsewhere in the region. Labor historian Robert Kern attributes this in part to the fact that the "[s]tate government in Santa Fe never intervened into labor disputes with the same kind of probusiness bias as Denver or Phoenix did."[16] As mentioned earlier (Chapter 10), labor strife may also have been avoided in part because of the successful effort led by John L. Lewis, representing the American Federation of Labor, in getting labor reforms instituted in 1912.

During the war years, however, New Mexico showed a few signs of labor unrest. Mining unions and the IWW were active in Dawson and Gallup, and in the latter thirty alleged Wobblies were deported from the town in 1917.[17] Members of the United Mine Workers (UMW) were deported from Gallup along with the Wobblies—a fact that prompted UMW locals, such as one in Tioga, Colorado, to declare the deportation "one of the most dastardly acts that could be committed by the capitalistic class against the working class."[18] Two weeks later a conservative paper reported from Gallup:

> As a result of the complete break down of the treasonable strike many of
> the men are hustling back to the mines to get on the pay roll. . . . These men
> are going back to their jobs and all that is left is a few aliens, mostly Austrians
> and Mexicans. . . . Patriotism has won over pro-Germanism, the little plan of
> the hyphenates and the pro-Germans to tie up the coal output of the Gallup
> district and thereby tie up the Santa Fe railroad and hinder the movement
> of troops and war material over that line has proved a miserable failure and
> the leaders are leaving for other parts to carry on their work of assisting the
> German kaiser and render the conduct of war for human liberty more dif-
> ficult for the United States.[19]

That same year authorities in Colfax County arrested a Wobbly organizer name Jack Diamond on the grounds that his attempts to recruit members for the union conflicted with a New Mexico law that prohibited actions aimed at the "destruction of organized government."[20] More important in New Mexico than actual labor strife was the fear of such industrial conflict because of an invasion of troublemaking radical types being chased out of the neighboring states of Colorado and Arizona.

Two events involving the IWW that had regionwide impacts on the radical cause were the deportation of workers out of Bisbee and the murder of Frank Little. The first of these took place in Arizona where, sensing trouble, George Powell wrote to fellow labor official Henry S. McCluskey on February 8, 1917, that while he was in Phoenix he had come across an IWW official named Perry who said he had $35,000 to organize the state. Powell wrote that he did not know if they could organize Arizona, but he was sure they could stir up a lot of trouble with that amount of money.[21] IWW organizer Grover H. Perry had, indeed, arrived in Phoenix and was hard at work as secretary-treasurer of the IWW's Metal Mine Workers' Industrial Union. The IWW had made progress in places such as Globe and Miami; in the latter there were several hundred Wobblies, many of whom were Finns. In a handout to miners Perry argued: "The Western Federation of Miners, while it has had its bright spots in the history of the militant working class, is now decadent. It has lost its once militant membership and its officials today are spending more time in legislative halls and company offices than they are at the mouth of the shaft. It has lost its punch. All the red blood that once was in that organization has come into the Metal Mine Workers."[22]

Under Perry's direction the IWW began a process of "boring from within" the Western Federation of Miners (WFM), infiltrating and taking over WFM locals. In 1917 strikes took place throughout the state, all attributed by the mainstream press to the IWW. Discontent was particularly high in Mexican mining camps. Mexican workers told *New York Evening Post* investigative reporter Robert W. Bruere that they were striking for "an American standard of living" and greater control over working conditions in the mines.[23] Arizona newspapers and government officials, however, depicted the striking miners as part of a pro-German conspiracy. Mining company officials refused to meet with union organizers for the International Union of Mine, Mill, and Smelter Workers (the new official name for the WFM), whom they considered no better than agitators who ought to be taken into the desert and shot. The acknowledged leader of the copper group, Walter Douglas of the Phelps-Dodge Corporation, was quoted as saying, "We will not compromise with rattle-snakes; this goes for the International of the A.F. of L. organization as well as the I.W.W."[24]

The first major mining strike attributed to IWW conspirators occurred in May 1917 in Jerome, where it was reported that fewer than 100 Wobblies were able to convince around 6,000 miners to walk off the job at the United Verde Copper Company, a property of former senator William Clark.[25] With the company's backing, early on the morning of July 10, 1917, a so-called citizens' group—armed with clubs and guns—rounded up 70 of the strikers, placed them in cattle cars, and deported them to California. After California authorities refused to accept the deportees, they were returned to Arizona, ending up in Kingman. No legal action was instituted against the deportation, and, because of this, union opponents may have felt encouraged to use the method again. They did so a few days later.

On June 27, 1917, at the call of the IWW, copper workers in the Warren district south of Bisbee went on strike against Phelps-Dodge and some smaller companies in the area. Miners called for the abolishment of the shifting scale—which linked pay to the price of copper—in favor of a flat wage of six dollars for eight hours of work, more safety reforms, and the elimination of medical examinations. In regard to the latter, the union claimed company physicians had used required examinations to declare workers suspected of being troublemakers unfit and thus unable to stay on the payroll. Mining company officials at Phelps-Dodge refused to meet with union organizers. Although there had been no violence—strike leaders stressed avoiding violence, and strikers went without coats to show they were not carrying arms—Cochise County sheriff Harry S. Wheeler came from nearby Tombstone "to preserve order" and protect mining properties.[26] Many in the area, including the newspapers, felt such action was necessary because the striking miners had stashed away vast amounts of dynamite and numerous rifles for later use.[27] Wheeler swore in a number of armed deputy sheriffs, including many people who continued to work for the mining companies. The sheriff arrested striking workers one at a time and hauled them before a makeshift "kangaroo" court where they were given the choice of going back to work or leaving town.

Mine owners believed even more drastic action was needed, and they had a willing accomplice in Sheriff Wheeler. Under Wheeler's direction a band of men, early in the morning of July 12, 1917, rounded up 1,200 persons in Bisbee they felt were Wobblies or professional labor agitators. Moving quickly through the dark several hours before daybreak, they broke into homes, dragged suspected workers out of bed, marched them to a ballpark in nearby Warren, loaded them into cattle and freight cars provided by the El Paso and Southwestern Railroad—a railway owned by Phelps-Dodge—and, with gunmen on top of the train, sent them on their way to Columbus, New Mexico. The idea was that the deported were to be handed over to military authorities for internment in Columbus. Civil and military authorities in Columbus, however, refused to allow the vigilantes in charge of the deportation to leave the men there. Faced with this resistance, the vigilantes left the deportees in the nearby desert town of Hermanas, New

Mexico—a place with a store and a half dozen houses and no city marshal to get in the way of their plans. The vigilantes backed up the train to the Hermanas station and sidetracked it there. The guards got off and awaited the first chance to get back to Bisbee. A local reporter thought the deportees might try to do the same thing, that is, "hold up the west bound train that passes through Hermanas at night and return to Bisbee," but this did not materialize.[28] The reporter also warned, "The feeling in Columbus is running high against Sheriff Harry Wheeler . . . and against the officials of the E.P.&S.W. for sending the I.W.W.'s to Columbus and it is openly charged that Wheeler knew that the military at Columbus would have nothing to do with interning the agitators."[29]

On July 13 New Mexico governor Washington E. Lindsey ordered the sheriff of Luna County to go to Hermanas and take charge of the deportees. The sheriff rounded up fifty well-armed deputies and, according to the local newspaper, "went forth prepared to meet a ravening horde of anarchists, I.W.W.'s and other menaces to the established social and economic conditions of Luna County, but when the posse arrived at Hermanas all they found was a mob of men who were more interested in getting something to eat and drink than [in] upsetting the peace and dignity of this or any other part of the southwest."[30] The sheriff talked to the deportees' leader W. B. Cleary, a Bisbee lawyer who had also been deported, and found no sign of trouble. The strikers were living peacefully, although short on food in the cattle trucks and boxcars.

Arizona governor Thomas Campbell wired Woodrow Wilson on July 12, giving his version of what had happened and asking the president to send troops. Said Campbell: "Industrial conditions throughout Arizona, due to the presence of large numbers of members of the Industrial Workers of the World, coming from outside the state and agitating their propaganda, are rapidly getting beyond the control of peace officers. There are no state troops under my authority, all Arizona National Guard being in Federal Service, making it impossible for me to use this force for the preservation of peace." The governor went on, "It is generally believed that strong pro-German influence is back of this movement, as the I.W.W. appear well financed and are daily getting (into) their ranks many aliens, particularly Austrians."[31] Wilson, on July 12, 1917, wired back to Campbell that the situation was under investigation. He added: "Meantime may I not respectfully urge the great danger of citizens taking the law in their own hands as you report their having done. I look upon such action with grave apprehension. A very serious responsibility is assumed when such precedents are set."[32] The president made this message available to Phoenix newspapers the following day.

On July 14, 1917, the War Department sent federal troops to escort the deportees back to Columbus. A few days later an army officer told the refugees they were free to leave whenever they wanted. Cleary, though, advised the refugees against leaving. He suggested that they stay together because there was a possibility that President Wilson would order the army to escort them back to Bisbee. On July 22 the deportees voted unanimously to stay in camp, pending federal action. Labor spokesmen in Arizona and elsewhere wired the White House demanding that federal troops escort the deportees back to their homes. Irritated by the lack of federal action, petitioners wired the president in August: "Are we to assume that Phelps Dodge interests are superior to the principles of democracy?"[33] This did not move the president, and the offer of an escort never materialized. The deportees began to drift away, although many remained in camp under federal protection until the middle of September. Meanwhile, in Bisbee the Citizens Protection League stayed on alert to prevent the troublemakers from returning to town.

A month after the event Mrs. Rosa McKay, a left-leaning member of the state house from Bisbee, wrote: "For fourteen years I have claimed Bisbee as my home. But after Thursday, the twelfth of July, I hang my head in shame and sorrow for the sights I have witnessed here."[34] At about the same time, the editor of *The Wyoming Weekly Labor Journal* declared, "When a mob can seize hundreds of men and force them to leave their homes and families, awed and intimidated by weapons of murder, the time has arrived for the people to make inquiry as to what has become of democracy in the United States."[35] The deportations, though, were praised in some quarters. The editor of a mining industry paper, for example, had this to say: "The citizens of Bisbee, Ariz. on Thursday set a fine example of how to handle the lawless I.W.W. The people of the famous Arizona copper camp simply took a day off to purge their city of the I.W.W. plague and they did it very thoroughly. The whole thing was very simple. . . . The Bisbee people have quickly learned of the one and only way to handle the I.W.W. It should become known as the 'Bisbee system of disposing of organized vagrants.' "[36]

Officials outside of Arizona may have been happy to see the strong stand taken against the IWW, but they were not overly pleased with the thought that Arizona was dumping its undesirables into their states. The Bisbee deportations set off rumors in Nevada that an army of 1,200 Wobblies, sidetracked at Hermanas, was planning an invasion of the state. Notified by the sheriffs in Esmeralda and Clark counties that the invasion was imminent, Nevada governor Emmet D. Boyle ordered that these men not be allowed to cross the Nevada line and sent a detachment of state police to the southern part of the state to keep an eye on incoming trains.

New Mexico officials were even more concerned. Writing to Governor Lindsey, A. M. Pollard, head of the Luna County Council of Defense, whose jurisdiction included Columbus, asked the governor and the State Council of Defense to do something about the deportees who had flooded the village of Columbus. He was concerned that the deportees, who may have been undesirable citizens, would take up jobs in New Mexico mines and cause the same types of labor troubles that had occurred in Arizona—the types of problems New Mexico had so far largely avoided.

He added, "These men outnumber the citizens of Columbus, and owning to remarks and threats which have been made by these men against some of the citizens of Columbus, these citizens have necessarily become alarmed and desire their removal."[37] Pollard wrote another letter to the governor on August 4, 1917, warning of the impending clash between the citizens of Columbus and the deportees, and he suggested that the governor either put the deportees under military guard (they were presently free to roam around the village) or remove them from the area. Pollard claimed, "They [the deportees] are disloyal to the State and Government and their chief aim in life at present is to try and cause some trouble or out break that would involve the State or Government."[38] Tensions seem to have died down a few weeks later, however, even though 900 deportees were left in the village. Even Pollard seemed to think the situation had gotten better and, indeed, had been exaggerated in the first place. Pollard blamed the panic over the deportees on false reports to the local Council of Defense from El Paso and Southwestern Railroad officials—the railroad used to ship the deportees to New Mexico.[39]

In August 1917, Governor George W.P. Hunt visited the deportees in Columbus. He found between 900 and 1,000 of them. He reported to President Wilson, "I spent five days in camp, talking to the refugees, singly and in groups, receiving their confidences and learning their views, judiciously questioning them when necessary to ascertain their real frame of mind."[40] He found that about half of the deportees were Wobblies. Some had joined the IWW since, and largely because of, the deportation. At the same time, Hunt concluded, the deportees as a whole were not pro-German or unpatriotic. Rather, "They are just ordinary human beings, struggling in their own ways and according to their own lights for a betterment of the conditions which they expect will be their lot through life."[41] They were people, Hunt continued, who had a "rather personal outlook upon affairs" rather than acting out of concern for mankind in general: "The situation to them seems very simple and practical, and they are wholly unable to comprehend why their strike should be associated with the war, or held by anyone to be an act of unfaithfulness to the government in its emergency."[42] Those who went on strike simply wanted a share of the additional profits the copper companies were enjoying because of the war: "They cannot understand why the war should be so one-sided in its effect upon capital and labor, as to justify extraordinary gain to the former while denying to the latter the right of organized action to secure a living wage."[43]

As to the cause of the deportation, Hunt concluded, "I am possessed of the firm conviction—a conviction supported by the scarcely veiled utterances of the mining companies' chief spokesman—that these incidents are manifestations of a determination entered into by the great copper mine operators of Arizona to crush organized labor in this State, and that, while employing the 'camouflage' of patriotic protestations they are in reality using the nation's extremity to serve their selfish ends, and they are going about their enterprise in a manner that would shame the Prussian autocracy."[44] Mine managers who helped plan and execute this clearly unlawful act, on the other hand, were proud of their involvement.[45] They defended their action based on the need to head off violent acts planned by the strikers.

A presidential commission looking into the matter roundly condemned the deportation as an action "wholly illegal and without authority in law either State or Federal."[46] Writing to Felix Frankfurter, counsel for the presidential commission, Theodore Roosevelt took exception to the report. He noted that John Greenway, a personal friend and onetime Bull Moose spokesman in Arizona, was a prominent leader in the deportation. Based on what he had learned from Greenway and others, he believed the federal report was "thoroughly misleading." For Roosevelt, "[N]o human being in his senses doubts that the men deported from Bisbee were bent on destruction and murder." The president felt local citizens had the right to protect themselves and had acted properly.[47] Similarly, a Cochise County jury acquitted a deputy who participated in the deportation on the grounds that while his actions may have been illegal under normal conditions, they were appropriate because he had acted in accordance with "the law of necessity" in a time of danger. In his instructions to the jury, the judge explained that the law of necessity "protects a man in his invasion of the rights of others when his fear of his own safety or welfare is great enough to force him to a drastic step, and his fear does not have to be fear of really existent dangers but only apparent danger is compelling as to be real to him who views it."[48]

In December 1917, about a month after the federal commission's report, Hunt returned to the governorship when a dispute over the 1916 contest was resolved in his favor. Anti-Wobbly hysteria, however, did not diminish, and Hunt was increasingly the target of attacks questioning his affiliation with the IWW and his loyalty to the nation. Several newspapers published a picture of Hunt between two indicted IWW leaders, Chas McKinnon and Grover H. Perry. *The Bisbee Daily Review*, on Friday, June 7, 1918, ran the picture, taken from an IWW publication, along with statements declaring its indignation that the state's chief executive had been "hobnobbing with traitors and enemies of society."[49] Hostile papers also declared that Hunt had made statements indicating that he opposed the war.[50]

During the summer of 1918, while mulling over his political future, Hunt's friend Alfred Maddern warned him that he could not count on the support of the Socialists, even though they posed as his friend. Hunt, he argued, should not believe the Socialists' promise of support because Socialists only voted for nominees of their own party. He reminded Hunt that the Socialists had nearly cost Hunt the election in 1916. Maddern considered the Socialists a "bunch of political highbinders" whose principles were ideal but whose "practices are not clean."[51] Hunt, perhaps in part for this reason, decided not to run again in 1918. He was a political realist who saw that his Republican opponent, Thomas Campbell, would probably win and that a defeat might permanently damage his political career. Drawing upon his status as a long-standing leader of the Democratic party, Hunt was able to secure an appointment from President Wilson as ambassador to Siam (present-day Thailand).

While Wobbly hysteria was reshaping Arizona politics, it was also being manifested harshly in Montana. Events following the miners' riot in 1914 had left Butte an open-shop town in which the miners were unorganized. Because the rustling card system suppressed the expression of grievances about the lack of enforcement of safety laws, mining conditions became less safe. Proof of this came on June 8, 1917, when a fire broke out in the Speculator Mine in Butte, claiming the lives of 160 miners. The tragedy stimulated a movement for better safety conditions, better wages, and a new, so-called independent union. That union, the Metal Mine Workers' Union, in which Wobblies assumed leadership roles, came into existence on June 13 and led to a general strike in all Butte mines. Mine owners refused to deal with the strike leaders, claiming they were German sympathizers. Acting on behalf of the miners, Congresswoman Jeanette Rankin appealed to John D. Ryan, president of the Anaconda Mining Company, to abolish the rustling card system. Ryan ignored her appeal.[52]

In July 1917, while the strike was coming to an end—some miners had given up and, out of money, gone back to work—Frank Little, an IWW organizer, arrived in town. Little had been in Missoula with Elizabeth Gurley Flynn in the free-speech campaign and, more recently, in Arizona leading strikes. Little, a small, frail man in his late thirties, was on crutches when he arrived in Butte as the result of a car accident. He pulled no punches while addressing union rallies in Butte—referring to the soldiers sent to Ludlow as "scabs" and "thugs" in uniform, condemning President Wilson for his handling of the deportation of miners in Bisbee, Arizona, and declaring "[t]he IWW do not object to the war but the way they want to fight it is to put the capitalists in the front trenches and if the Germans don't get them the IWW will. Then the IWW will clean the Germans."[53] The mainstream press denounced Little as a traitor and saboteur. Companies joined in his condemnation, fearing he stood in the way of a strike settlement on their terms.

On August 1, 1917, Little was murdered. The *Montana Socialist* reported, "In the gray of the morning of August 1, Frank Little, an I.W.W. organizer, was taken from his room in the Steele Block by six masked men, hurried into an automobile, with no covering but his underclothes, driven swiftly to the Milwaukee railroad trestle near the Centennial Brewery and hanged to the trestle."[54] The paper, no friend of the IWW, described the killing as "one of the most brutal, cruel, cowardly murders that ever disgraced an American city."[55] Nine days after the lynching, Wyoming Socialist B. Stewart wrote the *Wyoming Weekly Labor Journal* and noted that capitalistic press and officials in Montana had suddenly become very quiet about the evils of direct action, the tactic of violence they had regularly associated with the IWW. Apparently, he went on, "it is all very well for capitalists to use direct action on a member of the working class." If, however, "the case had been reversed and some prominent mine owner or banker had been kidnapped at night and direct action had been used on him by the working class . . . all the capitalist papers would be howling to hang every working man in Butte. . . . If capitalism is going to be allowed to use direct action[,] then the workers to defend themselves will be compelled to use direct action."[56]

Little's murder intensified the hysteria over the IWW and fed fears that once again brought federal troops to Butte. Fear also prompted passage of the state's anti-sedition law in 1918 and several acts of suppression. The IWW in Montana became the victim of mob actions and raids on its hall.[57] Montana Non-Partisan Leaguers, meanwhile, had to cope with groups led by businessmen who tried to prevent them from speaking.[58] Montanans charged that the Germans were behind the IWW and the NPL. U.S. Senator Burton Wheeler, a witness to all this, later recalled: "[T]he most bizarre element of the war hysteria was the spy fever, which made many people completely lose their sense of justice. All labor leaders, miners, and discontented farmers were regarded by these super-patriots as pacifists—and ipso facto agents of the Kaiser. There were increasing reports of enemy airplanes operating out of mountain hideaways south of Missoula in the Bitterroot Valley. Just how and why the German High Command expected to launch an invasion of the United States through western Montana, 6000 miles from Berlin, never made the slightest bit of sense to me, but the reports generated by this kind of emotion could not always be brushed aside."[59]

As a target in the campaign aimed at radicalism in general, Socialists and their organizations had a hard time throughout the region during the war years. During this period, the Colorado Socialist party's official paper was put out of business by vigilantes and the post office. In some parts of the state, particularly farming areas, party members were afraid to hand out literature. Elsewhere, the party continued to organize, although very quietly.[60] The NPL, however, newer and bolder, energetically organized the state during these years, much to the concern of conservative forces.[61] Socialist party leaders such as Secretary Jennie McGehe were not altogether upset by the NPL activity because it was at least keeping the radical movement alive.[62] Very little came of the league's effort, though, except for the election of a handful of state legislators.

By 1917 many Idaho Socialists had moved on to the Idaho version of the NPL, although, by doing so, they contributed to Idahoans' distrust of the organization.[63] The Idaho Non-Partisan League (INPL) began organizing in May 1917 and by August of that year had enrolled around 4,000 farmers. On August 23, 1918, a gang called the "Defense League" attempted to mob the NPL's founding father Arthur C. Townley, who was about to hold a rally in Boise. Before they could act, however, a group of farmers beat up the Defense Leaguers, some of whom were among Boise's leading citizens. Townley spoke for two hours from the capitol steps.[64] At about the same time, however, in Kootenai County in northern Idaho, a local merchant who rented a hall to INPL leaders for a public meeting received a visit from some business associates that convinced him to back away from the agreement, leaving the INPL out in the cold.[65]

The INPL had an anti-corporate component in its platform and emphasized securing such measures as state-owned facilities to process farm products, state-owned rural credit banks, and state-owned electrical power systems. Leaders of the Idaho movement, taking their cue from Townley, argued that farmers would get nowhere through third-party activity and that their best bet was to infiltrate and take over one of the major parties. In Idaho the repeated failure of third-party efforts by Populists, Socialists, and Bull Moosers seemed to prove the point. The INPL successfully invaded the Democratic party primary in 1918, with the support of miners' unions and the state Socialist party. To help the league's ticket, the Socialists stayed off the 1918 ballot. At the general election, though, the INPL ticket lost because conservative Democrats deserted the party and helped the Republicans sweep the state. The following year the legislature eliminated the direct primary for state offices, making it impossible for the NPL to repeat what it had done in 1918.

In Montana, things had gone bad for the Socialists even before the United States entered World War I. In early 1917 *The American Socialist* reported:

"Socialists and men who think ahead of the crowd are 'persona non grata' to the mine owners of Butte. To keep them out of the diggings the big companies have wooden barriers, a rigid rustling card process and the finest spotting and blacklist system in the world. Practically every man who was ever identified with Socialists by card, friendship or sympathy has been driven from Silver Bow county. . . . They could get no jobs."[66] The same article described Lewis Duncan, the former mayor and Socialist candidate for governor, as "a tired man with blistering hands and feet" who was working as a mucker with an independent company in the Butte mines. Duncan told reporters that the job, which a friend had found for him, was the only one he could find in the area, adding that "I'm going to stay, stay and muck, stay and wait for an inevitable day."[67] The exposure to the people around him, according to his son, was quite an eye-opener: "I remember him saying that he had no idea that the working day laborer was so vulgar and gauche. It was a shock to him."[68] When his health failed, Duncan gave up his work in the mines.

By 1918 the Montana Non-Partisan League (MNPL) had, in effect, displaced the Socialist party as the third party on the left. On the surface, the Socialist party was hostile to the newcomers. However, many Socialists had turned to the Montana version of the NPL, and suspicion grew that at least some of the party's opposition to the league was intended to help the league avoid the Socialist stigma.[69] The MNPL was particularly strong in Sheridan County in the northeastern corner of the state. Charles E. ("Red Flag") Taylor, editor of *The Producer News* in Plentywood, was the key figure in the league's movement in the area. He used his NPL paper to stir up farmers in the predominantly Scandinavian community. In 1918 the MNPL took over the county government. Taylor later joined the Communist cause.[70] During the war years, Bill Dunne had greater prominence than Taylor among Montana radicals. Born in Kansas City, Missouri, in 1887, Dunne joined the Socialist party in 1910 and moved to Butte in 1916, where he worked for several copper mining companies. In 1918 he was secretary of the Electrical Workers' branch of the IWW; vice president of the Montana Federation of Labor; a member of the Montana state legislature, to which he had been elected as a Democrat on a radical platform; an organizer for the MNPL; and founding editor of *The Butte Daily Bulletin*, the official organ of the Butte Central Labor Council.[71] Dunne also later became a Communist.

In 1918 the MNPL and many Socialists backed Montana congresswoman Jeanette Rankin, who opposed the war. Along with her war views, Rankin had been praised by leftist papers for her stand on economic issues. The *Appeal to Reason*, for example, praised Rankin for a speech in which she declared: "Together with our material improvement has grown the most widespread misery. The workers have no control over the product of their labor. There must be democracy in industry. Economic problems exist not because of the perversity of human nature, but because the laws are made for the protection and special privileges of a few."[72] Addressing a Butte audience in 1918 along with Arthur C. Townley, Rankin reaffirmed her commitment to the cause of workers, both male and female, and singled out for criticism "a certain group of wealthy men in Montana" who opposed fuller democracy in the state.[73] Rankin lost the GOP primary for a U.S. Senate seat and ran in the general election on a national ticket, finishing third. The Socialists had no candidates on the ballot in 1918, and national party records for that year show that only 123 people remained in the Montana Socialist party. The party, however, did have a platform. One section of this document suggests that the party had retreated from its firm antiwar stand: "We are, first, for Winning the War. We shall indulge only in legitimate criticism, and then only at times when it will be harmless to the government in its prosecution of war plans, and harmful to those whose conduct is inimical thereto."[74]

In Nevada the relatively good showing by Socialists in 1914 and 1916 encouraged nationally prominent radicals to establish a Socialist colony called Nevada City on land reclaimed by the Newlands Reclamation Project. They anticipated that the colony would eventually add around 5,000 party supporters to the state's electorate and thus help swing the state to Socialism. Promoters also hoped the colony would provide a haven for radicals who had been taking unpopular anti-militarist stands. Despite advertising in Socialist journals throughout the country, the colony failed to reach the targeted number (although the amount of growth is difficult to tell because of rapid turnover in membership). The colony added to the state party's ranks—making its base far more agricultural in nature—but, after the United States entered World War I, the Socialists' antiwar stand aroused considerable antagonism toward the colony, forcing most of the residents to leave.[75] Nevada officials, meanwhile, as illustrated in the Bisbee deportation episode, did what they could to prevent radicals from entering the state.

By 1917 Nevadans, Socialists included, were caught up in the tide of national patriotism. Many Nevada Socialists appeared to favor the war and quickly dissociated themselves from the national party. A particularly severe blow was A. Grant Miller's decision to leave the party. Tendering his resignation on September 1, 1917, Miller said he was doing so in part in the belief that Germany had to be defeated: "As I view it, the success of Germany means the triumph of autocracy to such a degree that the emancipation of the working and producing class would be set back fifty years at least."[76] Miller not only quit but did a complete turnabout: he joined the Republican party and helped ferret out subversives as head of Nevada's wartime Defense Council.[77]

One incident that captured considerable attention in the state involved a Socialist named Al Shidler, a smelter worker who lost his job in 1916 for his vocal opposition to conscription. Nye County sheriff William H. Thomas, also a Socialist, gave Shidler a job as a deputy. Upon hearing this, the Loyalty League complained to the county commissioners, who removed Shidler from office. Shidler was later convicted of sedition and sent to federal prison. Thomas, in trouble for helping Shidler and for using striking miners as deputies in a labor disturbance in Tonopah, lost his 1918 reelection bid. In that election the Socialist candidate for the U.S. Senate received only 710 votes out of 25,563 cast.

From Utah, New Mexico, and Arizona, the story was equally grim. While meeting with his cohorts from around the country in Chicago during the summer of 1918, Utah Socialist party secretary C. T. Stoney reported that comrades outside the cities were afraid to call or attend meetings. The members, Stoney proclaimed, "are scared breathless."[78] At that, conditions even in the cities were not ideal, and the party's activities there had been cut to a minimum awaiting the end of the war. Party members, Stoney concluded, "are afraid of their jobs and they do not dare to come out. Thousands of people throughout the state have lost their jobs because they have leaned toward Socialism."[79] Stoney also ventured the belief that Mormons were attracted to Socialism but felt they did not need the party because they could get everything Socialism had to offer through the church: "They tell us, 'Yes, these things are all true, but we will get them through the church, outside of Socialism.'"[80] In 1918 the Utah party held on, with an average membership of 324 members; that number had been as high as 772 in 1912 (Appendix, Table 3).

In New Mexico, chambers of commerce and leading citizens, fearful of radical activity, flooded the governor's office from 1917–1919 with mail offering exposés of revolutionary plots and making demands for protection.[81] The chair of the New Mexico Council of Defense warned Senator Albert B. Fall in 1918: "There are a great many Socialists in New Mexico, particularly among the homesteaders and farmers who have recently come here from Oklahoma and Texas. We hear vague rumors of their meeting and organizing to destroy property and interfere with the production of food and other things necessary to carry on the war, and we are having this matter investigated."[82] A New Mexico newspaper in the heart of the area where such activity was suspected noted that citizens had been somewhat tolerant of Socialists in the past, willing to "permit them to rant and roar" because "it was thought their vociferous hog wash could do no harm." Now, the editor continued, with the country in crisis, criticism of the war will not be tolerated, and Socialist meetings "at which the government of the United States is being roundly criticized and belabored for having entered the war" must come to an end, "peaceably if possible, forcibly if necessary."[83] In 1918 the state party secretary reported he had lost several members and was having difficulty holding on to or even making contact with the remaining 167 members in the four active locals in the state.[84] In 1918 the Socialist candidate for governor polled only 1.8 percent of the state vote. The party was well on its way to becoming a small, secretive sect.

Arizona featured an assortment of legal actions aimed at Socialists. A newspaper account of July 15, 1917, for example, related that in Globe, "Councilman P. H. Brouilett, Socialist member of the City Council," had been "arrested by a city policeman to complete a quorum for the purpose of passing a new ordinance forbidding incendiary speeches."[85] The following year brought accounts of a man arrested in Arizona simply for possessing a supply of the Socialist party's assessment stamps. The government failed to get an indictment, but indictments were forthcoming to a Socialist for possessing a pamphlet titled "War, What For" and to another who loaned the same pamphlet to a woman who turned out to be a government agent. At about this same time the government also charged a Socialist war protestor in Oatman with attempting to interfere with the national government's recruitment program. The Socialist admitted that he had approached men of draft age and urged resistance. On advice of his attorney he pleaded guilty and was sentenced to thirteen months in Leavenworth.[86] Witnessing all this, Arizona Socialist party secretary Alice Eddy, in 1918, painted a bleak picture. In mining areas, where the party had built its strongest locals, she reported that party members were being deported and driven out of the state, and those who remained were very timid, afraid even to hold meetings. Eddy concluded: "We have to keep still and cannot do much, and I do not think I could recommend anything that can be done in the state until after the war. . . . It is possible to hold meetings in Phoenix, but I doubt whether that is so in other parts of the state."[87]

By 1918 the Socialist party in much of the region had disappeared. In 1912 there had been more than 8,000 party members in the Mountain West region; by 1918 there were fewer than 2,000 (Appendix, Table 3). Over the years there had been a general tendency for parties in the region to lose 30–34 percent of their members in the year following a general election (1912, 1914, 1916) and to have membership rebound slightly in the next general election year. In 1918, however, there was no rebound. From 1917 to 1918, the number of party members in the region declined by 1,325, more than 40 percent. In the longer period between 1916 and 1918, membership in the region dropped off by around 60 percent. In Arizona, Idaho, Montana, and Nevada, membership losses hovered at around 80 percent. In an understatement, Chairman Stoney concluded in 1918: "The possibilities in the State of Utah at the present time are not very great."[88] Socialists around the region could have said the same thing, although each would have had slightly different explanations for this state of affairs, as did future scholars.

Concluding Note
Aftermath and Legacy

From 1912 to 1917, when the United States entered World War I, Socialists in the Mountain West were in a situation where people were rejecting their party but, at the same time, were unconsciously moving toward Socialism. After 1917 even the unconscious movement had abated, however, and to be a Socialist was not only unpopular but dangerous. War branded them as anti-American, prompting repression. Matters became even worse following the Red Scare that set in at the war's end. The Bolshevik Revolution in Russia in October 1917 not only frightened the powers that be, bringing more repression, but also sparked the emergence of a powerful and disruptive new left wing within the Socialist party. Most of the people who left the Socialist party either dropped out of politics or joined one of the major parties. A few from the far left became Communists.

The Russian Revolution propelled many leftists into a state of exuberance. They felt that revolution in the United States was also at hand. To hasten the day, they called for "revolutionary mass action." The strength of the new left

287

revolutionary movement was in the rapidly growing foreign language federations (Russians, Poles, Ukrainians, Finns) that were loosely allied with the national party. The left wing showed its strength in 1919 by winning twelve of the fifteen seats on the National Executive Committee (NEC). However, the existing NEC, under the control of the right wing, cried "fraud" and declared the election invalid. On May 24, 1919, the NEC expelled seven left-wing foreign language federations and the Socialist party of Michigan. As another blow to the left wing, the NEC refused to participate in the Third International called by the Russian Communist (Bolshevist) party. The left wing retaliated by boycotting the 1919 Socialist party convention, which, it charged, had been stacked in favor of its enemies. The left wing evolved into two new parties, which differed less in terms of objectives than over who should lead the new cause—the foreign language federations or English-speaking leftists with deeper roots in the country. The larger group, dominated by foreign language federations, formed the Communist party. The native-born, or "Americanized," Communists, fearing the movement could not survive under the leadership of foreign-born radicals because they were unfamiliar with conditions in the country, gravitated toward the Communist Labor party. Both of the warring parties were so strongly persecuted by the government in the Red Scare of the postwar years—locals raided, leaders arrested, members deported—that they were driven underground.

In the Mountain West, the new left wing made inroads in Colorado, Utah, Montana, and New Mexico, although some critics on the right dismissed the strength of the movement in these places.[1] According to U.S. military intelligence reports, ultra-radical delegates from Colorado and Utah attended the founding Communist Labor party convention in Chicago in 1919.[2] That same year a large section of the Butte Socialist party followed Bill Dunne into a Communist group.

One of the best-recorded accounts of the shift in radical activity involves the New Mexico party. Up to the war, New Mexico Socialists were relatively conservative. The territory and the state had never been much of a stronghold for radical labor; neither the Western Federation of Miners (WFM) nor the Industrial Workers of the World (IWW) was well established there. Most New Mexico members who voted on Haywood's removal from the executive committee favored removal. Under A. James McDonald, the party had a leader who favored craft unions and argued that Socialism and Catholicism were not in conflict with each other. During the war, however, leadership shifted to left-winger and far more militant Secretary-Treasurer W. B. Dillon from Las Vegas, who later bolted the national party. Writing to National Secretary Adolph Germer on July 29, 1919, Dillon accused the right wing of gaining control of the national party by unlawful means and forcing a split.[3] He concluded: "We are not afraid of a split if it becomes necessary, but we are placing the onus of the split on you, and having given you plenty of rope you are proceeding to hang yourself. We should worry. Go to it."[4]

A few days later the New Mexico party officially protested the NEC's decisions regarding expulsions, adding that if it was going to expel "every radical in the Socialist Party," New Mexico should be included in the sweep.[5] On August 15, 1919, Dillon followed up by writing to the national secretary: "Now that we are recognized as eligible for Left Wing membership, I presume the next step is to expel us. Well, you will find that our 100 members are Socialists, not reformists. The reformists were driven out of our ranks long ago, and we prefer to have the cream. If you want the skim you can have them." Germer responded by taking potshots at Dillon's "sterling leadership," which had brought the New Mexico party to its knees.[6] The saga ended with a resolution by the state executive committee of the New Mexico party in April 1920 to leave the Socialist party and affiliate with the Communist Labor party—although, apparently in protest, longtime Socialist leader W. P. Metcalf decided to withdraw from all participation in the organization. The majority declared: "The willful actions of a few reactionaries of the Socialist Party who refused to abide by the will of the rank and file forced the split, and while we are all sorry the split occurred, we are probably purged of all those who looked upon the socialist movement as a stepping stone to political power. . . . The revolution is here comrades; no longer is it an event of the future. LINE UP. Days now count where years counted before. Right now is the test of your class consciousness in your willingness to be counted in THE FINAL CONFLICT."[7]

Throughout the region in 1919–1920 one found not only new Communist groups but radical organizations such as the Workers, Soldiers, and Sailors Council of Salt Lake City and County, which was warmly supportive of the Russian Revolution and passionately dedicated to the overthrow of capitalism and restoring political and economic power to workers. A similar group—a Council of Workers, Soldiers, and Sailors—held rallies in Phoenix.

Active in 1919 in Butte was the Soldiers', Sailors', and Workers' Council, put together by the IWW and with which nearly every craft union in the city was affiliated. The organization, which radicals considered a "Soviet" after the Russian model, controlled a miners' strike that took place on February 6, 1919, following a cut in wages.[8] *The Butte Daily Bulletin,* founded and owned by the American Federation of Labor but under the editorship of the radical Bill Dunne, gave the strike great publicity and support. Harold Lord Varney, an IWW official and spokesman, pointed with pride to Butte as one of the American cities steeped in "revolutionary traditions."[9] Varney wrote on March 1, 1919: "In Butte, ideas which are wildly new elsewhere are traditional and common place. Proletarianism is an accepted theory. Class consciousness is surprisingly strong. Even the dreaded letters I.W.W. are a badge of popularity, and the I.W.W. feels here all the familiarity of home, for Butte claims the honor of being the birthplace of the 'Wobbly.'"[10]

The region in 1919–1920 continued to be marked by labor tension. Responding to a call from the United Mine Workers, coal miners went on strike in Wyoming, Utah, and New Mexico in November 1919. The War Department responded by sending troops into these states at the request of the governors, who anticipated violence. Soldiers patrolled the coalfields to protect miners who stayed on the job and to safeguard mine property. Governors, such as Joseph M. Carey of Wyoming, saw radicals and agitators to be at work in the mines and had several people suspected of such activity arrested. Throughout the region, meanwhile, operatives warned company owners to stay on guard against IWW agitators.[11] The actual extent of IWW infiltration into mines and other places is difficult to determine. During this period radicals did have some success within the trade union movement. In 1919 they took over the Utah Federation of Labor Convention long enough to persuade the organization to endorse the Soviet government of Russia. The following year radicals took over the Montana Federation of Labor and adopted a similar resolution, along with one calling for the release of Eugene Debs and other radicals from jail. The Montana federation also resolved in favor of political action with the Non-Partisan League (NPL) and decided to make *The Butte Daily Bulletin,* managed by Bill Dunne, its official organ.[12]

In late 1919 radicals in the Mountain West, as elsewhere, experienced a new wave of repression, best illustrated on the national level by raids conducted by U.S. attorney general A. Mitchell Palmer on radical organizations. In December 1919 Dunne's paper declared: "Hundreds of workers are literally rotting in the jails of this country because of their activity in the cause of Labor. . . . Some of the prisoners have escaped by death, others are dying, many have contracted tuberculosis and other loathsome diseases, and all are suffering untold agony from close confinement in the fetid atmosphere, from insanitary and unhealthy surroundings, from poor and insufficient food, and from inhumane treatment accorded them by brutalized guards."[13]

Sitting in a federal penitentiary in Atlanta, Debs received 913,664 votes for president in 1920, 3.4 percent of the total cast (Appendix, Table 2). His best showing in the Mountain West was 6.8 percent in Nevada. Elsewhere, he was not even on the ballot, or, if he was, he fell below his national average. The NPL picked up the slack in some states. Membership in the general NPL organization mushroomed from 25,000 in March 1916 to more than 210,000 in the fall of 1919. In September 1919 more than 200 organizers spread the group's message in the Northwest through "farm-to-farm canvas and man-to-man propaganda," as well as in open meetings. Although damaged by World War I hysteria, harassment from councils of defense, and vigilante and mob assaults, the NPL enjoyed some success in electing state legislators—twenty-one in Montana, twenty-four in Idaho, and four in Colorado.[14]

In Colorado the Republican party entered the 1920 election with a platform plank that read: "The Republican party recognizes that farmers and industrial workers have many grievances. These grievances can and will be righted by just executive and legislative action, which can only be accomplished when the nation returns to those methods of government designed by the fathers and designated in the constitution. They can never be righted by or thru any organization of socialistic principles or tendencies."[15] For the Republicans the chief threat to "Americanism" was the NPL, which was well organized and had been able to capture the Democratic primary. The league, though, wound up winning only a few offices. In Wyoming the NPL also played only a minor role, thwarted in part by the effort of an organization called the Wyoming American Association, formed by business interests to educate people against the league's Socialistic ideas.[16]

The showdown in Montana came in 1920. The NPL took over the Democratic party primary and nominated Burton K. Wheeler of Butte for governor. Republicans nominated Joseph M. Dixon and, eager to "fight sovietism in Montana," assailed the NPL and its candidates as "enemies of American institutions and ideals."[17] Dixon's speech kicking off the campaign called the NPL an offshoot of the old Socialist party in Montana, which had taken over the Democratic party. Dixon warned that "the Republican organization is the only one that now stands between the socialistic organization and the complete control of state and county government in Montana."[18] Pro-Dixon newspapers call the Democratic ticket headed by Wheeler "the I.W.W. ticket." Full-page ads featured quotes from clergymen who denounced the NPL movement in Montana and its radical leader Bill Dunne, who, along with all his other faults, "scoffs in his paper at religion and the men who lead and sustain religious thought in Montana."[19] Members of the clergy saw it as their duty to denounce the "red movement" in Montana. On election day around 103,000 people voted for Dixon, while 68,000 voted for Wheeler. In explaining the defeat, NPL leaders pointed to the tide for the Republican party nationally and the loss of population in places where the NPL was the strongest. Leaders also noted that throughout the state, banks had threatened foreclosures and industries said jobs would be lost if Dixon did not win.[20]

By the 1920s Arizona, Colorado, Idaho, Nevada, Utah, and Wyoming had enacted syndicalism laws aimed at radicals. Backers of syndicalism laws in several of these states had the NPL as well as the IWW and Socialists in mind, but a more direct attack on the NPL came in the form of attempts to abolish the direct primary system and return to the older method of making party nominations by convention. Supporters envisioned that this would make it far more difficult for the NPL to take over existing parties. Bills to abolish direct primaries failed in Colorado but were successful in Montana and Idaho, although the system was later restored in those states.[21]

Meanwhile, various federal agencies continued to keep an eye on radical activities in the Mountain West. In 1920–1921 agents reported to U.S. military intelligence from Butte, Denver, Reno, Salt Lake City, Douglas (Arizona), Nampa (Idaho), Pocatello (Idaho), and Trinidad (Colorado), among other places.[22] The reports, though, generally disclosed that little was going on. The Denver report in April 1920, for example, found that about all that was left of the radical bunch were twenty-five members of the Communist Labor party and a "very few" Wobblies.[23] The prime concern in some places was with the NPL and the emergence of the various World War I veterans' groups that had been organized by radicals. The latter often met stiff resistance. From Nampa, Idaho, in December 1920, for example, came the report: "The World War Veterans and the I.W.W. tried to organize here about a year ago, but were successfully opposed and wiped out by the American Legion."[24] A report from Nevada, on the other hand, stated that IWW radicals were "very strong and active in the Mining districts of Ely, McGill, Tonopah, Nevada, and Westwood, California just across the Nevada line, the total strength of which [is] between four (4) and five (5) hundred in the above mentioned places."[25] In various places throughout the region, anti-radical propaganda was distributed by military recruiters, various church leaders, and organizations such as the American Legion, Knights of Columbus, and Salvation Army.[26] Observers noted that the American Legion was particularly influential in Colorado and Wyoming, where the general public was seen as "antagonistic to extreme radicalism."[27]

Writing to Debs on January 8, 1920, Mae Bishop, then living in Salt Lake City, reminded the Socialist leader that she had had the pleasure of meeting him in 1908 when the Red Special stopped in Glenwood Springs, Colorado. Bringing him up to date, she reported: "Since coming to Salt Lake City I have become more active and for three years have helped in my small way in the Socialist party and also in the People's Council, so much so that I have been found important enough to be blacklisted, to have my home raided, and to be brought before the Dept. of Justice, and at the present I am about to be expelled from the stenographer's union because I carry a card in a 'red organization,' those are the things that hurt the most coming from my own class, fellow wage-slaves, but my small troubles are trifles compared to the ordeals faced by some of the comrades who are now behind prison walls."[28] (At the time, Bishop was a member of the Communist Labor party.)

The use of force against radicals continued well after the war. On July 1, 1921, for example, a group of men kidnapped Socialist Kate Richards O'Hare from a private residence in Twin Falls, Idaho, where she had a speaking engagement. They took her by automobile over the state line to Nevada, where they dropped her off. O'Hare said the leader of the group, who identified himself as the commander of the American Legion, threatened her with personal violence if she came back to Idaho and pressed charges against them for what they had done.[29] According to her account, three men "grabbed me, carried me out of the house and threw me on the floor of a waiting tour car. Another touring car was behind the one I was in and a roadster [was] in front. I was held on the floor of the car and prevented from making an outcry until the car was some distance out of town, when I was put on the back seat, between two men."[30]

By the late 1910s, many of the radicals who had organized and agitated in the Mountain West were in prison. Although Vincent St. John had retired to operate a small copper claim in New Mexico and was no longer a member of the IWW, in 1917 he was arrested, tried, and convicted along with hundreds of Wobblies. He was sent to Leavenworth and stayed there until freed by President William G. Harding in 1923. Haywood was also convicted under the federal Espionage Act, but, while out on bail pending his appeal, he fled to Russia. Other radicals left the region to continue their work in other parts of the country. Duncan became a teacher and an organizer for the Non-Partisan League in South Dakota. Ida Crouch Hazlett shifted her operations to Baltimore, Maryland, and continued to agitate for the party throughout the East and to express her opinions in various radical publications. Working in Newton, Iowa, in 1921 as an organizer for the Socialist party, she was set upon by an angry mob and escorted out of town by the American Legion.[31] Joseph Cannon headed for New York, where he accepted the state Socialist party's nomination for U.S. senator in 1916 and for governor in 1920. Herman Groesbeck was still in Wyoming in 1922, running on a nonpartisan ticket for a seat on the state supreme court. A labor journal declared that he was so "eminently fitted" for the position that his election "should be unanimous." His election, the paper added, "will enable him to round out a career as a valiant soldier for the common good." Groesbeck lost and moved to New York two years later.[32]

Much of the radicalism emerging in the area in earlier years had had its roots in the experiences of miners and, in particular, in the development of a set of leaders in the Western Federation of Miners who saw the interests of the min- ers—indeed, of all working people—as best promoted by the Populist party and, later, the Socialist party. The movement lost much of its driving force as miners and their leaders gravitated to more traditional interest group politics. Over the next several decades one could still find patches of radicalism in the region, such as in the far northeastern "red corner" of Montana where Communist candi- dates did relatively well. By and large, though, the Mountain West area, once so promising to the radical cause, was on its way to becoming among the more conservative areas of the country.[33] Although a number of factors may have been involved in this shift to the right, public reaction to the real or imagined threat of radicalism, which reached its peak during the war and the immediate postwar period, helped propel this trend.

Socialists in much of the Mountain West owed a great deal to the Populists. Both movements had an advantage over similar movements in other parts of the country because they emerged in a political climate that was relatively friendly to third-party activity and where industrial conditions encouraged radi- cal activity. These factors helped account for the fact that Socialist candidates in the region generally did better than they did elsewhere. Strategic mistakes and blown opportunities accounted for some setbacks. Socialists also faced numer- ous obstacles, not the least of which were a strong and widespread commit- ment to economic development no matter what the cost in terms of corporate control, the opposition of church groups, the successful policy of co-optation by the major parties, debilitating divisions within the movement, and a pattern of state-supported repression. The movement was torn between those who emphasized political action and those who favored direct action in the industrial field. Ultimately, the direction actionists went their own way, but the resulting violence in the industrial field rebounded not only against the industrial radicals but also against those trying to build conventional political parties. With World War I and the Red Scare, repression became even more pronounced because it was backed by the force of patriotism.

Socialists, though, like the Populists before them, played active and impor- tant roles in expressing economic and social discontent, agitating for reform, educating the public, building support for innovation, and compelling the major parties to change their policy positions. On the electoral level they functioned as a means through which ordinary people protested conditions and tried to regain control over their lives, their jobs, and their government. In a sense they "were the by-products of an economic transition that imbued in many Americans the feeling that they had been left behind."[34] The contributions of the Populists,

Socialists, and radical labor unions rested largely in building the agenda for change and, perhaps most of all, in frightening the powers that be into making reforms that helped democratize the political system, increase public control of corporations, and further protection of the working people.

Notes

ABBREVIATIONS

AFL	American Federation of Labor
ATR	*Appeal to Reason*
ISR	*International Socialist Review*
MM	*Miners Magazine*
SDH	*Social-Democratic Herald*
SPC	Socialist Party Collection, Duke University
UMW	United Mine Workers (aka United Mine Workers of America)
WFM	Western Federation of Miners

PREFACE

1. W. J. Cash, *The Mind of the South* (New York: Alfred A. Knopf, 1941): 2.

INTRODUCTION

1. Eugene V. Debs to Frank P. O'Hare, February 14, 1915, in J. Robert Constantine, ed., *Letters of Eugene V. Debs*, Vol. 2, 1913–1919 (Urbana: University of Illinois Press, 1990): 128.

2. Eugene V. Debs to Frank P. O'Hare, December 31, 1915 in ibid, 217.

3. This definition of radicalism is comparable to that used by other scholars. Elizabeth Jameson, for example, defines "a radical as one who advocates fundamental social and economic change." Elizabeth Jameson, *All That Glitters: Class, Conflict, and Community in Cripple Creek* (Urbana: University of Illinois Press, 1998): 194. Similarly, Aileen S. Kraditor uses the term radicalism "to apply to those who would change a society at its roots rather than reform it to conform more faithfully to its professed values and ideals." Aileen S. Kraditor, *The Radical Persuasion* (Baton Rouge: Louisiana State University Press, 1981): 8. A. Ross McCormick uses a more restricted definition of radicalism as "a commitment to social change and a design for modifying society which were based ultimately on a Marxian analysis of capitalism." A. Ross McCormick, *Reformers, Rebels, and Revolutionaries: The Western Canadian Radical Movement 1899–1919* (Toronto: University of Toronto Press, 1977): ix.

4. David A. Shannon, *The Socialist Party of America* (Chicago: Quadrangle Books, 1955): 38.

5. Nick Salvatore, *Eugene V. Debs: Citizen and Socialist* (Urbana: University of Illinois Press, 1982): 198.

6. In this respect the story is comparable to McCormick's account of radicalism in western Canada during a comparable time period. See McCormick, *Reformers, Rebels, and Revolutionaries*.

7. Among the most useful regional or state studies are James R. Green, *Grass-Roots Socialism: Radical Movements in the Southwest, 1895–1943* (Baton Rouge: Louisiana State University Press, 1978); Donald T. Critchlow, ed., *Socialism in the Heartland: The Midwestern Experience, 1900–1925* (Notre Dame, Ind.: University of Notre Dame Press, 1986); Henry F. Bedford, *Socialism and the Workers in Massachusetts, 1886–1912* (Amherst: University of Massachusetts Press, 1966); Garin Burbank, *When Farmers Voted Red: The Gospel of Socialism in the Oklahoma Country Side, 1910–1924* (Westport, Conn.: Greenwood, 1976); Lee M. Wolfle and Robert W. Hodge, "Radical-Party Politics in Illinois, 1880–1924," *Sociological Inquiry* 53 (Winter 1983): 33–60. One of the few attempts to provide an overview of the various regions is Shannon, *Socialist Party of America*. For a contemporary account of regional variations see Robert F. Hoxie, "The Rising Tide of Socialism," *The Journal of Political Economy* 19 (October 1911): 609–631.

8. Studies on Socialist parties in various places in the Mountain West include Jameson, *All That Glitters*; Jerry W. Calvert, *The Gibraltar: Socialism and Labor in Butte, Montana, 1895–1920* (Helena: Montana Historical Society Press, 1988); James Hulse, "Socialism in Nevada, 1904–1918: Faint Echoes of an Idealistic National Movement," *Nevada Historical Society Quarterly* 31 (Winter 1988): 247–258; John S. McCormick, "Hornets in the Hive: Socialists in Early Twentieth Century Utah," *Utah Historical Quarterly* 50 (Summer 1982): 225–240; John S. McCormick and John R. Sillito, "Socialism and Utah Labor: 1900–1920," *Southwest Economy and Society* 6 (Fall 1983): 15–29; John S. McCormick and John R. Sillito, "America's Socialist Heritage, Socialism in Utah, 1900–1920," *The Socialist Tribune* (April-May 1978): n.p.; John R. Sillito, "Women and the Socialist Party in Utah, 1900–1920," *Utah Historical Quarterly* 49 (Summer 1981): 220–237.

9. Seymour Martin Lipset and Gary Marks, *It Didn't Happen Here: Why Socialism Failed in the United States* (New York: W. W. Norton, 2000): 10.

10. On specific states see Robert W. Larson, *New Mexico Populism: A Study of Radical Protest in a Western Territory* (Boulder: Colorado Associated University Press, 1974); Thomas A. Clinch, *Urban Populism and Free Silver in Montana* (Missoula: University of Montana Press, 1970); James Wright, *The Politics of Populism: Dissent in Colorado* (New Haven, Conn.: Yale University Press, 1974); David R. Berman, *Reformers, Corporations, and the Electorate* (Niwot: University Press of Colorado, 1992); David B. Griffiths, "Far Western Populism: The Case of Utah, 1893–1900," *Utah Historical Quarterly* 37 (1969): 396–407. See also Robert W. Larson, *Populism in the Mountain West* (Albuquerque: University of New Mexico Press, 1986); David B. Griffiths, *Populism in the Far West, 1890–1900*, 2 vols. (Lewiston, N.Y.: Edwin Mellen, 1992). The earlier silver-only theme is found in John D. Hicks, *The Populist Revolt* (Minneapolis: University of Minnesota Press, 1931); Richard Hofstadter, *The Age of Reform* (New York: Knopf, 1955); Lawrence Goodwyn, *Democratic Promise: The Populist Moment in America* (New York: Oxford University Press, 1976).

11. Norman Pollack, *The Populist Response to Industrial America, Midwest Populist Thought* (Cambridge, Mass.: Harvard University Press, 1962); see also Pollack, *The Humane Society: Populism, Capitalism, and Democracy* (New Brunswick, N.J.: Rutgers University Press, 1990).

12. In this tradition see Vernon Jensen, *Heritage of Conflict: Labor Relations in the Nonferrous Metals Industry up to 1930* (New York: Greenwood, 1968; original pub. Ithaca, N.Y.: Cornell University Press, 1950); Melvyn Dubofsky, "The Origins of Western Working Class Radicalism, 1890–1905," *Labor History* 7 (Spring 1966): 131–154; George S. McGovern and Leonard F. Guttridge, *The Great Coal Field War* (Boston: Houghton Mifflin, 1972); A. Dudley Gardner and Verla R. Flores, *Forgotten Frontier: A History of Wyoming Coal Mining* (Boulder: Westview, 1989); Priscilla Long, *Where the Sun Never Shines* (New York: Paragon House, 1989); Zeese Papanikolas, *Buried Unsung: Louis Tikas and the Ludlow Massacre* (Salt Lake City: University of Utah Press, 1982). For the view that labor conditions were better than commonly depicted and the workers less radical than commonly depicted, see, for example, David M. Emmons, *The Butte Irish: Class and Ethnicity in an American Mining Town* (Urbana: University of Illinois Press, 1989); Richard H. Peterson, *The Bonanza Kings* (Lincoln: University of Nebraska Press, 1977); Mark W. Wyman, *Hard Rock Epic: Western Miners and the Industrial Revolution, 1860–1910* (Berkeley: University of California Press, 1979); David A. Wolff, *Industrializing the Rockies: Growth, Competition, and Turmoil in the Coalfields of Colorado and Wyoming, 1868–1914* (Boulder: University Press of Colorado, 2003). A useful review of literature on American workers and their political potential as far as Socialism was concerned is Julie Greene, *Pure and Simple Politics: The American Federation of Labor and Political Activism, 1881–1917* (New York: Cambridge University Press, 1998).

13. Jameson, *All That Glitters.*

14. Lincoln Steffens, "Eugene V. Debs," *Everybody's* (October 1908): 458.

15. Hicks, *Populist Revolt,* 291.

16. Karel D. Bicha, *Western Populism: Studies in an Ambivalent Conservatism* (Lawrence, Kans.: Coronado, 1976): 67.

17. Ibid., 71.

18. Editorial, *Inter-Mountain Advocate* (July 17, 1896): 1.

19. "Death of Warren Foster," *ATR* (November 6, 1909): 3.

20. Joseph R. Buchanan, *The Story of a Labor Agitator* (New York: Outlook, 1903): 67.

21. Ibid., 101. See also material on Buchanan in Robert E. Weir, *Knights Unhorsed: Internal Conflict in a Gilded Age Social Movement* (Detroit: Wayne State University Press, 2000.)

22. Elizabeth Gurley Flynn, *Rebel Girl: An Autobiography, My First Life (1906–1926)* (New York: International, 1973): 88.

23. Ibid., 97.

24. Ibid., 191.

25. Quoted in Ray Stannard Baker, "The Reign of Lawlessness: Anarchy and Despotism in Colorado," *McClure's Magazine* (October 1904): 49.

26. Operative report of January 14, 1906, from Wallace, Idaho, M65, Stanley Easton Papers, Box 1, Folder 3, of the Special Collections, Archives, University of Idaho Library, Moscow.

27. Ibid.

28. Letter from Eugene Debs to Adolph F. Germer, December 15, 1909, in Constantine, ed., *Letters of Eugene V. Debs,* Vol. 1, 1874–1912, 315.

29. Mari Jo Buhle, *Women and American Socialism, 1870–1920* (Urbana: University of Illinois Press, 1981): 25.

30. The term "brainworkers" is used by Leon Fink, *Workingmen's Democracy: The Knights of Labor and American Politics* (Urbana: University of Illinois Press, 1983).

31. See James A. Denton, *Rocky Mountain Radical: Myron W. Reed, Christian Socialist* (Albuquerque: University of New Mexico Press, 1997).

32. "The Bishop's Pleadings for Socialism Revealed in Intimate Letters," *The Christian Socialist* (Chicago, November 1914): 8–9.

33. John R. Sillito, "Prove All Things, Hold Fast That Which Is Good," *Weber Studies* (Spring 1984): n.p.

34. William E. Brooks to Anna Parker Merriam Brooks, August 21, 1904, William Eugene Brooks Letters, Arizona Collection, Arizona State University Libraries, Tempe.

35. Ibid., September 18, 1904.

36. "A Ringing Document from Nevada's Candidate for Congress on the Socialist Ticket," *MM* (October 16, 1906): 18.

37. Salvatore, *Eugene V. Debs*, 105, 226–227.

38. Ibid., 228.

CHAPTER 1

1. John W. Caughey, "Toward an Understanding of the West," *Utah Historical Quarterly* 28 (January 1959): 8–24.

2. Harvey Fergusson, *Home in the West: An Inquiry into My Origins* (New York: Duell, Sloan and Pearce, 1944): 3–4.

3. Ibid., 7.

4. Richard D. Lamm and Michael McCarthy, *The Angry West: A Vulnerable Land and Its Future* (Boston: Houghton Mifflin, 1982): 6.

5. Paul W. Rodman, *California Gold: The Beginning of Mining in the Far West* (Cambridge: Harvard University Press, 1947): 332.

6. Many of these points are found in the *Report of the President's Mediation Commission to the President of the United States* (Washington, D.C.: Government Printing Office, 1918), which looked into strikes in copper districts in 1917.

7. Duane A. Smith, *Rocky Mountain Mining Camps: The Urban Frontier* (Bloomington: Indiana University Press, 1967): 39.

8. W. G. Henry, "Bingham Canyon," *ISR* 13 (October 1912): 341.

9. See generally John Bodnar *The Transplanted: A History of Immigrants in Urban America* (Bloomington: Indiana University Press, 1985); Peter Kivisto, *Immigrant Socialists in the United States: The Case of the Finns and the Left* (Cranbury, N.J.: Associated University Presses, 1984).

10. See generally Zeese Papanikolas, *Buried Unsung: Louis Tikas and the Ludlow Massacre* (Salt Lake City: University of Utah Press, 1982).

11. James C. Foster, "The Impact of Labor on the Development of the West," in James C. Foster, ed., *American Labor in the Southwest, the First Hundred Years* (Tucson: University of Arizona Press, 1982): 4–5.

12. See generally Emilio Zamora, *The World of the Mexican Worker in Texas* (College Station: Texas A&M University Press, 1993).

13. Gunther Peck, *Reinventing Free Labor: Padrones and Immigrant Workers in the North American West, 1880–1930* (New York: Cambridge University Press, 2000).

14. Report from Leadville, Colorado, July 1, 1899, John F. Champion Papers, Western History Collection, University of Colorado, Boulder.

15. Report from Thiel Detective Agency, November 1, 1903, United Verde Copper Company Collection, MS 199, Cline Library, Northern Arizona University, Flagstaff.

16. Emma F. Langdon, *The Cripple Creek Strike: A History of Industrial Wars in Colorado* (New York: Arno, 1969): 351. This is a reprint of the 1904–1905 edition by Great Western, with new introduction.

17. Harry A. Mills and Royal E. Montgomery, *Organized Labor* (New York: McGraw-Hill, 1945): 60–75.

18. Robert E. Weir, *Knights Unhorsed: Internal Conflict in a Gilded Age Social Movement* (Detroit: Wayne State University Press, 2000): 17–18.

19. See Leo Wolman, *The Growth of American Trade Unions 1880–1923* (New York: National Bureau of Economic Research, 1924): 110–111.

20. Report of Special Employee Claude McCaleb at Globe, Arizona, for period June 1–15, 1917, to R. L. Barnes, Special Agent in Charge, in U.S. Military Intelligence Reports, Washington, D.C., 1984.

21. Ibid.

22. Paul Kleppner, "Voters and Parties in the Western United States, 1876–1900," *The Western Political Quarterly* (January 1983): 49–68.

23. Ibid.

24. David R. Berman, *Reformers, Corporations, and the Electorate* (Niwot: University Press of Colorado, 1992).

25. Gretchen Ritter, *Goldbugs and Greenbacks: The Antimonopoly Tradition and the Politics of Finance in America* (New York: Cambridge University Press, 1997).

26. See Ira Kipnis, *The American Socialist Movement 1897–1912* (New York: Columbia University Press, 1952): 50–61; David A. Shannon, *The Socialist Party of America* (Chicago: Quadrangle Books, 1955): 38.

27. Harold Lord Varney, "The Story of the I.W.W.," *The One Big Union Monthly* (May 1919): 49–53.

28. Ibid.

29. In this respect Mountain West Socialism resembled that found by James R. Green in his study of radical movements in the Southwest—Oklahoma, Texas, Louisiana, and Arkansas. See James R. Green, *Grass-Roots Socialism: Radical Movements in the Southwest, 1895–1943* (Baton Rouge: Louisiana State University Press, 1978).

30. Shannon, *Socialist Party of America*, 37–39.

31. Elizabeth Gurley Flynn, "Memories of the Industrial Workers of the World (IWW)," Occasional Papers Series, American Institute for Marxist Studies, Web Edition (1997): 2.

32. Ralph Chaplin, *Wobbly: The Rough-and-Tumble Story of an American Radical* (Chicago: University of Chicago Press, 1948): 85.

33. Much of what is speculated about the composition of the national party is based on a membership survey it conducted in early 1908, to which 6,310 of the 41,751 members responded. Results of the survey are in "Socialists in America—Who and What They Are," *Wilshire's Magazine* (June 1909): 6. The figures in this article were drawn from the April 1909 issue of the *Official Bulletin* of the Socialist party. This survey indicated that Socialists on a national basis were rather diverse as to age, income, and occupational status, although with a solid base of skilled workers, many of whom belonged to unions. On the composition of specific Mountain West parties, see Elizabeth Jameson, *All That Glitters: Class, Conflict, and Community in Cripple Creek* (Urbana: University of Illinois Press, 1998); Jerry W. Calvert, *The Gibraltar: Socialism and Labor in Butte, Montana, 1895–1920* (Helena: Montana Historical Society Press, 1988); James Hulse, "Socialism in Nevada, 1904–1918: Faint Echoes of an Idealistic National Movement," *Nevada Historical Society Quarterly* 31 (Winter 1988): 247–258; John S. McCormick and John R. Sillito, "America's Socialist Heritage, Socialism in Utah, 1900–1920," *The Socialist Tribune* (April-May 1978): n.p.

34. Jameson, *All That Glitters*.

35. David M. Emmons, *The Butte Irish: Class and Ethnicity in an American Mining Town* (Urbana: University of Illinois Press, 1989).

36. Quoted in "A Word of Appreciation," *Annual Labor Review of the Inter-Mountain Worker* (June 19, 1915): 10.

37. See J. Kenneth Davies, *Deseret's Sons of Toil* (Salt Lake City: Olympus, 1977).

38. John S. McCormick and John R. Sillito, "Socialism and Utah Labor: 1900–1920," *Southwest Economy and Society* 6 (Fall 1983): 15–29.

39. Ibid., 27.

40. "Socialist Convention," *Utah Labor Journal* (January 10, 1902): 2.

41. Remarks of Arizona Socialist party secretary Alice Eddy, Minutes of Joint Conference of National Executive Committee and State Secretaries, 1918, 34–35, SPC, Duke University, Durham, North Carolina.

42. McCaleb, June 1–15, 1917, U.S. Military Intelligence Reports.

43. The vote for Socialist candidates falls far short of perfection as an indicator of support for radicalism: there are a number of reasons why nonradicals might vote for Socialist candidates and radicals might vote for candidates of other parties or not vote at all. The size of the Socialist party vote as a percentage of all votes, however, does give

us some idea of the success of a party that, in fact, was dedicated to the replacement of the capitalistic system and, thus, of its potential to make a difference. Party vote data also give us a measure of what messages seemed to be working, for example, the tactical value of reform-orientated platforms versus those that emphasized the class struggle and the overthrow of the system.

CHAPTER 2

1. Joseph H. Kibbey, "Republican Outlook," *The Rita* 2 (February 23, 1896): 3.

2. "The Omaha Preamble, Platform and Resolutions" *The New Nation* (October 29, 1892): 657.

3. Ibid.

4. Frank Basil Tracy, "Menacing Socialism in the Western States," *Forum* (May 1893): 332.

5. Ibid., 333.

6. "Socialist Labor Rally," *The New Nation* (October 29, 1892): 656.

7. Address delivered by Gen. James B. Weaver, People's party candidate for president, at the Auditorium in Helena, Montana, August 16, 1892, MC 55, Thomas C. Power Papers, Montana State Archives, Helena.

8. Ibid.

9. Ibid.

10. Ibid.

11. Joseph R. Buchanan, *The Story of a Labor Agitator* (New York: Outlook, 1903): 33.

12. Ibid., 34.

13. Robert E. Weir, *Knights Unhorsed: Internal Conflict in a Gilded Age Social Movement* (Detroit: Wayne State University Press, 2000): 75.

14. "Omaha Preamble," 657.

15. "The 'Rustlers' and the Cattlemen," *The New Nation* (April 30, 1892): 276.

16. William J. Gaboury, *Dissension in the Rockies: A History of Idaho Populism* (New York: Garland, 1988): 27.

17. William D. Haywood, *Bill Haywood's Book: The Autobiography of William D. Haywood* (New York: International, 1929): 62.

18. Item, *Arizona Silver Belt* (November 15, 1890): 1. See also Lawrence Goodwyn, *Democratic Promise: The Populist Moment in America* (New York: Oxford University Press, 1976): 173, 226.

19. David B. Griffiths, "Populism in Wyoming," *Annals of Wyoming* 40 (April 1968): 59.

20. "Resolutions of the People's Party, Gila County, Ariz.," *Arizona Silver Belt* (October 15, 1892): 1.

21. John R. Morris, *Davis H. Waite: The Ideology of a Western Populist* (Washington, D.C.: University Press of America, 1982): 12.

22. "News from the Various States," *The New Nation* (July 9, 1892): 440.

23. Editorial, *The Independent-Journal* (August 4, 1892): 2.

24. Letter from Davis Waite to Hon. Albert Nance, November 18, 1892, in "The Populists Celebrate," *San Luis Valley Courier* (November 26, 1892): 2.

25. Ibid.

26. Joel F. Vaile, "Colorado's Experiment with Populism," *Forum* 18 (February 1895): 714.

27. James Wright, *The Politics of Populism: Dissent in Colorado* (New Haven, Conn.: Yale University Press, 1974): 146–147.

28. Robert W. Larson, *Populism in the Mountain West* (Albuquerque: University of New Mexico Press, 1986): 37.

29. David Brundage, *The Making of Western Labor Radicalism: Denver's Organized Workers, 1878–1905* (Urbana: University of Illinois Press, 1994): 102–103.

30. See Leon W. Fuller, "Colorado's Revolt against Capitalism," *The Mississippi Valley Historical Review* 21 (December 1934): 343–360.

31. G. Michael McCarthy, "Colorado's Populist Party and the Progressive Movement," *Journal of the West* 15 (January 1976): 54–75.

32. James A. Denton, *Rocky Mountain Radical: Myron W. Reed, Christian Socialist* (Albuquerque: University of New Mexico Press, 1997): 72.

33. Howard H. Quint, "Julius A. Wayland, Pioneer Socialist Propagandist," *The Mississippi Valley Historical Review* 35 (March 1949): 585–606.

34. Letter from J. A. Wayland, "The Farmers of the West Falling into Line," *The New Nation* (December 24, 1892): 755.

35. Ibid.

36. Leonard Schlup, "I Am Not a Cuckoo Democrat! The Congressional Career of Henry A. Coffeen," *Annals of Wyoming* (Fall 1994): 30–47.

37. Griffiths, "Populism in Wyoming," 63–65.

38. See Larson, *Populism in the Mountain West*, 55. The standard work is Thomas A. Krueger, "Populism in Wyoming" (M.A. thesis, University of Wyoming, 1960).

39. Schlup, "I Am Not a Cuckoo Democrat," 50.

40. "We Are in It," *The Reform* (1892): 1.

41. Gaboury, *Dissension in the Rockies*.

42. David B. Griffiths, *Populism in the Western United States, 1890–1900* (Lewiston, N.Y.: Edwin Mellen, 1992): 442.

43. From "The Platforms," *Great Falls News* (October 22, 1892): 6.

44. "News from the Various States," *The New Nation* (July 9, 1892): 440–441.

45. Ibid.

46. "The Reason Why," *Great Falls News* (October 22, 1892): 6.

47. "Outlook in Montana," *The New Nation* (July 9, 1892): 441.

48. Griffiths, *Populism in the Western United States*, 283–285.

49. Ellis Waldron and Paul B. Wilson, *Atlas of Montana Elections, 1876–1976*. University of Montana Publications in History (Missoula: University of Montana Press, 1978): 15–17; Thomas A. Clinch, *Urban Populism and Free Silver in Montana* (Missoula: University of Montana Press, 1970): 65.

50. "Nevada's Silver Men," *New York Times* (October 31, 1892): 5.

51. Russell R. Elliott, *History of Nevada*, 2nd revised ed. (Lincoln: University of Nebraska Press, 1987): 186. See also Mary Ellen Glass, *Silver and Politics in Nevada* (Reno: University of Nevada Press, 1969): 63–64.

52. Frank J. Jonas, "Utah, the Different State," in Frank J. Jonas, ed. *Politics in the American West* (Salt Lake City: University of Utah Press, 1969): 327–379.

53. David Griffiths, "Far Western Populism: The Case of Utah, 1893–1900," *Utah Historical Quarterly* 37 (1969): 396–407.

54. Labor developments in Utah during this period are discussed in Allan Kent Powell, *The Next Time We Strike: Labor in Utah's Coal Fields* (Logan: Utah State University Press, 1985); Paul A. Frisch, "Labor Conflict at Eureka, 1886–97," *Utah Historical Quarterly* 49 (Spring 1981): 145–156; J. Kenneth Davies, "Mormonism and the Closed Shop," *Labor History* (Spring 1962): 169–187.

55. J. Kenneth Davies, *Deseret's Sons of Toil* (Salt Lake City: Olympus, 1977): 110–111.

56. See Powell, *Next Time We Strike*; Frisch, "Labor Conflict at Eureka."

57. Griffiths, "Far Western Populism," 397.

58. Calvin A. Roberts, "H. B. Fergusson, 1848–1915: New Mexico Spokesman for Political Reform," *New Mexico Historical Review* 57 (July 1982): 237–255.

59. Carole Larson, *Forgotten Frontier: The Story of Southeastern New Mexico* (Albuquerque: University of New Mexico Press, 1993).

60. See, for example, "Honest Labor Speaks," *Santa Fe New Mexican* (October 31, 1890): 4.

61. Robert J. Rosenbaum, *Mexican Resistance in the Southwest* (Austin: University of Texas Press, 1981).

62. *Weekly Phoenix Herald* (October 11, 1894): 1. Other commentary on the limited organization and effectiveness of the People's Party in Arizona is found in letters to George W.P. Hunt from Frank L. Gates, September 28, 1892, and from Henry C. Roemer to Hunt, July 7, 1892. Both in George W.P. Hunt Papers, Arizona Collection, Box 5, Arizona State University Libraries, Tempe.

63. *Arizona Daily Gazette* (October 7, 1892): 1.

64. *Mohave County Miner* (July 23, 1892): 2.

65. Ibid.

66. Larson, *Populism in the Mountain West*.

67. Sally S. Zanjani, "The Election of 1890: The Last Hurrah for the Old Regime," *Nevada Historical Quarterly* (Spring 1977): 46–56.

68. "Party Platforms," *Arizona Silver Belt* (September 13, 1890): 1. Taken from *Globe-Democrat*, n.d.

69. Ibid.

70. Leon W. Fuller, "Colorado's Revolt against Capitalism," *The Mississippi Valley Historical Review* 21 (December 1934): 352–353.

CHAPTER 3

1. "Silver and Socialism," *New York Times* (October 18, 1893): 4.

2. *Mohave County Miner* (August 12, 1893): 3.

3. Ibid.

4. Michael P. Malone, *The Battle for Butte* (Seattle: University of Washington Press, 1981): 54–55.

5. Newspaper clippings from T. C. Powers Scrapbook, Montana State Historical Society, Helena, "Long List in Montana," Dateline, Bozeman, May 29, 1894, and "Our Congressional Nominee," *The Butte Bystander*, n.d.

6. See generally Richard Schneirov, Shelton Stromquist, and Nick Salvatore, eds., *The Pullman Strike and the Crisis of the 1890s, Essays on Labor and Politics* (Urbana: University of Illinois Press, 1999).

7. Letter from John W. Judd, U.S. Attorney, Utah, to Attorney General, U.S., Salt Lake City, July 16, 1894, Strike Files of the U.S. Department of Justice, Washington, D.C.

8. Letter from Joseph A. Small, marshal of the Colorado District, to Attorney General, Denver, December 7, 1895, Strike Files.

9. Ibid. See also letter from W. K. Meade, U.S. marshal, to Attorney General, Prescott, Arizona, July 8, 1894; letter from Joseph Pinkhause, former U.S. marshal, District of Idaho, to Attorney General, July 13, 1895, Strike Files.

10. Letter from Geo. M. Humprey, U.S. marshal, Nevada, to Attorney General, Carson City, Nevada, August 30, 1894, Strike Files.

11. William D. Haywood, *Bill Haywood's Book: The Autobiography of William D. Haywood* (New York: International, 1929): 53.

12. "Populist Convention," *The Coeur d'Alene Miner* (July 28, 1894): 3.

13. Robert Wayne Smith, *The Coeur d'Alene Mining War of 1892: A Case Study of an Industrial Dispute.* Oregon State Monographs (Corvallis: Oregon State University Press, 1961).

14. See Harold Lord Varney, "The Story of the I.W.W.," *The One Big Union Monthly* (May 1919): 49–53; Haywood, *Bill Haywood's Book*, 63.

15. Waite quoted in Percy Stanley Fritz, *Colorado: The Centennial State* (New York: Prentice-Hall, 1941): 354.

16. Ibid.

17. Davis H. Waite and Lorenzo Crounse, "Woman Suffrage in Practice," *The North American Review* 158 (June 1894): 740.

18. "Populists and the People," *New York Times* (April 1, 1894): 4.

19. Fritz, *Colorado,* 354.

20. See generally Marshall Sprague, *Money Mountain: The Story of Cripple Creek Gold* (Boston: Little, Brown, 1953).

21. Nick Salvatore, *Eugene V. Debs: Citizen and Socialist* (Urbana: University of Illinois Press, 1982): 203.

22. B. M. Rastall, *The Cripple Creek Strike of 1893* (Colorado Springs: Colorado College Studies, June 1905): 42.

23. "A Populist Scheme," *The Independent Journal* (March 8, 1894): 2.

24. Ibid.

25. Extract from *The Denver News* in "'Terrible Arraignment," *The Evening Journal* (November 5, 1894): 2.

26. James Wright, *The Politics of Populism: Dissent in Colorado* (New Haven, Conn.: Yale University Press, 1974): 199.

27. "Colorado Is Redeemed," *Idaho Daily Statesman* (November 7, 1894): 1.

28. Jennie A. McGehe, "Jennie A. McGehe Attends Woman's Party Meeting," *American Socialist* (August 26, 1916): 3. At the time she wrote this, McGehe was state secretary of the Colorado Socialist party.

29. Wright, *Politics of Populism*, 194–195.

30. David H. Waite, "Ex-Governor Waite Hits the One Hoss," *ATR* (August 7, 1897): 2.

31. Ibid.

32. Lewis L. Gould, *Wyoming: A Political History, 1868–1896* (New Haven, Conn.: Yale University Press, 1968): 186.

33. *The Populist* (October 20, 1894): 3, printing dispatch from Cheyenne, Wyoming, October 12, 1894.

34. Ibid.

35. Gould, *Wyoming*, 215.

36. "Populist Convention," *The Coeur d'Alene Miner* (July 28, 1894): 3.

37. "Where Are You?" unidentified paper clipping published in Moscow, Idaho, September 21, 1894, Scrapbook, George C. Pickett Collection, University of Idaho, Moscow.

38. "For Fiat Money," unidentified Idaho paper clipping, September 21, 1894, Scrapbook, George C. Pickett Collection, University of Idaho, Moscow.

39. Editorial, *Idaho Dailey Statesman* (September 22, 1894): 2.

40. "Workingmen in Politics," *Idaho State Tribune* (October 18, 1894): 1.

41. Boyd A. Martin, *Idaho Voting Trends* (Moscow: Idaho Research Foundation, 1975): 2.

42. William J. Gaboury, "From Statehouse to Bull Pen: Idaho Populism and the Coeur d'Alene Troubles of the 1890s," *Pacific Northwest Quarterly* (January 1967): 16.

43. Karel D. Bicha, *Western Populism: Studies in an Ambivalent Conservatism* (Lawrence, Kans.: Coronado, 1976).

44. Ellis Waldron and Paul B. Wilson. *Atlas of Montana Elections, 1876–1976* (Missoula: University of Montana Publications in History, 1978): 18–19.

45. Newspaper clippings from T. C. Power Scrapbook, Montana State Historical Society, Helena, "Long List in Montana," Dateline, Bozeman, May 29, 1894, and "Our Congressional Nominee," *The Butte Bystander*, n.d.

46. "Nevada Populist Nominations," *New York Times* (September 8, 1894): 5.

47. R. A. Maynard, "How I Became a Socialist," *The Comrade* (September 1903): 8.

48. Mary Ellen Glass, *Silver and Politics in Nevada* (Reno: University of Nevada Press, 1969): 88.

49. Maynard, "How I Became a Socialist," 8.

50. David Griffiths, "Far Western Populism: The Case of Utah, 1893–1900," *Utah Historical Quarterly* 37 (1969): 397.

51. Ibid.

52. "The Populist Movement," *The Silver City Enterprise* (August 24, 1894): 2.

53. Ibid.

54. "Political Grist," *Santa Fe Daily New Mexican* (September 15, 1894): 1.

55. Platform of the People's Party of Grant County, adopted in Silver City, October 8, 1894. Reprinted in "The Other Side," *The Silver City Enterprise* (October 12, 1894): 2.

56. "The Populist Primary," *The Silver City Enterprise* (October 5, 1894): 2.

57. Carole Larson, *Forgotten Frontier: The Story of Southeastern New Mexico* (Albuquerque: University of New Mexico Press, 1993): 87–88.

58. *Arizona Populist* (September 22, 1894): 2.

59. Ibid. (October 20, 1894): 3.

60. David R. Berman, *Reformers, Corporations, and the Electorate* (Niwot: University Press of Colorado, 1992): 35.

61. Buckey O'Neill, *An Open Letter* (October 12, 1894), Sharlot Hall Museum, Prescott, Arizona.

62. *Arizona Weekly Journal Miner* (September 19, 1894): n.p.

63. "The Populist Meeting," *Arizona Silver Belt* (November 3, 1894): 2.

64. Editorial, *Mohave County Miner* (December 29, 1894): 2.

65. Item from *Arizona Gazette,* n.d., in O'Neill Scrapbook, Sharlot Hall Museum, Prescott, Arizona.

66. *Phoenix Herald* editorial, quoted in *Arizona Journal Miner* (November 28, 1894): 2.

67. Buckey O'Neill, *The Rita* (February 23, 1896): 2–3.

68. David R. Berman, "Electoral Support for Populism in the Mountain States: Some Evidence from Arizona," *Social Science Journal* 24 (January 1987): 43–52.

69. J. S. Hilizinger, "The People's Party," *Arizona Magazine* 1 (1893): 20–22.

CHAPTER 4

1. Michael P. Malone, *The Battle for Butte* (Seattle: University of Washington Press, 1981): 106.

2. Teller quoted in "It Is McKinley," *El Paso Times* (June 19, 1896): 1.

3. "The People's Party Platform," *Tombstone Epitaph* (November 2, 1896): n.p.

4. Letter from Henry Demarest Lloyd to Bayard Holmes, July 13, 1896, Henry Demarest Lloyd Papers, State Historical Society of Wisconsin, Madison.

5. Letter from Hogan to Henry Lloyd, July 29, 1896, ibid.

6. Views of Socialist editor J. A. Wayland, "Matchett and Maguire," *ATR* (August 15, 1896): 1.

7. Ibid.

8. Proceedings of the Ninth Annual Convention of the Socialist Labor Party, 10, Socialist Labor Party of America Records (microfilm edition), State Historical Society of Wisconsin, Madison.

9. "'Bloody Bridles' Talks," *Inter-Mountain Advocate* (July 17, 1896): 1. Reprinted from *Denver New Road,* n.d.

10. Edward O. Wolcott, "Senator E.O. Wolcott to the Voters," *The Cheyenne Daily Sun-Leader* (August 14, 1896): 1.

11. Quote in Louis W. Koenig, *Bryan: A Political Biography of William Jennings Bryan* (New York: G. P. Putnam's Sons, 1975): 245.

12. Ibid., 218

13. Donnelly quoted in Paul W. Glad, *McKinley, Bryan, and the People* (Philadelphia: J. B. Lippincott, 1964): 197.

14. Nick Salvatore, *Eugene V. Debs: Citizen and Socialist* (Urbana: University of Illinois Press, 1982): 161.

15. "The Pop's Convention," *The Wyoming Tribune* (July 18, 1896): 4.

16. Glad, *McKinley, Bryan, and the People,* 156–157.

17. Letter from Edgar T. Tucker, secretary of the People's party in Leadville, Colorado, to Henry Kuhn, secretary of the Socialist Labor party, September 5, 1896, Socialist

Labor Party Papers (microfilm edition), Reel 9, State Historical Society of Wisconsin, Madison.

18. David B. Griffiths, *Populism in the Western United States, 1890–1900*, 2 vols. (Lewiston, N.Y.: Edwin Mellen, 1992): vol. 2, 466–467.

19. *The Populist Tribune* 4 (February 2, 1894): 4.

20. "Populists Opportunity," *Montana Populist* (September 28, 1893): 2.

21. "State's Disgrace,' *Montana Silverite* (January 18, 1895): 1.

22. "The Pop's Convention," *The Wyoming Tribune* (July 18, 1896): 4.

23. "An Open Letter to Chairman Hasbrouck," *Inter-Mountain Advocate* (July 17, 1896): 1.

24. Ibid.

25. Ibid., 2.

26. Letter from R. A. Hasbrouck to Henry Kuhn, September 1, 1896, Socialist Labor Party Papers (microfilm edition), Reel 9, State Historical Society of Wisconsin, Madison.

27. See "Withdrawal of Gov. Prince," *Santa Fe New Mexican* (October 9, 1896): 1.

28. William A. Keleher, *Memoirs: 1892–1969* (Santa Fe: Rydal, 1969): 38.

29. Unidentified clipping in L. Bradford Prince Papers, Series 1, Box 1, New Mexico Records Center and Archives, Santa Fe.

30. "Candidates of the People," *Albuquerque Morning Democrat* (November 1, 1896): 3.

31. Ibid.

32. "People's Party Convention," *The Silver Belt* (September 17, 1896): 3.

33. Griffiths, *Populism in the Western United States*, vol. 2, 517.

34. Communication from O. Erickson to Comrade Wayland, "Slavery in Wyoming," *ATR* (June 5, 1897): 3.

35. "Machine, Man and Mammon," *ATR* (July 3, 1897): 2.

36. Interview reprinted in the *Great Fall News* (November 14, 1896): 1.

37. Doris Buck Ward, "The Winning of Woman Suffrage in Montana" (M.A. thesis, Montana State University, June 1974): 64–65.

38. *The Silver Advocate* (October 27, 1898): n.p.

39. Jerry W. Calvert, *The Gibraltar: Socialism and Labor in Butte, Montana, 1895–1920* (Helena: Montana Historical Society Press, 1988): 20.

40. Thomas A. Clinch, *Urban Populism and Free Silver in Montana* (Missoula: University of Montana Press, 1970): 167.

41. "Progress in Montana," *SDH* (July 7, 1900): 3.

42. Griffiths, *Populism in the Western United States*, vol. 2, 403.

43. Ibid.

44. Item, *Living Issues* (October 1, 1897): n.p.

45. On the relation between the People's party and the Socialist party in Nevada, see Joseph Sullivan, "Rising from the Ranks, Socialism in Nye County," *Nevada Historical Quarterly* 34, no. 2 (Summer 1991): 340–349.

46. T. B. Catron to Hon. Pedro Sanchez, September 17, 1896, Marion Dargan Papers, Zimmerman Library, Special Collections, University of New Mexico, Albuquerque.

47. Robert W. Larson, *Populism in the Mountain West* (Albuquerque: University of New Mexico Press, 1986): 132.

48. Elvis E. Flemming, "'Sockless' Jerry Simpson: The New Mexico Years, 1902–1905," *New Mexico Historical Review* 69 (January 1994): 49–70.

49. Harvey Fergusson, *Home in the West: An Inquiry into My Origins* (New York: Duell, Sloan and Pearce, 1944): 73–74.

50. Ibid., 73.

51. "Populistic Convention," *Arizona Republican* (August 19, 1896): 1.

52. "The People's Party Platform," *Tombstone Epitaph* (November 2, 1896): n.p.

53. Buckey O'Neill, "An Open Letter," written in 1896. Reprinted in *MM* (August 1900): 10–18.

54. David R. Berman, "Electoral Support for Populism in the Mountain States," *Social Science Journal* 24 (January 1987): 43–52.

55. Letter from Harry Nash to G. W. Hunt, August 21, 1898, George W.P. Hunt Papers, Arizona Collection, Arizona State University Libraries, Tempe.

56. "A Day of Disorder," *Arizona Republican* (August 19, 1898): 1, 8.

57. Editorial, "For the Voters to Decide," *Arizona Silver Belt* (October 13, 1898): 2.

58. Item, *Arizona Silver Belt* (November 17, 1898): 1.

59. Sally S. Zanjani, "The Election of 1890: The Last Hurrah for the Old Regime," *Nevada Historical Quarterly* 20 (Spring 1977): 46–56.

60. Karel D. Bicha, "Western Populists: Marginal Reformers of the 1890s," *Agricultural History* (October 1976): 626–635.

61. Berman, "Electoral Support."

CHAPTER 5

1. David B. Griffiths, "Far Western Populism: The Case of Utah, 1893–1900," *Utah Historical Quarterly* 37 (1969): 406.

2. Eugene Debs, "Social Democrats in Convention," *ATR* (March 24, 1900): 3.

3. "Comrades, the Clock Has Struck," *SDH* (December 10, 1898): 1.

4. "First Annual Convention Social Democratic Party," *SDH* (March 17, 1900): 1.

5. Figures from "Official Vote" in *ATR* (January 12, 1901): 4.

6. Algie Simons, "The Socialist Outlook," *ISR* 5 (1904–1905): 203.

7. William Morris Feigenbaum, "Great Battles of Bygone Days," *American Socialist* (July 29, 1916): 3.

8. "First Platform of Socialist Party, Adopted by the Unity Convention in 1901," SPC.

9. Ibid.

10. Harry A. Mills and Royal E. Montgomery, *Organized Labor* (New York: McGraw-Hill, 1945): 83. See also "Great Growth of the A.F.L.," *SDH* (August 13, 1903): 5.

11. Algie Simons, "Socialism and the Trade Union Movement," *ISR* 3 (July 1902): 46–49.

12. Editorial, "National Organization," *ISR* (February 1902): 636–637.

13. Letter from William Mailly to J. W. Martin, Denver, May 11, 1903, SPC. The same message is found in a letter from acting National Secretary W. E. Clark to L. H. McGill, Morrison, Colorado, May 12, 1903, SPC.

14. This type of argument appears, among other places, in an editorial by John Spargo in *The Comrade* (December 1902): 60.

15. John C. Chase, "Organization Is Weak, But Sentiment Is Very Strong," *The Labor World* (September 19, 1902): 3.

16. Ibid.

17. Ibid.

18. Letter from W. E. Clark to Arizona Socialist J. B. Barnett, June 4, 1903, SPC.

19. Editorial, "National Organization," *ISR* (February 1902): 636–637.

20. Ibid.

21. See letter from William Mailly to D. G. Bruce, Sheridan, Wyoming, 1903 (no other date given), SPC.

22. See, for example, William Mailly letters to Kenneth Clayton in Globe, Arizona, February 2, 23, 1903, and to E. S. Lund, organizer in Lehi, Utah, March 3, 1903, SPC.

23. Conflict within Mountain West state organizations is frequently referred to in the SPC correspondence. See, for example, letters from W. E. Clark to A. Hastings, Cheyenne, Wyoming, June 5, 1907; William Mailly to J. W. Martin, Denver, Colorado, March 6, 1903; Mailly to J. Edward Morgan, Denver, July 10, 1908; Mailly to W. H. Tawney, national committeeman, Salt Lake City, March 3, 1903; Mailly to E. S. Lund, organizer, Lehi, Utah, March 3, 1903; Mailly to W. H. Tawney, April 14, 1903; W. E. Clark to Kate Hilliard, June 9, 1907; and Mailly to Tawney, June 9, 1908.

24. See, for example, Mailly correspondence with secretary of the Wyoming state party, July, 28, 1903, SPC.

25. Resolution adopted by Utah Socialist Party, no date, SPC.

26. Helen F. Sanders, *A History of Montana*, Vol. 1 (Chicago: Lewis, 1913): 430.

27. "The Tide Is Setting In," *ATR* (November 17, 1900): 4.

28. Ibid.

29. William Philpott, *The Lessons of Leadville*. Monograph 10 (Denver: Colorado Historical Society, 1995).

30. "The Populist Manifesto," *Utah Socialist* (October 25, 1900): 2.

31. Elder quoted in J. W. Martin, "The Socialist Movement in Colorado," *ATR* (September 5, 1903): 4.

32. Simons, "Socialist Outlook," 203–217.

33. Martin, "Socialist Movement in Colorado," 4.

34. See "Socialists Name Candidates and Adopt a Platform," *Colorado Springs Gazette* (July 6, 1902), 1; "David C. Coates' Sensational Debut and Retirement as a Socialist," *Rocky Mountain News* (July 6, 1902): 1.

35. "Remains a Socialist," *Idaho Springs News* (July 11, 1902): 3.

36. "No Fusion Is UKASE of Socialists," *The Denver Times* (July 4, 1902): 1.

37. "The Socialists Condemn Their Own Theory," *The Denver Times* (July 7, 1902): 4.

38. Ibid.

39. "Socialists Name Candidates and Adopt a Platform," *Colorado Springs Gazette* (July 6, 1902): 1.

40. "Socialists Have Completed Their Ticket," *The Denver Times* (September 4, 1902): 2.

41. Letter from Boyce to *The Socialist* (September 8, 1902), reproduced in "Will Boyce Stand?" *The Socialist* (September 21, 1902): 3.

42. "Ticket in Field," *The Daily News* (July 5, 1902): 7.

43. See "Two Tickets Claim the Name Socialist," *The Denver Times* (September 26, 1902), 2; "Put up a Ticket," *The Daily News* (July 5, 1902): 9.

44. "Minority Political Parties Making Strenuous Fight for Recognition," *The Denver Times* (October 16, 1902): 3.

45. James Wright, *The Politics of Populism: Dissent in Colorado* (New Haven, Conn.: Yale University Press, 1974): 228–229.

46. Editorial, "He Don't Like Socialism," *MM* (September 1902): 30.

47. See Patterson's reply to a challenge from Colorado Socialists for a debate in "Senator Patterson Replies to Challenge of Socialist Party," *The Denver Times* (October 18, 1902): 10.

48. Ibid.

49. Editorial, "The Defeat and Its Causes," *The Daily News* (November 6, 1902): 4.

50. "400,000 Socialist Votes Cast," *ATR* (November 22, 1902): 1.

51. Moyer quoted in Emma F. Langdon, *The Cripple Creek Strike: A History of Industrial Wars in Colorado* (New York: Arno, 1969): 76.

52. Editorial "The Political Situation," *The Labor News* (April 3, 1903): 2.

53. Sanders, *History of Montana*, 1, 427–430.

54. Eugene V. Debs, "Eugene Debs' Visit to the Northwest," *SDH* (November 4, 1899): 1.

55. Ibid.

56. "Montana Is Moving," *SDH* (November 4, 1899): 2. Reprint of editorial from the October 21, 1899, *Butte Labor Advocate*.

57. Sanders, *History of Montana*, 1, 430. Membership estimates also found in Terrence D. McGlynn, "Lewis J. Duncan, Socialist: The Man and His Work," paper presented to the Social Science Section, Montana Academy of Sciences, April 18, 1970, 10; Jerry W. Calvert, *The Gibraltar: Socialism and Labor in Butte, Montana, 1895–1920* (Helena: Montana Historical Society Press, 1988): 17.

58. Report from P. J. Cooney of Butte, one of the party's founding members, in "Progress in Montana," *SDH* (July 7, 1900): 3.

59. Ellis Waldron and Paul B. Wilson, *Atlas of Montana Elections, 1876–1976.* University of Montana Publications in History (Missoula: University of Montana Press, 1978).

60. Sanders, *History of Montana*, 1, 430.

61. Chase, "Organization Is Weak," 3.

62. P. J. Cooney, "Socialist Movement in Butte," *The Labor World* (July 4, 1902): 7.

63. "State Socialist Convention of Montana," *The Socialist* (August 10, 1902): 3.

64. See account by James D. Graham, "Corporate Corruption in the Socialist Party," *The Montana News* (October 21, 1909): 2–3.

65. P. J. Cooney, "Full County Ticket at Butte," *The Socialist* (September 14, 1902): 3. See also Clarence Smith, "Immense Enthusiasm in Butte," *The Socialist* (September 21, 1902): 3.

66. "Montana 'Socialist' Legislators Not Representatives of the Socialist Party," letter from P. J. Cooney, state secretary, Socialist party, November 30, 1903, published in *The Socialist* (December 6, 1903): 3.

67. John Morrissey, "Some Suggestions," *ATR* (December 13, 1902): 5.

68. "From Montana," report by Dr. Geo A. Willett, state secretary, *ATR* (September 5, 1903): 4.

69. Benj. F. Wilson, "Buried the Old Parties in Montana," *SDH* (April 18, 1903): 2. See also letter from William Mailly to J. H. Frincks, Socialist mayor-elect, Anaconda, Montana, April 9, 1903, SPC.

70. "A Tribute to Socialists" *ATR* (January 17, 1903): 2. Reprint of article from the *Anaconda Montana Standard,* n.d.

71. "Gleanings from Busy Socialistic Fields!" *SDH* (August 15, 1903): 3. See also "News of the World of Socialism," *American Labor Union Journal* (April 16, 1903): 8; letter from William Mailly to J. H. Frincks, Socialist mayor-elect, Anaconda, Montana, April 9, 1903, SPC.

72. Graham, "Corporate Corruption," 2–3.

73. Duane A. Smith, *Rocky Mountain West: Colorado, Wyoming, and Montana, 1859–1915* (Albuquerque: University of New Mexico Press, 1992): 189.

74. See, for example, "Shall Butte Also Whisper?" *The Butte Socialist* (April 4, 1915), 4; Sanders, *History of Montana,* 1, 43.

75. Report from Local Butte, in Simons, "Socialist Outlook," 212.

76. Daniel J. LaGrande, "Voice of a Copper King: A Study of the (Butte) *Reveille,* 1903–1906" (M.A. thesis, University of Montana, 1971).

77. Graham, "Corporate Corruption," 2–3.

78. Chase, "Organization Is Weak," 3.

79. Stanley Stewart Phipps, "The Coeur d'Alene Miners' Unions in the Post Bullpen Era, 1900 to 1916: The Socialist Party and I.W.W. Connections" (M.A. thesis, University of Idaho Graduate School, May 1980).

80. "Same Trick of 'Silence,'" Report of D. W. Smith, September 15, 1902, published in *The Socialist* (September 21, 1902): 3.

81. Phipps, "Coeur d'Alene Miners' Unions," 53.

82. "Canyon County Convention, Idaho," *The Socialist* (September 21, 1902): 3.

83. Letter from William Mailly to A. M. Slattery, March 9, 1903, and letter from Clarke to Slattery, June 15, 1907, both in SPC. In 1902 Slattery was the Idaho party's nominee for governor.

84. "Workingmen Unite," *Idaho State Tribune* (November 3, 1903): 5. The evidence is inconclusive as to whether the A. G. Miller quoted here was the A. Grant Miller who later became a prominent Socialist in Nevada.

85. A. B. Elder, "Introductory," *Utah Socialist* (October 25, 1900): 2.

86. "Elder Out of Politics," *Utah Labor Journal* (February 15, 1902): 1.

87. "Utah State Convention," *SDH* (July 21, 1900): 1.

88. Remarks of Joseph Gilbert, editor, *The Crisis,* a Utah Socialist paper, in Simons, "Socialist Outlook," 216.

89. "They Nailed the Lie!" *Utah Labor Journal* (April 3, 1902): 1.

90. "Elder Out of Politics," 1.

91. A. B. Elder, "A Reply to Opportunists," *Utah Labor Journal* (April 17, 1902): 1.

92. Ibid.

93. Ibid.

94. "The Utah Factions," *The Socialist* (May 4, 1902): 3.

95. W. H. Tawney, "'As Near Nothing as Possible'" *The Socialist* (May 24, 1903), 3; E. S. Lund, state secretary Socialist party, Utah, May 27, 1903, published in "Side by Side," *The Socialist* (June 21, 1903): 3.

96. John R. Sillito, "Women and the Socialist Party in Utah, 1900–1920," *Utah Historical Quarterly* (Summer 1981): 220–237; Editorial, *ISR* 3 (October 1902): 232.

97. John S. McCormick and John R. Sillito, "Socialism and Utah Labor: 1900–1920," *Southwest Economy and Society* 6 (Fall 1983): 15–30.

98. "Moses Thatcher" *ATR* (November 10, 1900): 4. Reprinted from *Salt Lake City Tribune*, n.d.

99. McCormick and Sillito, "Socialism and Utah Labor," 25.

100. E. L. Lund, "Socialists in Utah," *ATR* (September 5, 1903): 5.

101. "Local Labor Notes," *Utah Labor Journal* (January 10, 1902): 3.

102. Joseph Stipanovich, *The South Slavs in Utah: A Social History* (San Francisco: R and E Research Associates, 1975).

103. David B. Griffiths, *Populism in the Western United States, 1890–1900* (Lewiston, N.Y.: Edwin Mellen, 1992): 327–328.

104. Carl V. Hallberg, "Finding His Niche: F. W. Ott, a German Publisher," *Annals of Wyoming* 72 (Spring 2000): 2–13.

105. *ATR* (December 20, 1902): 3.

106. Letter from William Mailly to F. W. Ott, July 10, 1903, SPC.

107. Letter from William Mailly to J. T. Gates, secretary, Rock Springs, Wyoming, August 4, 1903, SPC.

108. Simons, "Socialist Outlook," 203–217.

109. Letter from William Mailly to Kenneth Clayton, Globe, Arizona, February 23, 1903, SPC.

110. "Conditions in Globe, Arizona," *MM* (October 1902): 15.

CHAPTER 6

1. K. Ross Toole, *Twentieth-Century Montana: A State of Extremes* (Norman: University of Oklahoma Press, 1972): 124–125.

2. John H.M. Laslett, *Labor and the Left: A Study of Socialist and Radical Influences in the American Labor Movement, 1881–1924* (New York: Basic Books, 1970): 241.

3. Ray Ginger, *Eugene V. Debs: A Biography* (New York: Collier Books, 1949): 209 ff.

4. See John Fahey, "Ed Boyce and the Western Federation of Miners," *Idaho Yesterdays* 25 (1981): 18–30.

5. Reports of operatives supplied by the Thiel Detective Agency in Leadville, February 1 and April 1, 1899, John F. Champion Papers, Western History Collection, University of Colorado, Boulder.

6. Eugene V. Debs, "Current Events Passed in Review," *SDH* (September 2, 1899): 1.

7. "Gross Outrages in Idaho," *SDH* (September 9, 1899): 4.

8. Claudius O. Johnson, *Borah of Idaho* (New York: Longmans, Green, 1936): 75.

9. William J. Gaboury, "From Statehouse to Bull Pen: Idaho Populism and the Coeur d'Alene Troubles of the 1890s," *Pacific Northwest Quarterly* (January 1967): 14–22.

10. Eugene V. Debs, "Eugene Deb's Visit to the Northwest," *SDH* (November 4, 1899): 1.

11. Ibid.

12. Debs, "Current Events," 1.

13. Proceedings of 7th Western Federation of Miners Convention, 1899, 20, Western Federation of Miners Papers, Western History Collection, University of Colorado, Boulder.

14. Ibid.

15. "Salutatory," *MM* (January 1900): 16.

16. Ibid.

17. Ibid., 17.

18. Ibid.

19. "The Coming Election," *MM* (November 1900): 6.

20. Ibid.

21. Ibid.

22. "A Letter from Wardner," *MM* (July 1900): 40–41.

23. Proceedings of the Western Federation of Miners, 1901, 91, Western Federation of Miners Papers, Western History Collection, University of Colorado, Boulder.

24. Ibid., 91–92.

25. Accounts of the meeting are in *The Denver Times* (May 27, 1902): 3. See also A. B. Elder, Utah Socialist, "Progress and Reaction Meet Face to Face," *ATR* (June 21, 1902): 2.

26. Elder, "Progress and Reaction," 2.

27. Ibid.

28. Ibid.

29. Algie Simons, "Socialism and the Trade Union Movement," *ISR* 3 (July 1902): 46–49.

30. Letter from F. W. Ott to Algie Simons, "Concerning the American Labor Union," *ISR* 3 (August 1902): 107–108.

31. Eugene V. Debs, "The Western Labor Movement," *ISR* 3 (November 1902): 257.

32. Proceedings of 10th Western Federation of Miners Convention, 1902, 13, Western Federation of Miners Papers, Western History Collection, University of Colorado, Boulder.

33. Ott to Simons, "Concerning the American Labor Union," 108.

34. Elder, "Progress and Reaction."

35. Ibid.

36. "Unionism in Socialism," *MM* (November 1902): 7.

37. See, for example, "A Patriot for Socialism," *MM* (December 1902): 50–51. This is a report from M. L. Salter, Park City Socialist Club, dated November 11, 1902.

38. Proceedings of 10th Western Federation of Miners Convention, 1902, 9.

39. Mark Wyman, *Hard Rock Epic: Western Miners and the Industrial Revolution, 1860–1910* (Berkeley: University of California Press, 1979).

40. Proceedings of 7th Western Federation of Miners Convention, 1899, 16, Western Federation of Miners Papers, Western History Collection, University of Colorado, Boulder.

41. Remarks of Guy E. Miller at Western Federation of Miners Convention, 1914, 128, Western Federation of Miners Papers, Western History Collection, University of Colorado, Boulder.

42. "War in Colorado" *ATR* (August 22, 1903): 1.

43. George G. Suggs, *Colorado's War on Militant Unionism: James H. Peabody and the Western Federation of Miners* (Detroit: Wayne State University Press, 1972): 180.

44. Guy E. Miller, "The Telluride Strike," in Emma F. Langdon, *The Cripple Creek Strike: A History of Industrial Wars in Colorado* (New York: Arno, 1969): 205.

45. Haywood quoted in Langdon, *Cripple Creek Strike,* 77.

46. Ibid., 34.

47. Report of President Moyer, May 24, 1904, Proceedings of the Western Federation of Miners Convention, 1904, 204, Western Federation of Miners Papers, Western History Collection, University of Colorado, Boulder.

48. Ida Crouch Hazlett, "Meaning of the Colorado Strike," *Wilshire's Magazine* 6 (March 1904): 140.

49. Harold Lord Varney, "The Story of the I.W.W.," *The One Big Union Monthly* (May 1919): 51.

50. Morris Hillquit, *Recent Progress of the Socialist and Labor Movements in the United States* (Chicago: Charles H. Kerr, 1907): 25. See also Marshall Sprague, *Money Mountain: The Story of Cripple Creek Gold* (Boston: Little, Brown, 1953).

51. Langdon, *Cripple Creek Strike,* 383.

52. "McCabe Socialist Club," *MM* (July 1904): 13.

53. Ibid.

54. Report from Thiel Detective Agency, December 2, 1903, United Verde Copper Company Collection, MS 199, Cline Library, Northern Arizona University, Flagstaff.

55. Report from Thiel Detective Agency, October 28, 1903, United Verde Copper Company Collection, MS 199, Cline Library, Northern Arizona University, Flagstaff.

56. Mary Field Parton, ed., *Autobiography of Mother Jones* (Chicago: Charles H. Kerr, 1925): 94.

57. "Agitators Not Needed in Labor Politics," *The Daily News* (July 7, 1902): 10.

58. George G. Suggs, "Religion and Labor in the Rocky Mountain West: Bishop Nicholas C. Matz and the Western Federation of Miners," *Labor History* 11 (Spring 1970): 190–206.

59. "Debs Sees Hard Times," *The Spokesman Review* (October 1, 1904): 2.

60. Priscilla Long, *Where the Sun Never Shines* (New York: Paragon House, 1989): 218–219.

61. Ibid., 230–231.

62. Ibid., 250. See also Bill Bryans, "Coal Mining in Twentieth Century Wyoming: A Brief History," *Journal of the West* 21 (October 1982): 24–35.

63. Long, *Where the Sun Never Shines,* 211.

64. Ibid., 222.

65. "A Letter from Wardner," *MM* (July 1900): 40–41. See also "Miners Keep Away," *Idaho State Tribune.* Reprinted in *SDH* (July 21, 1900): 1.

66. See generally Allan Kent Powell, *The Next Time We Strike: Labor in Utah's Coal Fields* (Logan: Utah State University Press, 1985).

67. "Just an Incident," *ATR* (May 12, 1900): 1.

68. Joseph Stipanovich, *The South Slavs in Utah: A Social History* (San Francisco: R and E Research Associates, 1975): 88.

69. "Another Capitalistic Governor," *ATR* (January 30, 1904): 6.

70. "Mother Jones Is Sensation in Utah," *Idaho Capital News* (May 5, 1904): 1.

71. Ibid.

72. Mary Field Parton, ed., *Autobiography of Mother Jones*, 105–106.

73. "Opposition to W.F.M. in Arizona," *MM* (December 1901): 8.

74. Jay Wagoner, *Arizona Territory: 1863–1912* (Tucson: University of Arizona Press, 1970): 384–390.

75. Long, *Where the Sun Never Shines*, 212.

CHAPTER 7

1. In Idaho there seems to have been a particularly heavy vote, higher than in any other state in the region, even though voting returns suggest there were more Socialists in some other states such as Montana and Utah. No returns were tabulated from Nevada and New Mexico.

2. J. W. Martin, "The Socialist Movement in Colorado," *ATR* (September 5, 1903): 4.

3. See letter from J. A. Easton in "Bleeding the Movement to Death," *The Socialist* (November 23, 1902): 3; letter from William Huffman in "Another Word from Denver," *The Socialist* (March 27, 1903): 3; letter from Cripple Creek local, February 8, 1904, in "Colorado," *The Socialist* (February 21, 1904): 4.

4. Ira Kipnis, *The American Socialist Movement 1897–1912* (New York: Columbia University Press, 1952): 150–151, 181–182. See also Editorial, "Head Hunting in Colorado," *SDH* (February 7, 1903): 2.

5. Kipnis, *American Socialist Movement*, 180–182.

6. See, for example, "Trifling with Justice in Denver, But Socialism Refuses to Down!" *SDH* (August 22, 1903): 1.

7. "The Political Situation in Colorado," *MM* (October 20, 1904): 5.

8. Ibid.

9. "The Mine Owners' Campaign Document," *MM* (August 25, 1904): 6–8.

10. Ibid.

11. Ibid.

12. J. W. Martin, state secretary, Colorado Socialist party, "Plutocracy vs. Socialism," *ATR* (April 23, 1904): 5.

13. Ibid.

14. Ibid.

15. Ibid.

16. Ibid.

17. Ibid.

18. Walter Hurt, "Who's Who in the Colorado Campaign," *ATR* (September 22, 1906): 5 ff.

19. Ibid.

20. "A. H. Floaten's Letter of Acceptance," SPC. Floaten's experiences were recorded in greater detail by Guy E. Miller, "Telluride Strike," in Emma F. Langdon, *The Cripple Creek Strike: A History of Industrial Wars in Colorado* (New York: Arno, 1969): 275–295.

21. "Gleanings from Busy Socialistic Fields!" *SDH* (October 24, 1903): 2.

22. Item, *SDH* (February 6, 1904): A3.

23. Royal A. Southworth quoted by Algie Simons, "The Socialist Outlook," *ISR* 5 (October 1904): 207–208.

24. "Wonderful Progress of the Campaign," *SDH* (October 15, 1904): 1.

25. "Preparing for Fall Campaign," *The Butte Miner* (July 16, 1904): 7.

26. Langdon, *Cripple Creek Strike*, 392.

27. "Governor Adams' Statement," in ibid., 424.

28. Editorial, "Lessons from the Socialist Vote," *ISR* 5 (December 1904): 340–344.

29. "We Coincide," *MM* (December 8, 1904): 6.

30. A. H. Floaten, "'Peace' in Colorado," *SDH* (April 1, 1905): 3 (original emphasis).

31. Ibid.

32. "The Colorado Socialist Vote," *ATR* (December 17, 1904): 3.

33. Simons, "Socialist Outlook," 207.

34. Letter from H. C. Darrah, El Paso County, to William Pen Collins, February 10, 1905, William Pen Collins Papers, Western History Collection, University of Colorado, Boulder.

35. K. Ross Toole, *Twentieth-Century Montana: A State of Extremes* (Norman: University of Oklahoma Press, 1972): 113–122.

36. Heinze quoted in Michael P. Malone, *The Battle for Butte: Mining and Politics on the Northern Frontier, 1864–1906* (Seattle: University of Washington Press, 1981): 176.

37. "Gleanings from Busy Socialistic Fields!" *SDH* (October 24, 1903): 3.

38. Ibid.

39. "Wilkins's Montana Report," *The Socialist* (February 21, 1904): 4.

40. Ibid.

41. Sanders, *History of Montana*, 1, 430–431.

42. Thomas A. Jacobson, "The Battle for Direct Legislation: Montana Politics beyond the Copper Kings, 1902–1906" (M.A. thesis, University of Montana, 1987).

43. "Geo. O'Malley, Butte, to Run for Governor," *The Butte Miner* (June 8, 1904): 11.

44. Debs quoted in "Wonderful Progress of the Campaign," *SDH* (October 15, 1904): 1.

45. "Trend of Montana Politics: Socialist-Labor Meeting in This City Very Warm," *Butte Inter Mountain* (October 21, 1904): 2.

46. Jacobson, "Battle for Direct Legislation."

47. Jerry W. Calvert, *The Gibraltar: Socialism and Labor in Butte, Montana, 1895–1920* (Helena: Montana Historical Society Press, 1988): 31.

48. Editorial from *Bozeman Chronicle*, November 23, 1904. Reprinted in *The Montana News* (November 30, 1904): 1.

49. Ibid.

50. Ibid.

51. Ibid.

52. Ida Crouch Hazlett, "Montana to Be Next!" *The Socialist* (September 9, 1905): 1.

53. See "Gleanings from Busy Socialistic Fields!" *SDH* (June 10, 1905): 3, for an example from Local Bozeman; "Socialist in Bad," *Butte Inter Mountain* (October 4, 1904): 8, for an example from the Anaconda local.

54. Hazlett, "Agitation in Montana," *The Socialist* (July 22, 1905): 4.

55. Ibid.

56. Wrigley quoted in "Socialism in Idaho," *The Socialist* (March 13, 1904): 3.

57. Wilkins quoted in "Party News," *ATR* (April 23, 1904): 3.

58. Brief note in "Socialist Outlook," *ISR* 5 (1904–1905): 208.

59. Stanley Stewart Phipps, "The Coeur d'Alene Miners' Union in the Post Bullpen Era, 1900 to 1916: The Socialist Party and I.W.W. Connections" (M.A. thesis, University of Idaho Graduate School, May 1980): 59.

60. "Why Are We Organized?" *The Socialist* (April 3, 1904): 2.

61. "From Salt Lake Itself," letter from J. H. Zenger, Salt Lake City, to *Seattle Socialist*, March 27, 1904, printed in *The Socialist* (April 3, 1904): 2.

62. Report of Jos. MacLaulan, Utah secretary, in "News and Views," *ISR* 9 (October 1908.): 313.

63. Report from Thiel Detective Agency, December 15, 1903, United Verde Copper Company Collection, MS 199, Cline Library, Northern Arizona University, Flagstaff.

64. Report from Thiel Detective Agency, November 1, 1903, United Verde Copper Company Collection, MS 199, Cline Library, Northern Arizona University, Flagstaff.

65. Reports from Thiel Detective Agency, September 22 and October 6, 1903, United Verde Copper Company Collection, MS 199, Cline Library, Northern Arizona University, Flagstaff.

66. Editorial, *Arizona Daily Star* (August 18, 1904): 4.

67. "Safford Items," *The Graham County Worker* (October 10, 1904): 1.

68. Editorial, "The Socialists," *Arizona Daily Star* (August 25, 1904): 4.

69. Editorial, "Socialism in Arizona Politics," *Arizona Daily Star* (August 28, 1904): 4.

70. "Nevada to the Front," *ATR* (December 24, 1904): 3.

71. "Debs' Tour a Big Triumph," *SDH* (October 8, 1904): 1.

CHAPTER 8

1. John Curtis Kennedy, "Socialistic Tendencies in American Trade Unions," *ISR* 8 (1907–1908): 330–345. Reprinted from *Journal of Political Economy,* n.d.

2. See Proceedings of Western Federation of Miners Convention, 1903, 86–89; and 1905, 204–209, both in Western Federation of Miners Papers, Western History Collection, University of Colorado, Boulder.

3. Proceedings of the First Convention of the Industrial Workers of the World, *The Founding Convention of the IWW: Proceedings* (New York: New York Labor News, 1905; reprint Merit, 1969): 1.

4. Ibid., 2.

5. Ibid., 163.

6. See Nick Salvatore, *Eugene V. Debs: Citizen and Socialist* (Urbana: University of Illinois Press, 1982): 208.

7. Hagerty quoted in *Founding Convention of the IWW,* 152.

8. Melvin Dubofsky, *We Shall Be All: A History of the Industrial Workers of the World* (Chicago: Quadrangle Books, 1969): 139.

9. *The Industrial Union Bulletin* (March 30, 1907): 2.

10. Proceedings of 14th Western Federation of Miners Convention, 1906, 211 (original emphasis), Western Federation of Miners Papers, Western History Collection, University of Colorado, Boulder.

11. *Founding Convention of the IWW*, 155.

12. J. Anthony Lukas, *Big Trouble* (New York: Simon and Schuster, 1997): 261, 270.

13. "From Goldfield, Nevada," *MM* (May 17, 1906): 12.

14. Editorial, "The Battle at Boise," *ISR* 7 (May 1907): 688.

15. Simons quoted in "The Western Federation of Miners," *ISR* 6 (May 1906): 643.

16. Ibid., 644.

17. "They Are But the Cat's Paw," *Caldwell News* (August 15, 1906), Defendants' Exhibit, Haywood Trial, Division of Manuscripts and Idaho State Archives, Idaho State Historical Society, Boise.

18. Theodore Roosevelt, letter from the White House, April 22, 1907, in *Theodore Roosevelt: An Autobiography* (New York: Charles Scribner's Sons, 1925): 489.

19. "Colorado Socialist State Convention," *MM* (July 12, 1906): 7–8.

20. Ibid.

21. Editorial, "The Coming Campaign," *ISR* (August 1906): 113.

22. Ira Kipnis, *The American Socialist Movement 1897–1912* (New York: Columbia University Press, 1952): 330.

23. "What Socialism Is," *Caldwell News* (July 18, 1906): n.p.

24. Report of Lewis E. Floaten, secretary, Colorado party, "News and Views," *ISR* 9 (October 1908): 309–315.

25. Editorial, "Socialism in the Present Campaign," *ISR* 7 (October 6, 1906): 242–243.

26. Guy E. Miller, "The Day of Deeds," *ATR* (October 27, 1906): 6.

27. Eugene V. Debs, "Haywood, the Standard Bearer," *ATR* (August 11, 1906): 1.

28. Ernest Untermann, "Business Administration or Working Class Administration?" *ATR* (August 11, 1906): 4.

29. "Haywood's Bold Challenge," *Wilshire's Magazine* (September 1906): 18.

30. Ibid.

31. George H. Shoaf, "Colorado Is Ready," *ATR* (December 3, 1906): 2.

32. Ibid.

33. State Campaign Committee of the Socialist Party, "An Address to the Voters of Colorado," *MM* (August 23, 1906): 6.

34. "Colorado Socialist State Convention," *MM* (July 12, 1906): 8.

35. Report in "Gleanings from Busy Fields," *SDH* (October 13, 1906): 4.

36. See Lindsey's comments on this contest in Ben B. Lindsey, *The Rule of Plutocracy in Colorado* (Denver: Hick's Printing House, 1908).

37. "Idaho," *The Socialist* (January 27, 1906): 5.

38. "Idaho," *The Socialist* (July 8, 1905): 4.

39. Operative Reports, March 31 and April 11, 1906, Stanley Easton Papers, University of Idaho, Moscow.

40. I. W. Wright, "Idaho Is Hustling," *ATR* (August 25, 1906): 2.

41. "To Win a State for Socialism," *The Socialist* (July 21, 1906): 6.

42. "Compromise in Idaho," *The Socialist* (October 20, 1906): 1.

43. Operative Report, April 30, 1906, Stanley Easton Papers, University of Idaho, Moscow.

44. "Titus' Meeting at Wallace, Idaho," *The Socialist* (May 19, 1906): 1.

45. Operative Report, April 30, 1906, Stanley Easton Papers, University of Idaho, Moscow.

46. Wright, "Idaho Is Hustling," 2.

47. Operative Report from Burke, Idaho, August 15, 1906, Stanley Easton Papers, University of Idaho, Moscow.

48. "Socialists in Convention," *St. Maries Gazette* (August 31, 1906): 1.

49. Stanley S. Phipps, "The Coeur d'Alene Miners' Unions in the Post Bullpen Era, 1900 to 1916: The Socialist Party and I.W.W. Connections" (M.A. thesis, University of Idaho Graduate School, May 1980): 58.

50. Ibid.

51. Operative Reports, April 11 and April 25, 1906, Stanley Easton Papers, University of Idaho, Moscow.

52. See report in "Gleanings from Busy Fields," *SDH* (October 13, 1906): 4, and Operative Report from Burke, Idaho, July 30, 1906, Stanley Easton Papers, University of Idaho, Moscow.

53. "For the Fall Campaign," *The Socialist* (August 25, 1906): 2.

54. Phipps, "Coeur d'Alene Miners' Unions," 59.

55. Lukas, *Big Trouble*, 453–454.

56. "Moyer-Haywood Trial in March," *Wilshire's Magazine* (February 1907): 22.

57. Margherita Arlina Hamm, "How Socialists Fare at Boise," *Wilshire's Magazine* (July 1907): 14. See also "Socialist Women Reporting the Haywood Trial," *The Socialist Woman* (August 1907): 5.

58. "Haywood Is Not Guilty, So Says the Boise Jury," *The Caldwell Tribune* (August 3, 1907): 1.

59. Editorial, "The Verdict," *The Caldwell Tribune* (August 3, 1907): 4.

60. "Haywood Is Acquitted," *The Goldfield Daily Tribune* (July 29, 1907): 1, 4.

61. Thos. J. Coonrod, state secretary, Socialist party of Idaho, "Mrs. Hazlett's Work in Idaho," *The Socialist* (September 14, 1907): 3.

62. Quoted in editorial, "An Exhibition of Solidarity," *ISR* 6 (April 1906): 623.

63. "Haywood Is Acquitted."

64. "Haywood Acquitted by Honest Jury!" *The Industrial Union Bulletin* (August 3, 1907): 1.

65. John R. McMahon, "Aftermath of the Haywood Trial," *Wilshire's Magazine* (September 1907): 11.

66. Ibid.

67. Kennedy, "Socialistic Tendencies," 330–345.

68. "Haywood Acquitted by Honest Jury!" 1.

69. See discussion in Dubofsky, *We Shall Be All*, 105.

70. "A Ringing Document from Nevada's Candidate for Congress on the Socialist Ticket," *MM* (October 16, 1906): 18.

71. Quoted in Guy Louis Rocha, "Radical Labor Struggles in the Tonopah-Goldfield Mining District, 1901–1922," *Nevada Historical Quarterly* 20 (Spring 1977): 3.

72. St. John quoted in Sally S. Zanjani and Guy Louis Rocha, *Ignoble Conspiracy: Radicalism on Trial in Nevada* (Reno: University of Nevada Press, 1986): 20.

73. Sally S. Zanjani, *The Unspiked Rail: Memoir of a Nevada Rebel* (Reno: University of Nevada Press, 1981): 118.

74. Zanjani and Rocha, *Ignoble Conspiracy*, 13.

75. Zanjani, *Unspiked Rail*, 117.

76. Anne Ellis, *The Life of an Ordinary Woman* (Boston: Houghton Mifflin, 1929): 263.

77. Ida Crouch Hazlett, "The Fight in Goldfield," *The Socialist* (January 18, 1908): 4.

78. Ibid.

79. "An Infamous Enactment," article from the *Nevada Workman,* n.d. Reprinted in *The Industrial Union Bulletin* (February 15, 1908): 3.

80. Ibid.

81. Russell R. Elliott, *Nevada's Twentieth-Century Mining Boom* (Reno: University of Nevada Press, 1966): 143.

82. Russell R. Elliott, *Radical Labor in the Nevada Mining Booms, 1900–1920* (Carson City, Nev.: State Printing Office, 1963): 9.

83. Report of the Executive Board, WFM, December 19, 1907, 47, Western Federation of Miners Papers, Western History Collection, University of Colorado, Boulder.

84. Ibid., 48.

85. Letter from Marion W. Moor to Chas. H. Moyer, Western Federation of Miners, April 10, 1906, in Proceedings of the Western Federation of Miners Convention, 1906, 218.

86. J. Albert Mallory, "The Class Struggle in Bisbee," *MM* (April 5, 1906): 14.

87. Ibid.

88. "Report from Bisbee, Arizona" *MM* (April 26, 1906): 12.

89. Ibid.

90. David R. Berman, *Reformers, Corporations, and the Electorate* (Niwot: University Press of Colorado, 1992): 71.

91. Proceedings of the Western Federation of Miners Convention, 1907, 389, Western Federation of Miners Papers, Western History Collection, University of Colorado, Boulder.

92. Ibid., 202.

93. H. S. McCluskey, *Absentee Capitalists Menace Popular Government in Arizona.* Bound reprint of articles appearing in the *Miami Daily Silver Belt* (August 27–October 21, 1921): 7. Henry S. McCluskey Papers, Arizona Collection, Arizona State University Libraries, Tempe.

94. Ibid., 8.

CHAPTER 9

1. Proceedings of the National Convention of the Socialist Party, 1908, 31–32, SPC.

2. Ibid., 28.

3. Ibid., 23.

4. Ibid., 113.

5. Ibid., 111.

6. Proceedings of the National Convention of the Socialist Party, 1910, 87, SPC.

7. Ira Kipnis, *The American Socialist Movement 1897–1912* (New York: Columbia University Press, 1952): 204–210. Left-wing revolutionary Haywood praised the 1908 platform because he felt the class struggle was at its foundation. See William D. Haywood, *Bill Haywood's Book: The Autobiography of William D. Haywood* (New York: International, 1929): 230.

8. See Kipnis, *American Socialist Movement,* 213; "Westward with Debs on the 'Red Special,'" *Wilshire's Magazine* (October 1908): 7; "Debs Red Special Here Wednesday," *The Spokesman Review* (September 14, 1908): 1.

9. Charles Lapworth, "The Tour of the Red Special," *ISR* 9 (December 1908): 409.

10. Lewis J. Duncan, "West Is for Debs," *The New York Evening Call* (September 24, 1908): 1.

11. "Debs Denounces the Old Parties in Speech Here," *The Daily Times* (September 18, 1908): 1; "Debs Opens up on Nebraskan," *The Spokesman Review* (September 8, 1908): 6.

12. "Socialist Leaders Speak from Rear Platform of 'Red Special'" *Las Vegas Age* (September 12, 1908): 6.

13. Ibid.

14. Ibid.

15. Lapworth, "Tour of the Red Special," 404.

16. Lewis E. Floaten, "Colorado," in "News and Views," *ISR* 9 (October 1908): 310.

17. Memo, "Standing of Locals and Members at Large in Colorado," May 1, 1908, Western History Collection, University of Colorado, Boulder.

18. David A. Wolff, *Industrializing the Rockies: Growth, Competition, and Turmoil in the Coalfields of Colorado and Wyoming, 1868–1914* (Boulder: University Press of Colorado, 2003).

19. Editorial in *The Montana News* (August 29, 1907): n.p.

20. "Socialists Hold Big Convention," *Rock Springs Rocket* (June 25, 1908): 1.

21. Notes, Herman V.S. Groesbeck Papers, American Heritage Center, University of Wyoming, Laramie.

22. A. Dudley Gardner and Verla R. Flores, *Forgotten Frontier: A History of Wyoming Coal Mining* (Boulder: Westview, 1989): 124–126.

23. Ida Crouch Hazlett, "Field Work in Idaho," *Montana News* (April 25, 1907): 1–2.

24. Editorial, "Party Work," *Montana News* (April 25, 1907): 3.

25. Thos. J. Coonrod, state secretary, Socialist party of Idaho, "Mrs. Hazlett's Work in Idaho," *The Socialist* (September 14, 1907): 3.

26. Stanley Stewart Phipps, "The Coeur d'Alene Miners' Unions in the Post Bullpen Era, 1900 to 1916: The Socialist Party and I.W.W. Connections" (M.A. thesis, University of Idaho Graduate School, May 1980): 61.

27. Report of Thos. J. Coonrod, "News and Views," *ISR* 9 (October 1908): 310.

28. Phipps, "Coeur d'Alene Miners' Union," 62.

29. See, for example, "Socialists May Have Ticket," *The Spokesman Review* (May 19, 1908): 6, mentioning activity in Idaho County; and "Red Flag Down: Old Glory Flies," *The Spokesman Review* (June 3, 1908): 1, in regard to Socialist activity in Nez Perce County.

30. "Red Flag Down."

31. "Another Fallen Idol!" *ATR* (June 20, 1908): 4.

32. Phipps, "Coeur d'Alene Miners' Union," 64.

33. "Idaho Notes," *The Montana News* (July 8, 1909): 2.

34. Phipps, "Coeur d'Alene Miners' Union," 69.

35. F. L. Runyon, Rathdrum (Kootenai County), Idaho, quoted in "The Farmer Division of the Appeal Army," *ATR* (December 26, 1908): 3.

36. Letter from John Imthurn, Julietta, Idaho, in ibid, 3.

37. Ellis Waldron and Paul B. Wilson, *Atlas of Montana Elections, 1876–1976,* University of Montana Publications in History (Missoula: University of Montana Press, 1978): 35–36.

38. Coonrod, "News and Views," 310; Helen F. Sanders, *A History of Montana* (Chicago: Lewis, 1913): 431.

39. Remarks of George H. Ambrose, Proceedings of the National Convention of the Socialist Party, 1908, 291, SPC.

40. Remarks of Ida Crouch Hazlett, in ibid., 299.

41. Sally S. Zanjani and Guy Louis Rocha, *Ignoble Conspiracy: Radicalism on Trial in Nevada* (Reno: University of Nevada Press, 1986).

42. Ibid., 150.

43. Ibid.

44. Proceedings of the National Convention of the Socialist Party, 1908, 298–299; Ida Crouch Hazlett, "The Fight in Goldfield," *The Socialist* (January 18, 1908): 4.

45. "Full Text of the Socialist Platform as Adopted by the State Convention at Sparks," *Nevada Forum* (July 13, 1908): 1–2.

46. Harris quoted in "Demands of Party Seek Human Good," *Nevada Forum* (December 2, 1906): 2.

47. "Nevada List Growing," *Nevada Forum* (September 21, 1908): 4.

48. "Socialists Giving Old Parties a Shake Down," *Nevada Forum* (September 4, 1908): 4.

49. Editor's Note, "Labor in Nevada," *The Socialist* (January 25, 1908): 1.

50. Secretary of State of Nevada, *Political History of Nevada* (Carson City: State Printing Office, 8th ed., 1986): 260.

51. "Utah Compromise—State Autonomy," *The Socialist* (December 8, 1906): 4.

52. Report of Jos. MacLaulan, Utah secretary, "News and Views," *ISR* 9 (October 1908): 313.

53. Brad E. Hainsworth, "Utah State Elections, 1916–1924" (PhD dissertation, University of Utah, August 1968): 341.

54. "Gleanings from Busy Field," *SDH* (September 29, 1906): 4.

55. Report of Geneva M. Fryer, in ibid., 309.

56. "George W. Williams' Letter to Posterity," in Betty Graham Lee, ed., *Cornerstones of the 1908 LDS Academy: A Research Guide* (Thatcher: Eastern Arizona College, 1981): 43.

57. H. F. Kane Comments, Thatcher, Arizona, September 18, 1908, in Lee, ed., *Cornerstones,* 49.

58. Ibid.

59. Ibid.

60. "Editor's Chair," *ISR* 9 (January 1909): 533.

61. Ibid.

62. Ibid., 534.

63. Ida Crouch Hazlett, "Local Work," *The Montana News* (July 8, 1909): 2.

64. "No Fusion—No Collusion," *The Montana News* (May 12, 1909): 2.

65. Ida Crouch Hazlett, Editorial, "The Labor Phase of the Socialist Movement," *The Montana News* (July 8, 1909): 2.

66. See, for example, "Socialist Party Turns Populist," *The Socialist* (October 14, 1909): 1.

67. Cannon quoted in Proceedings of the National Convention of the Socialist Party, 1908, 175, SPC.

68. Vincent St. John, "Political Parties Not Endorsed by Us," *The Industrial Worker* (August 12, 1909): 3,

69. Melvin Dubofsky, *We Shall Be All: A History of the Industrial Workers of the World* (Chicago: Quadrangle Books, 1969): 139.

70. B. H. Williams, "The East and West," *The Industrial Union Bulletin* (November 9, 1907): 1.

71. "Forty New Members a Week," *The Industrial Worker* (April 15, 1909): 4.

72. "May Day in Arizona, Red Flag at Globe," *The Industrial Worker* (June 3, 1909): 1.

73. Ibid.

74. Elizabeth Gurley Flynn, *The Rebel Girl: An Autobiography, My First Life (1906–1926)* (New York: International, 1973): 104.

75. "I.W.W. Defies Law Busy Bulls in Missoula," *The Industrial Worker* (October 7, 1909): 1.

76. Ibid.

77. Elizabeth Gurley Flynn and J. A. Jones, "Free Speech Is Won in Missoula, Mont.," *The Industrial Worker* (October 20, 1909): 1.

CHAPTER 10

1. Robert F. Hoxie, "The Rising Tide of Socialism," *The Journal of Political Economy* 19 (October 1911): 624.

2. Ibid. Of the two factors mentioned by Hoxie, empirical research suggests that the support Socialists were receiving in places like Arizona and Nevada during this period probably had more to do with the occupational conditions the miners faced than with their nativity, that is, than with the fact that they were European-born. See David R. Berman, "Environment, Culture, and Radical Third Parties: Electoral Support for the Socialists in Arizona and Nevada 1912–1916," *The Social Science Journal* 27 (1990): 147–158.

3. David A. Shannon, *The Socialist Party of America* (Chicago: Quadrangle Books, 1955): 12, 38.

4. Proceedings of the National Convention of the Socialist Party, May 18, 1910, 151, SPC.

5. Guy E. Miller quoted in Proceedings of the National Convention of the Socialist Party, 1908, 210, SPC.

6. A. Grant Miller, "Fractional Socialists," *The Voice of the People* (November 2, 1910): 1.

7. A. Grant Miller, editorial, *The Voice of the People* (October 10, 1910): 2.

8. A. Grant Miller, "Thunder Stealers," *The Voice of the People* (November 2, 1910): 1.

9. A. Grant Miller, editorial, *The Voice of the People* (November 2, 1910): 2.

10. Carl Ubbelohde, *A Colorado History* (Boulder: Pruett, 1965): 269–270.

11. "Hopeful Signs and New Duties," *Colorado Socialist Bulletin* (July 1910): 1.

12. Ibid.

13. Letter from W. P. Collins, Boulder, Colorado, February 14, 1911, Socialist Party of Montana Records, Montana State Archives and Historical Society, Helena.

14. Joseph M. Carey, "What's the Matter with Wyoming?" *Grand Encampment Herald* (supplement) (October 14, 1910): 1.

15. Ibid.

16. "Miss Maley's Letter of Protest," *Rock Springs Rocket* (July 8, 1910): 8.

17. Ibid.

18. Anna A. Maley, "One Wyoming Mining Town," *ISR* 11 (July 1910): 20–21.

19. A. Dudley Gardner and Verla R. Flores, *Forgotten Frontier: A History of Wyoming Coal Mining* (Boulder: Westview, 1989): 125.

20. Betsy Ross Peters, "Joseph M. Carey and the Progressive Movement in Wyoming" (PhD dissertation, University of Wyoming, May 1971): 80; David L. Kindler, "The Progressive Movement in Wyoming, 1910–1913" (M.A. thesis, University of Wyoming, January 1970).

21. Gardner and Flores, *Forgotten Frontier*, 125.

22. F. Ross Peterson, *Idaho: A Bicentennial History* (New York: W. W. Norton, 1976): 163.

23. Eugene Debs to Theodore Debs, November 1, 1910, in J. Robert Constantine, *Letters of Eugene V. Debs* (Urbana: University of Illinois Press, 1990): vol. 1, 385.

24. Stanley S. Phipps, "The Coeur d'Alene Miners' Unions in the Post Bullpen Era, 1900 to 1916: The Socialist Party and I.W.W. Connections" (M.A. thesis, University of Idaho Graduate School, May 1980): 74.

25. James D. Graham, "Corporate Corruption in the Socialist Party," *The Montana News* (October 21, 1909): 2–3.

26. Letter from Duncan to W. C. Snow, August 12, 1910, in Terrence D. McGlynn, "Lewis J. Duncan, Socialist: The Man and His Work," paper presented to the Social Science Section, Montana Academy of Sciences, April 18, 1970, 2.

27. Letter from Duncan to J. F. Mabie, September 26, 1910, in ibid., 7.

28. Letter from Duncan to J. Kruse, October 3, 1910, in ibid., 12.

29. Ibid.

30. On Utah Socialists see John R. Sillito, "Women and the Socialist Party in Utah, 1900–1920," *Utah Historical Quarterly* 49 (Summer 1981): 220–238; John S. McCormick, "Hornets in the Hive: Socialists in Early Twentieth Century Utah," *Utah Historical Quarterly* 50 (Summer 1982): 225–240; John S. McCormick and John R. Sillito, "Socialism and Utah Labor: 1900–1920," *Southwest Economy and Society* 6 (Fall 1983): 15–30.

31. McCormick and Sillito, "Socialism and Utah Labor."

32. A. Grant Miller, "Socialist Vote in Nevada," *The Voice of the People* (December 10, 1910): 1.

33. Ibid.

34. James Hulse, "Socialism in Nevada, 1904–1918: Faint Echoes of an Idealistic National Movement," *Nevada Historical Society Quarterly* 31 (Winter 1988): 252.

35. Letter from A. A. Hibbard to Professor Jeanne Wier, January 25, 1911, Suffrage Materials, Wier Collection, Nevada Historical Society, Reno.

36. Anne Bail Howard, *The Long Campaign: A Biography of Anne Martin* (Reno: University of Nevada Press, 1985): 97.

37. Susan Lee Kendall, "Women in Goldfield, 1903–1916" (M.A. thesis, University of Nevada, Las Vegas, April 1980): 49.

38. "Taft Lectures Arizona," *Wilshire's Magazine* (February 1910): 17.

39. Reuben W. Heflin, "New Mexico Constitutional Convention," *The New Mexico Historical Review* 31 (January 1946): 60–68.

40. *Columbus News* (August 12, 1910): 3.

41. "Will the Socialists Fuse?" *Columbus News* (August 26, 1910): 2.

42. Item in *Santa Fe New Mexican* (September 29, 1910): 4.

43. Heflin, "New Mexico Constitutional Convention," 66.

44. Thomas J. Mabry, "New Mexico's Constitutional Convention in the Making—Reminiscences of 1910," *The New Mexico Historical Review* 19 (April 1944): 178.

45. Quoted in "Political Highwaymen," *Roswell Daily Record* (September 29, 1910): 2.

46. See Dwight M. Ramsay Jr., "A Statistical Survey of Voting Behavior in New Mexico" (M.A. thesis, University of New Mexico, August 1951); Jack E. Holmes, *Politics in New Mexico* (Albuquerque: University of New Mexico Press, 1967): 12.

47. *The Times* [El Paso, Texas] (October 31, 1911), William C. McDonald Papers, New Mexico State Records and Archives, Santa Fe, n.p.

48. Robert Kern, "Labor Struggle, 1900–1936," in Robert Kern, ed., *Labor in New Mexico: Unions, Strikes, and Social History Since 1881* (Albuquerque: University of New Mexico Press, 1983): 86.

49. "Labor Taking Political Action in Arizona," *MM* (July 28, 1910): 4.

50. "Arizona Socialists Forced Constitution on Old Line Politicians," *California Social Democrat* (January 27, 1912): 1, 5.

51. Charles Foster Todd, "The Initiative and Referendum in Arizona" (M.A. thesis, University of Arizona, 1931): 16.

52. Letter from Mulford Winsor to Hunt, September 22, 1910, Box 1, Folder 10, George W.P. Hunt Papers, Arizona Collection, Arizona State University Libraries, Tempe.

53. Report of the Executive Board of the Western Federation of Miners, Denver, Colorado, January 14, 1911, 68–69, Western Federation of Miners Papers, Western History Collection, University of Colorado, Boulder.

54. W. S. Bradford, "Growth in Arizona," *ISR* (May 12, 1912): 789. See also letter from Bradford to Carl D. Thompson, April 10, 1913, SPC.

55. J. N. Morrison, *Weekly Bulletin* (September 3, 1910): 3.

56. See items in the Socialist Party of America Papers, Series III, Part C, Arizona, 1912–1960, Duke University, William R. Perkins Library, Durham, North Carolina.

57. Joseph D. Cannon, "What Has the Western Federation of Miners or President Moyer Ever Done?" *MM* (August 17, 1916): 7.

58. Letter from Joseph D. Cannon to Mother Jones, January 7, 1911, in Edward M. Steel, ed., *The Correspondence of Mother Jones* (Pittsburgh: University of Pittsburgh Press, 1985): 85–86.

59. Letter from W. S. Bradford to Carl D. Thompson, April 10, 1913, SPC.

60. Ibid.

61. Ernest Lebel, "The Appeal in Arizona," *ATR* (December 3, 1910): 3.

62. Ibid.

63. Ibid.

64. "Arizona Socialists Are Waging Magnificent Campaign," *California Social Democrat* (November 4, 1911): 5.

65. Ibid.

66. George Hunter, "John Greenway and the Bull Moose Movement in Arizona" (M.A. thesis, University of Arizona, 1966): 29.

67. Editorial, *The Observer* (November 18, 1911): 2.

68. See "A Communication Answered," *MM* (December 7, 1911): 10.

69. Copy of letter from J. W. Stimsom to Jerome Miner's Union, November 14, 1911, urging support for Hunt, Carl T. Hayden Papers, Arizona Collection, Arizona State University Libraries, Tempe.

70. Letter from Ernest Lebel to George Hunt, December 13, 1911, George W.P. Hunt Papers, Arizona Collection, Arizona State University Libraries, Tempe.

71. Ibid.

72. Ibid.

73. Ibid.

74. David R. Berman, *Reformers, Corporations, and the Electorate* (Niwot: University Press of Colorado, 1992).

CHAPTER 11

1. Unidentified article, "Read Carefully before You Vote," includes the Socialist Party platform adopted by the Socialist party at Great Falls, Montana, March 1911, SPC.

2. "Socialist Party Pledge," *Arizona Socialist Bulletin* (December 27, 1912): 1.

3. Ibid., 4.

4. Lists of local victories compiled by the national party are in various party records in the SPC.

5. "Victor, Colorado, Socialist Administration," Information Department, SPA, from letter from J. B. Bitterly, mayor, March 1913, SPC. On his election see "Victorious Socialism," *ATR* (May 13, 1911): 1.

6. "Progressive Municipality," *Arizona Socialist Bulletin* (December 27, 1912): 4.

7. John S. McCormick, "Hornets in the Hive: Socialists in Early Twentieth Century Utah," *Utah Historical Quarterly* 50 (Summer 1982): 226–227.

8. J. L. Engdahl, "Socialist Vice Presidential Candidate Seidel Swinging through the Rockies on Strenuous Trip," *The New York Call* (October 10, 1912), 5; J. L. Engdahl, "The Socialist Vote," *SDH* (October 19, 1914): 4.

9. John S. McCormick and John R. Sillito, "Socialists in Power: The Eureka, Utah, Experience—1907–1925," *Weber Studies* 6 (Spring 1989): 55–67.

10. Ibid.

11. Ibid.

12. "Eureka Makes Progress," *The Party Builder* (November 8, 1913): 2.

13. Davis Wilkins, "Nampa's Flirtation with Socialism," *Idaho Yesterdays* (Winter 1987): 15–17.

14. Ibid.

15. Stanley Stewart Phipps, "Building Socialism in One City: Coeur d'Alene, Idaho's 1911 Municipal Government," *Museum of North Idaho Quarterly Newsletter* 7 (Winter 1986): 1–5.

16. Editorial, "Will We Endorse Socialism?" *Coeur d'Alene Evening Press* (March 29, 1911): 2. The same theme is expressed in "Revolution or Government," *Coeur d'Alene Evening Press* (March 28, 1911): 2; and "Which Shall It Be?" *Coeur d'Alene Evening Press* (March 27, 1911): 2.

17. "A Problem for Coeur d'Alene to Solve," *Coeur d'Alene Evening Press* (April 3, 1911): 1.

18. Editorial, "Will We Endorse Socialism," 2.

19. "Friction in Socialist Local over Police Recall," *Coeur d'Alene Evening Press* (April 17, 1911): 1, 4.

20. Ibid.

21. From Coeur d'Alene, Idaho, Socialist party platform, "News and Views," *ISR* 11 (May 1911): 719.

22. "Socialists Demand Mayor Wood's Scalp," *Coeur d'Alene Evening Press* (June 5, 1911): 1.

23. Phipps, "Building Socialism in One City."

24. Jack Keister, "Why the Socialists Won in Butte," *ISR* 11 (June 1911): 731.

25. Jerry W. Calvert, *The Gibraltar: Socialism and Labor in Butte, Montana, 1895–1920* (Helena: Montana Historical Society Press, 1988): 35–37.

26. Lewis J. Duncan, "Socialist Politics in Butte, Montana," *ISR* 12 (November 1911): 288. See also Lewis J. Duncan, "The Trouble in Butte, Mayor Duncan's Statement to the Socialist Party and Press of America," July 21, 1913, SPC.

27. Letter from Duncan to Wm. Thurston Brown, April 12, 1911, cited in Terrence D. McGlynn, "Lewis J. Duncan, Socialist: The Man and His Work," paper presented to the Social Science Section, Montana Academy of Sciences, April 18, 1970, 9.

28. Calvert bases his membership statistics on an analysis of Montana party membership roles in 1913–1915. See Calvert, *The Gibraltar*, 58, 63.

29. David M. Emmons, *The Butte Irish: Ethnicity in an American Mining Town* (Urbana: University of Illinois Press, 1989): 103, 265.

30. Keister, "Why the Socialists Won," 732.

31. "Press Comments on Election," *The Montana News* (April 6, 1911): 2. Reprint of editorial from *Montana Outlook,* n.d.

32. Mary Stevens Carroll Reminiscence, Montana State Archives and Historical Society, Helena.

33. A. G. Edmunds, "Butte Socialists Hand Smashing Blow to Capitalistic Ring Rulers," *California Social Democrat* (August 26, 1911): 2.

34. Keister, "Why the Socialists Won," 731.

35. Frank Bohn, "Butte," *ISR* 13 (August 1912): 128.

36. "Municipal Problems," *The Montana News* (October 5, 1911): 2.

37. Ibid.

38. Duncan, "Socialist Politics in Butte," 290–291.

39. Ibid., 288.

40. Letter from Duncan to Hiram Pratt, May 20, 1911, Lewis Duncan Papers, Montana State Archives and Historical Society, Helena.

41. See Calvert, *The Gibraltar*, 37.

42. See letter from Duncan to Carl D. Thompson, city clerk, Milwaukee, Wisconsin, May 19, 1911, Lewis Duncan Papers, Montana State Archives and Historical Society, Helena.

43. Letter from Lewis Duncan to Mr. H. A. Barton, May 12, 1911, Lewis Duncan Papers, Montana State Archives and Historical Society, Helena.

44. Emmons, *Butte Irish*, 247.

45. Ibid., 266.

46. Lewis Duncan, "Socialist Administration: Butte, Montana," May 1, 1911–April 30, 1912, SPC. Duncan's accomplishments are also listed in "The Butte Municipal Administration," *The American Labor Year Book* (New York: Rand School of Social Science, 1916): 116–117.

47. "Butte Beats a Fusion," *ATR* (April 13, 1912): 2.

48. Thomas Campbell, Proceedings of the Western Federation of Miners, Twentieth Conference, 1912, 235, Western Federation of Miners Papers, Western History Collection, University of Colorado, Boulder.

49. Calvert, *The Gibraltar*, 43.

50. Mary Stevens Carroll Reminiscence.

51. Editorial, "Socialist Victory in Butte," *ISR* 13 (May 1913): 829.

52. Clarence A. Smith, "Miners' Union Day in Butte," *ISR* 12 (July 1911): 5–6.

53. "Butte Socialist Administration Commendable," *National Municipal Review* 2 (January 1913): 134. See also "Butte Administration a Success," *The Party Builder* (August 20, 1913): 2.

54. From the *Inter-Mountain Worker*, quoted in *MM* (October 2, 1913): 4.

55. Anna A. Maley, "Work among Women in the West," *The Progressive Woman* (July 1911): 9.

56. "The City of the Dead," *Arizona Socialist Bulletin* (December 27, 1912): 3.

57. See John Bodnar, *The Transplanted: A History of Immigrants in Urban America* (Bloomington: Indiana University Press, 1985).

CHAPTER 12

1. *American Labor Year Book 1916–1917* (New York: Rand School of Social Science, 1912): n.p., clipping in Morris Hillquit Papers, State Historical Society of Wisconsin, Madison.

2. John M. Work, "The Party Machinery," *The Progressive Woman* (July 1911): 10.

3. Bernard J. Brommel, *Eugene V. Debs: Spokesman for Labor and Socialism* (Chicago: Charles H. Kerr, 1978): 137.

4. Frank Bohn, "The National Progressive Party," *ISR* 13 (September 1912): 229.

5. "Emil Seidel Preaches Socialism before a Large Sunday Audience," *The Missoulian* (October 14, 1912): 3.

6. Quoted in H. Wayne Morgan, *Eugene V. Debs: Socialist for President* (Syracuse, N.Y.: Syracuse University Press, 1962): 130.

7. David R. Berman, *Reformers, Corporations, and the Electorate* (Niwot: University Press of Colorado, 1992).

8. James Wright, *The Politics of Populism: Dissent in Colorado* (New Haven, Conn.: Yale University Press, 1974). Also Colin B. Goodykoontz, "The Progressive Movement in Colorado, 1910–1912," *University of Colorado Studies,* Series C, Vol. 1, no. 2 (May 1941): 145–157.

9. David Sarashon, "The Election of 1916: Realigning the Rockies," *The Western Historical Quarterly* 11 (July 1980): 285–305.

10. John Spargo, *Report of the Non-Partisan League of North Dakota and Various Other States,* 1912, 5, SPC.

11. Ibid., 9.

12. Melvin Dubofsky, *"Big Bill" Haywood* (New York: St. Martin's, 1987): 58.

13. Harry A. Mills and Royal E. Montgomery, *Organized Labor* (New York: McGraw-Hill, 1945): 122.

14. Berger quoted in *New York Press* (May 13, 1912), clipping from Morris Hillquit Papers, State Historical Society of Wisconsin, Madison.

15. "Socialists Will Open Campaign at Chicago," *Indianapolis News* (May 20, 1912): n.p., clipping in ibid.

16. Note in *MM* (December 26, 1912): 5, referring to an article in *The National Socialist* (Washington, D.C., n.d.) under the caption "Expel Haywood."

17. Henry L. Slobodin, "The State of the Socialist Party," *ISR* 17 (March 1917): 539–541.

18. Nick Salvatore, *Eugene V. Debs: Citizen and Socialist* (Urbana: University of Illinois Press, 1982): 256.

19. See, for example, "Reflections on the Debs Vote," *Wilshire's Magazine* (December 1912): 1.

20. "The Election," *ISR* 13 (December 1912): 461–463.

21. "A Campaign for Membership," *MM* (November 27, 1913): 12–13.

22. L. E. Katterfield, "The Essentials of Organization," *Arizona Socialist Bulletin* (July 11, 1913): 3.

23. "Emil Seidel Preaches Socialism before a Large Sunday Audience," *The Missoulian* (October 14, 1912): 3.

24. "Seidel in Nevada," *SDH* (December 2, 1912): 1–2.

25. "The National Campaign," *SDH* (December 2, 1912): 1.

26. "Our Sixty Speakers," *The Party Builder* (October 16, 1912): 4.

27. Wright, *Politics of Populism,* 269.

28. "Demanding His Recall," *MM* (December 26, 1912): 5–6.

29. Concerns of this nature regarding Colorado are found in "Urging Organization," *The Party Builder* (September 27, 1913): 4.

30. "National Socialist Campaign Winning Men as Never Before," *SDH* (October 19, 1912): 4.

31. "Riot in Butte, Mont.," *The Industrial Worker* (November 21, 1912): 4.

32. Helen F. Sanders, *A History of Montana* 1 (Chicago: Lewis, 1913): 430.

33. Boyd A. Martin, *Idaho Voting Trends* (Moscow: Idaho Research Foundation, 1975).

34. I. F. Stewart, "Idaho Encampments," *ISR* 13 (May 12, 1912): 792–793; J. L. Engdahl, "Exploited Idaho Farmers Are Ready for Socialism," *The New York Call* (October 17, 1912): 5; Hugh T. Lovin, "The Farmer Revolt in Idaho, 1914–1922," *Idaho Yesterdays* (Fall 1976): 2–15.

35. Letter from I. F. Stewart to Carl D. Thompson, August 26, 1914, SPC.

36. Stewart, "Idaho Encampments."

37. "The Socialist Vote in Idaho," *Evening Capital News* (November 12, 1912): 4.

38. "Denunciation of Socialism from David Goldstein," *Evening Capital News* (November 14, 1912): 12.

39. *Tonopah Nevadan* (October 19, 1912): 3.

40. "The National Campaign," *SDH* (December 2, 1912): 1.

41. Russell R. Eliott, *History of Nevada* (Lincoln: University of Nebraska Press, 1987): 236.

42. Debs got 16.5 percent of the vote in Nevada. Oklahoma was second with 16.4 percent. See Congressional Quarterly, *Guide to U.S. Elections* (Washington, D.C.: Congressional Quarterly, Inc., 1975): 284.

43. "News and Views," *ISR* (January 1913): 571.

44. Thos. M. Fagan, "Socialism Sweeping on to Victory in Nevada," *American Socialist* (October 17, 1914): 3.

45. James Hulse, "Socialism in Nevada, 1904–1918: Faint Echoes of an Idealistic National Movement," *Nevada Historical Society Quarterly* 31 (Winter 1988): 247–258.

46. Ibid., 249.

47. Quoted in Betty Glad, *Key Pittman: The Tragedy of a Senate Insider* (New York: Columbia University Press, 1986): 231, note 7.

48. Report of P. J. Holt, state secretary, Utah, in "News and Views", *ISR* 12 (April 1912): 690.

49. J. L. Engdahl, "Socialist Party Growing among Mormon Workers," *The New York Call* (October 16, 1912): 4.

50. *The Deseret News* (November 7, 1912).

51. "News and Views," *ISR* 14 (September 1913): 183.

52. "Utah Labor Federation for Socialism," *The Party Builder* (October 25, 1913): 5. See also John S. McCormick and John R. Sillito, "America's Socialist Heritage, Socialism in Utah, 1900–1920," *The Socialist Tribune* (April-May 1978): n.p.

53. Story related in M. E. King, "Among His Own People," *The Christian Socialist* (Chicago, November 1914): 4.

54. Layne quoted in "Growing in New Mexico," *ISR* 12 (June 1912): 888.

55. Report from A. James McDonald, "For Sparsely Settled Regions," *The Party Builder* (October 16, 1912): 4.

56. John Doe, "The Santa Fe R.R.," *California Social Democrat* (March 6, 1912): 7.

57. "Growing in New Mexico," 888.

58. J. N. Morrison, "Joseph D. Cannon and the Arizona Movement," n.d., SPC.

59. "An Arizona School Mistress," *California Social Democrat* (April 13, 1912): 3.

60. Ibid.

61. See W. S. Bradford, "Arizona Trade Unions Declare for Socialism," *California Social Democrat* (February 17, 1912): 1; E. B. Simanton, "Arizona Unions for Socialism," February 29, 1912, published in "Arizona Unions for Socialism," *California Social Democrat* (March 9, 1912): 4.

62. James D. McBride, "The Development of Labor Unions in Arizona Mining, 1884 to 1919" (M.A. thesis, Arizona State University, 1974).

63. W. S. Bradford, "Growth in Arizona," *ISR* 12 (May 12, 1912): 789.

64. "Socialist Candidate Here," *Coconino Sun* (October 18, 1912): 1.

65. "Prohibitionists and Socialists Hold Political Meetings," *Arizona Republic* (November 1, 1912): 5.

66. *Arizona Socialist Bulletin* (December 1912).

67. "Growth of Socialism," *Arizona Gazette* (November 21, 1912): 4.

68. "The Oration of Governor Hunt Delivered July 4th at Bisbee, Arizona," *MM* (July 17, 1913): 8.

69. "Phoenix Street Railway Co.," *Arizona Socialist Bulletin* (July 11, 1913): 1.

70. "Arizona Will Not Tolerate Law-Defying Corporation Guards," *Arizona Socialist Bulletin* (May 23, 1913): n.p.

71. Editorial, "Capital Punishment," *Arizona Socialist Bulletin* (May 23, 1913): n.p.

72. Debs to Robert B. Sims, May 23, 1913, in J. Robert Constantine, ed., *Letters of Eugene V. Debs*, Vol. 2 (Urbana: University of Illinois Press, 1990): 31–32.

73. "Local Yuma Correspondence," *Arizona Socialist Bulletin* (July 11, 1913): 4.

74. "The Race of the States toward Socialism," *The Party Builder* (December 4, 1912): 1.

75. Proceedings of the National Convention of the Socialist Party, 1912, 136, SPC.

76. "Woman's Record," *The Party Builder* (June 27, 1914): 5.

77. Ibid.

78. Letter from A. Carlson, Sheridan, Wyoming, to CDT (Carl D. Thompson), August 18, 1914, SPC.

79. J. L. Engdahl, "Exploited Idaho Farmers Are Ready for Socialism," *The New York Call* (October 17, 1912): 5.

80. Anna A. Maley, "Work among Women in the West," *The Progressive Woman* (July 1911): 9.

81. Letter from Francis Marshall Elliott, member at large, Arizona Socialist Party, *Arizona Socialist Bulletin* (July 11, 1913): 3.

82. Comments of Mila Tupper Maynard, Proceedings of the First National Congress of the Socialist Party, 1910, 196, SPC.

83. Ibid.

84. Ibid., 186.

85. On increased filing fees, see Thos M. Fagan, Socialist state secretary in Nevada, "Socialism Sweeping to Victory in Nevada," *American Socialist* (October 17, 1914): 3, and complaints by Socialists in Arizona, "Arizona Socialists Forced Constitution on the Old Line Politicians," reproduced from *California Social Democrat* (January 22, 1912) in Socialist Party Papers, Series III, Part C, Arizona, 1912–1960, SPC.

86. Letter from W. S. Bradford to Carl D. Thompson, June 6, 1913, SPC.

87. Letter from Peter J. Holt, Utah state secretary, to Carl D. Thompson, June 7, 1913, SPC.

88. Letter from J. Block, secretary pro-tem of Colorado party, to Carl D. Thompson, June 7, 1913, SPC.

CHAPTER 13

1. J. L. Engdahl, "The Underground War," *MM* (October 23, 1913): 9.

2. "Queer Action of W.F.M. Officials," *MM* (April 10, 1913): 7–8.

3. "Miners Declare for Socialism," *ATR* (February 6, 1909): 1.

4. George S. McGovern and Leonard F. Guttridge, *The Great Coal Field War* (Boston: Houghton Mifflin, 1972).

5. "Marching on Denver to Fight for Free Speech," *The Industrial Worker* (March 27, 1913): 1.

6. Ted Fraser, "Denver Starts Organization Work in Earnest," *The Industrial Worker* (June 12, 1913): 1.

7. Priscilla Long, "The 1913–1914 Colorado Fuel and Iron Strike, with Reflections on the Causes of Coal-Strike Violence," in John H.M. Laslett, ed., *The United Mine Workers of America: A Model of Industrial Solidarity?* (University Park: Pennsylvania State University Press, 1996): 348.

8. Bowers quoted in McGovern and Guttridge, *Great Coal Field War,* 69.

9. Ibid., 353.

10. Upton Sinclair, "How Coal Barons Were Protected by Press and Politicians in Crushing Colorado Workers," *ATR* (December 20, 1919): n.p.

11. Letter from Adolph Germer to Walter Lanfersiek, November 30, 1913, SPC.

12. George N. Falconer, "Machine Guns and Coal Miners," *ISR* 14 (December 1913): 327–329.

13. Ibid., 328.

14. Mary Field Parton, ed., *Autobiography of Mother Jones* (Chicago: Charles H. Kerr, 1925): 182.

15. Quoted in *MM* (April 2, 1914): 4.

16. General John Chase, "The Military Occupation," in Leon Stein and Philip Taft, eds., *Massacre at Ludlow: Four Reports* (New York: Arno and *The New York Times,* 1971): 28.

17. Ibid., 46.

18. Ibid.

19. Quoted in "Coal Field Investigators Allege Shocking Conditions," *The Hooper-Mosca Tribune* (March 10, 1914): 1.

20. "Miners Demand Federal Intervention—General Chase Protests," *The Hooper-Mosca Tribune* (March 14, 1914): 1.

21. George N. Falconer, "The Miner's War in Colorado," *ISR* 14 (February 1914): 480.

22. Ibid.

23. Ibid.

24. Ibid.

25. Ella Reeve Bloor, *We Are Many* (New York: International, 1940): 132.

26. Stein and Taft, eds., *Massacre at Ludlow*, 1 (statement of husband).

27. Long, "1913–1914 Colorado Fuel and Iron Strike," 346.

28. "Major Holbrook Promises to Disarm Mine Guards First," *The Hooper-Mosca Tribune* (May 9, 1914): 1.

29. Vincent St. John, "The Lesson of Ludlow," *ISR* 14 (June 1914): 725.

30. Sinclair quoted in "Colorado," *ISR* 15 (July 1914): 44.

31. Jones quoted in "Colorado Will Have War Till U.S. Gets Mines," *The New York Call* (July 18, 1914): 1.

32. Frank Bohn, "After Ludlow—Facts and Thoughts," *ISR* 15 (August 1914): 114–116.

33. "Abandon Peace Hope in Colorado Mines," *The New York Times* (June 13, 1914): 2.

34. Zeese Papanikolas, *Buried Unsung: Louis Tikas and the Ludlow Massacre* (Salt Lake City: University of Utah Press, 1982): 164–166.

35. Helen Schloss, "Women Picket in Ludlow, Are Maltreated by Soldiers," *The New York Call* (September 18, 1914): 4.

36. Ibid.

37. See "Mother Jones Sends Thrilling Message to the Appeal Army," *ATR* (August 8, 1914): 1.

38. See discussion in McGovern and Guttridge, *Great Coal Field War,* 284–289.

39. Mary R. Alspaugh, "The Reward of the Miners," *ISR* 15 (April 1915): 604.

40. Letter from Edwin A. Miller, secretary of the Progressive party of Larimer County, to Edward P. Costigan, June 4, 1914, Edward P. Costigan Papers, Western History Collection, University of Colorado, Boulder.

41. Ibid.

42. "Justice for Lawson," letter from T. J. Brown, Denver, Colorado, *American Socialist* (October 30, 1915): 3.

43. Alspaugh, "Reward of the Miners," 604.

44. "Fiendish Scheme of Utah Fuel to Crush Unionism Fully Exposed," *MM* (April 19, 1914): 5.

45. Gunther Peck, *Reinventing Free Labor: Padrones and Immigrant Workers in the North American West, 1880–1930* (New York: Cambridge University Press, 2000): 213–214.

46. Phillip J. Mellinger, *Race and Labor in Western Copper: The Fight for Equality, 1896–1918* (Tucson: University of Arizona Press, 1995).

47. "Utah Metal Miners Armed to the Teeth," *The Industrial Worker* (September 26, 1912): 4.

48. "John Houland," *The Industrial Worker* (November 23, 1912): 6.

49. "Mormon Town Waking Up," *The Industrial Worker* (October 3, 1912): 4.

50. See, for example, letter from William H. Henry to Governor William Spry, November 12, 1915, William Spry Correspondence, Joe Hill Case, Utah State Archives and Record Service, Salt Lake City.

51. Letter from officials of the Tonopah Miners Union to Governor Spry, July 28, 1914, in ibid.

52. Letter from Socialist Party of America, Local Ogden, to Governor Spry, September 18, 1915, in ibid.

53. Jerry W. Calvert, *The Gibraltar: Socialism and Labor in Butte, Montana, 1895–1920* (Helena: Montana Historical Society Press, 1988): 54.

54. See William D. Haywood, "The Revolt at Butte," *ISR* 15 (August 1914): 89–95; M. Rhea, "The Revolt in Butte," *ISR* 15 (September 1914): 538–542; and account by former secretary of the Montana state party, Alma M. Kriger, in "Story of Events Which Precipitated Trouble," *The New York Call* (July 4, 1914): 1–2.

55. Many of these events are described in detail in Terrence D. McGlynn, "Lewis J. Duncan, Socialist: The Man and His Work," paper presented to the Social Science Section, Montana Academy of Sciences, April 21, 1972.

56. From *The Butte Socialist* (September 26, 1914), quoted in ibid., 24.

57. See Melvin Dubofsky, *We Shall Be All: A History of the Industrial Workers of the World* (Urbana: University of Illinois Press, 1988): 305; Burton K. Wheeler with Paul F. Healy, *Yankee from the West* (Garden City, N.Y.: Doubleday, 1962): 116; "Some History and Comments That May Be Interesting to the Miners of Butte, Montana," *MM* (July 16, 1914): 7–10.

58. Contemporary newspaper accounts are in Clarence Smith, "Mayor Duncan Stabbed in Butte Mine Trouble, Shoots His Assailant," *The New York Call* (July 4, 1914): 1; "The Stabbing of Duncan," *MM* (July 9, 1914): 8.

59. Proceedings of the National Convention of the Western Federation of Miners, 1914, 94–115, Western Federation of Miners Papers, Western History Collection, University of Colorado, Boulder.

60. Ibid., 106–107.

61. William D. Haywood, "Butte Better," *ISR* 15 (February 1915): 473–475.

62. "For Inquiry in Butte Outrage," *The New York Call* (September 25, 1914): 4.

63. Duncan quoted in Mary Stevens Carroll Reminiscence, Montana State Archives and Historical Society, Helena.

64. "W.F.M. Elects Moyer Again," *The New York Call* (August 3, 1914): 5.

65. Letter from John Striegel to Ernest Mills, August 2, 1914, Western Federation of Miners Papers, Western History Collection, University of Colorado, Boulder.

66. See generally James R. Kluger, *The Clifton-Morenci Strike: Labor Difficulty in Arizona* (Tucson: University of Arizona Press, 1970), and report on wages in Charles H. Moyer, "Strike in the Clifton District of Arizona," *MM* (October 17, 1915): 5.

67. Letter from Guy E. Miller to Charles Moyer, July 15, 1915, Western Federation of Mining, Report of the Executive Board, 20.

68. *Coconino Sun* (October 22, 1915): 7.

69. See "Militia Called out in Arizona Strike," *MM* (October 7, 1915): 6; "A Unique Strike," *ATR* (November 20, 1915): 4.

70. Mellinger, *Race and Labor in Western Copper*, 157–158.

71. Annual Report of James Lord, president of Mining Department, American Federation of Labor, submitted to the Baltimore Convention of the Mining Department, AFL, 1916, 5, 10.

72. Mary Field Parton, ed., *Autobiography of Mother Jones* (Chicago: Charles H. Kerr, 1925): 172–177.

73. See "A Unique Strike," *ATR* (November 20, 1915): 4; "Struggle in Arizona," *MM* (February 3, 1916): 1, 5.

74. "Hunt No Good as Mediator," *Arizona Daily Star,* n.d., quoted in James M. Patton, *History of Clifton* (Greenlee County, Ariz.: Chamber of Commerce, 1977): 37.

75. "A Unique Strike," 4.

76. Alice S. Eddy, "Unique Copper Strike," *American Socialist* (November 27, 1915): 1.

CHAPTER 14

1. "Socialist Gain as War's Result," *The New York Call* (September 8, 1914): 1.

2. "1914 Election Figures," *ISR* 15 (February 1915): 485–486.

3. "Socialist Assails Wilson," *The New York Times* (March 20, 1916): 4.

4. Ira Kipnis, *The American Socialist Movement 1897–1912* (New York: Columbia University Press, 1952): 418.

5. "Socialist Leadership Un-American Says Allan L. Benson, Quitting Party," *Wyoming Weekly Labor Journal* (July 12, 1918): 1.

6. Ibid.

7. Henry L. Slobodin, "The State of the Socialist Party," *ISR* 17 (March 1917): 539–541.

8. See Appendix, Table 2, and Congressional Quarterly, *Guide to U.S. Elections* (Washington, D.C.: Congressional Quarterly, Inc., 1975): 487.

9. Letter from C. T. Stoney to Archibald Hunter, October 14, 1914, Archibald Hunter Collection, Utah Historical Society, Salt Lake City.

10. Brad E. Hainsworth, "Utah State Elections, 1916–1924" (PhD dissertation, University of Utah, August 1968): 345–346.

11. Letter from C. T. Stoney, editor of the *Inter-Mountain Worker,* to Archibald Hunter, February 20, 1915, Archibald Hunter Collection, Utah Historical Society, Salt Lake City.

12. C. T. Stoney, "Man's Emancipation," *Inter-Mountain Worker* (June 19, 1915): 4.

13. Letter from W. P. Metcalf to Charles D. Thompson, December 25, 1914, SPC.

14. Remarks of A. James McDonald in "Letters from 'American Socialist' Readers," *American Socialist* (June 10, 1916): 3.

15. A. James McDonald, "A Spanish Weekly," *ISR* 16 (January 1916): 445.

16. Report of Secretary-Treasurer W. B. Dillon, Las Vegas, Minutes of Joint Conference of National Executive Committee and State Secretaries, August 10–12, 1918, 87, SPC.

17. A. James McDonald to members, State Committee, New Mexico Socialist Party, February 2, 1915, SPC.

18. Dwight M. Ramsey Jr., "A Statistical Survey of Voting Behavior in New Mexico" (M.A. thesis, University of New Mexico, August 1951).

19. Elda B. Conly, "The Idaho State Convention," *ISR* 15 (September 1914): 184–185.

20. L. A. Coblentz and A. B. Clark, *Official Information for Voters* (Nampa: Idaho Socialist Party, 1914): 1, SPC.

21. Ibid., 17.

22. Elda B. Conly, "Hope to Invade State Legislature of Idaho," *American Socialist* (October 24, 1914): 4.

23. Coblentz and Clark, *Official Information for Voters*, 17–18.

24. Boyd A. Martin, *Idaho Voting Trends* (Moscow: Idaho Research Foundation, 1975): 5.

25. Arguments of Committees for the Election of Candidates for State Office, General Election, 1914, secretary of state, State of Montana, Helena, Montana, October 1914, 16.

26. "Non-Partisan Organization Inaugurated among Farmers, Sinister Movement on Foot in North Dakota to Divide the Farmer Vote," *Montana Socialist* (December 11, 1915): 1.

27. Ellis Waldron and Paul B. Wilson, *Atlas of Montana Elections, 1876–1976*, University of Montana Publications in History (Missoula: University of Montana Press, 1978): 62–66.

28. Advertisement, *The Butte Socialist* (April 4, 1915): 4.

29. Jerry W. Calvert, *The Gibraltar: Socialism and Labor in Butte, Montana, 1895–1920* (Helena: Montana Historical Society Press, 1988): 10.

30. State Secretary Thomas M. Fagan, "Socialism Sweeping on to Victory in Nevada," *American Socialist* (October 17, 1914): 3.

31. Ibid.

32. "A. Grant Miller," *Nevada Socialist* (September 1914): 2.

33. Fagan, "Socialism."

34. See State of Nevada, *Official Returns of the Election of November 1914* (Carson City, Nev.: State Printing Office, 1915).

35. Justus E. Taylor, state secretary, "Nevada's Opportunity," *Nevada Socialist* (August 1, 1916): 3.

36. Ibid.

37. See State of Nevada, *Official Returns of the Election of November 1916* (Carson City, Nev.: State Printing Office, 1917).

38. Eddy, "Situation in Arizona Aids Socialist Fight," 3.

39. Letter from Eddy to Thompson, August 21, 1914, SPC.

40. W. S. Bradford, "Is Hunt for the Workers?" *Arizona Socialist Bulletin* (October 11, 1916): 1.

41. Ibid.

42. F. Reaves, "Gila County Comment," *Arizona Socialist Bulletin* (October 11, 1916): 4.

43. C. A. Peterson in *Arizona Socialist Bulletin*, n.d. Reprinted in "Governor Hunt Is Commended," *California Social Democrat* (February 19, 1916): 1.

44. Reaves, "Gila County Government," 4.

45. Letter from Alfred Maddern to George W.P. Hunt, June 2, 1918, George W.P. Hunt Papers, Arizona Collection, Arizona State University Libraries, Tempe.

46. "State Party Directory," *Arizona Socialist Bulletin* (October 11, 1916): 4.

47. Mari Jo Buhle, *Women and American Socialism, 1870–1920* (Urbana: University of Illinois Press, 1981).

48. Platform of the Socialist Party of New Mexico, 1914, SPC.

49. "Manifesto on Equal Suffrage in Nevada," *Nevada Socialist* (July 1, 1916): 1.

50. James Weinstein, *The Decline of Socialism in America, 1912–1919* (New York: Monthly Review, 1967): 60.

51. See "Woman's Record," *The Party Builder* (June 27, 1914): 5; Max Sherover, "Hope and Work for the Socialist U.S. Senator from Nevada," *American Socialist* (September 9, 1916): 3.

52. "Resolutions Adopted by the State Executive Committee, Socialist Party of Nevada, February 15, 1916," Emmet D. Boyle, Executive Records, Nevada State Division of Archives and Records, Carson City.

53. Debs quoted in Sherover, "Hope and Work," 3.

54. "Men of the West Praise Suffrage," *New York Morning Telegraph* (August 12, 1915), clipping from Emmet D. Boyle, Scrapbooks, Nevada State Division of Archives and Records, Carson City, n.p.

55. David R. Berman, "Gender and Issue Voting: The Policy Effects of Suffrage Expansion in Arizona," *Social Science Quarterly* 74 (December 1993): 838–850.

56. Letter from Emma F. Langdon to Carl D. Thompson, August 17, 1914, SPC. This letter came in response to a letter from the national secretary who was trying to assess the effects of suffrage. Other, less definite answers from Socialists in the region came from I. F. Stewart, Idaho, to Thompson, August 26, 1914; Alice Eddy of Arizona to Thompson, August 21, 1914; and A. Carlson from Wyoming, August 18, 1914, all in SPC.

57. Jennie A. McGehe, "Jennie A. McGehe Attends Woman's Party Meeting," *American Socialist* (August 26, 1916): 3.

58. "Montana Suffragists Confident of Winning," *The New York Call* (September 7, 1914): 5.

59. "For Inquiry in Butte Outrage," *The New York Call* (September 25, 1914): 4.

60. "Overwhelmed But Undismayed Are the Socialists of Butte," *Montana Socialist* (April 10, 1915): 1.

61. A. James McDonald, New Mexico state secretary, to Carl D. Thompson, April 22, 1915, SPC.

62. Letter from George Lindsay, businessman (a director of the Farnsworth Canal and Reservoir Company) in Mountain Home, Utah, November 24, 1914, to national party headquarters in Chicago, SPC.

63. "Arizona Farmers Now Ready to Fight for Socialism," *American Socialist* (August 28, 1915): 2. See also "Contest Globe Election: Two Aldermen Elected," *American Socialist* (July 18, 1914): 1; Robert Logan, "Victory in Arizona," *American Socialist* (June 5, 1915): 4.

64. Logan, "Victory in Arizona."

65. "Note from Nevada," *ISR* 17 (October 1916): 247.

66. See letters from Earl W. Bowman to Carl D. Thompson, February 21, 1915, and from W. C. Tharp to Thompson, March 24, 1915, both in SPC.

67. Ethelwyn Mills, "Legislative Program of the Socialist Party," Socialist Party National Office, Chicago, 1914, SPC.

68. "How Socialist Legislators Served the Working People," *ATR* (June 19, 1915): 3.

69. Letter from Earl W. Bowman to *American Socialist,* January 25, 1915, SPC.

70. Letters from Earl W. Bowman, senator, Adams County, Idaho, to Carl D. Thompson, January 29 and February 21, 1915, both in SPC; "Idaho Socialist Legislator Fights for Unemployment," *American Socialist* (February 6, 1915): 1.

71. Carol Cross, "Idaho's Only Socialist Legislator 35 Years Ago Anticipated Work Relief," *The Idaho Sunday Statesman* (March 5, 1950). Reprinted in Gladys Bowman Knight, *A Biographical Sketch of Earl Wayland Bowman, 'The Ramlin' Kid' "* (Caldwell, Idaho: Caxton, 1967): 20.

72. Letter from Earl W. Bowman to Carl D. Thompson, February 21, 1915, SPC.

73. Interview in *The Idaho Statesman*, n.d., unidentified document, SPC.

74. Ibid.; also letter from Earl W. Bowman to *American Socialist*, January 25, 1915, SPC.

75. "Force Idaho to Grant Man the Right to Work," *American Socialist* (March 20, 1915): 1. See also "How Socialist Legislators Served the Working People," *ATR* (June 19, 1951): 3.

76. "In Nevada's Legislature," *American Socialist* (February 6, 1915): 4.

77. The expulsion is discussed in a letter from Justice E. Taylor, state secretary of the Nevada Socialist party, to Carl D. Thompson, February 11, 1913, SPC.

78. M. J. Scanlan, "Fighting the Good Fight in the Nevada Legislature," *American Socialist* (May 8, 1915): 2.

79. "Socialist Legislation in Nevada," in *The American Labor Year Book, 1916* (New York: Rand School of Social Science, 1916): 108.

80. "How Socialist Legislators Served the Working People," 3.

81. Conner quoted in Mills, "Legislative Program of the Socialist Party," 38.

82. Ibid., 21.

83. Letter from Conner to Carl D. Thompson, February 17, 1913, SPC.

84. Mills, "Legislative Program of the Socialist Party," 38–39.

85. "Democratic Platform Pledges Brutally Broken at Helena," *Montana Socialist* (February 6, 1915): 1.

86. Ibid.

87. See untitled notes in *American Socialist* (February 6, 1915): 1.

88. Untitled note in *American Socialist* (March 27, 1915): 4.

89. "Here's Brilliant Record of Lone Socialist Legislator in Utah," *American Socialist* (April 17, 1915): 4. See also E. D. MacDougall, "Bevan in the Legislature," *Annual Labor Review of the Inter-Mountain Worker* (June 19, 1915): 10.

90. Letter from J. Alex Bevan to Carl D. Thompson, December 26, 1914, SPC.

91. MacDougall, "Bevan in the Legislature," 10–11.

92. Letter from W. C. Tharp to Carl D. Thompson, December 26, 1914, SPC.

93. Ibid.

94. "Republican Victory," *The Clovis Journal* (November 6, 1914): 1.

95. Letter Thomas J. Mabry, editor of *The Clovis Journal*, to Governor W. C. McDonald, November 16, 1914, William C. McDonald Papers, New Mexico State Records Center and Archives, Santa Fe.

96. Letter from W. C. Tharp to Charles D. Thompson, December 26, 1914, SPC.

97. Letter from W. C. Tharp to Socialist headquarters, January 15, 1915, SPC.

98. Letter from A. James McDonald to members, State Committee, New Mexico Socialist party, February 2, 1915, SPC.

99. Ibid.

100. Letter from state party secretary A. James McDonald to W. C. Tharp, February 2, 1915, SPC.

101. "In New Mexico's Legislature," *American Socialist* (January 30, 1915): 1.

102. *New Mexico Bluebook of 1915* (Santa Fe: State of New Mexico, 1916): 31.

103. "Socialists and Statehood," *Arizona Daily Star* (September 25, 1906): 7.

104. "Industrial Pursuits Advocated for State," *Arizona Gazette* (April 16, 1912): 1.

105. Editorial, *Coconino Sun* (June 30, 1916): 6.

106. David R. Berman, *Reformers, Corporations, and the Electorate* (Niwot: University Press of Colorado, 1992).

107. T. A. Larson, *History of Wyoming* (Lincoln: University of Nebraska Press, 1978): 334.

108. Ibid.

CHAPTER 15

1. "The Socialist Party and the War," in *The American Labor Year Book* (New York: Rand School of Social Science, 1917–1918): 50.

2. Harry A. Mills and Royal E. Montgomery, *Organized Labor* (New York: McGraw-Hill, 1945): 137.

3. Benson quoted in "Socialist Leadership Un-American Says Allan L. Benson, Quitting Party," *Wyoming Weekly Labor Journal* (July 12, 1918): 1.

4. Ibid.

5. Ibid.

6. Hugh T. Lovin, "The Banishment of Kate Richards O'Hare," *Idaho Yesterdays* 22 (Spring 1978): 20–25.

7. Report of Special Employee Claude McCaleb at Globe, Arizona, for 1917, to R. L. Barnes, special agent in charge, Military Intelligence, Washington, D.C.

8. William D. Haywood, *Bill Haywood's Book: The Autobiography of William D. Haywood* (New York: International, 1929): 299.

9. T. A. Larson, *History of Wyoming* (Lincoln: University of Nebraska Press, 1978): 394.

10. John R. Sillito and Timothy S. Hearn, "A Question of Conscience: The Resignation of Bishop Paul Jones," *Utah Historical Quarterly* 50 (Summer 1982): 209–223.

11. See generally, F. Ross Peterson, *Idaho: A Bicentennial History* (New York: Norton, 1976).

12. H. C. Peterson and Gilbert C. Fite, *Opponents of War 1917–1918* (Madison: University of Wisconsin Press, 1957).

13 "No Pacifists in New Mexico, Declares Jones," *The Silver City Independent* (February 27, 1917): 1.

14. Letter attached to letter written to local councils by the Guadalupe County Council of Defense, State of New Mexico, August 13, 1917, Governor Washington E. Lindsey Collection, New Mexico State Records Center and Archives, Santa Fe.

15. Report of the Executive Secretary, NEC, August 8, 1912, 23, SPC.

16. Robert Kern, "Labor Struggle, 1900–1936," in Robert Kern, ed., *Labor in New Mexico: Unions, Strikes, and Social History Since 1881* (Albuquerque: University of New Mexico Press, 1983): 86.

17. Peterson and Fite, *Opponents of War,* 55.

18. "Big Four Local 3053," *Wyoming Weekly Labor Journal* (August 17, 1917): 3.

19. "Strike Is Failing, Leaders Are Leaving," *The Gallup Herald* (September 1, 1917): 1.

20. Robert Kern, "A Century of Labor in New Mexico," in Kern, ed., *Labor in New Mexico*, 8.

21. Letter from George Powell to Henry S. McCluskey, February 8, 1917, Henry S. McCluskey Papers, Arizona Collection, Arizona State University Libraries, Tempe.

22. Grover H. Perry, secretary-treasurer, "To All Metal Mine Workers: The I.W.W. Is Coming, Join the One Big Union," pamphlet, IWW's Metal Mine Workers' Industrial Union, Phoenix, Arizona.

23. Robert W. Bruere, *Following the Trial of the IWW* (New York: *New York Evening Post*, 1918): 3.

24. Douglas quoted in ibid., 7.

25. Will Robinson, *The Story of Arizona* (Phoenix: Berryhill, 1919): 299.

26. See account by Thomas McGuinness, real estate developer in Bisbee, in "Truth about Bisbee," *ATR* (August 25, 1917): 1.

27. Harold Callander, "Bosses Turn Bisbee into Armed Camp," *The New York Call* (September 6, 1917): 2.

28. "Dumping I.W.W. at Columbus," *The Deming Headlight* (July 13, 1917): 1.

29. Ibid.

30. "Nothing Doing at Hermanas," *The Deming Headlight* (July 20, 1917): 1.

31. Enclosure attached to letter from Joseph Patrick Tumulty to Woodrow Wilson, July 12, 1917, in Arthur S. Link, ed., *The Papers of Woodrow Wilson,* vol. 43 (Princeton: Princeton University Press, 1966–1988): 158.

32. Telegram from Woodrow Wilson to Thomas E. Campbell, July 12, 1917, ibid.

33. Letter from J. L. Donnelly and Thomas A. French to Wilson, August 6, 1917, ibid., 373.

34. Rosa McKay, "Butte and Bisbee Outrages Scored by Brave Women Representatives," *ATR* (August 18, 1917): 2.

35. "What Has Become of Democracy in the State of Arizona," *Wyoming Weekly Labor Journal* (August 17, 1917): 3.

36. Item from *Skillings Mining Review,* n.d. Reprinted as "The Bisbee System," *The Silver City Enterprise* (July 20, 1917): 1.

37. Letter from A. M. Pollard to Governor Lindsey, August 1, 1917, Governor Washington E. Lindsey Collection, New Mexico State Records Center and Archives, Santa Fe.

38. Letter from Pollard to Washington Lindsey, August 4, 1917, ibid.

39. Letter from Fred Fosoff, special representative, to Washington Lindsey, August 12, 1917, ibid.

40. Letter from George Wylie Paul Hunt to Woodrow Wilson, September 3, 1917, in Link, ed., *Papers of Woodrow Wilson,* vol. 43, 136.

41. Ibid., 137.

42. Ibid.

43. Ibid.

44. Ibid., 139.

45. Bruere, *Following the Trial of the IWW*, 8.

46. Department of Labor, Office of the Secretary, *Report on the Bisbee Deportations, Made by the President's Mediation Commission to the President of the United States,* November 6, 1917 (Washington, D.C.: Government Printing Office, 1918).

47. Letter from Theodore Roosevelt to Felix Frankfurter, December 19, 1917, in Elting E. Morrison, John Blum, Alfred D. Chandler Jr., and Sylvia Rice, eds., *The Letters of Theodore Roosevelt* (Cambridge, Mass.: Harvard University Press, 1951–1954): 1264.

48. True Copy of the Notes of the Hon. Thomas E. Campbell (written between 1934 and 1939), MS 132, 59, Campbell Family Papers, Arizona Historical Society Library, Tucson.

49. "Gov. Hunt Has His Picture Taken with Indicted Leaders of I.W.W.," *The Bisbee Daily Review* (June 7, 1918): 4.

50. Ibid.

51. Letter to George W.P. Hunt from Alfred Maddern, June 2, 1918, George W.P. Hunt Papers, Arizona Collection, Arizona State University Libraries, Tempe.

52. Jeanette Rankin, "Butte and Bisbee Outrages Scored by Brave Women Representatives," *ATR* (August 18, 1917): 2.

53. Little quoted in Burton K. Wheeler with Paul F. Healy, *Yankee from the West* (Garden City, N.Y.: Doubleday, 1962): 139.

54. "Will This Trump Win?" *Montana Socialist* (August 4, 1917): 1.

55. Ibid.

56. B. Stewart, "Communication," *Wyoming Weekly Labor Journal* (August 17, 1917): 3.

57. H. C. Peterson and Gilbert C. Fite, *Opponents of War 1917–1918* (Madison: University of Wisconsin Press, 1957): 169–170.

58. Robert L. Morlan, *Political Prairie Fire: The Nonpartisan League, 1915–1922* (St. Paul: Minnesota Historical Society Press, 1985): 173–174.

59. Wheeler and Healy, *Yankee from the West,* 142.

60. Minutes of Joint Conference of National Executive Committee and State Secretaries, August 10–12, 1918, Chicago, Illinois, 37.

61. "Non-Partisan League Given Poor Recommendation by Attorney Frank C. Goudy," *The Alamosa Courier* (October 13, 1917): 1.

62. Minutes of Joint Conference, 37.

63. J.C.H. Reynolds, division secretary of American Patriotic Conference, Northwestern Territory, to Jerome J. Day, August 13, 1918, Jerome James Day Papers, University of Idaho, Moscow.

64. The story is told in "The Associated Press Again," *ATR* (October 15, 1921): 2.

65. Reynolds to Day, August 13, 1918.

66. "Duncan Now Mucker in Copper Mines of Butte," *American Socialist* (February 10, 1917): 3.

67. Ibid.

68. Quoted in Terrence D. McGlynn, "Lewis J. Duncan, Socialist: The Man and His Work," paper presented to the Social Science Section, Montana Academy of Sciences, April 18, 1970, 31.

69. William C. Pratt, "Radicalism on the Northern Plains, 1912–1950," *Montana: The Magazine of Western History* (Winter 1992): 44, note.

70. Ibid.; Charles Vindex, "Radical Rule in Montana," *Montana: The Magazine of Western History* 18 (January 1968): 5–8; Verlaine Stoner McDonald, "A Paper of, by, and for the People," *Montana: The Magazine of Western History* 48 (Winter 1998): 18–33; Dave Walter, "Montana's Prairie Radicals: 1918–1937, "*Montana Magazine* (November-December 1996): 78–84.

71. Letter from Office of the Traveling Examiner, Hercules Mining Company, to Harry L. Day, March 4, 1918, Jerome Jones Day Papers, University of Idaho, Moscow.

72. "First Woman Member of Congress Is a Radical," *ATR* (March 24, 1917): 2.

73. "Jeannette Rankin and Townley Hit Hard at Big Business Tories," *The New York Call* (August 26, 1918): 2.

74. Montana Party platform, adopted September 14, 1918, Melinda Alexander Papers, Montana State Archives and Historical Society, Helena.

75. William S. Shepperson, *Retreat to Nevada: A Socialist Colony of World War I* (Reno: University of Nevada Press, 1966).

76. "Not in Harmony with Socialists' Policy, A. Grant Miller Withdraws from Party," *Carson City Daily Appeal* (September 10, 1917): n.p.

77. Ted Louis DeCorte Jr., "The 'Red Scare' in Nevada, 1919–1920" (M.A. thesis, University of Nevada, Las Vegas, August 1979).

78. Stone quoted in Minutes of Joint Conference, 1918, 101.

79. Ibid.

80. Ibid.

81. Robert Kern, "A Century of Labor in New Mexico," in Kern, ed., *Labor in New Mexico*, 3–24.

82. Letter from Charles Springer to Albert B. Fall, May 3, 1918, FA Box 37, Folder 9, Albert Fall Collection, Huntington Library, San Marino, California.

83. Editorial, "You Can't Do It Here," *Portales Journal* (July 16, 1917): n.p., attached to a letter from J. R. Sanders to Governor Lindsey, August 13, 1917, Governor Washington E. Lindsey Collection, New Mexico State Records Center and Archives, Santa Fe.

84. Minutes of Joint Conference, 1918, 85.

85. Unidentified article in True Copy of the Notes of Hon. Thomas E. Campbell (written between 1934 and 1939), MS 132, 59, Campbell Family Papers, Arizona Historical Society Library, Tucson.

86. Report of Executive Secretary to the National Executive Committee, August 8, 1918 (Chicago, Illinois): 17–23, SPC.

87. Eddy quote in Minutes of Joint Conference, 1918, 35.

88. Ibid., 101.

CONCLUDING NOTE

1. See, for example, James Oneal, "The Convention Aftermath," *The Eye Opener* (September 15, 1919): 6.

2. Report, Department of Intelligence Office, Chicago, Illinois, September 13, 1919, in Randolph Boehm and Robert Lester, eds., *U.S. Military Intelligence Reports: Surveillance of Radicals in the United States, 1917–1941* (Washington, D.C.: U.S. Government Document).

3. Letter from W. B. Dillon to Adolph Germer, July 29, 1919, SPC.

4. Ibid.

5. Resolutions of Socialist Party of New Mexico, received at national headquarters of the Socialist Party of America, August 1, 1919, SPC.

6. Letter from Adolph Germer to W. B. Dillon, August 15, 1919, SPC.

7. FBI Bulletin of Radical Activities, week ending April 24, 1920 (mislabeled on file as May 1, 1920), in Boehm and Lester, eds., *U.S. Military Intelligence Reports.*

8. Harold Lord Varney, "Butte—A Soviet Strike," *The Revolutionary Age* (March 1, 1919): 8.

9. Ibid.

10. Ibid.

11. See, for example, Report to John H. Wourms, November 12, 1919, MG 315, Box 2, Folder 54, Jerome James Day Papers, 1876–1941, University of Idaho, Moscow.

12. "State Federation Concludes Session," *The Free-Lance* (March 3, 1920): 1.

13. "Bail Is Wanted without Fail for the Men Who Are in Jail," *Butte Daily Bulletin* (December 6, 1919): 2.

14. John W. Gunn, "Awakening of Farmers Is Shown in Growth of Nonpartisan League," *ATR* (September 6, 1919): 2.

15. "Colorado Republicans Endorse Americanism," *Rocky Mountain News* (October 3, 1920): 4.

16. T. A. Larson, *History of Wyoming* (Lincoln: University of Nebraska Press, 1978): 454–455.

17. "United Republican Party Declares War on League," *Montana Record-Herald* (September 11, 1920): 1.

18. "In Forceful Language Republican Candidate Sounds Campaign Keynote," *Montana Record-Herald* (September 11, 1920): 1.

19. Full-page ad in *The Daily Missoulian* (October 31, 1920): 7.

20. Editorial, "The Future of the League in Montana," *The Montana Nonpartisan* (November 6, 1920): 4.

21. Robert L. Morlan, *Political Prairie Fire: The Nonpartisan League, 1915–1922* (St. Paul: Minnesota Historical Society Press, 1985): 239.

22. Boehm and Lester, eds., *U.S. Military Intelligence Reports.*

23. U.S. Military Intelligence Report from Denver District, Army RCTG Service, April 17, 1920, ibid.

24. Letter from Claude F. Wiley, Nampa, Idaho, to director of Military Intelligence Division, Washington D.C., December 2, 1920, ibid.

25. Letter from Sergeant Joseph G. Zimmerman, Reno, Nevada, to director of Military Intelligence Division, San Francisco, November 26, 1920, Military files, ibid.

26. Material from ibid.

27. U.S. Military Intelligence Report from Denver District, ibid.

28. Letter from Mae Bishop to Eugene V. Debs, January 8, 1920, in Constantine, Vol. 2, 46–47.

29. "Kate O'Hare to Prosecute Idaho Mob," *ATR* (July 16, 1921): 2. See also "Kate O'Hare Kidnapped," *The New Day* (July 9, 1921): 6.

30. "Kate O'Hare's Own Story of Kidnapping," *ATR* (July 16, 1921): 2.

31. "Legion Lawlessness Growing, Mrs. Hazlett Mobbed!" *The New Day* (August 6, 1921): 2–3.

32. "Grossbeck for Justice of the Supreme Court," *Wyoming Weekly Labor Journal* (November 3, 1922): 4.

33. See, for example, Peter F. Galderisi, Michael S. Lyons, Randy T. Simmons, and John G. Francis, *The Politics of Realignment: Party Change in the Mountain West* (Boulder: Westview, 1987).

34. Steven J. Rosenstone, Roy L. Behr, and Edward H. Lazorus, *Third Parties in America: Citizen Response to Major Party Failure* (Princeton, N.J.: Princeton University Press, 1984): 89.

Appendix

Table 1. Number of Western Federation of Miners Locals, 1900–1909

Area	1900	1901	1902	1903	1904	1905	1906	1907	1908	1909
Arizona	2	5	7	16	17	14	14	14	17	16
Colorado	27	28	32	43	43	38	35	30	24	22
Idaho	8	10	10	9	10	10	9	8	10	13
Montana	16	20	28	27	27	28	26	25	28	26
Nevada	4	4	10	10	11	13	15	20	38	36
New Mexico	0	0	0	0	1	1	0	0	0	0
Utah	0	2	3	4	12	10	10	12	13	11
Wyoming	1	1	0	2	3	3	3	3	1	1
Total	58	70	90	111	124	117	112	112	131	125

Source: January issues of *The Miners Magazine* for each year.

Table 2. Votes for Socialist Party Candidates for President, Total and as Percentage of Total Votes, 1900–1920*

Area	1900	1904	1908	1912	1916	1920
Arizona	—	—	—	3,163	3,174	—
	—	—	—	(13.4)	(5.5)	—
Colorado	686	4,303	7,960	16,366	9,951	7,860
	(0.3)	(1.8)	(3.0)	(6.2)	(3.4)	(2.7)
Idaho	—	4,949	6, 400	11,960	8,066	38
	—	(6.8)	(6.6)	(11.3)	(6.0)	—
Montana	711	5,675	5,920	10,811	9,634	—
	(1.1)	(8.9)	(8.6)	(13.5)	(5.4)	—
Nevada	—	925	2,103	3,313	3,065	1,864
	—	(7.6)	(8.6)	(16.5)	(9.2)	(6.9)
New Mexico	—	—	—	2,859	1,997	—
	—	—	—	(5.9)	(3.0)	—
Utah	717	5,767	4,890	8,899	4,460	3,159
	(0.8)	(5.7)	(4.5)	(8.0)	(3.1)	(2.2)
Wyoming	21	987	1,715	2,760	1,459	—
	(0.1)	(3.2)	(4.6)	(6.5)	(2.8)	—
National	86,935	402,489	420,380	900,369	589,924	913,664
	(0.62)	(2.9)	(2.8)	(5.99)	(3.18)	(3.42)

*1900 figures are for Debs as the nominee of the Social Democratic party.
Source: Congressional Quarterly, *Guide to U.S. Elections* (Washington, D.C.: Congressional Quarterly, Inc., 1975): 281–286; *The American Labor Year Book 1917–1918* (New York: Rand School of Social Science, 1919): 338–339.

Table 3. Socialist Party Yearly Membership Averages, Selected Years, 1909–1918

Area	1909	1912	1913	1914	1915	1916	1917	1918
Arizona	280	687	498	460	441	549	437	180
Colorado	881	1,976	1,030	1,237	714	797	848	583
Idaho	673	1,667	818	905	765	884	495	190
Montana	711	1,647	1,428	1,589	1,057	721	461	123
Nevada	240	652	670	614	330	443	98	91
New Mexico	175	278	140	191	182	278	138	91
Utah	341	772	518	448	252	401	346	324
Wyoming	533	685	690	648	495	751	383	299
Region	3,834	8,364	5,792	6,092	4,236	4,824	3,206	1,881
National	41,479	113,371	92,173	93,579	79,374	83,138	80,128	NA

Sources: "Membership," *The Socialist* (January 16, 1909): 2; *The American Labor Year Book 1916–1917* (New York: Rand School of Social Science, 1918): 95–96; random party records in Socialist Party of America Papers, 1897–1963 (on microfilm), William R. Perkins Library, Duke University, Durham, N.C.

Table 4. Subscribers *Appeal to Reason*, Total Number and as Percentage of Population, Selected Dates, 1906–1912

Area	December 1906	March 1907	January 1909	January 1912	May 1912
Arizona	2,775	3,319	1,765	1,999	2,126
	(16.3)	(18.6)	(9.09)	(8.69)	(9.24)
Colorado	8,201	8,676	5,559	7,654	9,355
	(11.8)	(12.0)	(7.18)	(9.26)	(11.31)
Idaho	2,604	2,867	1,788	4,946	6,144
	(10.1)	(10.5)	(5.84)	(14.2)	(17.7)
Montana	3,578	3,936	4,136	3,733	5,506
	(11.1)	(11.8)	(11.4)	(9.10)	(13.4)
Nevada	1,206	1,498	1,501	1,659	1,544
	(18.3)	(21.4)	(19.2)	(20.5)	(19.1)
New Mexico	1,261	1,498	2,526	3,171	3,325
	(4.6)	(5.24)	(8.09)	(9.52)	(9.98)
Utah	2,645	2,944	2,493	896	1,485
	(7.8)	(8.63)	(6.79)	(2.3)	(3.82)
Wyoming	1,095	1,265	1,098	1,357	1,407
	(8.9)	(9.96)	(8.01)	(8.7)	(9.02)
National	271,563	300,506	293,746	465,362	533,054
	(3.2)	(3.5)	(3.3)	(4.9)	(5.65)

Sources: Subscription figures from *The Appeal to Reason* (April 13, 1907): 3; (January 23, 1909): 4; (January 13, 1912): 4; (May 25, 1912): 4; also U.S. Census estimates for 1906, 1907, 1909, and 1912.

Table 5. Persons per Subscriber to *Appeal to Reason*, Socialist Party Member, and Vote for Debs, 1908–1909

Area	Per Subscriber to *Appeal*, January 1909	Per Party Member Avg. 1909	Per Vote for Debs 1908
Arizona*	116	730	107
Colorado	144	907	100
Idaho	182	484	51
Montana	91	529	64
Nevada	54	341	39
New Mexico**	130	1,870	310
Utah	150	1,095	76
Wyoming	133	274	85
Region	126	687	82
Nation	311	2,209	216

* Vote for governor in 1908 (1,912).
** Vote for representative to Congress in 1908 (1,056).
Sources: Information in Tables 2–4; U.S. Census for 1910; "The Vote for Socialist Party Ticket in the United States," *International Socialist Review* 15 (February 1915): 486.

Table 6. Party Membership and Debs Vote, 1912

Area	Party Membership 1912	Debs Vote 1912	Membership as a Percentage of Debs Vote	Debs Votes Per Member
Arizona	687	3,163	22	4.6
Colorado	1,976	16,366	12	8.3
Idaho	1,667	11,960	14	7.2
Montana	1,647	10,811	15	6.6
Nevada	652	3,313	20	5.1
New Mexico	278	2,859	10	10.3
Utah	772	8,899	9	11.5
Wyoming	685	2,760	25	4.3
Region	8,364	60,131	14	7.2
Nation	113,371	900,369	13	7.9

Source: Information in Tables 2 and 3.

Table 7. Membership Vote on Removal of Berger from the National Executive Committee, 1905

Area	Yes	No	Percent Yes
Arizona	38	19	67
Colorado	92	24	79
Idaho	87	93	48
Montana	82	48	63
Nevada	—	—	—
New Mexico	—	—	—
Utah	35	28	56
Wyoming	25	21	54
Region	359	233	61
National	4,215	4,718	47

Source: *Social Democratic Herald* (September 23, 1905): 1.

Table 8. Membership Vote on Removal of Haywood from the National Executive Committee, 1913

State	Yes	No	Percent Yes
Arizona	174	54	75
Colorado	404	332	55
Idaho	270	175	61
Montana	245	436	36
Nevada	116	164	41
New Mexico	58	9	87
Utah	70	90	44
Wyoming	95	50	66
Region	1,432	1,314	52
National	23,436	11,674	67

Source: *Weekly Bulletin*, Socialist Party (March 1, 1913): n.p., in Socialist Party of America Papers, 1897–1963 (on microfilm), William R. Perkins Library, Duke University, Durham, N.C.

Table 9. "Slackers" in World War I*

State	Number Called	Failed to Appear	Percentage Failed
Arizona	2,213	525	26
Colorado	24,547	1,888	8
Idaho	9,207	832	9
Montana	28,441	3,854	14
Nevada	5,474	1,179	22
New Mexico	10,491	1,334	13
Utah	12,416	1,053	8
Wyoming	2,733	399	7
Region	115,422	16,264	14
Nation	3,082,949	252,294	8

*Adapted from "First Complete Official Record of Draft," *The New York Times* (January 20, 1918): 1.

References

ARCHIVAL MATERIALS

Arizona Collection, Arizona State University Libraries, Tempe
    William E. Brooks Letters
    Carl T. Hayden Papers
    George W.P. Hunt Papers
    Henry S. McCluskey Papers
Arizona Historical Society, Tucson
    Campbell Family Papers
Butte–Silver Bow Public Archives, Butte, Montana
    Terrence McGlynn Collection
Denver Public Library, Western History Department
    John R. Lawson Papers
Duke University, William R. Perkins Library, Durham, North Carolina
    Socialist Party of America Papers, 1897–1963 (on microfilm)
Huntington Library, San Marino, California
    Albert Fall Collection

Idaho State Historical Society, Division of Manuscripts and Idaho State Archives, Boise
    W. E. Borah Papers
    Defendants' Exhibit, Haywood Trial
Montana State Archives and Historical Society, Helena
    Melinda Alexander Papers
    Mary Stevens Carroll Reminiscence
    Lewis Duncan Papers
    Thomas C. Power Papers
    Socialist Party of Montana Records
Nevada Historical Society, Reno
    Tasker Oddie Collection
    Jeanne Wier Collection
Nevada State Division of Archives and Records, Carson City
    Emmet D. Boyle, Executive Records, Scrapbooks
    Nevada State Council of Defense Records
New Mexico State Records Center and Archives, Santa Fe
    Governor Washington E. Lindsey Collection
    William C. McDonald Papers
    L. Bradford Prince Papers
Northern Arizona University, Cline Library, Flagstaff
    United Verde Copper Company Collection
Presidential Papers
    Link, Arthur S., ed. *The Papers of Woodrow Wilson.* 58 vols. Princeton: Princeton University Press, 1966–1988.
    Morrison, Elting E., John Blum, Alfred D. Chandler, and Sylvia Rice, eds. *The Letters of Theodore Roosevelt.* 8 vols. Cambridge, Mass.: Harvard University Press, 1951–1954.
Sharlot Hall Museum, Prescott, Arizona
    Buckey O'Neill Collection
    Buckey O'Neill Scrapbook
State Historical Society of Wisconsin, Madison
    Morris Hillquit Papers (microfilm edition)
    Henry Demarest Lloyd Papers (microfilm edition)
    Socialist Labor Party of America Papers (microfilm edition)
United States Government Files
    Strike Files of the U.S. Department of Justice
    Randolph Boehm and Robert Lester, eds., *U.S. Military Intelligence Reports: Surveillance of Radicals in the United States, 1917–1941* (microfilm). Washington, D.C.: 1984.
University of Colorado, Western History Collection, Boulder
    John F. Champion Papers (operative's reports, Leadville, Colorado)
    William Pen Collins Papers
    Edward P. Costigan Papers
    Western Federation of Miners Papers
University of Idaho, Moscow
    Jerome James Day Papers

Stanley Easton Papers
George C. Pickett Collection
University of Montana, Missoula
Joseph M. Dixon Papers
University of New Mexico, Zimmerman Library, Special Collections, Albuquerque
Marion Dargan Papers
Harvey Butler Fergusson Collection
University of Wyoming, American Heritage Center, Laramie
Herman V.S. Groesbeck Papers
Franics Warren Papers
Utah Historical Society, Salt Lake City
Governor Simon Bamberger Scrapbook
Archibald Hunter Collection
Utah State Archives and Record Service, Salt Lake City
William Spry Correspondence, Joe Hill Case
Wyoming State Archives, Laramie
Joseph M. Carey Papers

NEWSPAPERS, MAGAZINES, AND JOURNALS

The Age (Boulder, Montana)
The Alamosa Courier (Colorado)
Albuquerque Morning Democrat
American Labor Union Journal
American Socialist (Chicago, 1914–1917)
Annual Labor Review of the Inter-Mountain Worker
Appeal to Reason (Girard, Kansas, 1895–1917, 1919–1922)
Arizona Citizen (Tucson)
Arizona Daily Gazette
Arizona Daily Star (Tucson)
Arizona Gazette (Phoenix)
Arizona Journal Miner (Prescott)
Arizona Labor Union Journal (Phoenix)
Arizona Miner (Prescott)
Arizona Populist
Arizona Republic (Phoenix)
Arizona Republican (Phoenix)
Arizona Silver Belt (Globe)
Arizona Socialist Bulletin (Phoenix)
Arizona Weekly Journal Miner (Prescott)
The Bisbee Daily Review (Arizona)
Boise Evening Capitol News (Idaho)
Bozeman Chronicle (Montana)
The Butte Bystander

REFERENCES

Butte Daily Bulletin
Butte Inter Mountain
Butte Labor Advocate
The Butte Miner
The Butte Socialist
Caldwell News (Idaho)
The Caldwell Tribune (Idaho)
California Social Democrat (Los Angeles, 1911–1916)
Carson City Daily Appeal (Nevada)
The Cheyenne Daily Sun-Leader (Wyoming)
The Christian Socialist (Chicago)
The Clovis Journal (New Mexico)
Coconino Sun (Flagstaff, Arizona)
Coeur d'Alene Evening Press (Idaho)
The Coeur d'Alene Miner
Coeur d'Alene Press
Colorado Socialist Bulletin (Denver)
Colorado Springs Gazette
Columbus News (New Mexico)
The Commoner (Lincoln, Nebraska)
The Comrade (New York, 1901–1905)
The Crisis (Utah)
The Daily Missoulian (Montana)
The Daily News (Denver)
The Daily Populist (Denver)
The Daily Times (Wallace, Idaho)
The Deming Headlight (New Mexico)
Denver New Road
Denver News
The Denver Times
The Deseret Evening News (Salt Lake City)
The Eagle (Santa Fe, New Mexico)
El Paso Times
Evening Capital News (Boise)
The Evening Journal (Alamosa, Colorado)
The Eye Opener
Forum
The Free-Lance (Butte, Montana)
The Gallup Herald (New Mexico)
The Goldfield Daily Tribune (Nevada)
Graham County Advocate (Safford, Arizona)
The Graham County Worker (Safford, Arizona)
Grand Encampment Herald
Great Falls News (Montana)
The Hooper-Mosca Tribune (Hooper, Colorado)

Idaho Capital News (Boise)
Idaho Daily Statesman (Boise)
Idaho Springs News
Idaho State Tribune (Wallace)
Idaho Statesman
Independent-Journal (Alamosa, Colorado)
The Industrial Union Bulletin (Chicago, 1907–1909, IWW)
The Industrial Worker (Spokane and Seattle, Washington, 1909–1918)
Inter-Mountain Advocate (Salt Lake City)
Inter-Mountain Worker
International Socialist Review (Chicago, 1900–1918)
The Labor News (Colorado Springs)
The Labor World
Las Vegas Age (New Mexico)
Living Issues (Salt Lake City)
Miami Daily Silver Belt
The Miners Magazine (Denver, 1914–1921, WFM)
The Missoulian (Montana)
Mohave County Miner (Kingman, Arizona)
The Montana News (Helena)
The Montana Nonpartisan
Montana Populist
Montana Record-Herald
Montana Silverite
Montana Socialist (Butte)
The National Socialist
Nevada Forum (Reno, Sparks)
Nevada Socialist (Reno)
Nevada Workman (Goldfield)
The New Day
The New Nation (1891–1894)
The New York Call (1909–1918)
The New York Evening Call
New York Press
New York Times
The Observer
The One Big Union Monthly (Chicago, 1919–1921, IWW)
The Party Builder (Chicago, 1912–1914, official bulletin of the Socialist party)
Phoenix Herald
The Populist (Kalispell, Montana)
The Populist Tribune
Portales Journal (New Mexico)
The Progressive Woman
The Rathdrum Tribune (Kootenai County, Idaho)
The Reform (Sundance, Wyoming)

REFERENCES

The Revolutionary Age
Rock Springs Rocket (Wyoming)
Rocky Mountain News (Denver)
Roswell Daily Record (New Mexico)
Salt Lake Herald
San Luis Valley Courier (Alamosa, Colorado)
Santa Fe Daily New Mexican
Santa Fe New Mexican
The Silver Advocate
The Silver Belt
The Silver City Enterprise (New Mexico)
The Silver City Independent (New Mexico)
Social-Democratic Herald (Chicago and Milwaukee, 1898–1912)
The Socialist (Toledo, Ohio; Caldwell, Idaho; Seattle, Washington)
Socialist Party Monthly Bulletin (Chicago, 1904–1913)
The Socialist Woman (Chicago)
The Spokesman Review (Spokane)
St. Maries Gazette
St. Vrain Journal (New Mexico)
The Syndicalist (Chicago, 1913)
The Times (El Paso, Texas)
Tombstone Epitaph (Arizona)
Tonopah Miner
Tonopah Nevadan
Utah Labor Journal (Salt Lake City)
Utah Socialist (Salt Lake City)
The Voice of the People (Reno)
Weekly Bulletin (Arizona)
Weekly Phoenix Herald
Wilshire's Magazine (Toronto, New York, and Bishop, California; various years, 1900–1915)
The Wyoming Tribune
Wyoming Weekly Labor Journal (Cheyenne)

GOVERNMENT DOCUMENTS

Arguments of Committees for the Election of Candidates for State Offices, General Election 1914. Secretary of State, State of Montana, Helena, October 1914.

Department of Labor, Office of the Secretary. *Report on the Bisbee Deportations, Made by the President's Mediation Commission to the President of the United States,* November 6, 1917. Washington, D.C.: Government Printing Office, 1918.

New Mexico Blue Book. Santa Fe: State of New Mexico, various years.

Report of the President's Mediation Commission to the President of the United States. Washington, D.C.: Government Printing Office, 1918.

Secretary of State, State of Nevada. *Official Returns of the Election of November 1914.* Carson City, Nev.: State Printing Office, 1915.

———. *Official Returns of the Election of November 1916.* Carson City, Nev.: State Printing Office, 1917.

———. *Political History of Nevada.* Carson City: State Printing Office, 8th ed., 1986.

BOOKS, DOCUMENTS, AND ARTICLES

Address delivered by Gen. James B. Weaver, People's Party candidate for president, Auditorium, Helena, Montana, August 16, 1892, Montana State Archives.

The American Labor Year Book. New York: Rand School of Social Science (various years).

Baker, Ray Stannard. "The Reign of Lawlessness: Anarchy and Despotism in Colorado." *McClure's Magazine* (October 1904): 43–57.

Bedford, Henry F. *Socialism and the Workers in Massachusetts, 1886–1912.* Amherst: University of Massachusetts Press, 1966.

Berman, David R. "Electoral Support for Populism in the Mountain States: Some Evidence from Arizona." *Social Science Journal* 24 (January 1987): 43–52.

———. "Environment, Culture, and Radical Third Parties: Electoral Support for the Socialists in Arizona and Nevada 1912–1916." *Social Science Journal* 27 (1990): 147–158.

———. "Gender and Issue Voting: The Policy Effects of Suffrage Expansion in Arizona." *Social Science Quarterly* 74 (December 1993): 838–850.

———. *Reformers, Corporations, and the Electorate.* Niwot: University Press of Colorado, 1992.

Bicha, Karel D. *Western Populism: Studies in an Ambivalent Conservatism.* Lawrence, Kans.: Coronado, 1976.

———. "Western Populists: Marginal Reformers of the 1890s." *Agricultural History* (October 1976): 626–635.

Bloor, Ella Reeve. *We Are Many.* New York: International, 1940.

Bodnar, John. *The Transplanted: A History of Immigrants in Urban America.* Bloomington: Indiana University Press, 1985.

Brommel, Bernard J. *Eugene V. Debs: Spokesman for Labor and Socialism.* Chicago: Charles H. Kerr, 1978.

Bruere, Robert W. *Following the Trial of the IWW.* New York: New York Evening Post, 1918.

Brundage, David. *The Making of Western Labor Radicalism: Denver's Organized Workers, 1878–1905.* Urbana: University of Illinois Press, 1994.

Bryans, Bill. "Coal Mining in Twentieth Century Wyoming: A Brief History." *Journal of the West* 21 (October 1982): 24–35.

Buchanan, Joseph R. *The Story of a Labor Agitator.* New York: Outlook, 1903.

Buhle, Mari Jo. *Women and American Socialism, 1870–1920.* Urbana: University of Illinois Press, 1981.

Burbank, Garin. *When Farmers Voted Red: The Gospel of Socialism in the Oklahoma Country Side, 1910–1924.* Westport, Conn.: Greenwood, 1976.

"Butte Socialist Administration Commendable." *National Municipal Review* 2 (January 1913): 134.

Calvert, Jerry W. *The Gibraltar: Socialism and Labor in Butte, Montana, 1895–1920*. Helena: Montana Historical Society Press, 1988.

Cash, W. J. *The Mind of the South*. New York: Alfred A. Knopf, 1941.

Caughey, John W. "Toward an Understanding of the West." *Utah Historical Quarterly* 28 (January 1959): 8–24.

Chaplin, Ralph. *Wobbly: The Rough-and-Tumble Story of an American Radical*. Chicago: University of Chicago Press, 1948.

Chase, General John. "The Military Occupation," in Leon Stein and Philip Taft, eds., *Massacre at Ludlow: Four Reports*. New York: Arno and *The New York Times*, 1971.

Clinch, Thomas A. *Urban Populism and Free Silver in Montana*. Missoula: University of Montana Press, 1970.

Coblentz, L. A., and A. B. Clark. *Official Information for Voters*. Nampa: Idaho Socialist Party, 1914.

Congressional Quarterly. *Guide to U.S. Elections*. Washington, D.C.: Congressional Quarterly, Inc., 1975.

"Comrades, the Clock Has Struck." *Social-Democratic Herald* (December 10, 1898): 1.

Constantine, J. Robert, ed. *Letters of Eugene V. Debs*, 2 vols. Urbana: University of Illinois Press, 1990.

Critchlow, Donald T., ed. *Socialism in the Heartland: The Midwestern Experience, 1900–1925*. Notre Dame, Ind.: University of Notre Dame Press, 1986.

Davies, J. Kenneth. *Deseret's Sons of Toil*. Salt Lake City: Olympus, 1977.

———. "Mormonism and the Closed Shop." *Labor History* (Spring 1962): 169–187.

Debs, Eugene. "Social Democrats in Convention." *Appeal to Reason* (March 24, 1900): 3.

Denton, James A. *Rocky Mountain Radical: Myron W. Reed, Christian Socialist*. Albuquerque: University of New Mexico Press, 1997.

Dubofsky, Melvin. *"Big Bill" Haywood*. New York: St. Martin's, 1987.

———. "The Origins of Western Working Class Radicalism, 1890–1905." *Labor History* 7 (Spring 1966): 131–154.

———. *We Shall Be All: A History of the Industrial Workers of the World*. Chicago: Quadrangle Books, 1969.

Editorial. *The Independent Journal* (August 4, 1892): 2.

Elder, A. B. "Progress and Reaction Meet Face to Face." *Appeal to Reason* (June 21, 1902): 2.

Elliott, Russell R. *History of Nevada*. Lincoln: University of Nebraska Press, 2nd revised ed., 1987.

———. *Nevada's Twentieth-Century Mining Boom*. Reno: University of Nevada Press, 1966.

———. *Radical Labor in the Nevada Mining Booms, 1900–1920*. Carson City, Nev.: State Printing Office, 1963.

Ellis, Anne. *The Life of an Ordinary Woman*. Boston: Houghton Mifflin, 1929.

Emmons, David M. *The Butte Irish: Class and Ethnicity in an American Mining Town*. Urbana: University of Illinois Press, 1989.

Fahey, John. "Ed Boyce and the Western Federation of Miners." *Idaho Yesterdays* 25 (1981): 18–30.

Feigenbaum, William Morris. "Great Battles of Bygone Days." *American Socialist* (July 29, 1916): 3.

Fergusson, Harvey. *Home in the West: An Inquiry into My Origins.* New York: Duell, Sloan and Pearce, 1944.

Fink, Leon. *Workingmen's Democracy: The Knights of Labor and American Politics.* Urbana: University of Illinois Press, 1983.

"First Annual Convention Social Democratic Party." *Social-Democratic Herald* (March 17, 1900): 1.

Flemming, Elvis E. "'Sockless' Jerry Simpson: The New Mexico Years, 1902–1905." *New Mexico Historical Review* 69 (January 1994): 49–70.

Flynn, Elizabeth Gurley. "Memories of the Industrial Workers of the World (IWW)." Occasional Papers Series, American Institute for Marxist Studies, Web edition, 1997.

———. *The Rebel Girl: An Autobiography, My First Life (1906–1926).* New York: International, 1973.

Foster, James C. "The Impact of Labor on the Development of the West," in James C. Foster, ed., *American Labor in the Southwest: The First Hundred Years.* Tucson: University of Arizona Press, 1982.

Francis, John G. "The Political Landscape of the Mountain West," in Peter F. Galderisi, Michael S. Lyons, Randy T. Simmons, and John G. Francis, *The Politics of Realignment: Party Change in the Mountain West.* Boulder: Westview, 1987.

Frisch, Paul A. "Labor Conflict at Eureka, 1886–97." *Utah Historical Quarterly* 49 (Spring 1981): 145–156.

Fritz, Percy Stanley. *Colorado: The Centennial State.* New York: Prentice-Hall, 1941.

Fuller, Leon W. "Colorado's Revolt against Capitalism." *Mississippi Valley Historical Review* 21 (December 1934): 343–360.

Gaboury, William J. *Dissension in the Rockies: A History of Idaho Populism.* New York: Garland, 1988.

———. "From Statehouse to Bull Pen: Idaho Populism and the Coeur d'Alene Troubles of the 1890s." *Pacific Northwest Quarterly* (January 1967): 14–22.

Galderisi, Peter F., Michael S. Lyons, Randy T. Simmons, and John G. Francis. *The Politics of Realignment: Party Change in the Mountain West.* Boulder: Westview, 1987.

Gardner, A. Dudley, and Verla R. Flores. *Forgotten Frontier: A History of Wyoming Coal Mining.* Boulder: Westview, 1989.

Ginger, Ray. *Eugene V. Debs: A Biography.* New York: Collier Books, 1949.

Glad, Betty. *Key Pittman: The Tragedy of a Senate Insider.* New York: Columbia University Press, 1986.

Glad, Paul W. *McKinley, Bryan, and the People.* Philadelphia: J. B. Lippincott, 1964.

Glass, Mary Ellen. *Silver and Politics in Nevada.* Reno: University of Nevada Press, 1969.

Goodwyn, Lawrence. *Democratic Promise: The Populist Moment in America.* New York: Oxford University Press, 1976.

Goodykoontz, Colin B. "The Progressive Movement in Colorado, 1910–1912." *University of Colorado Studies,* Series C, Vol. 1, no. 2 (May 1941): 145–157.

Gould, Lewis L. *Wyoming: A Political History, 1868–1896.* New Haven: Yale University Press, 1968.

Green, James R. *Grass-Roots Socialism: Radical Movements in the Southwest, 1895–1943*. Baton Rouge: Louisiana State University Press, 1978.

Greene, Julie. *Pure and Simple Politics: The American Federation of Labor and Political Activism, 1881–1917*. New York: Cambridge University Press, 1998.

Griffiths, David B. "Far Western Populism: The Case of Utah, 1893–1900." *Utah Historical Quarterly* 37 (1969): 396–407.

———. *Populism in the Western United States, 1890–1900*, 2 vols. Lewiston, N.Y.: Edwin Mellen, 1992.

———. "Populism in Wyoming." *Annals of Wyoming* 40 (April 1968): 57–71.

Hallberg, Carl V. "Finding His Niche: F. W. Ott, a German Publisher." *Annals of Wyoming* 72 (Spring 2000): 2–13.

Haywood, William D. *Bill Haywood's Book: The Autobiography of William D. Haywood*. New York: International, 1929.

Heflin, Reuben W. "New Mexico Constitutional Convention." *New Mexico Historical Review* 31 (January 1946): 60–68.

Hicks, John D. *The Populist Revolt*. Minneapolis: University of Minnesota Press, 1931.

Hilizinger, J. S. "The People's Party." *Arizona Magazine* 1 (1893): 20–22.

Hillquit, Morris. *Recent Progress of the Socialist and Labor Movements in the United States*. Chicago: Charles H. Kerr, 1907.

Hofstadter, Richard. *The Age of Reform*. New York: Knopf, 1955.

Holmes, Jack E. *Politics in New Mexico*. Albuquerque: University of New Mexico Press, 1967.

Howard, Anne Bail. *The Long Campaign: A Biography of Anne Martin*. Reno: University of Nevada Press, 1985.

Hoxie, Robert F. "The Rising Tide of Socialism." *Journal of Political Economy* 19 (October 1911): 609–631.

Hulse, James. "Socialism in Nevada, 1904–1918: Faint Echoes of an Idealistic National Movement." *Nevada Historical Society Quarterly* 31 (Winter 1988): 247–258.

Industrial Workers of the World. *Proceedings of the First Convention of the Industrial Workers of the World*. New York: New York Labor News, 1905; 2nd ed., New York: Merit, 1969.

Jameson, Elizabeth. *All That Glitters: Class, Conflict, and Community in Cripple Creek*. Urbana: University of Illinois Press, 1998.

Jensen, Vernon. *Heritage of Conflict: Labor Relations in the Nonferrous Metals Industry up to 1930*. New York: Greenwood, 1968; original pub., Ithaca, N.Y.: Cornell University Press, 1950.

Johnson, Claudius O. *Borah of Idaho*. New York: Longmans, Green, 1936.

Jonas, Frank J. "Utah, the Different State," in Frank J. Jonas, ed., *Politics in the American West*. Salt Lake City: University of Utah Press, 1969.

Keister, Jack. "Why the Socialists Won in Butte." *International Socialist Review* 11 (June 1911): 731–733.

Keithly, Ralph. *Buckey O'Neill*. Caldwell, Idaho: Caxton, 1949.

Keleher, William A. *Memoirs: 1892–1969*. Santa Fe: Rydal, 1969.

Kennedy, John Curtis. "Socialistic Tendencies in American Trade Unions." *ISR* 8 (1907–1908): 330–345. Reprinted from *Journal of Political Economy*, n.d.

Kern, Robert, ed. *Labor in New Mexico: Unions, Strikes, and Social History Since 1881*. Albuquerque: University of New Mexico Press, 1983.

Kibbey, Joseph H. "Republican Outlook." *The Rita* 2 (February 23, 1896): 3.

Kipnis, Ira. *The American Socialist Movement 1897–1912*. New York: Columbia University Press, 1952.

Kivisto, Peter. *Immigrant Socialists in the United States: The Case of the Finns and the Left*. Cranbury, N.J.: Associated University Presses, 1984.

Kleppner, Paul. "Voters and Parties in the Western United States, 1876–1900." *Western Political Quarterly* (January 1983): 49–68.

Kluger, James R. *The Clifton-Morenci Strike: Labor Difficulty in Arizona*. Tucson: University of Arizona Press, 1970.

Knight, Gladys Bowman. *A Biographical Sketch of Earl Wayland Bowman, "The Ramlin' Kid."* Caldwell, Idaho: Caxton, 1967.

Koenig, Louis W. *Bryan: A Political Biography of William Jennings Bryan*. New York: G. P. Putnam's Sons, 1975.

Kraditor, Aileen S. *The Radical Persuasion*. Baton Rouge: Louisiana State University Press, 1981.

Lamm, Richard D., and Michael McCarthy. *The Angry West: A Vulnerable Land and Its Future*. Boston: Houghton Mifflin, 1982.

Langdon, Emma F. *The Cripple Creek Strike: A History of Industrial Wars in Colorado*. New York: Arno, 1969. Reprint of 1904–1905 ed. by Great Western with new introduction.

Larson, Carole. *Forgotten Frontier: The Story of Southeastern New Mexico*. Albuquerque: University of New Mexico Press, 1993.

Larson, Robert W. *New Mexico Populism: A Study of Radical Protest in a Western Territory*. Boulder: Colorado Associated University Press, 1974.

———. *Populism in the Mountain West*. Albuquerque: University of New Mexico Press, 1986.

———. "The White Caps of New Mexico: A Study in Ethnic Militancy in the Southwest." *Pacific Historical Review* 44, no. 2 (May 1975): 171–185.

Larson, T. A. *History of Wyoming*. Lincoln: University of Nebraska Press, 1978.

Laslett, John H.M. *Labor and the Left: A Study of Socialist and Radical Influences in the American Labor Movement, 1881–1924*. New York: Basic Books, 1970.

Lee, Betty Graham, ed. *Cornerstones of the 1908 LDS Academy: A Research Guide*. Thatcher: Eastern Arizona College, 1981.

Lindsey, Ben B. *The Rule of Plutocracy in Colorado*. Denver: Hick's, 1908.

Lipset, Seymour Martin, and Gary Marks. *It Didn't Happen Here: Why Socialism Failed in the United States*. New York: W. W. Norton, 2000.

Long, Priscilla. "The 1913–1914 Colorado Fuel and Iron Strike, with Reflections on the Causes of Coal-Strike Violence," in John H.M. Laslett, ed., *The United Mine Workers of America: A Model of Industrial Solidarity?* University Park: Pennsylvania State University Press, 1996.

———. *Where the Sun Never Shines*. New York: Paragon House, 1989.

Lovin, Hugh T. "The Banishment of Kate Richards O'Hare." *Idaho Yesterdays* 22 (Spring 1978): 20–25.

———. "The Farmer Revolt in Idaho, 1914–1922." *Idaho Yesterdays* (Fall 1976): 2–15.

Lukas, J. Anthony. *Big Trouble*. New York: Simon & Schuster, 1997.

Mabry, Thomas J. "New Mexico's Constitutional Convention in the Making—Reminiscences of 1910." *New Mexico Historical Review* 19 (April 1944): 168–184.

Malone, Michael P. *The Battle for Butte*. Seattle: University of Washington Press, 1981.

Martin, Boyd A. *Idaho Voting Trends*. Moscow: Idaho Research Foundation, 1975.

Maynard, R. A. "How I Became a Socialist." *The Comrade* (September 1903): 8.

McCarthy, G. Michael. "Colorado's Populist Party and the Progressive Movement." *Journal of the West* 15 (January 1976): 54–75.

McCluskey, H. S. *Absentee Capitalists Menace Popular Government in Arizona*. Bound reprint of articles from the *Miami Daily Silver Belt*, August 27–October 21, 1921. 30 pp. Henry S. McCluskey Papers, Arizona Collection, Arizona State University Libraries, Tempe.

McCormick, A. Ross. *Reformers, Rebels, and Revolutionaries: The Western Canadian Radical Movement 1899–1919*. Toronto: University of Toronto Press, 1977.

McCormick, John S. "Hornets in the Hive: Socialists in Early Twentieth Century Utah." *Utah Historical Quarterly* 50 (Summer 1982): 225–240.

McCormick, John S., and John R. Sillito. "America's Socialist Heritage: Socialism in Utah, 1900–1920." *The Socialist Tribune* (April-May 1978): n.p.

———. "Socialism and Utah Labor: 1900–1920." *Southwest Economy and Society* 6 (Fall 1983): 15–30.

———. "Socialists in Power: The Eureka, Utah, Experience, 1907–1925." *Weber Studies* 6 (Spring 1989): 55–67.

McDonald, Verlaine Stoner. "A Paper of, by, and for the People." *Montana: The Magazine of Western History* 48 (Winter 1998): 18–33.

McGehe, Jennie A. "Jennie A. McGehe Attends Woman's Party Meeting." *American Socialist* (August 26, 1916): 3.

McGovern, George S., and Leonard F. Guttridge. *The Great Coal Field War*. Boston: Houghton Mifflin, 1972.

Mellinger, Phillip J. *Race and Labor in Western Copper: The Fight for Equality, 1896–1918*. Tucson: University of Arizona Press, 1995.

Miller, Guy E. "The Telluride Strike," in Emma F. Langdon, *The Cripple Creek Strike: A History of Industrial Wars in Colorado*. New York: Arno, 1969.

Mills, Ethelwyn. "Legislative Program of the Socialist Party." Chicago: Socialist Party National Office, 1914.

Mills, Harry A., and Royal E. Montgomery. *Organized Labor*. New York: McGraw-Hill, 1945.

Morgan, H. Wayne. *Eugene V. Debs: Socialist for President*. Syracuse, N.Y.: Syracuse University Press, 1962.

Morlan, Robert L. *Political Prairie Fire: The Nonpartisan League, 1915–1922*. St. Paul: Minnesota Historical Society Press, 1985.

Morris, John R. *Davis H. Waite: The Ideology of a Western Populist*. Washington, D.C.: University Press of America, 1982.

O'Neill, Buckey. *An Open Letter* (October 12, 1894), printed in *Miners Magazine* (August 1900): 10–18.

―――. *The Rita* (February 23, 1896): 2–3.

Papanikolas, Zeese. *Buried Unsung: Louis Tikas and the Ludlow Massacre.* Salt Lake City: University of Utah Press, 1982.

Parton, Mary Field, ed. *Autobiography of Mother Jones.* Chicago: Charles H. Kerr, 1925.

Patton, James M. *History of Clifton.* Greenlee County, Ariz.: Chamber of Commerce, 1977.

Paul, Rodman W. *California Gold: The Beginning of Mining in the Far West.* Cambridge: Harvard University Press, 1947.

Peck, Gunther. *Reinventing Free Labor: Padrones and Immigrant Workers in the North American West, 1880–1930.* New York: Cambridge University Press, 2000.

Peterson, F. Ross. *Idaho: A Bicentennial History.* New York: W. W. Norton, 1976.

Peterson, H. C., and Gilbert C. Fite. *Opponents of War 1917–1918.* Madison: University of Wisconsin Press, 1957.

Peterson, Richard H. *The Bonanza Kings.* Lincoln: University of Nebraska Press, 1977.

Philpott, William. *The Lessons of Leadville.* Monograph 10. Denver: Colorado Historical Society, 1995.

Phipps, Stanley Stewart. "Building Socialism in One City: Coeur d'Alene, Idaho's 1911 Municipal Government." *Museum of North Idaho Quarterly Newsletter* 7 (Winter 1986): 1–5.

Pollack, Norman. *The Humane Society: Populism, Capitalism, and Democracy.* New Brunswick, N.J.: Rutgers University Press, 1990.

―――. *The Populist Response to Industrial America: Midwest Populist Thought.* Cambridge, Mass.: Harvard University Press, 1962.

"A Populist Scheme." *The Independent Journal* (March 8, 1894): 2.

Powell, Allan Kent. *The Next Time We Strike: Labor in Utah's Coal Fields.* Logan: Utah State University Press, 1985.

Pratt, William C. "Radicalism on the Northern Plains, 1912–1950." *Montana: The Magazine of Western History* (Winter 1992): 43–55.

Proceedings of the National Convention of the Socialist Labor Party (various years).

Proceedings of the National Convention of the Socialist Party (various years).

Proceedings of the National Convention of the Western Federation of Miners (various years).

Quint, Howard H. "Julius A. Wayland, Pioneer Socialist Propagandist." *Mississippi Valley Historical Review* 35 (March 1949): 585–606.

Rastall, B. M. *The Cripple Creek Strike of 1893.* Colorado Springs: Colorado College Studies, June 1905.

Report of the Executive Board of the Western Federation of Miners, Denver, Colorado, December 19, 1907; January 14, 1911.

Ritter, Gretchen. *Goldbugs and Greenbacks: The Antimonopoly Tradition and the Politics of Finance in America.* New York: Cambridge University Press, 1997.

Roberts, Calvin A. "H. B. Fergusson, 1848–1915: New Mexico Spokesman for Political Reform." *New Mexico Historical Review* 57 (July 1982): 237–255.

Robinson, Will. *The Story of Arizona.* Phoenix: Berryhill, 1919.

Rocha, Guy Louis. "Radical Labor Struggles in the Tonopah-Goldfield Mining District, 1901–1922." *Nevada Historical Quarterly* 20 (Spring 1977): 3–45.

Roosevelt, Theodore. *Theodore Roosevelt: An Autobiography*. New York: Charles Scribner's Sons, 1925.

Rosenbaum, Robert J. *Mexican Resistance in the Southwest*. Austin: University of Texas Press, 1981.

Rosenstone, Steven J., Roy L. Behr, and Edward H. Lazarus. *Third Parties in America: Citizen Response to Major Party Failure*. Princeton, N.J.: Princeton University Press, 1984.

Salvatore, Nick. *Eugene V. Debs: Citizen and Socialist*. Urbana: University of Illinois Press, 1982.

Sanders, Helen F. *A History of Montana*, I. Chicago: Lewis, 1913.

Sarashon, David. "The Election of 1916: Realigning the Rockies." *Western Historical Quarterly* 11 (July 1980): 285–305.

Schlup, Leonard. "I Am Not a Cuckoo Democrat! The Congressional Career of Henry A. Coffeen." *Annals of Wyoming* (Fall 1994): 30–47.

Schneirov, Richard, Shelton Stromquist, and Nick Salvatore, eds. *The Pullman Strike and the Crisis of the 1890s: Essays on Labor and Politics*. Urbana: University of Illinois Press, 1999.

Shannon, David A. *The Socialist Party of America*. Chicago: Quadrangle Books, 1955.

Shepperson, William S. *Retreat to Nevada: A Socialist Colony of World War I*. Reno: University of Nevada Press, 1966.

Sillito, John R. "Socialist Saints: Mormons and the Socialist Party, 1900–1920." *Dialogue: A Journal of Mormon Thought* 18 (Summer 1985): 121–131.

———. "Prove All Things, Hold Fast That Which Is Good." *Weber Studies* (Spring 1984): n.p.

———. "Women and the Socialist Party in Utah, 1900–1920." *Utah Historical Quarterly* 49 (Summer 1981): 220–237.

Sillito, John R., and Timothy S. Hearn. "A Question of Conscience: The Resignation of Bishop Paul Jones." *Utah Historical Quarterly* 50 (Summer 1982): 209–223.

Simons, Algie. "Socialism and the Trade Union Movement." *International Socialist Review* 3 (July 1902): 46–49.

———. "The Socialist Outlook." *International Socialist Review* 5 (1904–1905): 203.

Smith, Duane A. *Rocky Mountain Mining Camps: The Urban Frontier*. Bloomington: Indiana University Press, 1967.

———. *Rocky Mountain West: Colorado, Wyoming, and Montana, 1859–1915*. Albuquerque: University of New Mexico Press, 1992.

Smith, Robert Wayne. *The Coeur d'Alene Mining War of 1892: A Case Study of an Industrial Dispute*. Oregon State Monographs. Corvallis: Oregon State University Press, 1961.

Socialist Party of America, Minutes of Joint Conference of National Executive Committee and State Secretaries, Chicago, August 10–12, 1918, SPC.

Spargo, John. *Report of the Non-Partisan League of North Dakota and Various Other States, 1912*. Socialist Party of America Papers, 1897–1963 (microfilm), William R. Perkins Library, Duke University, Durham, N.C.

Sprague, Marshall. *Money Mountain: The Story of Cripple Creek Gold*. Boston: Little, Brown, 1953.

Steel, Edward M., ed. *The Correspondence of Mother Jones*. Pittsburgh: University of Pittsburgh Press, 1985.

Steffens, Lincoln. "Eugene V. Debs." *Everybody's* (October 1908): 458.

Stein, Leon, and Philip Taft, eds. *Massacre at Ludlow: Four Reports*. New York: Arno and The New York Times, 1971.

Stipanovich, Joseph. *The South Slavs in Utah: A Social History*. San Francisco: R&E Research Associates, 1975.

Suggs, George G. *Colorado's War on Militant Unionism: James H. Peabody and the Western Federation of Miners*. Detroit: Wayne State University Press, 1972.

———. "Religion and Labor in the Rocky Mountain West: Bishop Nicholas C. Matz and the Western Federation of Miners." *Labor History* 11 (Spring 1970): 190–206.

Sullivan, Joseph. "Rising from the Ranks, Socialism in Nye County." *Nevada Historical Quarterly* 34, no. 2 (Summer 1991): 340–349.

Toole, K. Ross. *Twentieth-Century Montana: A State of Extremes*. Norman: University of Oklahoma Press, 1972.

Tracy, Frank Basil. "Menacing Socialism in the Western States." *Forum* (May 1893): 322–342.

Ubbelohde, Carl. *A Colorado History*. Boulder: Pruett, 1965.

Vaile, Joel F. "Colorado's Experiment with Populism." *Forum* 18 (February 1895): 714–723.

Varney, Harold Lord. "The Story of the I.W.W." *The One Big Union Monthly* (May 1919): 49–53.

Vindex, Charles. "Radical Rule in Montana." *Montana: The Magazine of Western History* 18 (January 1968): 5–8.

Wagoner, Jay. *Arizona Territory: 1863–1912*. Tucson: University of Arizona Press, 1970.

Waite, Davis H., and Lorenzo Crounse. "Woman Suffrage in Practice." *North American Review* 158 (June 1894): 740.

Waldron, Ellis, and Paul B. Wilson. *Atlas of Montana Elections, 1876–1976*. University of Montana Publications in History. Missoula: University of Montana Press, 1978.

Walter, Dave. "Montana's Prairie Radicals: 1918–1937." *Montana Magazine* (November-December 1996): 78–84.

Weinstein, James. *The Decline of Socialism in America, 1912–1919*. New York: Monthly Review, 1967.

Weir, Robert E. *Knights Unhorsed: Internal Conflict in a Gilded Age Social Movement*. Detroit: Wayne State University Press, 2000.

Western Federation of Miners. Convention Proceedings (various years).

———. Report of the Executive Board (various years).

Wheeler, Burton K., with Paul F. Healy. *Yankee from the West*. Garden City, N.Y.: Doubleday, 1962.

Wilkins, Davis. "Nampa's Flirtation with Socialism." *Idaho Yesterdays* (Winter 1987): 15–17.

Wolff, David A. *Industrializing the Rockies: Growth, Competition, and Turmoil in the Coalfields of Colorado and Wyoming, 1868–1914*. Boulder: University Press of Colorado, 2003.

Wolfle, Lee M., and Robert W. Hodge. "Radical-Party Politics in Illinois, 1880–1924." *Sociological Inquiry* 53 (Winter 1983): 33–60.

Wolman, Leo. *The Growth of American Trade Unions 1880–1923.* New York: National Bureau of Economic Research, 1924.

Wright, James. *The Politics of Populism: Dissent in Colorado.* New Haven, Conn.: Yale University Press, 1974.

Wyman, Mark W. *Hard Rock Epic: Western Miners and the Industrial Revolution, 1860–1910.* Berkeley: University of California Press, 1979.

Zamora, Emilio. *The World of the Mexican Worker in Texas.* College Station: Texas A&M University Press, 1993.

Zanjani, Sally S. "The Election of 1890: The Last Hurrah for the Old Regime." *Nevada Historical Quarterly* 2 (Spring 1977): 46–56.

———. *The Unspiked Rail: Memoir of a Nevada Rebel.* Reno: University of Nevada Press, 1981.

Zanjani, Sally S., and Guy Louis Rocha. *Ignoble Conspiracy: Radicalism on Trial in Nevada.* Reno: University of Nevada Press, 1986.

UNPUBLISHED MATERIAL

DeCorte, Ted Louis, Jr. "The 'Red Scare' in Nevada, 1919–1920." M.A. thesis, University of Nevada, Las Vegas, August 1979.

Hainsworth, Brad E. "Utah State Elections, 1916–1924." PhD dissertation, University of Utah, August 1968.

Hunter, George. "John Greenway and the Bull Moose Movement in Arizona." M.A. thesis, University of Arizona, 1966.

Jacobson, Thomas A. "The Battle for Direct Legislation: Montana Politics beyond the Copper Kings, 1902–1906." M.A. thesis, University of Montana, 1987.

Kendall, Susan Lee. "Women in Goldfield, 1903–1916." M.A. thesis, University of Nevada, Las Vegas, April 1980.

Kindler, David L. "The Progressive Movement in Wyoming, 1910–1913." M.A. thesis, University of Wyoming, January 1970.

Krueger, Thomas A. "Populism in Wyoming." M.A. thesis, University of Wyoming, 1960.

LaGrande, Daniel J. "Voice of a Copper King: A Study of *The* (Butte) *Reveille*, 1903–1906." M.A. thesis, University of Montana, 1971.

McBride, James D. "The Development of Labor Unions in Arizona Mining, 1884 to 1919." M.A. thesis, Arizona State University, 1974.

McGlynn, Terrence D. "Lewis J. Duncan, Socialist: The Man and His Work." Paper presented to the Social Science Section, Montana Academy of Sciences, April 18, 1970.

———. "Socialist Organizers in Montana." Paper presented to the Social Science Section, Montana Academy of Sciences, April 21, 1972.

Peters, Betsy Ross. "Joseph M. Carey and the Progressive Movement in Wyoming." PhD dissertation, University of Wyoming, May 1971.

Phipps, Stanley Stewart. "The Coeur d'Alene Miners' Unions in the Post Bullpen Era, 1900 to 1916: The Socialist Party and I.W.W. Connections." M.A. thesis, University of Idaho Graduate School, May 1980.

Ramsay, Dwight M., Jr. "A Statistical Survey of Voting Behavior in New Mexico." M.A. thesis, University of New Mexico, August 1951.

Todd, Charles Foster. "The Initiative and Referendum in Arizona." M.A. thesis, University of Arizona, 1931.

Ward, Doris Buck. "The Winning of Woman Suffrage in Montana." M.A. thesis, Montana State University, June 1974.

Index